The Management of Child Protection Services

Context and Change

Robert Sanders
School of Social Sciences and International Development
University of Wales Swansea

Ashgate

ARENA

Aldershot • Brookfield USA • Singapore • Sydney

Published by
Ashgate Publishing Ltd
Gower House
Croft Road
Aldershot
Hants GU11 3HR
England

Ashgate Publishing Company
Old Post Road
Brookfield
Vermont 05036
USA

British Library Cataloguing in Publication Data
Sanders, Robert
    The management of child protection services : context and change
    1. Child welfare — Great Britain   2. Child welfare —Government policy—
    3. Abused children — Services for —Great Britain
    I. Title
    362.7′6′7′0941

Library of Congress Cataloging-in-Publication Data
Sanders, Robert, 1946–
    The management of child protection services : context and change /
    Robert Sanders.
        p. cm.
    ISBN 1-85742-392-5. — ISBN 1-85742-393-3 (pbk.)
    1. Child welfare—Great Britain.   2. Child welfare—Great Britain—
    Administration.   3. Abused children—Services for—Great Britain.
    4. Social work with children—Great Britain.   5. Child abuse—Great
    Britain—Prevention.   I. Title.
    HV751.A6S36   1999
    362.76′8′0941—dc21   98-40537
                                                                              CIP
ISBN 1 85742 392 5 (Hbk)
ISBN 1 85742 393 3 (Pbk)
Printed and bound in Great Britain by MPG Books Ltd, Bodmin, Cornwall

Contents

Figures and Tables	vii
Acknowledgements	ix
Note	x
Introduction	xi
1 An historical context of child protection	**1**
The history of child abuse: an overview	1
British approaches to protecting children from harm	16
A comparison of the British and American approaches	21
The history of interagency working in child protection	22
2 A cross-cultural context of child protection	**25**
Introduction	25
General considerations	26
The UN Convention on the Rights of the Child	35
Britain and North America	39
Britain and Europe	47
Britain and the rest of the world	54
Race, ethnicity and culture	65
3 The structural/policy context of child protection in England and Wales	**73**
From the top – central government policy	73
The role of the media and public opinion	75
Parliament and child protection	79
Crossing the central–local divide	85

Research and policy   103
Training and networking   112

4   Area Child Protection Committees   **117**
Executive authority of Area Child Protection Committees   117
The composition of Area Child Protection Committees   118
Area Child Protection Committees: roles and functions   122

5   The professional/agency context of child protection   **183**
Social services   183
Police and Crown Prosecution Service   196
The health agencies   214
Education   250

6   Conclusions   **263**

References   271
Index   301

Figures and Tables

Figure 1.1	'The Maiden Tribute of Modern Babylon', *Pall Mall Gazette*, 6 July 1885	19
Figure 1.2	William Stead's trial, *Pall Mall Gazette*, 24 October 1885	20
Figure 2.1	Filtering of child protection referrals	45
Figure 3.1	The structure of child protection services in England and Wales	74
Figure 3.2	Policy, research and practice	104
Figure 4.1	Child abuse inquiries by year	163
Table 1.1	Total deaths from homicide in England and Wales 1863–1887	3
Table 1.2	Infant mortality rates	4
Table 1.3	The growth of Societies for the Prevention of Cruelty to Children	13
Table 2.1	Cross-cultural studies of attachment behaviour	30
Table 2.2	Availability of resources	32
Table 2.3	Central registries in Europe	50
Table 2.4	Mandatory reporting in Europe	51
Table 2.5	Child abuse in Australia by state (1995–96)	54
Table 2.6	Australian substantiation rates (1995–96)	55
Table 2.7	Mandatory reporting in Australia	56
Table 2.8	Child protection referrals – Victoria, Australia (1993–94)	56
Table 2.9	The 16 countries with the lowest under 5s mortality	58
Table 2.10	The ten countries with the highest under 5s mortality	59
Table 3.1	Social Services Inspectorate Reports	96
Table 4.1	Use of legal orders in relations to children	125

Table 4.2   Generic/specialist divisions in social work   147
Table 4.3   Staff child protection training needs   158
Table 4.4   Regions for Part 8 Study   171
Table 4.5   Age at death   171
Table 4.6   Part 8 Reviews: Death by parent – ages   175
Table 5.1   Agency representation on eight Area Child Protection
              Committees   215
Table 5.2   Trends in public health   220
Table 5.3   Trends in school exclusions   253

Acknowledgements

I would like to thank my colleague Sonia Jackson with whom I have collaborated closely over the last five years and who has helped me immensely in my learning about and writing about the management and policy of child protection. I would like to thank her as well for her observations on this particular text. I would also like to express my gratitude to those colleagues and friends who have assisted me by engaging in dialogue, providing me with material (in some cases on a *very* long-term loan basis) and for giving me encouragement and support. In particular I would like to express my gratitude to Rhona Hunt and Dr Alison Maddocks, for their contributions to my understanding of some of the issues involved in the organisation of child psychiatric services and the role of paediatricians in child protection respectively. As is customary, when acknowledging the help of others, I must emphasise that any mistakes, omissions, out-of-date material, etc., are entirely my own responsibility.

The University of Wales Swansea has provided me with considerable support, not least a period of study leave in Spring 1997, during which the majority of the material for this book was put together. Finally I would like to acknowledge the forbearance of my family who coped well with a largely absent member of the family.

Material from *The Care of Children: Principles and Practice in Regulations and Guidance* is reprinted with permission from The Stationery Office.

Note

Frequent reference is made to Government guidance on child protection. To make the text flow more smoothly the two main publications will be abbreviated in the text. The earlier work, Department of Health and Social Security and the Welsh Office (1988) *Working Together: A guide to arrangements for inter-agency co-operation for the protection of children from abuse*, London: HMSO, will simply be referred to as '*Working Together* (1988)'.

The latter volume, Home Office, Department of Health, Department of Education and Science, and Welsh Office (1991) *Working Together Under the Children Act 1989: A guide to inter-agency co-operation for the protection of children from abuse*, London: HMSO, will be referred to as '*Working Together* (1991)'.

Introduction

This book is not about child abuse; it is about child protection. The main aim of this book is simple: to inform the reader about the kinds of forces that have shaped current child protection practice in the UK and, to a lesser extent, in the rest of the world. It is about change and it is about systems. One cannot change what one does not understand. It is all too easy to enter a system, become familiar with its internal operations, and believe that on that basis change can be achieved. But systems operate within systems, and those external systems, whether temporal, spatial, or social, operate to keep the system stable – that is, change resistant (homeostatic). As an example, with my colleagues, I have described some of the difficulties facing ACPCs as national problems not local ones, but having local effects:

> ACPCs are finding it frustrating trying to resolve at local level issues that are essentially national in character. One example of this is the participation of general practitioners in ACPCs and child protection case conferences. Another example would be developing policy with Education on the issue of abuse by professionals. These are not local issues, although they become local problems. There is a sense in which ACPCs are being used as a stage upon which are set issues and dilemmas, the resolution of which actually lies somewhere offstage. (Jackson et al. 1994: 35)

This is essentially a systems-within-systems issue. One of the aims of this book is to help child protection professionals to better understand the roles and responsibilities of other agencies in contributing to the collective process of managing child protection services. If you the reader were to pick up this book for a browse and begin by looking at what it says about your particular agency, you may not find anything that is particularly new to you. But you may find the material on other agencies of use. Therefore, the book could be said to contribute to what has now become an accepted bedrock principle of child protection: children are best protected when agencies work well together; children are more at risk and less well protected when agencies fail to resolve their obstacles to working collectively. Those obstacles are frequently related to a lack of understanding.

This book is more about the management of child protection services than about the practice of protecting children. I plan to look at issues and dilemmas for agencies when working with other agencies to provide an interagency service. I will describe the managerial context of the different agencies, hopefully highlighting differences and similarities which when better understood should contribute to better communication between agencies.

This book was begun at a particularly exciting and challenging time in the management of child protection services in England and Wales. The preceding five years have seen significant effort on the part of all child welfare agencies being devoted to the establishment of new systems of child protection to take into account massive changes brought about by the implementation, in October 1991, of the Children Act 1989. The introduction of the Act represented a complete reform and rationalisation of the legal framework dealing with children and required fundamental shifts in attitudes towards work with children and families. Research during the 1980s, for example, as contained in the government publication *Social Work Decisions in Child Care: Recent Research Findings and their Implications* (DHSS 1985b) highlighted serious shortcomings in the child care system. For example, that admission to care and subsequent care 'careers' were poorly managed, that compulsory powers were over-used, that parents of children in the care system felt pushed aside, and subsequently therefore lost contact with children, were all key issues that were addressed by the Children Act 1989.

The concept of a 'child in need' was introduced by the Act, and children in need of protection, whose development was likely to be significantly impaired without services being provided, were clearly located as one group of vulnerable children within this broader category. To assist with the integration of the Act and child protection, on the same date the Act came into force, the Department of Health published *Working Together* (1991), which has colloquially come to be known as 'the bible' of child protection.

At the same time that agencies were attempting to get to grips with the requirements of the Act in providing a local and comprehensive child protection service, 'new' forms of abuse were moving to centre stage. Child protection agencies were attempting to address organised abuse (and paedophile rings), ritual and satanic abuse, abuse of children by professionals having responsibility for their welfare (for example teachers, foster carers, residential care workers) and abuse by juveniles and siblings. These needed to be addressed by the newly emerging child protection coordinating machinery.

Area Child Protection Committees (ACPCs) have largely been the focus for these changes, and therefore their operation will be a focus of this book. Operating within government guidance, the ACPCs are a vehicle by which central government child protection policy is translated firstly into local child protection policy and then into practice. The means to achieve this is the development of child protection coordinating structures and the development, implementation and review of agreed inter-agency policies for child protection. Most, if not all, Area Child Protection Committees will have completely revised their local child protection procedures manuals in light of the Children Act 1989, and many will have changed their structures, developing functional and geographical subcommittees to function more effectively and efficiently.

Overlapping these developments, and following from the events in Cleveland in the summer of 1987 and the subsequent report (Butler-Sloss 1988), the Department of Health commissioned a programme of research into various aspects of child abuse and child protection. Although a number of the reports had previously appeared, in June 1995, an overview, *Child Protection: Messages from Research* (DoH 1995a), provided a brief synopsis of all of the commissioned studies and drew together some of the essential themes to emerge. As described by John Bowis, Parliamentary Under Secretary of State, in the Foreword to the 'Blue book', as it came to be known, an essential theme was that 'real benefits may arise if there is a focus on the needs of children and families rather than a narrow concentration on the alleged incident of abuse.' In the months that followed, despite a dissemination programme by the Department of Health and the Welsh Office to spread the main themes, there appeared to be a conspicuous lack of discussion about the 'Blue book'. The newly launched journal, *Child and Family Social Work*, carried a critique by Nigel Parton, (Parton 1996) and a reply by the former Department of Health assistant secretary Rupert Hughes (Hughes 1996). There was some coverage in *Children's Services News* (the successor to *Children Act News*, which was launched by the Department of Health to publicise the implementation of the Children Act 1989), which looked at how some authorities were attempting to implement the messages. Nevertheless, during the first two years of its existence, remarkably little notice appears to have been taken of the 'Blue book'.

The reason for this early 'low-key' approach to such fundamental material could possibly be the early stance taken by the Department of Health that *Working Together* (1991) would *not* be revised to take into consideration *Child Protection: Messages from Research*. It may have struck many that if the messages were really important, as important as the themes leading to the implementation of the Children Act 1989, then there would be a clear lead from the Department of Health, and in Wales, from the Welsh Office, addressing how to translate those messages into policy and from policy into practice.

More recently, the Department of Health has announced its intention to review and revise *Working Together* (1991), to incorporate the 'Blue book' messages and a consultation document (DoH 1998) has since appeared. In conjunction with previous works which have questioned the role of child protection services within a child welfare context (Audit Commission 1994c; Colton et al. 1993; Jones and Bilton 1994), we are beginning to see publications opening the dialogue on what is becoming termed the 'Refocusing Debate' (ADSS/NCH Action for Children 1996; NSPCC 1996).

This is why the current time in the management of child protection services has become so exciting and challenging; full of potential hazards but equally holding a promise of a better, more balanced, more comprehensive service for vulnerable children. Through lengthy negotiations, Area Child Protection Committees appear to have struggled, largely successfully, to get agencies to take on the pre-eminence of a child protection service as the means of best meeting the needs of children. The example comes to mind of a senior manager of a local education authority describing for herself the experience of taking on board the message being put forward at the ACPC: 'We are all child protection agencies now.' ACPCs have developed structures that are generally quite effective for administering that service (Jackson et al. 1994).

It remains to be seen how difficult it will be for those who have struggled in lengthy negotiations to get others to place emphasis within child welfare on protection to reverse that process and allow child protection to assume its place as a subsidiary to child welfare more generally. These struggles will almost certainly be taking place throughout England and Wales over the next five years.

The structure of this book is a consideration of various contexts of child protection work. In recent years with the development of more and more teaching derived from an ecological understanding of human behaviour, context has become very important to my thinking – in this book I have abstracted all I have learned about child protection as practitioner, lecturer and researcher and attempted to locate it in context, or to be precise in a number of different contexts. In Part One, I consider the historical context of child protection, primarily focusing on Britain and the US and exploring the links. In Part Two, cross-cultural contexts of child protection are considered. Part Three examines the structural context of child protection. This refers to the examination of the structures in place within each of the agencies involved in child protection to look at how policy developed at the very top governmental levels is transmitted down to practice. Part Four examines one stage of this structure in detail, Area Child Protection Committees. Part Five looks at the professional and agency contexts of child protection. The last part of the book draws together some of the conclusions derived from a consideration of the various contexts of child protection.

For those readers who are moving from the practice of protecting children into the management of those services to protect children, this book should contain much material that you will find useful. At the very least, it will highlight where to look to find further information that will help you to achieve your objectives in working with others to develop and maintain those services.

The book is also aimed at an overseas audience to promote awareness of how we in the UK manage child protection services. There is much that is good and innovative in British child protection, and I would not want the emphasis in the text on academic critique to hide that. For too long perhaps British child protection systems have looked to the US for initiatives in child protection. British bookshelves contain considerably more American child protection material than the other way around; American child protection articles contain fewer references to British sources than vice versa. As I comment in Part One, 'Historically, Britain has looked across the Atlantic rather than across the Channel for ideas and inspirations regarding child welfare practice.' Certainly the debates in which we are currently engaged are not restricted to the British Isles, but apply to the US, Europe and the rest of the world.

1 An historical context of child protection

London Bridge is falling down,
Falling down, falling down.
London Bridge is falling down,
My fair lady. (Children's Nursery Rhyme)

The history of child abuse: an overview

The abuse of children by adults is generally considered by any standards to be a very long-standing phenomenon. However, reflection on child abuse in an historical context almost always entails a retrospective evaluation of behaviours against contemporary standards. The types of illustrations of the way children were treated in the past, and which so often produce sadness, horror, pain and indeed, sometimes pure outrage, are probably best viewed as indicators of the types of behaviours that were permitted, condoned or even encouraged by the societies in which they took place. As described by a number of writers, childhood (and therefore child abuse as a particular experience of childhood), is a socially constructed phenomenon (Stainton Rogers 1989; Parton 1985). These social constructions are also a reflection of the relationship between the child and the state/society within which he or she lives. It will be helpful therefore to put some of the examples given of how children were abused in the past into a social context.

The beginning of any consideration of children in relation to society begins with the nature of childhood as viewed in society, a discussion following the work of Ariès (1962), DeMause (1976) and Pollock (1993). It is the contention

1

of Ariès that children were not viewed as children in medieval society because there was no conception of childhood as such: 'in medieval society the idea of childhood did not exist' (p.125). In such a model, children share the same fates as adults (wars, famines, plagues, etc.) without discrimination by virtue of their younger status. They may be newer individuals to arrive within that society, but other than that, they are not different.

Pollock considers that there are shortcomings in Ariès' contention, because of methodological considerations. She suggests there has been a conception of childhood in medieval times, even if reflection of that was absent in the kind of material used for data by Ariès. She is not alone in her refutation of Ariès' contention, and Cunningham suggests in relation to Ariès' quote above: 'Rarely can so few words have brought forth so many in refutation' (1995: 30)

DeMause (1976) noted the scarcity of material on parent–child relations in history, and considers the nature of parent–child relationships as an evolving phenomenon, the evolution of which is dependent upon a process he describes as 'psychogenic'. In this theoretical framework, the inter-generational processes influencing how people parent contribute to an overall development of parenting across the ages. He considers that this process contributes to an overall improvement for the welfare of children: '... if today in America there are less than a million abused children, there would be a point back in history where most children were what we would now consider abused'. (DeMause 1976: 3)

Let us look at some of the examples cited of child abuse in historical times. The most extreme form of abuse is child homicide. There are several references in the Bible to the large-scale extermination of children, by Pharaoh at the time of the birth of Moses, and by Herod at the time of the birth of Jesus. There are also biblical references to child sacrifice (Jericho 7: 32; 2 Chronicles 28: 3; Joshua 6: 26; 1 Kings 16: 34). Tower (1996) refers to the biblical story of Isaac, who was at the point of being sacrificed by his father, Abraham, and was only stopped by the intervention of an angel who told Abraham it had been a test of faith (Genesis 22: 1–19).

DeMause (1976) considers that the extent of infanticide in antiquity is generally under-recognised and he considers that the practice extended well into the Middle Ages:

> Thousands of bones of sacrificed children have been dug up by archaeologists, often with inscriptions identifying the victims as first-born sons of noble families, reaching in time all the way back to the Jericho of 7,000 B.C. Sealing children in walls, foundations of buildings, and bridges to strengthen the structure was also common from the building of the wall of Jericho to as late as 1843 in Germany. (DeMause 1976: 27)

The Bible also contains references to children being interred in the walls and gates of Jericho: 'In his days did Hiel the Bethelite build Jericho: he laid the foundation thereof in Abiram his firstborn, and set up the gates thereof in his youngest son Segub' (1 Kings 16: 34). Both Bakan (1971) and Radbill (1974) refer to the practice across centuries and cultures of interring newborn infants into walls of buildings and bridges to strengthen the structures. Several writers (DeMause 1976; Zigler and Hall 1989) refer to this practice as the basis for the children's nursery rhyme/song, '*London Bridge is Falling Down*'.

Tower (1996) refers the power of fathers in ancient Rome to kill, abandon or sell their children, although as pointed out by Doxiadis (1989) because of the Roman Empire's need for people to carry out its plans for conquest, measures were taken to forbid the practice of infanticide. Infanticide in some cultures (Hawaii, China and Japan, for example) was seen as a means of regulating the population, a form of survival of the fittest. Doxiadis (1989) suggests that whilst the practice in ancient Greece was forbidden, it was practised nevertheless. Others have considered it to be so extensive as to have been a cause for the very small population of ancient Greece. Doxiadis highlights the difference in attitudes towards infanticide in the ancient world being based on whether the society needed more people or not. Lee et al. (1994) note that the Qing lineage during the eighteenth century regularly used infanticide to control the number and sex of their infants. Radbill (1980) describes a number of cultures (British New Guinea, Germany, North American Indians) in which there was a test of viability of the newborn child, the consequences of failing the test being death. In other societies, the child was not protected until given a name. Zigler and Hall (1989) also give several examples of the child's right to live being determined shortly after being born, usually by the father. The practice of infanticide was so widespread as to render the first year of an individual's life as the time of greatest likelihood to be killed. The following table is reproduced from Rose (1986):

Table 1.1: Total deaths from homicide in England and Wales 1863–1887
(Rose 1986)

Age	Total
Under 1	3,225
1–2	106
2–3	70
3–4	54
4–5	40
All ages over 5	1,789

He notes 'Thus the under-l's formed 61 per cent of all homicide victims, at a time when they constituted 2.5–3 per cent of the population' (Rose 1986: 8). When combined with other causes of child mortality, (disease, starvation), it led Walvin to observe that 'the death of the young as well as the old, was an inescapable social reality in nineteenth-century England' (1982: 21–2). The death rate for children under one year of age, is shown in Table 1.2.

Table 1.2: Infant mortality rates (death of children under one year of age from all causes) (Parton 1985)

Year	Deaths under 1 year of age per 1000
1839–40	153
1896	156
1899	163

Interestingly, Cunningham (1995) notes that while infant mortality rose in England and Wales (along with Belgium and France), in other European countries (Austria, Denmark, Germany, Netherlands, Norway and Sweden) it fell during the same period. Parton (1985) notes that 1899 was a peak during the period when rates were recorded, followed by a decline, although Cunningham (1995) estimates that it was considerably higher (between 250 and 340) during the seventeenth and early eighteenth century.

Disability and illegitimacy were particularly likely to condemn a child to death in a wide range of cultures and societies. In Greece children with a disability could be especially vulnerable to infanticide; Aristotle in *The Politics* stated: 'With regard to the choice between abandoning an infant or rearing it, let there be a law that no cripple should be reared.' Zigler and Hall (1989) note that the Roman Laws of the Twelve Tables forbid the rearing of a child with a defect or deformity. As DeMause describes it: '... any child that was not perfect in shape and size, or cried too little or too much, or was otherwise than is described in the gynaecological writings on "How to Recognize the Newborn That is Worth Rearing", was generally killed' (1976: 25). In *Moral Essays*, Seneca wrote, 'sickly sheep we put to the knife to keep them from infecting the flock; unnatural progeny we destroy; we drown even children who at birth are weakly and abnormal.'

The connection between illegitimacy and infanticide was so strong in both England and America during the seventeenth and eighteenth centuries that where an unmarried mother gave birth to a child alone and the child was later found dead, the mother was regularly accused of murdering the child (Jackson 1996). In England, it was the presumption in law (a statute of 1624) that the child was deemed to have been murdered by the mother unless the mother was able to prove that the child was stillborn. This was reversed in 1803, so that evidence was required of the child's live birth before a woman could be convicted. Whilst many women were hanged for such an offence, the twentieth century saw a reversal of the previous severity. With the Infanticide Acts of 1922 and 1938, women were able to be convicted of a lesser offence, 'Infanticide', a variation of manslaughter, rather than murder.

Gender was another factor that in certain places at certain times may have condemned a child to a short life. Whereas illegitimate children, whether male or female, were always equally likely to have been exposed, in the case of legitimate children, only girls were vulnerable, a preference across most societies being an institutionalised preference for males over females. According to Payne (1928) the Chinese banned infanticide under the influence of European missionaries, but we have seen a resurrection of this practice in recent years with the advent of the one-child policy. It has been suggested that the exposing of female children may have accounted for the very large gender imbalances during the Middle Ages (156 males to 100 females in 801; 172 males to 100 females in 1391). Radbill comments, 'Girls were especially at risk ... far more likely [than brothers] to be killed, sold or exposed' (1980: 6). Poffenberger notes the extremity of the practice in India after the turn of the nineteenth century: 'The outstanding example of female infanticide in Gujarat was practised by the Jhareja Rajputs of Kathiwar and Kaach, where a census taken by the British administrators in 1805 found almost no daughters' (1981: 79).

The distressing sight of 'half-clad infants, sometimes alive, sometimes dead, and sometimes dying, who had been abandoned by their parents to the mercy of the streets' (Pettifer 1939: 31), led Thomas Coram to found the first British foundling hospital in 1739. Similar institutions had been, or were being set up in Paris (Rose 1986; Marvick 1976), Dublin (Rose 1986), Moscow (Dunn 1976), St Petersburg (Radbill 1980) and other European capitals. The first recorded foundling hospital was established in Milan in 1787 (Radbill 1980). As pointed out by Cunningham (1995), the foundling hospitals were predominantly set up in Catholic countries where policies facilitated the abandonment of infants. Despite the establishment of foundling hospitals, the chances of survival for foundling children were very small indeed. In the case of the London Foundling Hospital, for example, the survival rate for foundlings was 52 per cent, though Cunningham (1995) notes the rate was as low as one-third during the five years following the opening of the doors to larger numbers in 1756.

Although historically, children had a very difficult time of surviving, if they did survive, then the likelihood of being the target of sexual usage by adults was quite high: 'The child in antiquity lived his earliest years in an atmosphere of sexual abuse. Growing up in Greece and Rome often included being used sexually by older men' (DeMause 1976: 43). But the involvement of children in adult sexuality was by no means limited to those societies, and DeMause gives examples from other cultures as well. Tower (1996) notes the difference between the sexual usage of children in Rome and Greece: in Rome, sexual relations with children did not raise their status, as it did in Greece. Radbill (1980) describes a number of cultures in which daughters (as well as wives) were loaned to guests as an act of hospitality. Christianity, drawing on the teachings of Christ, was largely responsible for the development of the view of children as 'innocents', and therefore needing protection. DeMause (1976) highlights the parental role in the sexual usage of children, whether through the sale of children for sexual purposes or other means. He notes that one effect of such usage can be child prostitution, an issue which has raised concern recently, but is not new. Myers (1994) considers the work of Dr Ambrose Tardieu to be the first modern acknowledgement of child sexual abuse. In 1857, Tardieu published a book chronicling thousands of cases, but despite his eminence and prestige, his beliefs were challenged and dismissed by his successors. Cunningham (1988) notes that both Tardieu and later Binet (another nineteenth century child development specialist who pioneered work on children's intelligence) saw the seriousness of child sexual abuse, attempted to ascertain how widespread it was, and upheld the credibility of children's accounts about the abuse they had experienced.

There are other forms of ill-treatment of children which have come to be defined as abusive from a contemporary perspective. DeMause (1976) provides a very good overview of the severity of discipline meted out to children. The value of beating children was widespread and shared, ostensibly for the purpose of improving their character, but one wonders if it was not often administered for more sinister motivations. Child labour is another form of ill-usage of children that has been the subject of concerns in the past. Considerable campaigning and lobbying went into efforts to protect children from the relatively unrestrained application of market principles by employers during the Industrial Revolution. For many such employers, the lower wage costs associated with child labour was a sudden and welcome increase of profits, which more than balanced the cost in human misery of which they may or may not have been aware.

The philanthropic campaign to eliminate child labour is one point of similarity amongst many in the development of child welfare social policy between Britain and the US. At first, one is perhaps inclined to be surprised at how many similarities, despite very different governmental frameworks, there are between the way both British and American child protection measures have developed. And yet, despite hostilities arising from several wars (The War of Independence, the War of 1812, and even as late as the American Civil War), there have been strong affinities arising from a common background, a common language and considerable commercial interests. In comparing the British child protection system with those in Europe, I have suggested elsewhere that 'Historically, Britain has looked across the Atlantic rather than across the Channel for ideas and inspirations regarding child welfare practice' (Sanders et al. 1996b: 900). The remainder of this section should provide a foundation for that assertion. We now turn to consider those separate, but strikingly parallel developments.

American approaches to protecting children from harm

Although it is my intention to highlight similarities between the American and British approaches and backgrounds of child protection, we must begin with a big difference. Within the American framework, child protection is a state issue, and although there may be considerable consistency across states facilitated largely by federal legislation and funding (for example, on mandatory reporting), there is considerable scope for different states to vary how they undertake child protection (as we will see in the next section). The extent of similarity or difference in the UK framework depends upon the level of analysis. It would be fair to say that because there are different statutes applying to the three regions, Scotland, England and Wales, and Northern Ireland, they have different subsidiary guidance addressing how child protection work should be undertaken. However, if one draws the parallel between local authorities and central government, then the parallel breaks down, as local authorities work to the same set of legal guidelines, determined by central government.

Physical abuse in the US

It is tempting to consider that the major impetus for American child protection begins with the case of Mary Ellen in 1874, which I will consider shortly. First I wish to explore the preconditions that helped to make those events so significant. As pointed out by Walzner (1976), abandonment of children and infanticide, either through exposure or by other means, when compared with the very high rates in Britain, were relatively rare in colonial America. As in Britain, when infanticide did occur, it was likely to be in connection with an illegitimate child. Nevertheless, there were still concerns about how children were treated. Walzner considers, 'If one were to broaden the definition of children to all wholly dependent persons ... then it is clear that the rod and the whip found widespread application, indeed, in the eighteenth century' (1976: 369). Bremner (1970) cites several examples from American child welfare history to indicate that protective action was certainly able to be taken, and was taken, before 1874. In Massachusetts, in 1655 an individual was found guilty of causing death through mistreatment to his twelve-year-old apprentice. Part of his punishment for the offence was the confiscation all of his goods. In Tennessee, a state court judgement in 1840, whilst upholding the right of a parent to chastise a disobedient child, also recognised that exceeding the bounds of moderation became a criminal offence for which one could be punished. According to Thomas (1972) however, it was only if the punishment was considered to be 'grossly unreasonable ... cruel or merciless ... or permanently injured the child' that it was likely to be considered prosecutable. It should be noted that where children were beaten (with rods, whips or other implements), it was in the context of a society which, as in Britain, generally endorsed the view that such punishment was necessary for the child's moral and spiritual development. Therefore, parents were relatively immune from criminal prosecution, unless they very clearly crossed the line. Thomas (1972) also notes that whilst statutes were in place to protect children, they were not systematically enforced. Folks (1902) notes that as early as 1825 states were adopting laws to protect children, by establishing a public duty to intervene in cases of cruelty or neglect of children, and if necessary to remove them (to an almshouse). In 1833, New York City gave certain city officials (or their representatives) the authority to remove children who were neglected or suffering because of their parents, although it did not provide a responsibility to find children who were in need of this protection. Despite this, however, it would appear that this was insufficient: when the case of Mary Ellen did arise, in 1874, the starting point was that there was no statute that could enable her to be protected (perhaps because the people involved in her case were not her legal parents). In the previous year in New York, as pointed out by Thorpe (1994), a woman was charged with 'wholesale infanticide', allowing children who were boarded out with her (i.e. baby farming) to die.

The story of Mary Ellen Wilson is generally accepted as a watershed in American child protection. The situation as regards child protection after 1874 was certainly very different from before. The actual story of how Mary Ellen came to be in need of protection and was ultimately protected has been the target of some demythologising on the part of a number of writers. The kernel of the story is that Mary Ellen, a child in clear need of protection from her carers, was unable to be protected by the law because there was no law allowing the state to intervene to protect children. Therefore in order for her to be protected, an argument had to be made that Mary Ellen, by virtue of being human, was a member of the animal kingdom and as such was none the less eligible to be afforded the same protection as was at the time made available to protect animals from abuse at the hands of their owners. There was already a very active organisation, the New York Society for the Prevention of Cruelty to Animals (NYSPCA) established a few years before in April

1866 by Henry Bergh, which achieved considerable progress in its first years to protect animals from mistreatment. The story of Mary Ellen Wilson contains a mixture of both truth and fiction. The truth of it is that Henry Bergh, the founder of the NYSPCA, was involved in the legal application to protect Mary Ellen; the fiction is that she had to be considered to be a member of the animal kingdom in order to be protected.

Late in 1873, Mrs Etta Wheeler, variously described as a missionary, tenement worker and social worker, was visiting among the New York poor when she received accounts of a child who was living in dreadful circumstances, the victim of horrendous maltreatment. The reports said the child was cruelly whipped, kept as a prisoner in her home and frequently left on her own. A terminally ill woman that Mrs Wheeler was visiting, reported that she had repeatedly heard the desperate cries of the child and the sounds of beatings and verbal abuse through the thin walls of the tenement where she lived. Mrs Wheeler tried to see the child, and although not allowed entry by an aggressive male, was nevertheless able to glimpse Mary Ellen, a pale, thin child the size of a five-year-old (she was nine at the time), poorly and inadequately clad for the time of year (December). She noted numerous marks on the child's arms and legs from the whip she observed lying on the table. In the face of the child, Mrs Wheeler saw an unloved child facing misery and unhappiness. For several months, Wheeler attempted without success to enlist the aid of the child welfare organisations and the law enforcement agencies. Although she had previously considered approaching Mr Bergh, it was when her niece endorsed this action that she brought her concerns to him. Bergh expressed interest in the case, and asked Mrs Wheeler to return with more substantial evidence of the concerns, which she did the following day. Mr Bergh sent a NYSPCA investigator to the home, posing as a census worker, and on the following day, on the basis of what was found, Mary Ellen was forcibly removed from her home under a special warrant issued by the New York Supreme Court. Mary Ellen was brought to the court; her body was bruised and she had a gash over her eye where Mrs Connolly had struck her with a pair of shears. Mary Ellen related her story of abusive treatment by the Connollys, of beatings every day. Apart from the narration of the beatings, and equally disturbing, was the child's experience of lack of love, warmth and caring: 'I have no recollection of ever having been kissed by any one – have never been kissed by mamma. I have never been taken on my mamma's lap and caressed or petted. I never dared to speak to anybody, because if I did I would get whipped' (*New York Times*, 10 April 1874: 8).

Subsequent enquiries revealed that Mary Ellen, at the age of 18 months, was indentured (a practice of placing children for apprenticeship) with Mrs Mary Connolly and her deceased husband, Thomas McCormack, by the Department of Charities on 2 January 1866. She had been left at the

Department on 21 May 1864, by a woman who had received her from her parents, but who no longer knew where her parents could be located. She had stopped receiving payment in respect of the child and was therefore unable to continue to look after her.

As a result of the court case Mrs Connolly was sent to prison for one year. Her husband, Francis Connolly, was not indicted. Mary Ellen was placed in an orphanage, from which she was subsequently removed by Mrs Wheeler to live with the woman's mother in Rochester, New York.

During the case, Mr Bergh made it clear that he was acting in a private capacity, and not as a representative of the organisation which he had founded. Further, although there are indications that participants in the scenario may have made the link between Mary Ellen as a member of the animal kingdom and therefore being entitled to the same kind of protection, there is no evidence that the court took any similar view; indeed, the action taken was described by Thomas (1972) as an old English writ of law used to remove the custody of one person from another.

Apart from the need felt by some to clarify the contentious point of whether Mary Ellen was protected as a person, or as a member of the animal kingdom (Watkins 1990; Costin 1991; Lazoritz and Shelman 1996) – and one may reflect on why this issue should be considered so important as to warrant this – there are a number of other interesting aspects of the circumstances surrounding the Mary Ellen 'legend'. There is an attractive fancifulness about the idea of there being an ability to protect animals in a way that was not available for children, which would certainly appeal to those who were crusading for support (both public and financial) to rescue children from homes considered to be unsatisfactory.

We should consider a number of points to help us understand the significance of the case of Mary Ellen. It is possible that too much has been made of it, and that the resulting pressure to establish agencies to protect children was rather the result of a 'fortuitous coming together of a constellation of related factors that stimulated public receptivity to a view of child abuse and neglect as a social problem' (Costin 1991: 203). As described by Nelson, 'a single incident, however momentous, does not guarantee that concerned individuals will view the event as an example of a larger problem, and organise to solve it' (1984: 67).

First, this notion that we have described as fanciful, that Mary Ellen needed to be protected as a member of the animal kingdom, has certainly been misconstrued, although it was clear that this was present as a context factor. This conception of the 'human as animal' owes a considerable debt to the impact of Charles Darwin, whose writings reduced the distance between animals and humans, a notion with which some, especially those with very strong religious convictions, may have been very uncomfortable, but which would appeal to those wishing to be seen as contemporary. An earlier reference to this notion is contained in a letter to the *New York Telegram* (19 May 1868), which was a plea to Henry Bergh to extend his activities to protecting children. In it the value of protecting children is weighed against the value of protecting animals, and considered greater. Costin (1991) gives two further examples of the press explicitly describing children as members of the animal kingdom in order to make the case for better protection. It is difficult to tell whether the apparent indignation surrounding the contrast that was being made between the protection afforded to animals when children were still considered unprotected arose out of the sheer irony of the matter or out of a more fundamental concern for the plight of children, But it certainly appears clear that the case of Mary Ellen occurred in a context of a pre-existing concern about the welfare of ill-treated children.

A second interesting facet of the case of Mary Ellen was that Bergh himself had had prior involvement in requests to intercede on behalf of children. In one case, that of Emily Thompson, in June 1871, he acceded to the request, but generally he had shown himself resistant to pressures to involve his society in the protection of children. The case of Emily Thompson, which had remarkable similarities with the case of Mary Ellen, had a very different short-term outcome, in that although the child's keeper Mary Anne Larkin was convicted, given a suspended sentence, and the child returned to live with her. Part of the reason for this was the child's continued denial of the abuse, despite clear evidence from neighbours who had witnessed the incidents described to the court. Although the case was very unsatisfactory from Bergh's point of view, who possibly considered it an unsuccessful foray on his part into child welfare, it did have an ultimately more positive outcome, in that the publicity afforded to the case produced a grandmother, who had been described by Mrs Larkin as dead, and who resumed the care of Emily Thompson.

A third aspect of the Mary Ellen case, again supporting the contention that it alone was not responsible for the subsequent development of American child protection, was that previous cases of even more severe maltreatment did not result in the same public outcry. Costin notes the following, 'Earlier in the same year, the *New York Times* reported that John Fox, 13, had died from a cruel beating by his father for "refusing to go after beer without the money to pay for it"' (1991: 209). Despite the coroner's verdict that the death was due to the injuries, the *New York Times* took no further interest in the case. This leads to the fourth interesting aspect of the Mary Ellen case, the role of the media. Costin (1991) points out a very interesting aspect of the Mary Ellen case: that Etta Wheeler was married to a journalist. Whilst there is no evidence of the direct influence of this connection, it is highly suggestive. Nelson (1984) considers that the press applied a discretion as to which cases received more extensive coverage and which did not. Those that did involved three dimensions of parenting: status, class and gender. Incidents of ill treatment receiving more extensive coverage were likely to involve step-parents (or non-parents), from a working-class background, and the victims were likely to be girls rather than boys. Thus there is not only an interesting comparison between John Fox and Mary Ellen Wilson to highlight these differences, but an interesting comparison of a number of similarities between the case of Mary Ellen and that of Maria Colwell, over a hundred years later and three thousand miles away. A picture of the circumstances surrounding a high-profile incident emerges in which it is not the incident itself that touches the fuse, but rather the incident in a nexus of circumstances; a finding similar to that suggested by Parton (1985) in the case of Maria Colwell.

In the aftermath of the Mary Ellen case, there was very quick action to establish a child protection network. The solicitor for the NYSPCA, Elbridge Gerry, who was a significant actor in the Mary Ellen case, searched for a benefactor to establish a society whose exclusive objective would be the protection of children from maltreatment. He found it in the person of John Wright, a highly respected local figure, who had a great fondness for children. He gathered the 'names' of New York society, and some of the richest men in the US, for the new association which was established as the New York Society for the Prevention of Cruelty to Children (NYSPCC) with the aim to:

> ... to seek out and rescue from the dens and slums of the city those little unfortunates whose childish lives are rendered miserable by the constant abuse and cruelties practiced on them by the human brutes who happen to possess the custody or control of them. (Costin 1991: 212)

There is much in the language of that mission statement ('rescue', 'human brutes', 'happen to possess') that forecasts the conflicts that were to eventually emerge between the rescue approach of Berry and the NYSPCC, and the more integrative, family-preservation approach adopted by the Boston Society for the Prevention of Cruelty to Children. However, the initial impact was the immediate establishment and progressive expansion of an establishment of local SPCCs throughout the US. The first, in New York, was established in April 1875. This was soon followed by the establishment of similar societies in Philadelphia, Chicago and Boston. Table 1.3 shows the subsequent expansion of the organisation.

In 1909, the White House (under President Theodore Roosevelt) convened the Conference on the Care of Dependent Children, the first of a series of ten yearly conferences looking at child welfare. Arising from this was the establishment of the Children's Bureau in 1912.

Table 1.3: The growth of Societies for the Prevention of Cruelty to Children
(from Costin 1991, 1992)

Year	Number
1875	1
1876	8
1898	20
1908	55
1910	200

Twenty years later, however the movement had lost its momentum, and Costin (1992) considers the question of why for nearly four decades there was a hiatus in child protection awareness and activity. The diminished discussion of child protection in social work literature between 1900 and the 1950s is used as evidence to support this contention. There are several reasons suggested by Costin (1992) for this pattern. Most significantly was the emerging division between the two approaches to child protection endorsed by the New York branch ('Coercive Reform') and the Boston branch ('Assimilative Reform'). Other reasons for the hiatus suggested by Costin include:

- Divisions about who should do protective work (some workers were beginning to suggest it should be taken over by public rather than charitable agencies)
- The decline of feminism (Gordon, 1988a; 1988b)
- Increasing concerns about the wide range of social problems affecting children's welfare de-emphasised child abuse
- Disenchantment with the juvenile courts ability to safeguard children's welfare in a legal context
- The lack of overall direction of the SPCCs (giving rise to the Child Welfare League of America in 1921, established under the aegis of the Massachusetts SPCC)
- Difficulties in differentiating child welfare from family welfare
- The emerging emphasis within social casework on psychoanalytic understanding and methods, an approach which did not particularly lend itself to working with child abusers
- A reluctance to use authority in casework
- Antiquated practices and attitudes to the poor continuing into the Great Depression of the 1930s.

Many of these factors can be seen to have parallels within the development of British child protection which I consider below.

The advance call for the re-emergence of child protection in the late 1950s and early 1960s came when Caffey (1946), who had jointly trained as a paediatrician and radiologist, published a paper concluding the existence of a link between subdural haematomas and long bone fractures, which he considered to have a common cause of external trauma (although he did not define the source of the trauma, or give the condition a name). Others however, did begin to suggest that the cause of the common trauma was with the parents, culminating in the work of Wooley and Evans (1955), which compelled the medical community to consider parental causes of the trauma. In 1961, a conference with the provocative title 'The Battered-Child Syndrome', was organised by Dr Kempe in his capacity as chairman of the American Academy of Paediatrics. The effects of the conferences were electric. As described by Radbill (1980), it set in motion a 'bandwagon effect'. Parton's (1985) consideration of the political context of the inaugural conference, highlighted the flagging credibility, status and legitimacy of the Children's Bureau and the consistency of the theme of child abuse with their prime objectives, as significant factors. They provided support for research into child abuse, and particularly supported the work of Kempe and his colleagues in Denver. In 1974, the Child Abuse Prevention and Treatment Act was passed which established the National Center for Child Abuse and Neglect and provided a model statute for state child protective programmes. In 1977, Kempe and some of his colleagues created the International Society for the Prevention and Treatment of Child Abuse and Neglect, launching in that year the *International Journal of Child Abuse & Neglect*.

Sexual abuse in the US

The predominant emphasis in this section has so far been on physical abuse and neglect. Sexual abuse of children has many facets and issues:

- Intrafamilial sexual abuse of children
- Child pornography
- Child prostitution
- Less common forms of abuse (abuse of boys, abuse by females)
- Organised and ritualistic forms of sexual abuse
- Distinctions between incest (legal and cultural concepts) and child sexual abuse (a socio-legal concept).

Rush (1980) notes that in the early nineteenth century, American slave owners delighted in 'breaking in' their young slaves or using them for breeding. Girls as young as eleven were made pregnant. Gordon (1988b) has argued that the sexual abuse of children has undergone an 'historical amnesia' similar to that which appears to have applied in the case of physical abuse. This was not simply attributable to the decline of feminism between 1920 and 1970, but by an active reinterpretation of child sexual abuse. In a sample of the case records of the 'Boston child-saving agencies' (the Massachusetts SPCC), from 1880 onwards, she found ten per cent to contain incest, which were attributed by workers to 'male brutality and lack of sexual control'. There were hundreds of cases in which it was clear that the agencies were not only aware of sexual abuse, but taking action to address it. However the public was not made aware of it, as the agency considered the material too revolting to make public. An analysis of cases at a later stage in the 1930s showed a number of differences in the types of concerns, which Gordon considers the result of a threefold transformation. The locus had changed from the home to the streets; concerns about abusers had shifted from fathers or other paternal figure to perverted strangers, and the victims had gone from being abused innocents to being sexual delinquents. In fact, in the early twentieth century there was considerable concern about female juvenile sexual delinquency, as a social problem. However, Gordon notes 'The statistics about child sexual abuse remain what they were a century ago: the most dangerous place for children is the home, the most likely assailant their father' (1988b: 61).

Another factor to account for the delay in the renewed recognition of child sexual abuse was Freud's rejection of the validity of his female patients' accounts of being sexually abused:

> Almost all my women patients told me that they had been seduced by their fathers. I was driven to recognize in the end that these reports were untrue and so came to understand the hysterical symptoms are derived from phantasies and not from real occurrences. (Freud 1966: 584)

Thus Freud rejected the seduction theory in favour of the Oedipus complex. This conception, from someone whose work was beginning to exert a powerful influence on social work, particularly in the US, had the effect of altering the balance of psychological investigations from external trauma to internal longings and fantasies. Wigmore, a legal scholar at the turn of the century was convinced that in sex-offence cases, the legal system should not put weight on the evidence of women and girls: 'One form taken by these complexes is that of contriving false charges of sexual offenses by men ... The real victim, however, too often in such cases is the innocent man' (1970 [1904]: 736)

Sexual abuse of children emerged (or rather, like physical abuse, re-emerged) as an issue in the late 1970s. Finkelhor (1979) published his findings of a survey of New England students from six colleges which looked at their experiences of being sexually abused. Of the 796 students surveyed, 530 were female and 266 male. He found 19.2 per cent of women and 8.6 per cent of men had been abused as children, usually at around the age of ten or eleven. Russell (1983) interviewed 930 women in the San Francisco area and found that 38 per cent had experienced sexually abusive contact as a child, although the figure rose to 51 per cent when non-contact forms of abuse were included. Variations in definitions appear to account for the differences between the Finkelhor and Russell findings.

British approaches to protecting children from harm

Physical abuse in the UK

A consideration of the protection of children from harm of the worst kind could begin with looking at the practice of baby-farming which resulted in the deaths of so many children. Despite the presence of the Thomas Coram hospital for foundlings in the eighteenth century, it is noted by Cunningham that 'Some historians of the foundling system, when they look at England, wonder whether the English equivalents of the foundling hospitals were the privately-run baby farms' (1995: 126). The practice appears to have begun around the middle of the nineteenth century.

In the 1840s the London Poor Law unions had adopted a crude form of 'boarding-out', but for reasons of economy only, by concentrating their children in a private institution, namely Mr Bartholomew's 'Baby-Farm' at Tooting; this became notorious in 1848 during the cholera epidemic, for 155 of its 1300 inmates died in the 'appallingly crowded and insanitary conditions that were uncovered there' (Rose 1986: 49).

A series of scandals emerged in the nineteenth century when it was learned that so many of the children being farmed out were not surviving. In a number of cases this was clearly because the 'farmers', having once accepted children into their homes under agreements with parents to look after them and having collected the fee, either murdered or exposed them. Of course in many cases it may have been difficult to determine the balance between simply poor standards of care where the death was not intentional and homicide or abandonment. Concerns about the practice of 'baby-farming' (and certainly the beginning of the popular usage of the term) appears to have begun around 1865, when following the discovery of a number of murdered infants in the countryside surrounding Torquay, the police were alerted. The particular case of a Mary Jane Harris (the mother of an illegitimate child, Thomas) and Charlotte Winsor, attracted considerable publicity. It was the evidence of Harris, turned Queen's Evidence, which convicted Winsor. It transpired that Winsor had admitted to the child's mother that she had disposed of babies regularly. Another case, that of Mrs Jaggers, in 1867 also attracted considerable publicity; she admitted having had the care of 40 children in the preceding three years, three of whom were the subject of inquests. At the time of the third, she admitted caring for eight infants, although more were suspected. Another case described by Rose describes a woman, seen as more typical of the baby-farmer – 'not bad at heart' and not a wilful murderess, but rather a 'poor, ignorant, struggling' woman (1986: 80).

In 1868, Ernest Hart of the *British Medical Journal* launched an enquiry into baby-farming (and abortion), utilising undercover methods, in which individuals posed as parents wishing to arrange for care for their child. The articles attracted considerable press interest. A similar journalistic investigation was undertaken in Scotland by the *North British Daily Mail* in 1870, the articles appearing between February and April 1871. The public concern about this practice was heightened when in the space of only a few weeks in 1870, 16 dead babies were found in Camberwell, South London. Two baby farmers were charged with murder, and one, Mrs Waters, was subsequently hanged. The other, Agnes Norman, presented numerous bizarre features (including killing of animals), described by Lock (1993) as a form of Munchausen Syndrome by Proxy similar to that manifested by Beverley Allitt, the nurse convicted of killing several children in her charge in more recent times.

From October to December 1895, *The Sun* newspaper undertook a journalist investigation of the practice of baby-farming. Following a public campaign, 'The British Medical Journal in 1903 [17 January] chided the system of baby farming and urged the licensing of foster parents and inspectors to see that the children were properly cared for' (Radbill 1980: 14). Nevertheless, over a relatively long period of journalistic and public concern, Parliament took little action, the government's response being that it was a police matter, not requiring new legislation. And yet, the police had no real interest in the dead babies being found. As expressed by Mary Baines, 'they think no more of finding the dead body of a child in the street than of picking up a dead cat or dog' (Baines, *c.* 1865, quoted in Rose 1986: 93). However, the practice of baby-farming (and especially the South London case) did contribute to the establishment of the Infant Life Protection Society.

Sexual abuse in the UK

As pointed out by Conte and Shore (1982), protection for children from sexual abuse began in England as early as the sixteenth century. In 1548 a law was passed to protect boys from forced sodomy. Nearly 30 years later, in 1576, another law was enacted to prohibit the forcible rape of girls under the age of ten (Conte and Shore 1982: 22). One can speculate on the extent to which, in tandem with the Ariès thesis, this was an effort to protect children because of their particular vulnerabilities and the implications of rape for subsequent development. It seems more likely that in the context of children not being seen as different (the lack of a conception of childhood), that it represented an extension to one sector in society (children) a protection from rape that may have already been available to others. Alternatively, it may mark the beginning of children being seen as being different and having distinctive needs by virtue of their age and immaturity.

Child prostitution was a concern in nineteenth-century England. As noted by Radbill (1980: 8), 'The London Society for the Protection of Young Females recorded children no older than eleven entrapped in houses of prostitution' from which they were not allowed to escape until they were 'broken in'. On 6 July 1885, the *Pall Mall Gazette* shocked the London community with 'The Maiden Tribute of Modern Babylon', the revelation of the findings of its 'Secret Commission' concerning child prostitution in London (see Figure 1.1). The first of four in a series it contained horrific descriptions of young nursemaids abducted in London parks, of virgins inveigled into brothels with promises of fine clothes, and of parents selling their children's chastity for a few shillings. Thousands of children past the age of consent (then twelve) were bought by professional procurers from their poverty-stricken parents for the sexual use of gentlemen. Sometimes they were returned to their parents; sometimes they went into a brothel. As a result , the Criminal Law Amendment Act (1885) was passed, a piece of legislation which previously had substantial difficulty getting Parliamentary consideration. The Act raised the age of consent to 16, brought in new penalties for white slavery and introduced other measures to protect girls and young women from sexual violation. Ironically, the *Gazette*'s campaigning editor, William Stead (see Figure 1.2), was one of the first to be imprisoned (for nine months) under the legislation. Although well-intentioned, as part of the evidence collection for his 'Secret Commission' he had undertaken to procure a young woman.

In the UK, the Paedophile Information Exchange was set up in 1974, originally to campaign for the legal and social acceptance of paedophilia and for the rights of adults to have sexual relations with children. They subsequently reversed their strategy to campaign for the 'rights' of children to have sexual relations with adults, a move described as 'a skilful tactic' by Bowen and Hamblin (1981).

The growth of awareness by both professionals and members of the public of child sexual abuse in the late 1970s and early 1980s was slower in the UK than it was in the US. It has been argued that the reason for this is

THE

PALL MALL GAZETTE

An Evening Newspaper and Review.

No. 6336.—Vol. XLII.   *MONDAY, JULY* 6, 1885.   *Price One Penny.*

"WE BID YOU BE OF HOPE."

THE Report of our Secret Commission will be read to-day with a shuddering horror that will thrill throughout the world. After this awful picture of the crimes at present committed as it were under the very ægis of the law has been fully unfolded before the eyes of the public, we need not doubt that the House of Commons will find time to raise the age during which English girls are protected from inexpiable wrong. The evidence which we shall publish this week leaves no room for doubt—first, as to the reality of the crimes against which the Amendment Bill is directed, and, secondly, as to the efficacy of the protection extended by raising the age of consent. When the report is published, the case for the bill will be complete, and we do not believe that members on the eve of a general election will refuse to consider the bill protecting the daughters of the poor, which even the House of Lords has in three consecutive years declared to be imperatively necessary.

This, however, is but one, and that one of the smallest, of the considerations which justify the publication of the Report. The good it will do is manifest. These revelations, which we begin to publish to-day, cannot fail to touch the heart and rouse the conscience of the English people. Terrible as is the exposure, the very horror of it is an inspiration. It speaks not of leaden despair, but with a joyful promise of better things to come. *Wir heissen euch hoffen!* "We bid you be of hope," CARLYLE'S last message to his country, the rhythmic word with which GOETHE closes his modern psalm—that is what we have to repeat to-day, for assuredly these horrors, like others against which the conscience of mankind has revolted, are not eternal. "Am I my sister's keeper?" that paraphrase of the excuse of CAIN, will not dull the fierce smart of pain which will be felt by every decent man who learns the kind of atrocities which are being perpetrated in cool blood in the very shadow of our churches and within a stone's throw of our courts. It is a veritable slave trade that is going on around us; but, as it takes place in the heart of London, it is a scandal—an outrage on public morality—even to allude to it. We have kept silence far too long. There are a few devoted workers who have been labouring for years endeavouring to save those who might well address GORDON'S homely reproach to the "majority of us: "While you are eating and drinking and "resting on good beds, we, and those with me, are watching by night and by day"—working against this great wrong—happy, indeed, if they escaped obloquy and abuse for endeavouring to remind us of our duty. No longer will good men be able with easy conscience to join in that indignant "Hush!" by which the evil-doers have hitherto silenced every attempt to make articulate the smothered wail that rises unceasing from the woeful under-world. There is now an end to that conspiracy of silence by which, after every inquiry, "the door was each time quickly closed upon "the question, as the stone lid used to be shut down, in the "Campo Santo of Naples, upon the mass of human corpses that "lay festering beneath." That "stone lid" is raised now, never again, we may hope, to be closed until something has been done. Under the ruthless compulsion of publicity even those but indifferent honest will do more good than many of the most virtuous when the evil could be hidden out of sight.

That much may be done, we have good ground for hoping. If only because so little has hitherto been attempted. A dull despair has unnerved the hearts of those who face this monstrous evil, and good men have sorrowfully turned to other fields where their exertions might expect a better return. But the magnitude of this misery ought to lead to the redoubling, not to the benumbing of our exertions. No one can say how much suffering and wrong is irremediable until the whole of the moral and religious forces of the country are brought to bear upon it. Yet, in dealing with this subject, the forces upon which we rely in dealing with other evils are almost all paralysed. The Home, the School, the Church, the Press are silent. The law is actually accessory to crime. Parents culpably neglect even to warn their children of the existence of dangers of which many learn the first time when they have become their prey. The Press, which reports verbatim all the scabrous details of the divorce courts, recoils in pious horror from the duty of shedding a flood of light upon these dark places, which indeed are full of the habitations of cruelty. But the failure of the

Churches is, perhaps, the most conspicuous and the most complete. CHRIST'S mission was to restore man to a semblance of the Divine. The Child-Prostitute of our day is the image into which, with the tacit acquiescence of those who call themselves by His name, men have moulded the form once fashioned in the likeness of GOD.

If Chivalry is extinct and Christianity is effete, there is still another great enthusiasm to which we may with confidence appeal. The future belongs to the combined forces of Democracy and Socialism, which when united are irresistible. Divided on many points they will combine in protesting against the continued immolation of the daughters of the people as a sacrifice to the vices of the rich. Of the two, it is Socialism which will find the most powerful stimulus in this revelation of the extent to which under our present social system the wealthy are able to exercise all the worst abuses of power which disgraced the feudalism of the Middle Ages. Wealth is power, Poverty is weakness. The abuse of power leads directly to its destruction, and in all the annals of crime can there be found a more shameful abuse of the power of wealth than that by which in this nineteenth century of Christian civilization princes and dukes, and ministers and judges, and the rich of all classes, are purchasing for damnation, temporal if not eternal, the as yet uncorrupted daughters of the poor? It will be said they assent to their corruption. So did the female seris from whom the seigneur exacted the *jus primæ noctis.* And do our wealthy think that the assent wrung by wealth from poverty to its own undoing will avert the vengeance and the doom?

If people can only be got to think seriously about this matter progress will be made in the right direction. Evils once as universal and apparently inevitable as prostitution have disappeared. Vices almost universal are now regarded with shuddering horror by the least moral of men. Slavery has gone. A slave trader is treated as *hostis humani generis.* Piracy has disappeared. Intestine war is now almost unknown. Torture has been abolished. May we not hope, therefore, that if we try to do our duty to our sisters and to ourselves, we may greatly reduce, even although we never entirely extirpate, the plague of prostitution? For let us remember that—

    Every hope which rises and grows broad
    In the world's heart, by ordered impulse streams
    From the great heart of GOD.

And if that ideal seems too blinding bright for human eyes, we can at least do much to save the innocent victims who unwillingly are swept into the maelstrom of vice. And who is there among us bearing the name of man who will dare to sit down any longer with folded hands in the presence of so great a wrong?

THE MAIDEN TRIBUTE OF MODERN BABYLON.—I.

THE REPORT OF OUR SECRET COMMISSION.

IN ancient times, if we may believe the myths of Hellas, Athens, after a disastrous campaign, was compelled by her conqueror to send once every nine years a tribute to Crete of seven youths and seven maidens. The doomed fourteen, who were selected by lot amid the lamentations of the citizens, returned no more. The vessel that bore them to Crete unfurled black sails as the symbol of despair, and on arrival her passengers were flung into the famous Labyrinth of Dædalus, there to wander about blindly until such time as they were devoured by the Minotaur, a frightful monster, half man, half bull, the foul product of an unnatural lust. "The "labyrinth was as large as a town and had countless courts and galleries. "Those who entered it could never find their way out again. If they "hurried from one to another of the numberless rooms looking for "the entrance door, it was all in vain. They only became more hopelessly "lost in the bewildering labyrinth, until at last they were devoured by "the Minotaur." Twice at each ninth year the Athenians paid the maiden tribute to King Minos, lamenting sorely the dire necessity of bowing to his iron law. When the third tribute came to be exacted, the distress of the city of the Violet Crown was insupportable. From the King's palace to the peasant's hamlet, everywhere were heard cries and groans and the choking sob of despair, until the whole air seemed to vibrate with the sorrow of an unutterable anguish. Then it was that the hero Theseus volunteered to be offered up among those who drew the black balls from the brazen urn of destiny, and the story of his self-sacrifice, his victory, and his triumphant return, is among the most familiar of the tales which since the childhood of the world have kindled

Figure 1.1 'The Maiden Tribute of Modern Babylon', *Pall Mall Gazette*, 6 July 1885

8   *PALL MALL GAZETTE.*   [OCTOBER 24, 1885.

FOURTH EDITION.

A FRENCH POLITICAL AMNESTY.

(EXCHANGE TELEGRAPH COMPANY'S TELEGRAM.)

PARIS, Saturday.—It is reported that one of the first acts of the new Chamber when constituted will be to declare a general political amnesty. Many names are mentioned as likely to be included in this act of grace, but the most prominent are Louise Michel and Prince Krapotkin, the Nihilist.

THE ST. LOUIS MYSTERY.

(REUTER'S TELEGRAM.)

NEW YORK, Oct. 24.—The *New York Tribune* publishes a despatch from St. Louis stating that Mr. Samuel Brooks, of Hyde, has visited the prisoner Maxwell, who is charged with the murder of Mr. Preller, and has recognized him as his son Hugh.

THE ARMSTRONG CASE.

SECOND DAY'S PROCEEDINGS.

The knowledge of the difficulty in getting into the court prevented this morning anything in the nature of the crowd of yesterday, as depicted by our artist in the illustration below. And as a consequence, when the jury roll was called over at five minutes to ten o'clock, there were only the reporters, one or two barristers' clerks, one solitary barrister in a back seat, and two police constables in the dock awaiting the arrival of the defendants. In the five minutes that preceded the hour of commencing the counsel arrived,

tioning witness as to what took place at Wimbledon when her daughter was restored to her.

Cross-examined by Mr. Russell : There was considerable improvement in the child's appearance when she saw her at Wimbledon. It was at Mrs. Stead's suggestion that she saw her daughter alone. Mrs. Stead said that Mrs. Broughton was a very bad woman. When she wrote Mr. Booth asking him to return Eliza, and hoping that God would reward him for the trouble he had taken, she thought that he had been kind to the child and would return her. She did not say that she was satisfied with what the child had told her as to her not being outraged.

This answer was found not to be in accord with the witness's examination in chief before the magistrate. The question was repeated, and witness said it might be true that she said she was satisfied with what the child had told her.

You were a friend of Mrs. Broughton' —Yes.

How intimate? - Only as a neighbour.

To say good morning?—Yes, sir.

That was all ? -Yes, sir.

No further intimacy? No, sir.

You were not in the habit of going into each other's houses?—No, sir.

What her character or previous history had been you know nothing about?—No, sir.

And before Tuesday, the 2nd June, you had never seen the woman Mrs. Jarrett ?—No, sir.

You did not even know, I think, what her name was?—No, sir.

You did not know till when?—Till the first letter, a week after the child left.

Up to that time had you asked Mrs. Broughton what the name of this strange person was ?—Yes, sir ; I did.

MRS. ARMSTRONG.

ELIZA ARMSTRONG.

CHARLES ARMSTRONG.

MRS. JARRETT (" Becky.")

MRS. BROUGHTON (" Nancy").

MR. ARMSTRONG'S, 32, CHARLES STREET.

THE OLD BAILEY.

Above: Collage of Characters involved in Stead's trial as they appeared in the Pall Mall Gazette.

33

Figure 1.2   William Stead's trial, *Pall Mall Gazette*, 24 October 1885

attributable to avoidance and denial of the possibility of sexual abuse. This may be behind the claim by Mrazek et al. who considered the lack of take-up of the findings of previous research into child sexual abuse, that 'Despite these attempts to enlighten the professional community, no further efforts were made to determine the incidence of child sexual abuse or provide specialised treatment services for the children and their families' (1981: 48). After the events in Cleveland in 1987 and the subsequent inquiry (Butler-Sloss 1988) however, the sexual abuse of children became an issue that it would have been very difficult for most, whether professionals or public, to deny.

A comparison of the British and American approaches

There is a remarkable concordance of the pattern of awareness (late nineteenth century), loss of awareness – the hiatus – (early twentieth century) and re-emergence of awareness (late twentieth century) between the British approaches and the American approaches, for both physical abuse and sexual abuse. Two factors might account for a large part of this concordance. One is the common history and the shared language. The other is the operation of more global factors, for example, the depression of the 1930s and the emerging emphasis within social casework on psychoanalytic understanding as described by Costin (1992).

But how did the specific events in the US, and in particular the establishment of SPCCs, lead to a similar development in the UK? As noted by Hendrick (1994), by the 1880s child abuse was beginning to be seen as a social problem. In 1881, a reverend's letter to the *Liverpool Mercury* called for the establishment of a society to protect children in that city. A banker, Thomas Agnew, upon learning of the work of the SPCCs in the US, including that in New York, conferred with his Liberal MP (Samuel Smith) upon his return to the UK in 1882. The MP, in his turn, several weeks later at a meeting to consider the establishment of a dog's home, successfully lobbied for an appeal to protect children. On 19 April 1883, the Liverpool Society for the Prevention of Cruelty to Children was established. The emphasis appeared to follow the Boston model rather than the New York model: according to Hendrick, the SPCC 'put the emphasis not on removing the child from the home, but on compelling parents to be humane' (1994: 52). In 1889, the various SPCCs that had been established, with the exception of the founding branch at Liverpool, combined to form the National Society for the Prevention of Cruelty to Children (NSPCC). One of their first efforts was a vigorous campaign for the passage of the Prevention of Cruelty to and Protection of Children Act (1889).

The history of interagency working in child protection

The focus of this section will be to highlight the nature of interagency and interdisciplinary work to protect children in an historical perspective. How did agencies work together in the past to protect children? Or did they? These are difficult questions to address: not much has been written about this aspect of the history of child protection, and understanding must be gleaned from odd statements here and there in the literature. Yet the answers to these questions are vital when attempting to put current interagency work into a historical perspective.

The picture that emerges is one of good working relationships between various agencies in the broader child welfare working (judging from the source of referrals to organisations like the Charity Organisation Society (COS), and the membership of their boards of governors), but a less positive approach to working together with other agencies in the US between the child welfare charities and the child protection charities. As noted by Costin, Elbridge Gerry, 'frequently stated that the function of SPCCs was an exclusive one, with a clear demarcation from the work of children's charitable organizations. He did not make referrals to or seek collaboration with them' (1991: 180). This stance of separateness was supported by a New York Court of Appeal at the end of the nineteenth century, when the New York State Board of Charities proposed to exercise its charities' statutory inspection role in relation to the NYSPCC. Gerry refused to allow them to inspect the Society's shelter for children. The Appeal Court considered that the SPCC was a law-enforcing, rather than a charitable institution and was thus not subject to visitation. Whilst this may have been presented to the court as a decision about the nature and function of the NYSPCC, it also represents two aspects about how child abuse was coming to be viewed. First, it is an indication that the welfare needs of children in need of protection are different from their protection needs. The children in shelters were presumably no less in need of welfare safeguards than children looked after by charitable organisations for other reasons (perhaps even more so). This is emphasised here because of its relevance to contemporary debates in child protection. Second, it appeared as confirmation of Gerry's assertion that there was no overlap between destitute and dependent children and neglected and abused ones. The two problems were seen as separate and distinct (Gerry 1913). This speaks volumes about how the causes of child abuse were seen.

In his case study of a particular family at the turn of the century (a watershed in British child protection with the introduction of the Prevention of Cruelty to and Protection of Children Act in 1889), Ferguson noted the operation of interagency working:

In addition, child protection practice proceeded from the outset upon major collaborations with other state agencies not only in defining its object of intervention but in the pragmatics of ongoing casework. Two police officers, a general practitioner and the 'school board man' all rubbed shoulders with the inspector in the Pearson home in 1898. Add to this the involvement of the judiciary in the public sphere, and the 'child at risk' had already become a focal point of a variety of social practices, all claiming different levels of expertise. (1990: 133)

This suggests that at the turn of the century interagency working in Britain was more developed (or at least contained less antipathy) than in the US, despite the similarities between the structures that were being set up to protect children in the two countries. There is however, as I have indicated, very little direct evidence to draw upon to consider this.

2 A cross-cultural context of child protection

'Assessing the child abuse problem within any country is a major undertaking; assessing the child abuse problem world-wide can be overwhelming.' (Daro et al. 1996)

Introduction

This section will attempt to put the British management of child protection services into the context of child protection issues and management in other countries. The main focus is to address the question: 'What are the child protection concerns and how do agencies work together in other countries to protect children?' Because of the diversity of structures within the UK, it is important to re-emphasise that the term 'British' is mostly being used to refer to the system in England and Wales, the geographical area covered by *Working Together* (1991). Different systems apply in Northern Ireland and Scotland. Where these differences are significant to the issue under consideration, this will be made clear. In many respects, for example, as pointed out by Hetherington et al. (1997, below), the distinctive features of the Scottish system make it more akin to child protection systems in mainland Europe than to England. Murray and Hill (1991) compare the Scottish child welfare system with that found in England. Scottish children's hearings are described as fully committed to welfare principles, and keeping children in need of protection within a single system of decision making.

After a general introduction to some issues concerning child abuse and child protection in an international context, this section will address cross-cultural issues in four parts. First, the consideration of the history of British child protection has already laid a foundation for a comparison of contemporary British child protection with child protection in North America (the US and Canada). This is not to imply an equivalence between Canada and the US as regards child protection, but there are strong enough similarities warranting a consideration of both: '... the Canadian child welfare system has developed along similar lines to the American one ... Canadian legislative response to the problem of child abuse was generally later than in the US but followed similar lines' (Thompson-Cooper et al. 1993: 558). A second useful comparison is that between Britain and the rest of Europe. Very different perspectives have developed in Britain, for example historically, and in relation to the different types of judiciary systems, so that in a number of ways Britain stands out as being singular and apart from the other European countries. The role of language seems to be an obvious and significant factor accounting for this pattern. One may speculate on how different child protection in Britain would be if British education policy placed as great an emphasis on second-language acquisition as appears to be the case in other European countries. Another section will look at British child protection in the context of the rest of the world. In this sense, we can expect to find more similarities between Britain and both the US and the rest of Europe, as there are issues which affect the non-industrialised nations (child labour, child prostitution, sex tourism) more so than the industrialised ones, although issues such as child prostitution are not absent from Britain and Europe. In a presidential address to ISPCAN, Ferrier (1986) noted the differences between industrialised and developing countries in forms of abuse identified, although recognition of the extent of child abuse problems is made difficult by problems of definition. The final section in this part will consider the extent to which child protection services, in Britain and in other countries, address race, ethnicity and culture.

Of necessity, the material drawn upon here to highlight child protection in a cross-cultural context is selective. As the entire body of literature on child protection is located in some cultural or national context, one could easily be attempting to review the entire body of child abuse and child protection literature on the basis of location. This would clearly be impossible. Therefore material from different cultures and countries has been selected on the basis of relevance to themes developed in this book.

General considerations

A good place to begin is with the classic work on cross-cultural perspectives on child abuse and neglect by the anthropologist, Jill Korbin (1981). She edited a collection of nine papers presented at the 1978 symposium of the

American Anthropological Association, which were on the theme of exploring child abuse in an international context. She writes 'There is no universally accepted standard for optimal child rearing or for abusive and neglectful behaviours. Child maltreatment, like other categories of behaviour, must be defined by an aggregate of individuals, by a community or cultural group, to be meaningful' (Korbin 1981: 205). This places child abuse, along with many other social issues, right in the middle of an anthropological dimension with 'ethnocentrism' at one end and 'cultural relativism' at the other. Any consideration of child rearing (and consequently of child abuse) in an international context would be incomplete without a consideration of these two concepts.

What is ethnocentrism? Kottak has defined ethnocentrism as 'the tendency to view one's own culture as best and to judge the behaviour and beliefs of culturally different people by one's own standards' (1997: 48). Schulz and Lavenda go even further and suggest that it is 'the opinion that one's own way of life is natural or correct, indeed the only true way of being fully human' (1990: 32). From an ethnocentric perspective, there are universal standards, optimal ways of raising children, and right and wrong things to do with them, all judged from the perspective of a 'superior' society. Kincheloe and Steinberg note the connection between this kind of thinking and a 'colonial mind-set'. From this perspective, 'Everyone ... would be better off if they could be exposed to the glories of Western Civilization' (1997: 3).

Let us consider, by way of contrast, cultural relativism. Kottak defines cultural relativism as 'the position that the values and standards of cultures differ and deserve respect. Extreme relativism argues that cultures should be judged solely by their own standards' (1997: 48). It involves 'understanding another culture in its own terms sympathetically enough so that the culture appears to be a coherent and meaningful design for living' (Greenwood and Stini 1977: 182).

However, it would be an oversimplification to say that ethnocentrism is an unmitigated evil, and that cultural relativism is an unequivocal good. One simply has to look at the extremes of both positions to realise that a balance must be struck. The dangers of an ethnocentric perspective are relatively clear. It is a manifestation of the exercise of power imbalances between different cultures and societies. For this reason it is something which anthropologists have endeavoured to avoid. On the other hand, according to Korbin, 'a stance of extreme cultural relativism, in which all judgements of humane treatment of children are suspended in the name of cultural rights, may be used to justify a lesser standard of care for some children' (1991: 68). With ethnocentrism one has cultural hegemony; however, with cultural relativism one lacks a foundation from which to censure female circumcision, the internment of Jewish children (and adults) in concentration camps, the historical practice of foot-binding in China, and ultimately, the practice of child sacrifice as practised in some societies in former times. At its most extreme, cultural relativism would imply the acceptance of such practices on the basis of being only comprehensible within the culture in which they are/were practised, and not susceptible to external judgement. Channer and Parton are extremely critical of the concept of cultural relativism. This is because whilst defining the concept as 'the assumption that all cultures are equally valid' (1990: 111) they interpret it to entail a loss of individualisation within culture. They see it as a negative concept because it involves 'the failure to relate to the client as an individual, a subject rather than a typical object of that ethnic group' (1990: 113). They suggest that cultural relativism is subject to racist assumptions and should be abandoned because it 'leads to simplistic, polarized, and stereotypical views' (1990: 117). However, they also consider a Eurocentric view to be unhelpful.

There are other complexities (for anthropologists at least) as well. If ethnocentrism is an evil to be avoided, then to what extent should anthropologists be encouraged to engage in a type of meta-ethnocentrism, i.e. engaging cultures about the issue of ethnocentrism, (and of necessity, doing that from a particular cultural perspective)? This dilemma is described well by Seymour-Smith:

> Perhaps a more complex issue is that of whether anthropologists should also combat ethnocentrism in the peoples they study: should 'native ethnocentrism' be respected as part of the indigenous world view, or should the anthropologist combat prejudice and misinterpretation in the community by providing more information about the values and customs of other people. (1986: 97)

In terms of child abuse one can begin to see parallels on an anthropological level with the concept of 'good enough parenting' developed and amplified by Adcock and White (1985). The dilemma for practitioners, is: 'to what extent is the evaluation of not-good-enough parenting an expression of the different values between two cultures, middle class professionals and working class (or underclass) clients?' Are there universal standards that one can hold up as a standard? The resolution of the dilemma was found by adopting the needs of the child as the 'gold standard' against which parenting could be evaluated. It is based on the commonality of basic human needs influenced by early thinkers on the concepts of needs (Maslow 1943; Towle 1973; Kellmer Pringle 1975). In these models there is seen to be a hierarchy of needs, some more fundamental than others. Whilst children are seen as having a wide range of needs, many of which may be different for children in different circumstances (for example Black children may have specific needs arising from their ethnic identity; children with learning difficulties may have 'special' needs, etc.), those individualised needs rest on a foundation of needs that are shared by all children everywhere.

But the question to be asked is to what extent are these formulations of the 'commonality' of human needs themselves ethnocentric in their orientation? Do children all over the world have the same common needs? Clearly this question is almost impossible to answer, but one can suggest that perhaps some needs considered to be common and basic are actually culturally derived, and if not absent, certainly less strong in other cultures. A particular example might be autonomy. There appears to be a great emphasis on autonomy in Western conceptualisations of child development. It is the second of Erikson's (1963) eight stages of development (Autonomy vs. Shame/Doubt). Maslow's conception of needs (as described by Crain, 1992) suggested that an individual needed to achieve a cultural distance in order to achieve the highest level of need fulfilment, self-actualisation:

> ... self-actualizers, compared to most people, have maintained a certain independence from their society. Most people are so strongly motivated by needs such as belongingness, love, and respect that they are afraid to entertain any thought that others might disapprove of. (Crain 1992: 320)

Kellmer Pringle's (1975) development of the concept of 'responsibility' as one of the child's fundamental needs, is overlaid with overtones of 'independence' and 'autonomy', in such a way as to suggest that the ability of the child to learn to accept responsibility is for the purposes of being able to separate and function independently. It reflects an understanding perhaps based on the toddler's ambivalent motivation to leave the primary attachment figure (parent or carer) to seek new experiences. This can be seen as embedded in the concept of attachment, a fundamental concept in Western child care thinking, but not one with universal consistency throughout the world. There are very strong cultural variations in patterns of attachment. Woodhead (1998: 9) notes that 'Bowlby's original prescriptions for healthy emotional development reflect post-war family patterns and gender divisions as much as children's psychological needs.' Barnes (1995) summarises the work of Van IJzendoorn and Kroonenberg (1988), a meta-analysis of attachment studies across different cultures in Table 2.1. In the table, Secure, Avoidant and Ambivalent refer to the attachment-type measures developed by Ainsworth et al. (1978) using the technique known as the 'Strange Situation', a procedure in which young children were exposed to the presence of a stranger whilst their parent was present, separated from their parent while remaining with the stranger, and then reunited with the parent. Type B children, the most common, are those who are distressed upon their parent's departure but easily comforted upon

Table 2.1: Cross-cultural studies of attachment behaviour (from Barnes
1995; Van IJzendoorn and Kroonenberg 1988)

Country	No. of studies	Percentage of Attachment Types		
		Secure (Type B)	Avoidant (Type A)	Ambivalent (Type C)
West Germany	3	57	35	8
UK	1	75	22	3
Holland	4	67	26	6
Sweden	1	75	22	4
Israel	2	64	7	29
Japan	2	68	5	27
China	1	50	25	25
USA	18	65	21	14
Overall Average		65	21	14

reunion. Type A children are those who shunned contact when the parent
returned. Type C children, the least common, are those who although upset
when the parent left, were inconsolable when she returned, but at the same
time sought proximity with the parent.

The table highlights some very strong differences in the proportion of
these three types of attachment patterns in children in different cultures,
making a tendency to generalise about attachment across cultures something to be undertaken with extreme caution. As pointed out by Barnes
(1995), how children respond to the 'Strange Situation' may in itself be an
indication of the different child-rearing patterns across cultures to which
the children have been exposed. For example:

> ... one explanation of the pattern of results from Japanese studies is that the infants
> were very distressed in the Strange Situation because, in their culture, they are
> never normally left alone at 12 months ... There was no opportunity for them to
> show avoidance patterns (Type A) since at reunion the mothers typically went
> straight to them and picked them up immediately. This meant that an unusually
> high number of Japanese infants were scored as Type C at 12 months, yet in other
> settings they did not appear to be insecurely attached. (Barnes 1995: 17)

Outside Western nations the primacy of autonomy is less clear. In countries
where poverty is extreme and where infant mortality is high, there may
indeed be a high degree of emphasis placed on autonomy ('self-sufficiency'),

as found by LeVine (1977). In such societies, emphasis on the child's survival appears to preclude an emphasis on the child's cognitive development:

> Teaching interactions are de-emphasized ... a primary goal of parents who have scarce resources is to prepare infants for self-sufficiency. This belief results in early attempts to wean children and to teach them to walk and use the toilet. LeVine concludes, then, that parents in poor communities hold survival as the primary goal of infant care; once a child's survival is assured in older infancy, parents overriding concern is that the child become self sufficient'. (Trawick-Smith 1997: 580)

This would appear in some respects, although presumably for different reasons, to be similar to the Western emphasis on autonomy.

Compare that with the view of Boykin and Toms (1985), that models of child development such as Erikson's, which place an emphasis on autonomy reflect Anglo-Saxon ideals, and are not necessarily shared in other cultures. In some cultures, or at least in some families within other cultures, collectivism and social interdependence may be more valued than individualism and autonomy. Harrison et al. (1990) considered this to be the case in African American, Puerto Rican, and Native American cultures. Wagatsuma noted a similar state in Japan: 'Interdependence among people, instead of individual autonomy, characterizes Japanese social relations' (1981: 132). This is echoed by Yamamoto and Iga who note in comparing Japan and the US, 'In the American society independence is a virtue in itself; in Japan there is a pervasive awareness of mutual interdependence' (1983: 171). Caudill and Weinstein (1969) note that for Japanese mothers, who spend much of their time with their infants, the American practice of 'baby-sitting' may well be considered as neglect. Olson (1981) describes her experiences of raising a young daughter in Turkey, learning that her maid/nurse was extremely critical of subjecting her daughter 'to the loneliness of sleeping alone'.

Another example of child-rearing practice that might vary in different cultures is that of sibling caretaking, the practice of older siblings in a family assuming responsibility for younger ones. In Western societies, a family in which children are left too frequently in the care of older siblings run the risk of being considered neglectful. This is especially true if the sibling care-taker is quite young herself (the caretaking role usually, but not invariably falls to female children in the family rather than males). Weisner and Gallimore (1977) looked at sibling caretaking and noted that although the practice is widespread, there has been little study of its ethnographic incidence. Minturn and Lambert (1964) looked at mothers in six cultures, one of which was a Western culture (New England). Whilst not reporting direct measures of sibling caretaking, on the basis of interviews, they reported that the New

England mothers spent a greater proportion of their time in charge of infants than those of any of the other five cultures they studied. Whiting and Whiting (1975), also studying six different cultures, noted that the level of sibling caretaking is more frequent where women have more work to do, where mother's work takes her away from the home, and where circumstances (for example, residence, birth order and family size) make alternative caretakers available. Woodhead (1998) notes a number of differences between children's experiences in societies with resources and those without, summarised in the following table:

Table 2.2: Availability of resources (Woodhead 1998)

Where material resources are plentiful	Where material resources are scarce
Confident in using material in a playful way	Respect material resources as precious
Presented with choices	Few choices available
Feel powerful in negotiating, consuming and owning property	Feel privileged to use play equipment

Material status combines with survival prospects:

> While a mother from Boston might view the Gusii [Kenya] practice of demand feeding as 'spoiling' the child, the demand for obedience as 'repressive' and the use of young children as caregivers as 'abusive', the traditional Gusii mother might view the Western practice of leaving infants to cry as 'abusive', tolerating a toddler's challenging behaviour as 'spoiling' and encouraging playful fun as 'over indulgent'. (Woodhead 1998: 14)

Woodhead (1998), noting that 'With few exceptions, textbook child development originates mainly in Europe and North America' (p.8), gives examples of difficulties in applying Western notions of child development to non-Western cultures. He notes for example in comparing mother-child dyads in India, Guatemala, Turkey and the US, that 'While "guided participation" was a feature in all these settings, the goals and processes of learning and teaching varied.' Comparing the use of 'motherese' in twelve societies, US mothers ranked highest in the extent of their sociability with their children.

Clearly there are other examples one could cite to illustrate how different the experience of being a child is depending upon the culture in which one is brought up. These illustrations serve to remind the reader of the importance of being aware that decisions about what constitutes abuse are, as we are told in *Child Protection: Messages from Research* (DoH, 1995a), definitional ones; furthermore, the process of making a definition is, in itself, a socially powerful, and potentially abusive action. This applies in a cross-cultural context as well as in relation to individual children and families.

Finkelhor and Korbin (1988) have suggested a rather broad definition of child abuse which crosses national and cultural boundaries as that portion of harm that results from what people do that is 'proscribed, proximate, and preventable'. As pointed out by Korbin, 'definitional issues must be structured into a coherent framework so that child abuse and neglect can be identified within and across cultural contexts' (1991: 68). She describes three levels of definition formulation:

- Practices considered acceptable within a culture but considered unacceptable by those outside it
- Variations between cultures on the definitions of what falls within, and outside of, acceptable behaviour towards children
- The abuse of children by society, for example, through poverty, inadequate housing, poor maternal and child health care, and lack of nutritional resources (and Korbin considers these as factors beyond parental control).

Korbin then defines eight factors which may operate across cultures to make children more vulnerable to abuse:

- Health status
- Children who are deformed or handicapped
- Excess or unwanted children
- Children who are born under unusual, stigmatized, or difficult circumstances
- Vulnerabilities associated with particular developmental stages
- Gender
- Certain behaviours and personality characteristics, and
- Diminished social supports.

This approach to identifying factors applying across cultures to adopt universal standards can be compared with that adopted by Martin Woodhead (1998) addressing the slightly different, but relevant, question of how to identify standards for ensuring quality of provision for young children across cultures that have such different issues and concerns for the upbringing of children. Based on his study of early child care and education programmes in India, Mexico, France, Venezuela and Kenya, he observed that quality of care was a priority, and yet the programmes appeared to have little in common. Criticising the notion of Developmentally Appropriate Practice (DAP), which was an attempt to identify universals in child development, and criticised for being insensitive to cultural development, he puts forward principles of Practice Appropriate to the Context of Early Development (PACED) which is based on local variations in children's development and emphasises local stakeholders' interest in quality of child development.

Sexual abuse

The use of children for the sexual gratification of adults is a problem that causes difficulties not only within different countries around the world but raises issues about the ability to work across national boundaries to protect children through coordinated international efforts. But it also raises definitional issues in a cross-cultural context.

DeChesnay (1989) notes that although child sexual abuse is a global phenomenon, it is not always admitted to exist nor defined as a problem. Konker (1992) highlights the diversity in her specific consideration of sexual abuse from an anthropological perspective: 'There are cultural differences in what is defined as appropriate adult sexual conduct, sexual maturity, and sexual pleasure ... Valued adult-child sexual contact routinely occurs as a part of initiation activities in at least 20 countries throughout the world' (1992: 148). In Great Britain, before the study by Smith and Grocke (1995), little information was available about what were considered acceptable and unacceptable practices regarding sexual behaviour. Their starting point was that more was known about sexual deviance than about sexual normality or ordinariness. They found class and gender differences as well as offering observations on particular types of behaviour. They found that 'manual social class families tended to be more restrictive in their practice and attitudes towards sexuality. For example, they reported less nudity in their families and less discussion of sexual matters within the household ...'. Girls 'had more detailed knowledge about their own sex ... Mothers discussed sexual matters in more detail with their daughters so increasing their knowledge and vocabulary.' As regards indicators of abuse they found that:

> Excessive masturbation, oversexualised behaviour, an extensive sexual curiosity or sexual knowledge and genital touching are thought to be indicators of sexual abuse. But, as these behaviours are found to be common within a community sample, these behaviours are not *in themselves* sufficient to suggest abuse. (DoH 1995a: 82–3)

Finkelhor (1994) explored the epidemiology of child sexual abuse in 20 predominantly Caucasian, Western and Christian cultures, and found that whilst there were variations (in part at least attributable to the range of methodological approaches and definitional differences), 'In every country where researchers have asked about it ... an important percentage of the adult population ... acknowledged a history of sexual abuse' (1994: 413). Konker (1992) stresses that 'Each culture has a right to define appropriate social conduct on its own terms', which, while being a point that can hardly be disputed, raises considerable difficulties when people from one culture are resident in a different culture. It is also a difficulty when one considers an issue such as sex tourism, where people may travel (usually from more developed countries to less developed ones) for the express purpose of sexual relations with children in a society in which there are no legal prohibitions against such activities, or where existing sanctions are less actively pursued, either because of a lack of resources or for other reasons. At the BASPCAN Congress in Edinburgh, 1997, Professor DeSilva presented a video highlighting the child sex tourism problem in Sri Lanka, and the steps that were being taken to address it. The Philippines has been notorious for child prostitution, importing paedophiles from all over the globe for the purpose of sexual relations with children as young as five years old. Forbes has described child prostitution in the Philippines as 'a matter of national and international shame ... a stain that is particularly noticeable against the social fabric of the nation, which is family-oriented, with families central to social organization' (1989: 186).

The UN Convention on the Rights of the Child

Having described some of the difficulties inherent in the enterprise of identifying standards of child welfare that should prevail in a world-wide community of nations, let us now consider the most significant effort to date to achieve this, the adoption and ratification of the UN Convention on the Rights of the Child. On 20 November 1989, the Convention was unanimously adopted by the General Assembly of the United Nations, and within one year was ratified by a sufficient number of member nations to give it legal force. The origins of the Convention can be traced back to principles of child welfare and protection set out in the Declaration of Geneva in 1924, which were developed in 1948, and subsequently adopted by the UN General Assembly as a ten-point Declaration of the Rights of the Child in 1959. The Convention has clearly been a long time in the making, taking most of the twentieth century to reach ratification and adoption.

The lot of children around the world is not a happy one, although the overall picture is one of great variability. Some countries appoint an ombudsman for children – for example Sweden (Sylwander 1997) and Norway (Waage 1997) – who have responsibility to promote the interests of children in relation to public and private authorities. In Denmark, there is a National Council on

Children's Rights, which has very close links with children's groups around the country to keep a finger on the pulse of issues of concern to children (Muldkjaer 1997). On the other hand, Moorehead (1989) provides a range of examples of the exploitation of children in a world-wide context (street children, exploitative employment, children and war, imprisonment of children, child trafficking, sexual exploitation, 'disappeared' children). Lee-Wright (1990) and Sawyer (1988) have described the situations of children enslaved around the world. Nevertheless, it would be a mistake to see the principles of the Convention as applying to a greater extent to underdeveloped countries; there is no room for complacency concerning the position of children's welfare and rights in developed countries.

The Convention sets minimum standards against which the treatment of children in various countries can be judged. It is a comprehensive document containing 54 articles (1–41 in part I addressing the provisions relating to children; 42–54 in part II addressing how the convention should be implemented). Articles 1–41 address the following:

- Protection of children from discrimination
- Best interests of the child as a basis for actions
- Duty to respect rights and responsibilities
- The inherent right to life of all children
- The right to a name and nationality
- Protection for the child's identity
- Child's right to live with parents (unless not in best interest; to have contact if separated)
- Right of families to be reunited if necessary crossing frontiers
- Prevention of kidnapping and abduction of children
- Child's right to express views and opinions on matters concerning him or otherwise
- Child's right to freedom of thought, conscience and religion (subject to parental guidance and national law)
- Freedom of association
- Right to privacy
- Encouragement of appropriate media information to child; discouragement of inappropriate media information
- Support to both parents to bring up child
- Obligation to protect children from abuse and neglect
- Protection of children without families
- Adoption, where recognised, to be in child's best interest
- Special protection for refugee children
- Right of handicapped children to services to help them lead a full life
- Child's right to health; state's obligation to reduce infant mortality

- When children placed, to be reviewed
- Right of children to social security
- Child's right to an adequate standard of living
- Child's right to education (free and compulsory primary education)
- Education to foster respect for basic human rights; respect for child's cultural and national values
- Right of minority children to enjoy their own culture, religion and language
- Child's right to leisure, play and cultural activities
- State's obligation to protect children from labour that is harmful to their health, education or development (minimum age for employment; regulate employment)
- Protection from drugs
- Protection from sexual exploitation
- States to prevent sale, trafficking or abduction of children
- Protection from other forms of exploitation
- Prohibition of torture, cruel treatment or punishment, capital punishment, life imprisonment, etc. of children
- No child under 15 to take part in armed conflict; children affected by war to be protected
- Treatment for recovery of children affected by war
- Juvenile justice: avoidance of court proceedings and residential placements.

Melton (1991) maintains that the Convention confirms that children are persons, legally and morally, and that the state should ensure that they are treated with dignity. It requires of governments substantial reforms of most existing child protection systems. Some specific provisions of the Convention deal with child protection. These are Article 19 (protection from abuse and neglect), Article 24.3 (abolition of traditional practices prejudicial to children's health), Article 34 (protection from sexual exploitation) and Article 36 (protection from other forms of exploitation). Let us consider these more fully:

Article 19

1. States Parties shall take all appropriate legislative, administrative, social and educational measures to protect the child from all forms of physical or mental violence, injury or abuse, neglect or negligent treatment, maltreatment or exploitation including sexual abuse, while in the care of parent(s), legal guardian(s), or any other person who has the care of the child.

2. Such protective measures should, as appropriate, include effective procedures for the establishment of social programmes to provide necessary support for the child and for those who have the care of the child, as well as for other forms of prevention and for identification, reporting, referral, investigation, treatment, and follow-up of instances of child maltreatment described heretofore, and, as appropriate, for judicial involvement.

This Article makes it a responsibility of government to take action (through legislative and other means) to protect children from all forms of abuse. The addition of the phrase 'while in the care of parent(s), legal guardian(s), or any other person who has the care of the child' presumably does not mean to exclude children from whom there is no one in that position, but rather to define the type of abuse situation that this Article is directed at. The second part of the Article provides that government should establish social welfare programmes to support families and prevent abuse, as well as arrangements to identify, investigate, adjudicate, and provide treatment in respect of children who have been abused. The emphasis given to prevention is welcome, given the tendency in many countries (as I have earlier described in connection with the UK) for the emphasis on investigation to be at the expense of both prevention and treatment.

Article 24.3

States Parties shall take all effective and appropriate measures with a view to abolishing traditional practices prejudicial to the health of children.

Traditional practices such as the foot-binding of young girls in China would, if they were still being practised, come under this Article, as indeed would any ceremonial or ritual scarification or body-part piercing, provided it could be established that it was indeed, 'prejudicial to the health' of the child. Sawyer (1988) includes child marriage, force-feeding of children prior to sale by auction and female circumcision as exploitative traditional practice. Female circumcision, clitoridectomy, or 'female genital mutilation' as it has come to be termed is probably the most controversial form of traditional practice. As pointed out by Newell (1991) the need for circumcision of both young girls and boys is not supported by medical evidence, and is a practice which causes considerable pain and discomfort, especially if carried out without anaesthetic. The practice has been illegal in the UK (except on specific physical and mental health grounds) for more than a decade (under The Prohibition of Female Circumcision Act 1985). Nevertheless, despite the legal prohibition, it continues to be practised illegally. According to Black and Debelle (1995) although there is a considerable body of literature on the practice in Africa, little has been written about its existence in Britain. Unfortunately, prohibiting the practice in developed countries can become confused with issues about the will within the dominant culture to accept the cultural norms, customs and practices of ethnic minority communities. To avoid this, a strategy of involving members, and particularly leaders, of the ethnic minority community to address the issue will be useful to disentangling the ethical and moral issues of one culture exerting its will and power over another.

Article 34

> *States Parties undertake to protect the child from all forms of sexual exploitation and sexual abuse. For these purposes States Parties shall in particular take all appropriate national, bilateral and multilateral measures to prevent:*
> *(a) the inducement or coercion of a child to engage in any unlawful sexual activity;*
> *(b) the exploitative use of children in prostitution or other unlawful sexual practices;*
> *(c) the exploitative use of children in pornographic performances and materials.*

These provisions specifically address the responsibility that governments have to operate conjointly to prevent sexual activity involving children, including child prostitution and child pornography.

Article 36

> *States Parties shall protect the child against all other forms of exploitation prejudicial to any aspects of the child's welfare.*

This can be seen as a catch-all clause, designed to give governments considerable flexibility to safeguard the welfare of the child from harms that may not be addressed in the specific Articles.

Britain and North America

Two essential differences between child protection in North America and the UK are the diversity of arrangements in the US for protecting children arising from the federal structure, and mandatory reporting requirements.

Within the US there are 50 different sets of child protection arrangements; in the UK there are three (England and Wales, Scotland, Northern Ireland). Clearly, there are difficulties associated with different types of child protection arrangements, especially when families can freely move from one jurisdiction to the other. However, there is no evidence to suggest that parents under suspicion or investigation relocate to a different area on the basis of the prevailing legislative child protection arrangements (although they may simply relocate to avoid detection). It would be extremely difficult to undertake any type of comparative analysis of the variations between the states of the US within the scope of this book. Information however can be obtained from the National Clearinghouse on Child Abuse and Neglect Information which provides detailed information on the different child protection arrangements in each of the states. This information is available on the Internet:

http://www.calib.com/nccanch/services/statutes.htm

The information includes for each state the definitions of the various forms of abuse, the legislative statements requiring mandated reporting, penalties for failure to report, immunity from liability for reporting, malicious reporting, and more.

Bell and Tooman note that in Scotland there is a legislative requirement that 'any person who has knowledge or a reasonable suspicion that a child is being abused or is at risk of abuse should communicate their concern to one or more of the agencies with statutory duties and/or powers to investigate and intervene' (1994: 339), although whether the strength of this 'should' is equivalent to a legal compulsion is unclear.

Mandatory reporting

Mandatory reporting requires professionals (and in some cases members of the public) to report suspicions concerning child abuse to agencies that are in a position to intervene to protect the child. Where they are in effect they are usually accompanied by definitions as to what types of situations must be reported, sanctions for failure to report, provisions for immunity from liability arising from the reporting (usually providing protection provided the report is 'in good faith'), and frequently provisions concerning sanctions for malicious reporting (more commonly a problem with non-professional reporters of child abuse).

Mandatory reporting of child abuse, which began in the US in 1963, is an issue that divides child protection in the Western world. Gilbert (1997) looks at child protection in nine different countries, dividing them broadly into those with mandatory reporting requirements (US, Canada, Sweden, Denmark and Finland) and those without (England, Belgium, Netherlands and Germany). Within Europe, of 14 European countries described by Ruxton (1996), seven had mandatory reporting requirements, and seven did not (see below for more details).

In the US, mandatory reporting, which applies in every state, now has a 30-year history. Its origins can be traced to a Children's Bureau-sponsored conference in 1962 to consider the challenge of child abuse. At that time a model statute for mandatory reporting was put forward, and several others were suggested by other agencies in the years that followed (Hutchison

1993; Bell and Tooman 1994). Between 1963 and 1967 every state (and the District of Columbia) passed a law requiring the reporting of child abuse. In some cases, as in that of California, described by Lawrence-Karski (1997) this may have built on previous existing state legislation requiring the reporting by hospitals and physicians of *any* intentionally inflicted injuries (adopted by that state as early as 1929).

Canada also has mandatory reporting requirements. Unlike the US, in Canada there is little literature on the Canadian child protection systems and no central data collection system on the incidence of child abuse and the operation of child protection in the various provinces and territories (Thompson-Cooper et al. 1993). Both they and Swift (1997) report that in Canada, all jurisdictions except one, the Yukon, have mandatory reporting provisions in their child protection legislation.

In Britain, in the 1980s, an interdepartmental review of child care law (DHSS 1985a) considered, but did not support, the adoption of mandatory reporting requirements along similar lines to the US. It considered that such reporting would reduce the sense of professional responsibility and would put barriers between professionals and the public. It noted that 'anyone is free to pass information to responsible organisations'. Bell and Tooman describe this position as being based on a 'naive and idealistic understanding of professionalism'. They consider that studies of inquiry reports and of inter-professional work point to 'UK professionals being much less concerned about the welfare of children and much more concerned about their own power and status' (1994: 353). They argue that in Britain the emphasis has been on investigation, not reporting, and consider that this position should now be re-evaluated as there is a strong case for the implementation of mandatory reporting in the UK. Let us consider the arguments in favour and against mandatory reporting.

Arguments in favour of mandatory reporting

Bell and Tooman (1994) note that mandatory reporting leads to an increased level of reporting, increased involvement of other professionals in child protection, and an improvement of other professionals' knowledge and understanding of child protection. Fürniss (1996) considers that only a small minority of children needing protection will have parents insightful and motivated enough to seek treatment; it is the others however, that need it most. He considers that countries with mandatory reporting provide the highest protection and the most therapeutic developments. He also notes that the presence of mandatory reporting requirements means that the professional community cannot avoid dealing with the problem. Toth (1996) notes that without mandatory reporting children would continue to be victimised and abusers would not be accountable for their actions, and that through mandatory reporting public awareness of child abuse is raised. Echoing the point made by Fürniss (1996), Toth notes that before mandatory reporting, despite privileged communication, very few abusers came forth voluntarily. Finally, in relation to the point of high numbers of unsubstantiated cases, she notes that a good investigation can identify a false or mistaken accusation and vindicate the accused. Besharov (1990) considers that mandatory reporting requirements have resulted in both increased numbers of reports and fewer deaths of children from abuse.

Arguments against mandatory reporting

Marneffe (1996) notes that the main aim of child protection has been narrowed to investigation, removal if necessary of children, and exacting accountability of abusers. The larger social and psychological factors are 'not on the foreground'. Both she and Bell and Tooman (1994) note that mandatory reporting results in too many unsubstantiated reports and too many intrusive investigations, while children are not helped. Besharov (1990) estimates that nearly two-thirds of reports turn out to be unfounded, '... as many as 65 per cent of all reports are closed after an initial investigation reveals no evidence of maltreatment. This situation is in sharp contrast to 1975, when only about 35 per cent of all reports were unfounded' (1990: 10). The time comparison suggests that the increase in unfounded reports is due to the introduction of mandatory reporting.

Marneffe (1996: 42) also notes that mandatory reporting results in a distortion of resource allocation: the 'only form of child welfare service available in many countries is concentrated in a controlling child protection system', a point echoed by Thompson-Cooper et al. (1993). Belsey (1996) considers that the evidence for non-mandatory reporting is based on the effectiveness of health, social and judicial policies addressing the issue of child abuse and neglect in several communities and countries. The effectiveness of reporting is related to presence of treatment programmes and training of different disciplines. By implication, although he does not say this explicitly, this may be lacking. Bell and Tooman (1994) consider that mandatory reporting blurs the distinction between reporting and investigating (how much of what type of information is needed, by whom, in order to report). A further consideration noted by some authors (apart from the relative resource allocations referred to by Marneffe above) is the sheer expense of maintaining mandatory reporting. The proliferation of investigations necessitated by the introduction of mandatory reporting are putting child protection systems under strain. In connection with Canadian mandatory reporting, 'Because of the emphasis on case-finding, the limited resources have been stretched to the point where families with serious problems of child abuse do not get the services they require' Thompson-Cooper et al. (1993: 557). Between 1980 and 1985 reports of all forms of child abuse increased by 55 per cent, whereas the funding available for agencies to respond to child abuse reports only increased by two per cent (Thompson-Cooper et al. 1993). It needs to be acknowledged however, that this is not just a problem for those countries which have mandatory reporting requirements, but it is certainly made worse by the large numbers of unsubstantiated cases.

Under arguments against mandatory reporting might also be included reasons given why professionals do not report, despite the existence of reporting requirements. Besharov (1990) notes that professionals did not report as many as 40 per cent of sexual abuse cases, that nearly 30 per cent of fatal or serious abuse cases were not reported, that nearly 50 per cent of moderate physical abuse cases were not reported, and that as many as 70 per cent of fatal or serious neglect cases were not reported (rising to three-quarters for cases of moderate neglect). Bell and Tooman (1994) summarise some of the reasons why professionals might not report despite requirements to do so and sanctions for failure to report:

- Fear of physical retaliation
- View that reporting will not accomplish anything
- Inability to recognise indicators of abuse
- Fear of being sued by the family
- Fear of therapeutic relationship being jeopardised.

What are we to make of these arguments in favour and against mandatory reporting? In some ways it is like the optimist who sees a half glass of water as 'half full' while the pessimist sees it as 'half empty'. The concerns of the antagonists appear to be with different children. Those who advocate mandatory reporting are concerned that there should be no children who are being abused who are not drawn into a system designed to protect them. At its most extreme, it is the argument that the net may catch those who are less in need of protection, as long as it catches *all* of those who need to be protected. No child should be unprotected. Opponents of mandatory reporting, whilst not indifferent to the plight of those children who may be abused yet unprotected, are looking at the harm done to those children who are involved in a system designed to protect them. 'System abuse' is the phrase that has been used to note the harm done to children in the system, both to those who may clearly be in need of protection, and to those whose need for protection may be less significant. It is looking at the protection system as 'half empty'. It is not the intended effect that causes concern, but the unintended harm.

Any attempt to reconcile these differences cannot simply be based on the accepted standard of being 'child centred' because both are child-centred positions – they are concerned however with different children: 'Child-centredness is a principle with multiple meanings depending on context, and will have differential applications according to context' (Hetherington et al. 1997: 22). An attempt to reconcile these conflicting positions needs to be based on some type of compromise that will maximise the system's ability to provide for both groups of children. How is this to be achieved?

As one of the main issues in comparing the advantages and disadvantages of mandatory reporting is the number of unsubstantiated cases brought into the net, it may be useful to consider this particular point in comparison with the UK. Fortunately, we have material (Gibbons et al. 1995a) that tells us about what happens in the course of referrals to British child protection agencies and how many drop out along the various stages. Unfortunately, it is quite difficult to make direct comparisons because of the systems' different natures. At what point for example, in the British system, would a case be considered to be 'unfounded' or 'unsubstantiated' in the North American sense? Besharov (1990) describes reports as being unfounded 'after an initial investigation'. Thompson-Cooper (1993) notes that in Quebec a case is considered to be unfounded only after the family have been 'intensively interviewed'. How do these compare with British trends?

Gibbons et al. (1995a) examined the way eight local authorities operated their local child protection procedures. They looked at the number of children referred to child protection, the number that were subsequently investigated, the number that were the subject of a child protection conference, and finally, the number whose names were added to the child protection register. They found:

First Filter: Initial decision by duty social worker whether to investigate
  Investigated (3/4 of referrals)
  Not Investigated (1/4 of referrals)

Second Filter: Decision by manager whether to call conference
  Conferenced (1/3 of cases investigated)
  Not Conferenced (2/3 of cases investigated)

Third Filter: Decision by case conference whether to place the child's name on the child protection register
  Registered (2/3 of cases conferenced)
  Not Registered (1/3 of cases conferenced)

Figure 2.1 shows the successive drop-out rate from the system using those figures.

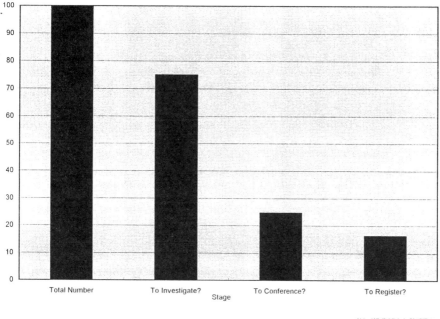

Figure 2.1   Filtering of child protection referrals (N = 100%)
(adapted from Gibbons et al. 1995)

Cumulatively, of all those referred, 75 per cent are investigated, 25 per cent
are subject of a child protection conference and 16 per cent are added to the
child protection register. This could be interpreted as non-substantiation rates
of 25 per cent, 75 per cent and 84 per cent respectively. Twenty-five per cent
are not even investigated. Seventy-five per cent are either not investigated, or
if investigated, do not warrant further child protection action (i.e. a child
protection conference). And finally, 84 per cent of children referred do not
need to have their names added to the child protection register, and do not
need the kind of interagency child protection plan that can be provided by a
child protection conference.

There are clear requirements for making the decision to place a child's name
on the register, and the need for a child protection conference, following from
the investigation undertaken under section 47 of the Children Act 1989, will
be evaluated on the basis of the likelihood of the child(ren)'s name needing to
be added to the register. The requirements in order for a child's name to be
added to the child protection register are:

One of the following requirements needs to be satisfied:

> i) there must be one or more identifiable incidents which can be described as having adversely affected the child. They may be acts of commission or omission. They can be either physical, sexual, emotional or neglectful. It is important to identify a specific occasion or occasions when the incident has occurred. Professional judgement is that further incidents are likely;

or

> ii) Significant harm is expected on the basis of professional judgement of findings of the investigation in this individual case or on research evidence. (*Working Together*, 1991 , paragraph 6.39)

Nevertheless, substantial numbers of children are being involved in the child protection system, where the need for this type of intervention is doubtful. And this would appear to be the case, when comparing Britain with North America, regardless of whether or not there is mandatory reporting.

As a final point, it needs to be noted that the lack of consensus concerning mandatory reporting continues. Some argue (for example, Bell and Tooman 1994) that Britain, having rejected mandatory reporting, should now reconsider introducing it. Others, like Hutchison (1993), argue that it is time to revise the definitions of abuse contained within the mandatory reporting requirements so that only the most serious cases are investigated. Others, like Thompson-Cooper et al. (1993), suggest that whilst mandatory reporting requirements may have been useful in their time (particularly for raising public awareness of the issue), they have now outlived their usefulness and it is time to dispose of them: 'In our desire to protect children, we have protected some, but we have also harmed many and intervened unnecessarily in the lives of families' (Thomson-Cooper et al. 1993: 561).

In the UK we have talked about 'refocusing' and a 'lighter touch'; in the US, Lindsey and Trocmé (1994) have described it using a 'red herring' metaphor:

> We have described child abuse as the 'red herring' of child welfare. The phrase derives from the practice of drawing a red herring across a trail pursued by hunting dogs in order to confuse them and set them off in the wrong direction. We use the phrase 'red herring' because concerns with the horror of child abuse has shifted the focus of the public child-welfare system away from a broad concern with the welfare of children to the increasingly narrow task of protecting children from severe assault. (1994: 91)

Both essentially indicate a basic 'taking one's eye off the ball', and losing sight of what is the essence of the issue.

Britain and Europe

If making a comparison with one or two countries in North America presents complexities, the task of undertaking a comparison between Britain and each European country is enormous, and beyond the scope of this book. However, it is possible to highlight similarities and differences between Britain and Europe, both taken collectively and using examples from individual countries. Though there are similarities, this is not to imply any homogeneity of approach to child protection within mainland Europe.

According to Hallett, European colleagues consider the British system to be 'punitive, coercive, unhelpful and anti-therapeutic' (1993: 145). Most European countries show far more interest in therapy and after-care than in punishing offenders. Boushel notes 'The British approach is viewed by many as continuing to be overly concerned with the identification and punishment of abusive behaviour, rather than the amelioration of the personal and social factors underlying it' (1994: 176). Sluckin and Dolan (1989) looking at child abuse intervention in the Netherlands, France and West Germany found less reliance on professional social workers with statutory powers than in the UK. Doek (1991) also found in Europe that state intervention is not directly linked to child abuse and neglect, although on this specific point, he was not making a direct comparison between the UK and European countries across the Channel.

The most comprehensive work so far undertaken comparing child protection in Britain with other European countries is that by Hetherington et al. (1997). Building on previous work undertaken comparing child protection in France and Britain (Cooper et al. 1995), they drew comparisons between eight European child protection systems: Belgium (Flemish and Francophone), France, Germany, Italy, the Netherlands, UK (England and Scotland). In order to make comparisons, the research was undertaken in two stages. They identified social workers in the eight countries (seven groups in England, one group in each of the other seven countries), and invited them to take part in two seminars on cross-cultural comparisons of child protection. Using case material (as far as possible devoid of national characteristics or features), the first seminar explored with workers how they would deal with the case material. The sessions were videotaped. The second stage involved taking the case material and the videotape and having it dubbed into the language of a different country and then showing both to social workers from that country. Workers were asked to comment on what they saw. This discussion was also videotaped. From the results of this investigation they extracted a number of themes of commonalities and differences. Considering first the commonalities:

1   All of the child protection systems considered operated within a wider legal/judicial framework administered by the state.
2   In all the states there was a division of providing child welfare services between the voluntary/independent agencies and the statutory agencies (and in Germany, the Netherlands and Belgium the voluntary sector is particularly strong).
3   All countries examined provided universal education from the age of five or six (this is important because of the significance of professional relationships with teachers and education staff).
4   All of the countries had universal health provision, although there were significant variations in the involvement of health agencies in child protection.
5   There was a commonality of professional assumptions, specifically, for example:

- promoting the autonomy of individuals and families
- preserving confidentiality
- social practice being based on knowledge of social sciences from all countries
- the situations of abusing families (case material) were complex and not easily understood.

Some of the differences are that in all countries except England:

- Judges involved with children have professional training for that role
- The judicial system is inquisitorial
- There is opportunity for informal dialogue between the social workers and the judge (or in Scotland, the reporter and the children's panel)
- There was a possibility of judicial intervention on the basis of the child's welfare alone.

England was the only country where child welfare and juvenile justice issues are separated, and where it was necessary to have evidence of significant harm related to parental responsibility to take legal action (other than on an emergency basis).

The English groups saw the other European child protection systems as being more flexible, offering more support to social workers, putting more pressure on parents, being less aware of parental rights, relying less on evidence, being less bureaucratic, and having a more user-friendly legal system. Inversely however, the English groups were seen by the European workers as spending too little time considering the family, not using theory or concepts freely, giving insufficient consideration to the needs and suffering of the children in their own right, spending too much time on procedural and evidential discussion, and operating a system that encouraged, or at least did not defuse, the level of conflict between professionals and the family.

Hetherington et al. (1997) conclude:

> ... in Europe, in countries with similar socio-economic circumstances, viable child protection systems exist in which:
>
> - the suffering of the child rather than the identification of abuse is seen as central. Children can, if it is considered to be in their interest, be interviewed without their parents' knowledge;
> - children can decide, up to a much further point than here, not to have action taken;
> - social workers can risk holding a situation so that a child has time to agree to intervention;
> - social workers are recognised both by parents and other professionals as having authority;
> - co-operation and co-ordination between agencies can happen without formal procedures;
> - children can be protected without a register;
> - social workers do not need procedures to cope with the inherent anxieties of the work;
> - voluntary organisations are structured into the system and seen as an integral part of the overall provision of service;
> - invoking the law to protect a child is seen as the responsibility of others as well as social workers;
> - the law can function in the discourse of welfare; working in partnership takes place with less emphasis on parental rights; and
> - working in partnership is facilitated by the social worker having confidence in their authority. (Hetherington et al. 1997: 180)

No standard statistical data is collected in Europe on child abuse and neglect (Armstrong and Hollows 1991) and there is variable recognition within different countries of the extent to which children are abused. In Sweden, Finland, Denmark and Austria, laws have been passed which explicitly prohibit physical punishment and other humiliating treatment of children. The rates of prosecution for physical punishment in these countries are not high; the legislation serves more as a marker of the kind of status that should be afforded to children within society than as a means of addressing a widespread social difficulty. Four main categories of abuse tend to be used throughout Europe – physical abuse, sexual abuse, emotional abuse and neglect (Ruxton 1996) – but the emphasis may be different between countries. For example, at the same time when the Netherlands were recording cases of emotional abuse through the confidential doctor service as being about 40 per cent of all cases of abuse, in England the rate for emotional abuse was five per cent. Ruxton looks at the keeping of central registers and mandatory reporting in Europe, and the following two tables are adapted from information supplied by her:

Table 2.3: Central registries in Europe (Ruxton 1996)

Central Registry?	Yes	No
Austria		✓
Belgium	✓	
Finland		✓
France		✓
Germany		✓
Greece		✓
Ireland		✓*
Italy		✓
Netherlands	✓	
Spain		✓
Sweden	✓	
UK	✓	

*but some report from local health boards

At the beginning of the 1990s, Doek (1991) observed that European nations had by and large decided not to introduce mandatory reporting legislation. However, as pointed out in Table 2.4, more recently, half of the European countries reported by Ruxton (1996) are considered to have mandatory reporting requirements. This contrast would suggest a trend towards the increased usage of, and reliance upon, mandatory reporting requirements.

Ruxton points out that some countries without mandatory reporting requirements nevertheless do have a reporting code. It may be this grey area which causes confusion as to whether a country has mandatory reporting or not. It is interesting to note for example that while Ruxton describes the UK as not having mandatory reporting requirements, Daro et al. (1996), on the basis of information supplied by Creighton of the NSPCC, describe the UK method or reporting abuse as 'mandatory'. While the system in the UK clearly does not rely on voluntary reporting, it is equally clear that it is not mandatory in the sense that the term is used in many other countries (that is, it being a criminal offense not to report, with criminal sanctions in place).

Table 2.4: Mandatory reporting in Europe (Ruxton 1996)

Child Abuse Reporting	Mandatory	Voluntary
Austria		✓
Belgium		✓
Denmark	✓	
Finland	✓	
France	✓†	
Germany		✓
Greece		✓
Italy	✓	
Luxembourg	✓	
Netherlands		✓
Portugal	✓	
Spain		✓
Sweden	✓	
UK		✓

† with the exception of doctors and midwives

Confidential doctor service

A consideration of the diversity of child protection arrangements in Europe would be incomplete without reference to the confidential doctor service that applies in several countries, most notably in Belgium and the Netherlands. The confidential doctor system is an arrangement for dealing with child abuse cases in a manner which is therapeutic rather than investigatory and forensic, and at the current time is unique to Europe. As described by Roelofs and Baartman in relation to the Netherlands, the goals of the service are 'to understand the parents and their problems and to influence family functioning in an effort to reinforce the parent-child bond' (1997: 194).

The work of the confidential centres in Belgium has been described by Marneffe (1992) and Marneffe and Broos (1997). There, the centres have three functions: to work directly with abused children and their families, to provide support, supervision and counselling for other professionals who are working with such children and families, and to change public opinion. They operate in an 'anonymous neutral environment' where the emphasis is on treatment, not investigation. Because the approach is multidisciplinary, the 'confidential doctor' is not necessarily a medical doctor, but can be another professional, for example, a social worker or other mental health professional.

In both countries these arrangements are built onto a pre-existing statutory framework to protect children (in Belgium since 1912; in the Netherlands since 1905) and represent the outcome of a debate about the relative merits of a therapeutic orientation towards child abuse compared with an approach that is more controlling and punitive. However, the statutory framework for protecting children remains as a background provision for those children who require it. A small percentage of those families being worked with by the confidential doctor centre may become involved with judicial intervention to protect the children. One of the key themes explored by Hetherington et al. (1997) in the various child protection systems they considered is the interface (described as 'intermediate institutions') between the administrative and legal domains. In other words, they explore what needs to happen in order for a child and family to cross the line from being a case in need of help and support (administrative) to one in need of control (legal).

The approach in Belgium is more diverse (Marneffe and Broos 1997) compared with the Netherlands because of the tripartite division of the country geographically (north–south), politically (Flanders, Wallonia and Brussels) and linguistically (French, Flemish and German all being official languages). In 1985, following four years of studies, commencing in 1979, eleven multidisciplinary teams for the prevention of child abuse and neglect were established in the French community. Two years later six more were established in Flanders. The whole of Belgium is covered by these 17 centres. The Flemish confidential doctor centres are provided by *Kind in Nood*, a specialist voluntary agency. The French-speaking centres are provided by *SOS Enfance*, a non-governmental organisation. Interestingly, Marneffe and Broos note differences between Flanders and Wallonia as follows:

> ... Flanders is influenced by the Netherlands, where progressive solutions are sought to social problems, while Wallonia is influenced by France, where repression plays an important role in solving social problems. The tendency of the Flemish teams to collaborate with judicial authorities, especially in cases of sexual abuse, is somewhat minimal ... while the rate is higher in Wallonia (1997: 171)

It would appear that the linguistic connection between Dutch-speaking Flanders and the Netherlands, and that between Wallonia (where a dialect of French is spoken) and France, are significant influences on the nature of child protection systems. Findlay (1987) has described the Dutch system of child protection as being essentially a therapeutic model. Statutory agencies and the police are only called in as a last resort. Two major organisations are concerned with child protection: the Dutch Society for the Prevention of Cruelty to Children (established in 1970), primarily concerned with preventing abuse through education of the public, and a therapeutic confidential doctor service (established in 1972), which works with families where abuse has occurred. Neither agency has a responsibility to pass information to the police.

Roelofs and Baartman (1997) describe the history of child abuse and child protection in the Netherlands, which although having a very different system has some very close parallels with child protection issues in Britain. For example, they describe a series of child protection watersheds, which have parallels with British child abuse inquiries: the 1987 unresolved Oude Pekela case (70 children investigated for extrafamilial sexual abuse), the 1988/89 Bolderkar affair where 15 of the children in a medical day care centre were investigated for intrafamilial sexual abuse (and nine were placed away from home), and the Epe incest case in which a woman's claim that she and her sister were sexually abused by parents and others outside the family led to a division of the population into 'believers' and 'non-believers'. Edwards and Soetenhorst-de Savornin Lohman (1994) have compared the impact on professional workers of the ensuing 'moral panic' following the Bolderkar affair in Vlaardingen with the events in Cleveland. Roelofs and Baartman (1997) note that whereas previously child care workers had been criticised for being too passive in respect of abuse, afterwards they were criticised for being too active – a very close analogy with the aftermath of Cleveland. They also note another impact on child protection in the Netherlands as a result of the emerging awareness of sexual abuse during the 1980s:

> In contrast to the strategy of compassion employed in cases of physical abuse and neglect, punishment of the perpetrator was called for ... Criminal prosecution made it clear that child sexual abuse is the full responsibility of the perpetrator; it was handled as a crime rather than as a family problem. Handling it as a family problem according to principles based on systems theory would mask the perpetrator's responsibility – something at which he or she was already adept – and would make the child, as a member of the family system, responsible for being a victim. (Roelofs and Baartman 1997: 194)

In the Netherlands however, compared with Belgium, the confidential doctor service is more limited in its remit. It operates alongside the Child Care and Protection Board, a statutory agency with a remit to protect children utilising court powers if necessary. Neither body undertake treatment of abusing families. The confidential doctor service undertakes assessment work, and then will refer on to the appropriate agency, following up at intervals to monitor the impact of intervention. The CCPB on the other hand can, if necessary, put the wheels in motion for children to be protected by the courts.

When comparing the relative merits of a 'confidential doctor' system of child protection with a system of mandatory reporting, it is useful to note that as they operate at present, both have a tendency to individualise and pathologise the difficulties experienced by abusing families. Neither address the societal/structural factors that cause abuse. How are agencies, dealing as they do with individual children and families, to get to grips with addressing the root causes locally of the problems that may lead families to abuse, and children to be abused? To start with it needs to be put on the agenda.

Britain and the rest of the world

English-speaking countries

Thorpe (1994) chronicles the history of child protection in Australia, describing the parallels between England, North America and Australia in the three phases of concern during the nineteenth century over the employment of children, baby-farming, and finally the care of children within their own family. The wide publicity surrounding the case of Alice Mitchell, who in the space of months had allowed 38 children farmed with her to die, led to the establishment of the Children's Protection Society, children's legislation in 1908, and the setting-up of a State Children's Department.

Like the US however, Australia has considerable local autonomy in child protection. As noted by the Steering Committee for the Review of Commonwealth/State Service Provisions (SCRCSSP), 'Despite common elements, jurisdictions vary in their legislation, definitions, policy and procedures' (1997, Vol. 2: 535). This can entail variations in what kinds of cases are investigated and what kinds of orders courts have available to them when considering abuse cases. The following table shows the very different levels of activity concerning child protection in the various Australian jurisdictions.

Table 2.5: Child abuse in Australia by state (1995–96) (SCRCSSP 1997)

Jurisdiction	Notifications	Rate per 1000	Substantiations
South Australia	8,935	18	2,415
New South Wales	28,930	16	14,063
Queensland	15,362	14	4,662
Tasmania	2,933	19	235
Victoria	29,914	22	6,663
Western Australia	3,748	7	1,095
Australia Capital Territory	1,437	15	445
Northern Territory	515	9	255

There are substantial variations in the rates: for example, the rate in Victoria is more than three times the rate in Western Australia. If one compares the rate of substantiated cases with the total number of notifications, the emerging disparities are even greater, with the highest rate being more than six times the lowest.

Table 2.6: Australian substantiation rates (1995–96) (SCRCSSP 1997)

Jurisdiction	Substantiation rate
South Australia	27.0
New South Wales	48.6
Queensland	30.3
Tasmania	8.0
Victoria	22.3
Western Australia	29.2
Australia Capital Territory	31.0
Northern Territory	49.5

The SCRCSSP (1997) has expressed concern about:

- the proportion of investigations which result in substantiation of abuse or neglect; and
- the impact of unnecessary investigations on families who may nevertheless benefit from family support. (1997: 538)

Briggs and Hawkins (1997) and Thorpe (1994) note the resistance in Victoria, for example, to mandatory reporting, which was only overcome in the end because of a high-profile child abuse fatality (two-year-old Daniel Valerio who was killed by his stepfather in 1990). The requirements concerning reporting are tabulated in Table 2.7.

Reflecting a theme that we have seen developed in the UK and elsewhere, Liddell (1989) describes a discontinuity between Victoria's policy and practice in so far as policy identifies the causes of child abuse as being multifactored (including societal factors as well as individual and family factors), but the practice (in terms of legislative initiatives) reflects an emphasis on the actions of the individual and the family. He considers that the main focus on community responsibility and accountability in child protection has been on mandatory reporting of child abuse and neglect by professionals.

Another similarity between Australia and the UK is the development of

Table 2.7: Mandatory reporting in Australia (Briggs and Hawkins 1997)

Jurisdiction	Mandatory reporting requirements
South Australia	Doctors and dentists from 1969; other professionals from 1976
New South Wales	Medical practitioners since 1977; other professionals from 1987
Queensland	Medical practitioners and family court staff must report; no requirements on other professionals
Tasmania	All professionals other than child care personnel explicitly required
Victoria	Most professionals from 1993
Western Australia	No mandatory reporting requirements
Australia Capital Territory	Voluntary notification arrangements
Northern Territory	Mandatory for anyone to report

performance indicators as a tool for monitoring the effectiveness of child protection services. Some of the indicators referred to:

- Reabuse rates
- Substantiation rates
- Response time to commence investigation
- Response time to complete investigation.

The SCRCSSP's 1997 Report highlights the socio-demographic characteristics of 10,000 families investigated by the child protection services during 1993–94. The following table is adapted from those findings.

Table 2.8: Child protection referrals – Victoria, Australia (1993–94)
(SCRCSSP 1997)

Socio-demographic characteristic	CPS referred families (per cent)	Population (per cent)
Living in rented accommodation	60	23
In receipt of pension or benefit	58	26
Single-parent household	46	17
Moved in last five years	90	42

In New Zealand the law makes it clear that all adults have a moral (but not a legal) responsibility to report suspicions that a child is being maltreated (Briggs and Hawkins 1997). A consideration of child protection in New Zealand would be incomplete without reference to family group conferences, a system for dealing with professional concerns about children and young people in a juvenile justice context as well as a child protection one. The main reason for the introduction of this novel scheme was extreme concern about the over-representation of Maori children in the state care system. As a result, legislation was passed in November 1989 which introduced a new method for dealing with young people in trouble. The process involves four stages. In the first stage the need for a conference is agreed and a coordinator is appointed (of the same race and speaking the same language as the family). In the second stage, in consultation with the immediate family and the child or young person, members of the extended family are identified and decisions made about who to invite. The timing and venue of the conference is arranged. In the third stage, at the actual conference, family members make a plan, on their own, although the coordinator is available to advise as necessary. The fourth stage entails communicating the plan to the professionals, which is arranged via a meeting between the family, the coordinator and the professionals. The plan should contain contingency plans and time-scales for review as well as a consideration of the necessary resources. The operation of the scheme has been considered to be quite successful, to the extent that experimental trials of family group conferences have taken place in Britain, (for example, in the former Welsh authority of Gwynedd, and the English county of Hereford and Worcester). The government consultation document on the revised *Working Together* (DoH 1998) has invited views on family group conferences, although making it clear that they see it as a potential supplement to the decision making of child protection conferences:

The Government doubts that it will be appropriate for Family Group Conferences to be used in the place of child protection conferences since the decision about whether to place a child on the child protection register must ultimately remain a matter for professionals. (DoH 1998: 48)

This suggests that, in this respect at least, the remit of the consultation document is limited by the necessity to ensure that child protection continues to operate within the same investigative priority as previously.

Non-English-speaking countries

Having considered primarily Western, developed countries up to this point, let us now look at Britain compared to the non-English-speaking part of the rest of the world. It takes a considerable leap of the imagination however to begin to appreciate the very extensive differences in the nature of concerns for children's welfare.

If we compare, for example, some of the developed countries with some of the poorer nations of the world in terms of under 5s mortality (defined as mortality of children under the age of five per 1000 live births in 1990), some striking differences emerge as shown in Table 2.9.

Table 2.9: The 16 countries with the lowest under 5s mortality
(Mackay 1993)

Country	Life expectancy (years)	Average births in a woman's lifetime	Under 5s mortality
Japan	78.8	1.7	6
Sweden	77.8	1.9	7
Ireland	75.1	2.4	7
Finland	75.9	1.7	7
Hong Kong	77.6	1.4	7
Taiwan	–	–	8
Austria	75.3	1.5	9
Belgium	75.6	1.6	9
Canada	77.3	1.7	9
Denmark	76.2	1.5	9
France	76.8	1.8	9
Germany	75.0	1.5	9
Netherlands	77.6	1.6	9
Singapore	74.5	1.8	9
Switzerland	77.8	1.5	9
UK	76.1	1.8	9

In the US, comparable under 5s mortality is 11 per 1000 and in Australia it is 10 per 1000.

A comparison with the ten countries with the highest level of under 5's mortality is both revealing and disturbing.

In all of these countries, at least two out of every ten children will not reach their fifth birthday and in the case of Mozambique, this figure is as high as three children out of ten. In Japan however, with the lowest under 5's mortality rate, only six out of 1000 children will die before their fifth birthday. The average births in a woman's lifetime, and under 5's mortality figures are connected: 'When women come to feel confident that their children are likely to survive, they then have fewer children' (Mackay 1993: 90). The

Table 2.10: The ten countries with the highest under 5s mortality
(Mackay 1993)

Country	Life expectancy (years)	Average births in a woman's lifetime	Under 5s mortality
Burkina Faso	49.2	6.5	228
Guinea	44.5	7.0	237
Gambia	45.0	–	238
Guinea-Bisseau	43.5	5.8	246
Malawi	49.1	7.6	253
Sierra Leone	43.0	6.5	257
Mali	46.0	7.1	284
Angola	46.5	6.4	292
Afghanistan	43.5	6.9	292
Mozambique	48.5	6.3	297

table also shows how different the life chances of children are depending upon where they are born in its most stark statistic: life expectancy. Whereas a child in Sierra Leone can only expect to live on average until the age of 43, in Japan, a child can expect to live nearly twice as long, to the age of 78. While disturbing, this picture represents an improvement, and the death rates among children has been declining throughout the world, in both developed and developing countries. Some countries have made remarkable progress during this century: in 1900 the average life expectancy in Japan was 45 years.

A similar picture emerges for infant mortality (deaths before the age of one year):

> In 1990, the rates ranged from five to six deaths per thousand live births in Japan, Sweden and Finland to over 150 in Afghanistan and some African countries ... The 1990 rates for the USA, about nine per 1000 births, or eight in England and Wales were even higher than the rates of five to seven in Japan and the Nordic countries. Nevertheless, the infant mortality rate for East European countries were two to three times higher, those for Latin American countries were eight to nine times higher and those for African countries were 15 to 20 times higher than the rates for the UK ... there were dramatic falls in infant mortality rates in all countries between 1960 and 1990. (Mackay 1993: 92)

The most dramatic declines were in Oman, Turkey, Egypt, Iran, China and the United Arab Emirates. However, the decline has been less dramatic in those countries with the highest rates (parts of Asia and sub-Saharan Africa).

Daro et al. (1996) compared 21 developed countries – Australia, Austria, Belgium, Czech Republic, Denmark, England, Estonia, Finland, France,

Germany, Greece, Ireland, Israel, Italy, Japan, the Netherlands, New Zealand, Norway, Spain, Sweden, and the US – and 12 developing countries – Argentina, Bangladesh, Dominican Republic, Ecuador, Hong Kong, Kenya, Malaysia, Pakistan, Philippines, Singapore, South Africa and Tunisia – on a number of different 'Risk Factors' relevant to abuse. They found the average under 5s mortality rate in those developed countries to be 7.1 per 1000, compared with a rate six times higher (41.7) in developing countries.

One might expect that given the very different survival opportunities of babies and young children throughout the world, concerns about child abuse and child protection are likely to be very different and reflected in different definitions of what constitutes abuse. Daro et al. (1996) interestingly suggest that perhaps the differences are not as marked as one might expect. At the core, most countries included physical abuse of children, parental failure to provide for children, and the use of children by adults for sexual gratification as abusive. Sixty per cent indicated that abuse included street children and the forced labour of children under the age of twelve years. Beyond the core of concerns however, were additional concerns. Those noted by the developing countries were: abandonment, child prostitution, female infanticide or circumcision and forcing a child to beg. However, this description of core and additional concerns may reflect distortion in the Daro et al. (1996) sample. Whilst they are not completely explicit about data collection, it appears that data was collected from representatives to the ISPCAN congress (first in 1992, then in 1996). They draw on only a very small sample of developing countries and this may reflect which countries are able to send delegates to such congresses. For the world at large, however, the number of developing countries (and the population of people contained within them) far exceeds those in the developed countries. In their sample this proportion is reversed. As noted by Mackay, 'Each year the world's population expands by 96 million ... Ninety million of these are born in poor countries and a mere 6 million in rich countries' (1993: 89). They also note that the trend is for increasing proportion of the world's population to be born in the poorer countries.

In effect this means that perhaps from a more global perspective what Daro et al. (1996) have construed as the core concerns may actually be the additional concerns, and what they have described as the additional concerns, coming proportionately from a larger proportion of the world's population may actually be the core concerns. This would be more consistent with the observation by Doek: 'Although some attention is given to intra-familial child abuse (e.g. physical abuse of children by step/foster parents) in developing countries, extrafamilial child maltreatment determines the child activity and concern of developing countries ...' (1991: 51). It is important to remember from an international perspective, as well as from a domestic perspective, that it is not only the clarity of the definitional process that is important, but a consideration of who makes the definitions.

For example, in looking at child abuse in Sierra Leone, Thompson (1991) notes that it is a very real problem which raises the type of conflict between foreign inherited norms and customary practice. Thompson notes the precedence of the exclusive authority of parents over the rights and privileges of children in Sierra Leone culture, but notes this is none the less at variance with the criminal liability attaching to parents and guardians for child abuse. Let us look briefly at some of these 'additional concerns' in developing countries.

Africa

In relation to Nigeria for example, Amdi (1990) considers that child abuse is a significant community problem, but one which historically has been ignored by the community. Uzodike (1990) describes child abuse as a social problem which only gained the attention of the Nigerian public in the late 1980s. In part, this was in response to the establishment of the African Network for the Prevention and Protection Against Child Abuse and Neglect (ANPPCAN) in 1984. Not surprisingly, he reports on initial definitional difficulties (for example, the extent to which child labour is abusive), and whilst drawing on American and British source material, emphasises that 'the norms and culture of a society should be considered when determining acts or omissions that amount to abuse ...' (Uzodike 1990: 85). He proceeds to describe excessive corporal punishment, child marriage, child labour and neglect as areas of concern in a Nigerian context. Whilst two of these might be seen as 'core' concerns for Daro et al. (1996), two of these, child marriage and child labour, are not. Child labour is also a problem in other parts of the world.

LeVine and LeVine look at the practice of ceremonial clitoridectomy (female circumcision) and the practice of arranged marriages in sub-Saharan Africa. They observe:

> By Western criteria these practices may be seen as abusive and coercive, but an ethnographic account of their institutional and ideological contexts shows how they conform to local ideals and how parents believe they are acting in the best interests of their children. (1981: 36)

The variation of the practice in tribes where it has in the past been traditional is in part related to the differential success of campaigns against the practice by early European missionaries. LeVine and LeVine comment on the emerging ambivalence towards the practice by Gusii parents: 'They surrender their own children to the ordeal, but they may privately hope that their grandchildren will be spared ...' (1981: 50).

South America

Johnson (1981) explores the treatment of children by Native South Americans, noting in particular a distinction between the relatively savage treatment by some tribes of the children of those groups seen as their enemies (including murder) when compared with the treatment of their own children. The relative lack of 'aberrant' abuse is, however, connected with the practice of infanticide of unwanted or difficult children. Salazar (1991) reviews the kinds and nature of child labour in Latin America. A pressing concern for a number of South American countries, related to the issue of child labour, is the large number of street children. In their consideration of developing a primary prevention approach to the issue, Tyler et al. relate the issue to the continuing prevalence of the notion of the family as a safe haven as a contrast to the experience of many of the street children they studied: 'Despite the increased frequency of child abuse cases ... we still assume the benevolence of the family' (1992: 209). Some of their subjects give interesting accounts of their conception of home. One girl considered that 'home' was a space into which her parents could not intrude. Another street youth, a boy, when asked about his dream house, described it as: 'It would be the same house that I left, except that my parents would have their hands tied behind their backs and tape over their mouths' (Tyler 1992: 209). Sometimes it is not family stresses, but poverty that forces children onto the streets. In some cases authorities may be extremely antagonistic towards street children, at its most extreme undertaking to eliminate the problem through murder.

Asia and the Pacific

In Asia there is a mixture of affluent and poor countries:

> ... in the developing countries where, despite aid from other parts of the world, poverty, sickness, disease and exploitation continue to ravage the underprivileged millions, making it foreseeably impossible for the citizens of many countries ... to have any immediate hope of equating their lifestyles with those of their richer neighbours in, for instance, Hong Kong, Japan, Singapore, South Korea and Taiwan. (Davis 1994: 49)

Langness (1981) looking at New Guinea considers the initiation ceremonies for both males and females as the main example of cultural practices which would be considered abusive from a Western perspective. Goddard reporting on the Tenth International Congress of the International Society for Prevention of Child Abuse and Neglect (ISPCAN) in Malaysia noted, 'Child prostitution and child labour are major problems in many parts of Asia' (1995: 146). Child prostitution was described as one of the pre-revolution concerns in China by Korbin (1981) who considered that the levels of child abuse since the revolution have been relatively low. Before the revolution, Chinese culture considered children as the sole property of their parents, and bound to their parents by obligations of filial piety: 'Severe beatings, infanticide, child slavery, the selling of young girls as prostitutes, child betrothal, and foot-binding were not uncommon' (Korbin 1981: 167). The practice of foot-binding involved tightly binding the feet of young girls with strips of linen to prevent growth and induce disability. Introduced at the beginning of the Sung Dynasty (960–1279 AD), the practice, which was initially restricted to the upper classes, gradually spread throughout the other social classes, becoming a requirement for marriage. It was banned by the Chinese government in 1912. Interestingly, low rates of child abuse in China, as described by Breiner (1992) are said to be related to a generally open, humanistic attitude towards sexuality, combined with a respect for women and their sexual rights. However, the more recent increases in infanticide related to the introduction of the one-child policy are noted.

Poffenberger (1981), looking at rural India, noted that a preference for boys was also related to female infanticide, a long-standing practice which persisted despite the efforts of the British administration to put an end to it (for example, by passing a law in 1870 providing for close examination of the causes of deaths in certain castes where the practice was known to be more common). He describes a number of forms of harsh (by Western standards) discipline, but notes: 'Discipline may be common in India, but the kind of battering abuse and neglect found in the US is not common' (Poffenberger 1981: 92).

O'Kane (1996) undertook a comparison between child abuse in the UK and India. She observed that intrafamilial child abuse is not seen as a problem in India, although there is awareness of the impact of poverty and deprivation on large numbers of India's children. This lack of awareness, or denial, would apparently be the reason for a lack of legislation to protect children from intrafamilial abuse. Indian legislation also does not appear to be child-centred. There is also a lack of research into the incidence and prevalence of abuse in India. Evidence for the existence of sexual abuse within Indian society for example comes from the increasing number of cases of sexually transmitted diseases in children (58 out of 362 patients in one study being under the age of 14). In connection with physical abuse, O'Kane notes the strong public support for the physical punishment of children. She also notes a form of abuse particular to India, that of branding children because of superstitious belief and notes the occasional, but infrequent, appearance of reports of child sacrifice.

In Turkey, Olson considered that there was a low incidence of 'classic child abuse' (that is, child abuse as defined using Western standards), within a cultural context of families being seen as 'warm and accepting towards infants and small children' (1981: 103). However, some cultural practices are described as possibly being seen as abusive from a Western perspective, including the custom of swaddling babies and strapping them in their cradles during the first six months, the attention focused on the genitals of young children ('much admired by adult relatives'), and the high rates of accidents and injuries due to a relatively unsafeguarded hazard-filled environment (open fires, open stairways).

A particular concern in other Asian countries is 'sex tourism', as described by Ireland in relation to the Philippines, Sri Lanka and Thailand. He found 'extensive evidence of the use of young boys for sex by adult males from the West, Australasia and other Asian countries' (1993: 266), although the gender balance appears to be more towards both boys and girls in Thailand and the Philippines. The predominance of boys in sexual abuse in Sri Lanka (in intrafamilial abuse as well as in sex tourism) was described by DeSilva (1997). Davis (1994) provides disturbing descriptions of the desperate circumstances of some children finding this to be their only way to survive. The extent to which child prostitution is a problem in developed countries is confused by a lack of clarity over the extent to which it is on the agenda for the developed countries. A number of European countries (for example, Sweden, France and Germany) have passed legislation to make it a criminal offence to travel abroad for the purpose of sexually abusing children. The Sex Offenders Act (1997) contains provision for British citizens or UK residents:

> any act done by a person in a country or territory outside the United Kingdom which a) constituted an offence under the law in force in that country or territory; and b) would constitute a sexual offence to which this section applied if it had been done in England and Wales, or in Northern Ireland, shall constitute that sexual offence under the law of that part of the United Kingdom. (section 7(1))

However, approaches to child prostitution within developed countries still lack consensus and support. A report by the Council of Europe (1991) advocated street work (targeted on railway stations, airports and seaports) to prevent children drifting into prostitution. Butler (1998) drew attention to the irony that agencies attempting to address the issue of children in care drifting into prostitution are pilloried by the press for their efforts when they identify that the problem exists. Shaw and Butler (1998) identify Bradford, Cardiff and Birmingham as areas that have attempted to address the issue of child prostitution. Barrett (1994) noted that in the three European capitals (London, Amsterdam and Paris) where he researched child prostitution, services were underfunded – particularly in Paris and London – and were provided by voluntary agencies.

Very little research has been undertaken into Arab approaches to child abuse and protection. Haj-Yahia and Shor (1995) looked at the attitudes towards child abuse of 353 West Bank students in the helping professions. Although there was considerable agreement about what situations were considered as abuse and neglect, there were differences in the willingness to report maltreatment (although physical abuse was more likely to be reported than neglect). In attempting to create services for children and families, they are mindful of the challenge inherent in trying to adapt knowledge of child abuse accumulated in Western countries to a different culture, and the need to build services that are congruent with that culture.

It is worth restating that any exploration or consideration of child abuse in an international context must not only address what definitions are used but who makes those definitions and how. Otherwise the international context of child protection could simply become another arena where the interests of developed countries are given predominance over the interests of the developing nations to determine their own priorities to protect children. It could be a little too easy, and perhaps glib, to consider that awareness of child abuse in developing countries is simply at the earlier stage of awareness as was manifest in developed countries before the 1960s. This could be a potentially patronising and disservicing assumption which fails to address the need for the poor nations to develop their own child protection agendas. Indeed by looking at the child protection needs arising in contexts of pervasive economic deprivation, it may be that developed countries will learn more about the relations between poverty and abuse which have perhaps not been sufficiently addressed or taken on board by child protection in developed countries.

Race, ethnicity and culture

Issues of race, ethnicity and culture are both cross-national and within-country issues. The emphasis so far has been on cross-national differences. But there are many issues raised by child protection concerns when addressing different cultures within the same society. If one considers within-society cultural differences, there are three sets of circumstances for consideration. First there are those societies in which a pre-existing indigenous population has been subjugated by the arrival of European settlers (for example, Native Americans; Samoan and Maori people in New Zealand; Aborigines in

Australia; Native Canadians). Second, there are multicultural societies developed out of later immigration of non-white populations into a predominantly white culture (for example, Indians, Pakistanis and West Indians in Britain). A third group would be the contemporaneous influx of white and non-white populations (for example Africans and Europeans into the US in the eighteenth century). Within a society there may be one, two, or all three of these different patterns contributing to the multicultural nature of the society.

These very different circumstances make it difficult to generalise concerning white and non-white populations when it comes to child protection issues. When teaching child protection to social work students, I have on occasion been struck by the difficulties of making parallels between the experiences of African Americans and Black Britons. Whilst the underlying commonality of the operation of racism within a predominantly white society is a unifying theme, the very different history of the Black people within those societies makes comparison a risky business. In the US, Black people have a three-hundred-year history, and the extremes of oppression encompass slavery and virtually legitimised murder. In the UK, whilst acknowledging that Black people have always had a presence within that society, the major influx of Black people, particularly West Indians, is a post-war phenomenon. The extremes of legitimised murder have never really been experienced in Britain. On the other hand, it would be fair to say that Britain has never experienced the organised resistance of oppression by Black people as was manifested in the Civil Rights and Black Power movements of the 1960s in the US. Finally, it should be noted that the Black community within the UK is also not a homogeneous group. In some cities, for example, Cardiff and Liverpool, the presence of large numbers of Black people considerably pre-dates the post-war wave of immigration.

Indigenous populations

In New Zealand, Kotch et al. (1993) looked at racial bias in child abuse reporting and found an association between the diagnosis of child abuse and race. They examined 92 cases of intentional injury fatalities and 393 cases of intentional injuries for evidence of physical and sexual abuse. They found that child abuse codings were more likely to be made in connection with Maori and Samoan children than others. This trend in New Zealand is not new, and Fergusson et al. noted that 'the reported incidence of abuse amongst Maori children was six times greater than amongst European children, that the incidence amongst Pacific Island children was nine times greater' (1972: 149). As previously noted, it was this over-representation that contributed to the development of family group conferences.

In Australia, Thorpe, based on his study of child protection outcomes, concludes:

> Child protection ... is concerned primarily with policing family settings which do not conform to a norm ... Given that children living in minority child-rearing settings (single parents, Aboriginal people) are a majority of cases in the programme, it is difficult to escape the conclusion that child protection investigations may not be the most appropriate responses to concerns that are expressed about children and families in need of help and support by virtue of their impoverished circumstances. (1997: 76)

Smallwood (1995) as well comments on abuse amongst Australia's Aboriginal people, noting that before colonisation child abuse was non-existent. Afterwards however, poverty and hopelessness have contributed to the kinds of societal conditions that promote child abuse, which Smallwood considers need to be addressed by more resources.

In Canada, the situation is exceedingly complex with two contrasting prevailing cultures (English Canada and French-speaking Quebec) as an overlay to both issues surrounding indigenous groups and immigrant populations. The two different traditions of child welfare in Canada, as described by Harris and Melichercik (1986) reflect the divisions of an emphasis on parents' rights (Quebec) and the so-called 'British' doctrine which permits the state to intervene in family life to protect children. It is interesting to consider the parallels between these divisions within Canada, and the contrasts between Britain and France, a reflection perhaps of both different historical legal traditions and languages. Swift (1997: 45) has described the child protection definitional difficulties in Canada arising from culturally diverse child-rearing practices in the 'main immigrant reception areas of Toronto, Montreal and Vancouver'. She notes that shifting the emphasis from parental behaviour to the effects on the child does not necessarily eliminate the difficulty, as what is considered harmful in one culture may be considered an important part of childhood in another.

One of the key areas in Canada concerns Native Canadians, who historically have been over-represented in the care system. This has been seen both as an extension of the colonial relationship between the communities and more dramatically as a form of genocide, entailing the continuing destruction of Native communities. Efforts to address this, described by Swift (1997) have involved power sharing between the communities; but concerns have continued because of the continuing high levels of 'abuse, addiction, domestic violence and poverty'. Large numbers of Native children continue to enter the care system.

Metcalf (1979) described a model for addressing child abuse and neglect with Native Americans in California. The approach views the causes of abuse and neglect as arising outside of the individual from social processes, derived from the nature of the relationship between Native American culture and Anglo society. The work focuses on building ethnic identity, solidifying families and combating social isolation. Horejsi and colleagues considered the barriers between Native Americans and child protection agencies and highlight the history of oppression and the different agendas for child welfare as two such barriers. They describe 'how the oppression suffered by Native Americans has undermined their culture and their ability to parent so that child abuse and neglect are frequent problems' (Horejsi et al. 1992: 329). The concerns of the Native American include poverty, racism and discrimination, short life expectancy (44 years), boarding school legacy, foster care legacy, reservation experience, substance abuse and the struggle to establish an identity.

Race in British child protection – the 'punitive' and 'liberal' approaches

In writing about child protection and the Black population in Britain, a number of writers have commented on the two extremes of concerns, over-intrusiveness and inaction when white workers are engaged with Black clients (Channer and Parton 1990; Okine 1992); this has been described as the 'punitive approach' and the 'liberal approach' by Gambe et al. 1992.

In the 'punitive approach', Black children and families are disadvantaged by the child protection system because of institutional and individual racism and as a result they become disproportionately represented in the system. As described by Channer and Parton (1990), evidence from the disadvantage of Black children comes from the disproportional numbers of Black children in special schools, the higher likelihood (particularly of Afro-Caribbeans) of suspension from school, the greater likelihood for Black young people of ending up in custody and receiving a longer sentence in connection with offences, and the higher proportion coming into care (22.5 per thousand compared with a national average of 7.5 per thousand), and spending longer in care. However, they do not provide evidence in relation to the child protection system, largely due to the fact that in the UK there have been virtually no attempts to look at the issue of race in relation to child protection. Butt (1996) has been critical of *Child Protection: Messages from Research* (DoH 1995a) for this omission. In relation to this issue of over-representation of Black children, Corby (1993) observes:

> One would expect black children to be over-represented in child abuse statistics, partly because their families are more open to surveillance as a result of figuring highly among indices of deprivation ... and partly because, until recently, cultural

misunderstanding and the operation of both institutional and direct racism may have increased the chances of suspicions of abuse in black families being confirmed. (1993: 68)

Narducci writes: 'We place expectations on black parents of providing certain standards while denying them a fair chance at achieving that possibility' (1992: 14).

In the US, Levine et al. (1996) looked at the over-representation of African American families among substantiated cases of child maltreatment and concluded that 'differential referral source and/or differential worker attention were inadequate explanations for the overrepresentation of AAm [African Americans] in the child protection system. In California, according to Barth et al. (1995) African American children are two to three times more likely to be referred for abuse or neglect than other racial groups. The trends in over-representation of Black children in child protection are difficult to understand because of conflicting findings. One of the very early studies by Gil found that:

> About one third of the children ... were nonwhite. Since only 15 percent of children under age 18 in the United States were nonwhite ... nonwhites were over-represented ... to a significant extent ... the reporting rate for white children was 6.7 per 100,000 and the corresponding rate for nonwhite children was 21.0. (1970: 106)

He accounted for this over-representation by three possibilities: discriminatory reporting, an actual higher incidence (due to structural inequalities), and different cultural child-rearing practices. Other early studies appeared to show less difference between ethnic groups. For example, Strauss et al. (1980) found no difference between black and white families in the level of violence, although Hampton et al. (1989) found that between 1975 and 1985, violence had increased in black families but was associated with a corresponding decrease in violence in white families. Howitt (1992) however, considers that survey evidence (from the US) is reasonably clear-cut, showing no difference between different ethnic groups on experiences of abuse. But despite this he suggests that there are clear patterns of difference for intervention with an over-representation of black families.

The 'liberal' tradition, on the other hand, entails social workers being blamed for failure to act to protect Black children because of fear of being labelled racist, in the worst cases allowing children to die at the hands of their Black parents by operating on the basis of stereotyped, rather than actual, understandings of the strengths of Black families. Corby noted that inquiries '... intimated that social workers have overcompensated for the structural disadvantages experienced by Black families in our society to the detriment of the needs of children within them' (1993: 152). Noyes' review of child abuse fatality inquiries notes, 'Despite the fact that seven of the inquiries relate to black and minority ethnic children issues relating to the recruitment of black staff are barely touched upon' (DoH 1991c: 37).

These seven out of the 19 cases reviewed comprise 36.8 per cent of the cases, a considerable over-representation compared to the proportion of Black people in the population. But only one of the inquiries, that into the death of Tyra Henry (London Borough of Lambeth 1987), addressed race issues to any extent. There are dangers inherent to this approach:

> We must also recognise that there is a danger in our attempting to be anti-racist and culturally sensitive that we may inadvertently overlook the abuse of a child simply to protect ourselves from being labelled as a racist ... Being anti-racist and culturally sensitive does not and cannot mean providing a lower level of care and protection to children from these groups. If anything it means the opposite ... (Narducci 1992: 21)

Both of these positions – the punitive and the liberal – are based on a misassessment of Black families by white workers:

> The misassessment of black children and their families, has its roots in a Euro-centric perspective of black children and family life that is judgemental in essence. It is racially biased, stereotypical in presence, and frequently full of mythology. (Okine 1992: 116)

It is also reflected in the observation of Heras (1992) who refers in connection with a case study of sexual abuse in a Filipino family to:

> ... common errors that are made when cultural factors are ignored or misunderstood in the assessment and treatment of sexual abuse (SA) with ethnic clients. A consideration of culture in assessing SA is crucial when working with ethnically diverse groups.

Conceptually, this understanding of the misassessment being both liberal and punitive is quite difficult. On the surface, it is confusing that the operation of racism within society would have the effect of both bringing more children into the child protection system, and at the same time, failing to protect the most vulnerable. There seems to be a parallel with the types of concerns about child protection that practitioners have more generally – being pilloried for failing to act (as in the case of child abuse fatality inquiries) and being pilloried for allegedly over-zealous intervention (as in Cleveland). But two main factors appear significant. One is the failure to recognise the strengths of Black families. The other is the failure to see Black people as individuals and thereby intervene on the basis of stereotypes (whether they be positive liberal stereotypes or negative racist stereotypes.

How are we to make sense of the very disparate issues that arise from a cross-cultural consideration of child abuse and child protection? Doek (1991) has considered the trends in child abuse and neglect across different nations. In looking at intrafamilial abuse he considers identification of abuse (mandatory reporting), treatment, primary prevention and management of child abuse between countries. In looking at extrafamilial abuse in an international context, he considers the role of non-governmental and international governmental organisations. He contends that the most important step for the international protection of children from abuse is the development of strong national societies to prevent child maltreatment in each country, which coordinate and liaise to learn from others. Lewington and Olsen (1994) in their description of international cooperation in protecting children (including the work of Interpol), distinguish between the international exchange of nationally-developed good practice in arrangements to protect children, from the need to protect children from types of abuse, such as child pornography and sex tourism, which crosses national frontiers.

There are four aspects to my interest in presenting this material. First, managers of child protection services may be involved in efforts to coordinate international action to protect children throughout the world. It has become increasingly common for child welfare managers to visit other countries. (Russia and Romania come to mind as two recent examples where, due to recent political upheaval, changes have been contemplated and Western managers invited to advise.) International conferences (ISPCAN, Stockholm) are increasingly addressing issues of how to coordinate efforts to protect children across national boundaries (for example, from sex tourism).

Second, managers are responsible for the delivery of an ethnically sensitive child protection service. That service must be based on an understanding that different cultural and ethnic groups, whilst almost invariably concerned about the overall welfare of their children, may have different agendas, priorities and types of concerns for them. Invariably, questions arise about the position of children within the culture and frequently 'ends and means' discussions and negotiations that need to take place. Whilst some (but probably not all!) of the objectives of child rearing between different cultures may be the same, even in such cases, the means to reach those objectives may be different.

Third, a culturally relativist position would allow for the possibility for developed countries to learn from developing countries about child protection. As has been suggested, it has been too easy to discount the significance of poverty, deprivation and social isolation in Western child protection, despite the efforts of some researchers to put it on the agenda. In keeping with the theme of this book, seeing child protection in context, we can locate Western child protection practice against a backdrop of child welfare concerns in countries that have dramatically less resources, but similar social and emotional investment in the well-being of their children. There are clearly lessons to be learned there.

Finally, if working with different cultures (both within the country and internationally) is to be effective, then a balance needs to be struck between ethnocentrism and cultural relativism. The positives and negatives of both have been highlighted in this section, but it is up to the reader to find this balance in the practice of managing child protection services.

3 The structural/policy context of child protection in England and Wales

From the top – central government policy

At the heart of the child protection system is the Area Child Protection Committee. As shown in Figure 3.1, Area Child Protection Committees are the intermediaries between Central Government (elected members and civil servants) and the practitioner.

The model described in Figure 3.1 is complex and highlights the various interactions that can influence the ultimate practice of child protection. At the top is shown the three-way interaction between public opinion, media influence and members of parliament (MPs). Below are various interactions between MPs in their roles as ministers and the civil servants within those ministries. What viewer of the television comedy *Yes, Minister* has not been intrigued by the humorously presented question of wherein lies the true power in determining the direction of government policy – whether with ministers, who change with successive governments and cabinet reshuffles or with senior civil servants who provide continuity through changes of government? In addition, at this level are the various interactions between the different government departments. There is no reason to believe that communications between the Home Office and the Department of Health for instance, are easier than communications between these agencies at other levels, for example between ACPC members (police and social services managers) or between professionals (police and social workers) at a child protection conference. Indeed, the NSPCC National Commission of Inquiry into the Prevention of Child Abuse suggested 'Locally, the planning and delivery of children's services reflects the lack of co-ordination at national levels' (Williams of Mostyn, Lord 1996: 55).

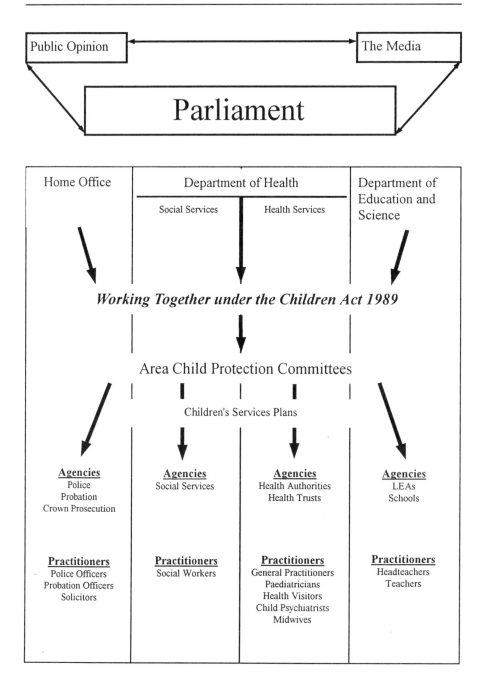

Figure 3.1   The structure of child protection services in England and Wales

Following down the model, there is a gap between the central and the local, highlighted in the figure in two ways by the direct connections between the government bodies and the local agencies, and also by the interface between *Working Together* (1991), *the* essential government guidance document, and Area Child Protection Committees, the local bodies charged with the responsibility of implementing that guidance. At the next level down, there is the interaction between agencies, which is likely to influence and reflect the interaction between the practitioners within those agencies.

Finally, if the complexity of the model were not sufficient, the dynamic properties must also be kept in mind – different parts of the system interact with other parts of the system, and the whole of the system and its components change over time. This section is going to explore these interactions and influences.

The role of the media and public opinion

The role of the media and of public opinion in child protection is not part of the structure as such, but it exerts very powerful influences on the development of child protection services. When Parton (1985) first began to consider the media role in child abuse, he considered that 'there is very little research available on the way social work and child abuse are presented in the media' (1985: 85). In fact he considered there was little study of the media impact on social issues more generally. But that situation has now been considerably addressed, and possibly in relation to issues raised in Parton's *Politics of Child Abuse*, the media portrayal of child abuse has now been extensively studied.

In his review of the literature on media interest in child abuse, Gough (1996) traces the interest of the media back to the case of Mary Ellen in New York during the 1870s, often cited as a watershed in child protection (Watkins 1990; Costin 1991), and considered here in Part One. A catalogue of events has aroused intensive media interest, including, among others:

- The Battered Baby Syndrome (1962)
- Particular Fatality Inquiries (Maria Colwell, 1974; Jasmine Beckford, 1985; Heidi Koseda, 1986; Tyra Henry, 1987)
- Cleveland (events 1987; Inquiry Report 1988)
- Rochdale (Report October 1990)
- Orkneys (events February 1991; Clyde Report October 1992)
- Staffordshire: 'Pindown' (events 1983–89; report, Levy and Kahan, 1991)
- Leicestershire: Frank Beck case (sentenced, 1991).

It is not my intent to convey the net influence of the media on child protection as completely negative. A balanced account should not fail to take into consideration the positive influence of the media and clearly some, if not all, of the events cited above needed to be reported. Hallett who considers media interest a mixed blessing, states, 'The inquiries are, of course, a legitimate source of public interest, and news reporting. They have undoubtedly heightened public awareness of child physical and sexual abuse' (1989: 137). Criticisms of the media's approach to child protection contend that by focusing on blame and individual culpability, the media has contributed to an atmosphere of defensiveness in the management and practice of child protection. This atmosphere has in turn led to a 'safety at all costs' approach, a 'cover your back' defensiveness that is now being re-evaluated as unhelpful.

The power of the media comes, logically enough, from its 'media-ting' role. That is, it acts as a go-between, or a transformer of information, and not simply as a transmitter. It should be clear here that we are considering the news media, and not other forms of media. There are at least three ways that the media can be seen to impact on information over and above the relatively straightforward process of relaying it from source to recipient. It *selects* information to be communicated using certain *terms*, from a particular *viewpoint*.

First, the media selects: the selection process is vital in bringing to public awareness certain issues (or aspects of issues), whilst at the same time consigning others to obscurity. Because of the need to attract public interest, the news media focuses on the unusual or sensational. As expressed by Charles Dana in 1882, 'When a dog bites a man that is not news, but when a man bites a dog that is news.' But the unusual is often, although not necessarily, atypical; it may be a reflection of the exception rather than the rule. In child protection, this is often lost sight of, and, as a result, the fairly good track record of a child protection system in protecting large numbers of children from the continuation of abuse and neglect and from the deaths that never happened, may be dramatically overshadowed, and even completely discounted, in the light of a single tragic event. The failure of the media to highlight the 'background' of good practice, when dealing with the 'figure' of a disturbing incident, may be a reflection of the way that agencies themselves often fail to address this sufficiently. But it may also derive from the media perspective that 'good news' is not news.

Second, the terms and language used define the issue in certain ways. It has been argued that the role of the media is not simply to transmit information but to transform it as well. Language is not simply a vehicle for the communication of ideas but serves as a conduit which shapes and filters those ideas. One way in which this happens is through the differentiation of concepts resulting in a complex hierarchy of concepts and sub-concepts. It is for this reason that some concepts lend themselves to easier expression in some languages than others.

Consider the following:

- 'Death of an Angel' (Australia, *Herald Sun*, 29.6.96) (Goddard, 1996)

and the following examples provided by Parton (1985: 88–9):

- 'Social Shirkers' (UK, *Daily Mail*, 21.2.80) (Golding and Middleton 1982)
- 'Early Victim Of Do-Nothing Welfare Team' (*Daily Mail*, 21.2.80) (Golding and Middleton 1982)
- 'Doomed Girl "Failed" By Welfare Worker' (*Daily Mail*, 13.11.82) (Golding and Middleton 1982)
- 'Why "Little Angel" Lucie Need Not Have Died' (*Daily Mirror*, 13.11.82) (Golding and Middleton 1982).

The use of emotive terms such as 'angel' and 'shirker' have two main impacts on the reader. First, they are intended to produce an indignant reaction in the reader, making them angry with those responsible for the death of the child and sympathetic to the newspaper's standpoint. The aim is to create a kind of alliance between the reader and the media, a type of 'we'-ness, as if to say, 'We (the media) are outraged by this, and surely you (the reader) will be as well.' Another impact of the use of such terms is to reduce the complexity of the issues. Shades of grey are reduced to black and white images. The complex interplay of factors that contribute to the causes of child abuse (as described for example by Belsky 1988) are reduced to a formulation wherein dichotomies are created between the innocent, good and helpless on the one hand, and the incompetent, feckless and evil on the other. Surely no one would believe from the phrase 'do-nothing' that the welfare agencies in question literally did nothing. Or would they? No one who had any intimate knowledge of children would believe that any child was an 'angel', i.e. totally good. But for the purpose of highlighting accountability, the media calls for a suspension of disbelief – a willingness to believe the unbelievable – that the actors are essentially uni-dimensional in relation to the particular issue. The news is printed in 'black and white' in more than one sense.

The third way in which the media exerts an influence on child protection is through presenting information from a particular value stance, which usually is not made explicit. The manner in which the information is conveyed implies certain assumptions about the causes, consequences and prescriptions of abuse. However, that value stance, which may be as influential on the receiver as the information itself, is less likely to be open to critical challenge because of its implicit nature. For example, it is virtually unknown for a newspaper when reporting on the death of a child through abuse to devote space to wider contextual issues such as the role of women in society, the prevalence of images of violence on television and in the cinema, the connections between social disadvantage (for example, poverty and isolation) and abuse, the role and status of children in society, etc. Rather the emphasis is almost invariably on the shortcomings of individuals. This tendency to hold the individual accountable for outcomes that are essentially a complex interplay between individual and contextual factors could be seen as a political manifestation of the changes that have taken place during the almost aggressive individualisation of the Thatcher years. Margaret Thatcher's famous declaration, 'There is no such thing as society, only individuals and their families' (*Sunday Times*, 9.11.88) highlights this dramatically (and casually sweeps away more than a century of study of sociology).

As a further example, one could cite the assumption of predictability. This is an issue over which the professionals and academics are still divided, although there would appear to be an agreement that predicting child abuse (and fatalities arising from abuse) is seen as less predictable today than perhaps 20 years ago. Kempe and Kempe (1978, cited in Parton 1985: 142) for example claimed to be able to 'predict with remarkable accuracy which families were at risk'. They do not mention however the rather high level of false positives (that is, identifying as at risk families that are not) that would follow from the use of their risk factors. Howitt (1992) too is critical of Kempe's early work on prediction, claiming it to be 'seriously misleading, a major error being claims of extremely high rates of success in predicting future abuse using "diagnostic" criteria' (1992: 20). In another study described by Parton (1985: 143), Lealman et al. (1983) assessed 511 families out of 2802 at the point of discharge from a maternity unit as being at risk. When subsequently looking at all the children on the register two-thirds were from those families assessed as at high risk but of the 511 families, 483 were not on the child protection register, an alarmingly high false positive rate. Brown and Saqi (1988) also consider prediction of child abuse to be difficult (because of the low prevalence). They suggest that using the most effective screening tools available on a hypothetical sample of 10,000 would yield 33 actual abusers identified against 1195 false positives (individuals classified as high risk but not showing evidence of abusing during the follow-up period).

The intention of these examples is not to provide a refutation of the premise of predictability in child abuse, but to show that it is not an area about which there is agreement yet. Some researchers do claim high success rates using screening tools such as the Child Abuse Potential Inventory (Milner 1986; Milner 1989). Rather the object is to illustrate that whilst there is as yet no agreement upon the extent to which abuse can be predicted, the media continues to portray such incidents as if they were predictable, requiring only a reasonable amount of 'common sense' to see what is coming, a commodity with which professionals are often credited as being astonishingly deficient.

The model in Figure 3.1 depicts the media as being powerful because of its position at the top. Both directly and indirectly, it influences the child protection system by exerting pressure on members of Parliament. Indirectly, it influences the public who in turn are also constituents and are able to inform their MPs of their concerns about child protection issues. Directly, it influences the attitudes and views of members of Parliament concerning child abuse. One of the curious anomalies of the public accountability of government-provided services is that within the professional structures one has a hierarchy that, on basis of promotion, should very broadly reflect a hierarchy of knowledge about the work of the agency. We would for example expect a Director of Social Services to have an understanding of the professional issues relevant to the provision of social services that is superior to that of a basic-grade social worker. But at the very top, both in central and local governmental structures, the systems are directed by lay people whose knowledge of the service is more likely to be derived from reading the news than from reading professional and trade journals and books. Whilst this is not intended as a criticism of the public accountability of government structures – a necessity in a democratic society – it once again highlights how powerful the influence of the media can be.

Parliament and child protection

The making of laws is the business of MPs, and clearly the role of the media described in the previous section is to influence legislation. This may be in the form of getting new legislation through Parliament or by lobbying to amend existing or pending legislation. Fox Harding (1991) describes four influences on the making of child care legislation:

- Scandals and enquiries and the response
- Interest groups and their thinking
- Reviews of legislation and policy, and
- Wider policies and changes.

In the following paragraphs are several examples where legislation was already in motion.

In 1972, one year before the death of Maria Colwell, the Report of the Departmental Committee on Adoption (the Houghton Report) appeared. The recommendations of the report, following concerns during the 1960s about the rights of foster parents (for example, in so-called 'tug of love' situations) and the pre-eminence of the 'blood tie' would have introduced profound changes to the arrangements for fostering and adopting children. One factor in the circumstances leading to the death of Maria Colwell was her removal from foster parents, against their will, to be returned to her mother and stepfather at whose hands she died in January 1973. However, the Houghton Report appeared likely to remain on the shelf without being given sufficient parliamentary time to become law. In November 1973, David Owen introduced a Private Member's Bill to implement the Houghton recommendations. Nevertheless, the future of the Bill seemed uncertain, and it was not until Mr Owen became Minister of State for Health in 1974 under the new Labour government, that a government-sponsored Bill was introduced and ultimately passed as the Children Act 1975. This Act, hailed as a children's charter, put much more emphasis on the rights of the child in contrast to the rights of the parents, setting out much more explicit provisions for the termination of parental rights in planning for children. It coincided with the increased emphasis on 'permanency planning' in social work practice for children living apart from their families.

During the spring of 1987, 121 children were removed from the care of their parents because of concerns about sexual abuse and placed in the care of the Cleveland local authority. This was the first occasion in the history of British child protection that such a large-scale operation had been conducted. The suspicions that large numbers of children were being sexually abused were based on a diagnostic procedure (reflex anal dilatation) which, whilst the subject of some medical controversy, was construed by the media as being incorrectly used as a conclusive indicator. However, many of the children involved had indicators of other forms of abuse (physical and emotional), and a number of the children had also made disclosures indicating that they were being sexually abused. The divergence of opinion between the police surgeon on the one hand, and two paediatricians involved on the other hand, fuelled the controversy. Whilst children were being removed from families on a large scale, a number of parents sought the intervention of the local MP, Stuart Bell, who took up the issue and campaigned vigorously on their behalf. He alleged that the paediatrician, Dr Marietta Higgs, and the social services manager responsible for child protection, Sue Richardson conspired to exclude the police. Bell also involved the media via the convening of a press conference at which he complained of the authorities abusing their powers.

The events in Cleveland were also a watershed in child protection because for the first time, social workers, who had been given increasing powers to intervene and protect children under the Children Act 1975 (which had not been dramatically diminished by the Child Care Act 1980), weren't being criticised for failing to intervene to save the life of a child (by this stage a number of inquiries had conducted into such matters – Susan Aukland, 1975; Wayne Brewer, 1977; Lester Chapman, 1979; Richard Fraser, 1982; Shirley Woodcock, 1984; Jasmine Beckford, 1985). Instead, social workers came under attack for intervening over-zealously and without due care as to the rights of the parents. During parliamentary debate, a parallel was drawn between the Cleveland social services department, and 'another body which carried the initials SS', (*Hansard*, HoC, 29 June 1987, col. 257). A cartoon appeared in the social work press which was to appear on the walls of many social services offices. In it are depicted two identical scenarios of a social worker being lynched by an angry mob. Under one is the caption 'the social worker who fails to remove a child'; under the other, 'the social worker who removes a child'. The events in Cleveland had clearly brought home to social workers that they were in a no-win situation, trying to find a balance between over-intervention and under-intervention that was particularly delicate and fraught with difficulty. The television documentary 'Death of Childhood' (ITV, 1997) provided an update on the individuals at the centre of the controversy, and concluded that the real tragedy of Cleveland was not that families were torn apart as alleged by Stuart Bell and the media, but that children who had experienced the trauma of abuse were not adequately protected because of the failure of the adults to agree on how to protect them. Examples were given in which, because of the controversy, police failed to bring charges against individuals even when there was sufficient evidence to do so, and the local authority failed to institute care proceedings to protect children when they had clear evidence of abuse from a number of different sources.

The events in Cleveland and the subsequent inquiry were to have an impact on the Children Act 1989. It is a common misconception that this Act came about as a result of the events in Cleveland in 1987. Leathard (1994: 11) for example states 'including the major Report of the Inquiry into Child Abuse in Cleveland (Butler-Sloss, 1988) which led directly to the Children Act 1989'. The reasons for this misconception are simple to understand. The events in Cleveland were followed by the Children Bill (1988), which eventually resulted in the Children Act 1989. However, a study of the roots of the Act reveals that its origins go back well before the events in Cleveland. Although one could begin with the emphasis on prevention contained in the Children and Young Person's Act 1963, a more obvious beginning would be in 1982 when the House of Commons Social Services Committee decided to undertake an enquiry into children in care. This resulted, in 1984, in the Report of the Social Services Select Committee, (the Short Report), which recommended

> ... a thorough-going review of the body of statute law, regulations and judicial decisions relating to children, with a view to the production of a simplified and coherent body of law ... it is for the sake of justice that the legal framework of the child care system must be rationalised. (House of Commons 1984)

As a result a joint Review of Child Care Law was undertaken by the Department of Health and the Law Commission which led to the White Paper *The Law on Child Care and Family Services*, published in January 1987. This outlined the basis of the Government's plan to reform the public part of child care law, 'a complete overhaul of the law in relation to children and families (in terms of both the provision of services for children and families and the protection of children at risk) to make the law both clearer and fairer.

While this activity was taking place in relation to how local authorities provide services to children and families, and in relation to how local authorities look after children, concerns were being expressed in the private law provisions for children as well. A review was undertaken by the Law Commission which, following from the joint review with the Department of Health, was able to integrate the two into a single proposed Bill which would entail the most thorough and comprehensive enactment in relation to children and families ever undertaken. This was the basis of the Children Bill, published in 1988.

If, as indicated, the Children Act 1989 did not come about because of the events in Cleveland, how did those events influence the Act? There are at least three identifiable influences: they resulted in the first *Working Together* (1988), were the basis for some amendment to the Act, and provided the necessary pressure to legislate. The first version of *Working Together* (1988) was expected to appear earlier, but its publication was delayed as a result of the events in Cleveland, and a decision was taken that it should appear after the Cleveland Inquiry results had been published. Both the Inquiry and the new guidance appeared in 1988. The Inquiry appeared in two versions, a full report and an abridged edition. Whilst this may have been helpful for some purposes, (for example easier access to practitioners), it has, according to Parton (1991), led to some confusion, as the shortened version, in contrast to the longer version, contained no criticisms of the police, police surgeons, magistrates or Stuart Bell, but does contain fuller descriptions of the roles of the paediatricians and the child abuse consultant. *Working Together* (1988) contained provisions to maximise interagency coordination in child protection by clarifying the roles of the various agencies (social services, health agencies, education, police, probation, NSPCC and other voluntary agencies, and where applicable the Armed Services). It provided guidance on how agencies should intervene in individual cases of child abuse, including a separate chapter on intervention when sexual abuse is suspected. It advised that consideration be given to the recommendation of the Cleveland Inquiry that Specialist Assessment Teams (SAT) be established, comprising a social worker, doctor and police officer to undertake the initial investigations of child sexual abuse. It endorsed joint policies and procedures under an Area Child Protection Committee, and joint training for practitioners, which was subsequently supported by central government funding under the Training Support Programme (TSP). Finally it established a new basis for local inquiries into cases of abuse resulting in death or serious harm to the child. These provisions were largely retained when *Working Together* (1988) was revised to implement the provisions of the Children Act 1989. The separate section for sexual abuse cases was removed, and the category of grave concern was dropped from the categories of the child protection register. A second influence of Cleveland on the Children Act 1989 was on amendments to the provisions of the Act as it was going through Parliament. The most conspicuous impact was on the provisions relating to the emergency protection of children. To understand this one must compare the Emergency Protection Order (EPO) provision of the Act with both its predecessor, the Place of Safety Order (POS), and with another order introduced at the same time by the Act, the Child Assessment Order (CAO). When introducing the Children Bill in November 1988, David Mellor indicated that the Bill addressed the problem of the devastating consequences that can arise for families when children are removed through over-zealous action of social workers, a clear indicator of the influence of Cleveland on the development of the EPO. In contrast to its predecessor the POS Order, the EPO contained certain provisions designed to reduce the amount of control the local authority could have, before the matter was referred to a court. The POS Order allowed a child to be removed for up to 28 days, without any right of redress. It also contained certain ambiguities as to whether or not the child could be made the subject of a POS Order when he or she was already in a safe place (for example in hospital), and the legality of medical examinations. The EPO, however, only lasted for eight days in the first instance, renewable for up to another seven days, and most importantly was open to challenge after 72 hours, (although not formally an appeal).

The Child Assessment Order provisions of the Act, especially as they related to Emergency Protection Orders were one of the most contested provisions of the Act, bringing on board a range of child welfare and social service agencies in shifting alliances and conflicts. Parton (1991: 177–90) provides a very full discussion of the politics of the CAO. In brief the issue of the need for a child assessment order arose out of the recommendations into the inquiry into the death of Kimberley Carlile (London Borough of Greenwich 1987) in which Kimberley's mother and her partner had denied social workers direct access to Kimberley, on one occasion only allowing a glimpse of the child through a glass panel over the door. The issue, a type of Catch-22, was how to ensure that children can be assessed to establish whether or not there is a basis for further legal intervention if parents are frustrating access in the first place. But the Cleveland Inquiry report made no mention of CAOs, considering instead that the needs of the child would be adequately served by the introduction of the EPO. As a result, a polarisation between the recommendations of the two enquiries emerged (Cleveland EPO vs Carlile CAO). The final result could be seen as a compromise. The provisions of the EPO were amended to include a ground of frustrated access – where investigations under section 47 of the Act were being 'frustrated by access to the child being unreasonably refused'. This meant that an EPO could be obtained without the child being seen where there was concern and where the parents were denying access to the child. In addition, provisions for a CAO were incorporated into the Act. This required the parents to produce the child for the purposes of assessment where the child was considered likely to suffer significant harm, and assessment was necessary to determine if the child was suffering (or likely to suffer) significant harm and an assessment was unlikely in the absence of an order. The date of the beginning of the assessment would be included in the order and the period of the order could be for up to seven days (only very exceptionally requiring the child to be accommodated away from home for any or all of that period).

The third impact of the Cleveland crisis was to create pressure to legislate. We have seen with the Maria Colwell situation that although much of the machinery for the potential legislation had already been in place (arising from the Houghton Committee report), it was very likely that owing to competition for parliamentary time for other issues, the White Paper would not have become a Bill and the Bill would not have become a law for lack of parliamentary debate. The same could be said to be true for the Children Act 1989. Prior to 1987 there was no great rush to get a new child statute on the books. Although people were aware of the iniquities and shortcomings of the child care system (for example the various routes via which children could enter the compulsory care of the local authority, and the different grounds applicable in different routes), it is possible that the provisions would have been delayed, introduced piecemeal (which they often are with Acts in any case), or relegated to the realms of guidance and regulations, rather than debated and introduced as the comprehensive piece of legislation which emerged.

Crossing the central–local divide

The relationship between local government and central government is often characterised by tension; this is especially true when different political parties are in power. It is useful to summarise the essential features of central government social policy in recent years under the Conservative administration. Flynn (1997) describes six themes:

1 A move from equality of treatment to the promotion of different treatment for different people.
2 Change from universal eligibility to rationing against strict eligibility criteria.
3 The move away from the presumption that public services should be provided by public bodies towards the development or private or mixed private and public provision.
4 The move from a position of no choice for the service user to some choice or the illusion of choice.
5 The move from local policy autonomy to central control and
6 Funding based on some measure of performance or volume of work.

Taking the fifth item, during the 18 years of Conservative administration there had been an almost unprecedented assault on the autonomy of local authorities, of which rate-capping was an early and dramatic example: 'Throughout the period of Conservative rule, local authorities spent as much energy trying to evade central government control as central government spent trying to subjugate them' (Flynn 1997: 70). The main control that central government exerts is through the funding of local authorities. Only about 20 per cent of local government funding is generated from local sources through the council tax. The bulk of local funding is provided through the revenue support grant, the size of which is determined by the Standard Spending Assessment, a formula derived from a collection of key indicators. The more direct implication of funding for child protection services is explored below when we consider the allocation of ring-fenced money.

In addition to the direct control of local government activities and funding, how can government, which is far removed from the working lives of most professionals, influence their practice? There are various means, some being the making of regulations and guidance, the use of inspection, the commissioning and publishing of research, ring-fenced funding of certain activities (for example, training), and networking (formal and informal mechanisms for meeting together to consider issues).

The making of regulations and guidance

There are differences between primary legislation, and regulations and guidance, and it is useful to be clear about the distinctions. In terms of the management of child abuse services, it is arguable that guidance has been more significant than primary legislation: 'The whole machinery of child-abuse procedures, area child-protection committees, case conferences, and at-risk registers, is based not on law but on circulars of guidance' (Hallet 1989: 139). The most lucid account of the differences between legislation, regulations and guidance is contained in *The Care of Children: Principles and Practice in Regulations and Guidance* (DoH 1989) which appeared at the same time as the Children Act 1989. The introduction contains the following:

> The status of principal legislation such as the Children Act 1989 is generally clearly understood. It is the law and must be obeyed. But the status of regulations, codes and guidance is less well appreciated.
>
> *Regulations* are what is called subordinate legislation. They are made by the Lord Chancellor or Secretary of State under the authority of an Act which is primary legislation. The Boarding-Out and Charge and Control Regulations 1988 were both made under the authority of the Child Care Act 1980 and the 1986 Amendment Act, and the Children Act 1989 gives the Secretary of State power to issue a wide range of regulations.
>
> Regulations have 'the full force of statute' (*Halsbury's 'Laws of England'*). This means that they must be obeyed as law under all circumstances. They include permissions and restrictions as to what may or may not be done and also requirements on what must be done.
>
> *Guidance documents and circulars* are usually issued as general guidance of the Secretary of State as described in S7(1) of the Local Authority Social Services Act 1970. Local authorities are required to act in accordance with such guidance which is intended to be a statement of what is held to be good practice. Though they are not in themselves law in the way that regulations are law, guidance documents are likely to be quoted or used in court proceedings as well as in local authority policy and practice papers. They could provide the basis for a legal challenge of an authority's action or inaction, including (in extreme cases) default action by the Secretary of State.
>
> Guidance is often issued alongside regulations, e.g. the handbooks that accompany the Boarding-Out and Charge and Control Regulations. But guidance may also stand alone, e.g. *Working Together* (1988, 1991).
>
> *Codes of practice* fall between regulations and guidance notes. They may be 'statutory' in that they are required by legislation and are laid before Parliament. They therefore carry more weight than other departmental guidance, but they are not law in the way that regulations are law. As with Section 7 guidance, courts expect detailed justification for not following codes of practice, but some flexibility to suit the needs of a particular case is allowed and expected.

One might sum up the differences between the requirements of these various official documents like this:– Regulations say '*You must/shall*'; codes say '*You ought/ should*'. When guidance explains regulations, it reaffirms the '*you must*' messages. However, when it goes beyond regulations in setting out good practice, it conveys the message that '*It is highly desirable to ...* ' or '*Unless there is good reason not to, you should ...* ' rather than '*You must*'. (DoH 1989: 2–3)

The guidance-making authority of government bodies such as the Department of Health, the Welsh Office, the Home Office, are therefore derived from, but not the same as, statute. Whilst guidance does not carry the full weight of statute, there is very strong weight attached to it, and it has been said that in the case of judicial review, for example, non-compliance with guidance on the part of the authority, could be extremely significant in determining the outcome. On the other hand, government guidance itself can in rare cases come under fire, for example from the courts. It is interesting that the above extract cites the Charge and Control Regulations of 1988 – it was precisely these regulations which, when challenged in a court, created some of the confusion about the status of regulations and guidance which subsequently needed to be clarified. In the case in question, the London Borough of Newham refused to allow a teenager to have a weekend stay with a relative under the Charge and Control Regulations because the checks required under the regulations had not been completed. The matter was referred to court, which decided that notwithstanding the government guidance requiring complete checks for even very short-term arrangements, some discretion should be allowed, and ruled in favour of the teenager and his family. The logic of this seems clear; whilst the provisions of the regulations were intended to ensure that the welfare of children in care were adequately safeguarded when being looked after by parents or relatives, it was not perhaps envisaged, or intended, that they should by their very nature eliminate the possibility of a short stay with relatives that might be very beneficial to the child, because it was planned at too short notice to fully implement the requirements of the regulations. Apart from the arguments about the requirements of the regulations, the interesting point was that the local authority was successfully challenged for attempting to comply with government guidance to the regulations, which raised the question of the status of guidance.

Reference to government bodies should not be taken simply to mean the Department of Health and the Welsh Office, and it is well to remember that the structures of governmental administration are quite different in those two bodies. Regulations and guidance produced by one can be taken to have equal standing in the other. Government bodies with an interest in child protection include as well the Home Office and the Department of Education and Science (now the Department for Education and Employment, DfEE). *Working Together* (1991) was produced by all four bodies working jointly. Another example of guidance, the *Memorandum of Good Practice* (Home Office and DoH 1992), was described as being produced by the Home Office 'in conjunction with' the Department of Health.

The quasi-compulsory nature of guidance issued by government departments makes it customary for draft documents on proposed guidance to be issued for consultation. There are potential difficulties with this process. Depending on the nature of the contents of the guidance, these will go to different statutory and voluntary agencies that have an interest in the issue, although occasionally they will not get to all those who consider they have an interest. The consultation periods are very variable. During the relatively hectic period of the introduction to the Children Act 1989, drafts on proposed guidance were appearing very frequently, occasionally with only a few weeks to respond. The timescales for responses were considerably reduced in Wales: the draft guidance was issued later than its appearance in England (because of the requirement of the Welsh Office to 'top and tail' the document to make it a Welsh Office document prior to distribution). In addition, the responses were required sooner in Wales than they were in England (in order for them to be compiled by the Welsh Office into a response to the Department of Health). In some cases the shortness of the timescale for consultation (for example with the proposed Adoption Bill) created frustration, because of the subsequent inaction following the consultation.

The interest of Government to ensure that agency practice conforms with government guidance was highlighted in the document *Patterns and Outcomes in Child Placement* (DoH 1991a) compiled by Jane Rowe as part of the introduction to the Children Act 1989. That publication contained a summary of the research into child placement, accompanied by a series of practical exercises that practitioners and managers could use to familiarise themselves with the principles of good practice contained in the Act. One exercise, 'Where did the guidance go?' using the hypothetical scenario of a child fatality in which non-adherence to procedures featured, asks the reader to focus on several questions relating to the availability of guidance to practitioners. It included such issues as where such documents are kept, how available they are, how they are updated, monitored and evaluated, and how new staff get to know about them. The introduction to the exercise contains the following:

> One of the responsibilities of managers of child care services is to develop and distribute policy, procedure and guidance materials for those who work face to face with children and families. Yet research and inquiries have shown that these essential documents may never reach the practitioners whom they were intended

to help. They may be successfully distributed when first issued, but due to the passage of time, staff changes and the lack of efficient storage and retrieval systems in some teams or area offices, they can become lost or forgotten. (DoH 1991a: 130)

Some examples of government guidance issued in the last decade are:

- Local Authority Circular [LAC (92) 18]: *Children's Services Plans*
- Local Authority Circular [LAC (94) 11]: *The Education of Children being looked after by Local Authorities*
- Welsh Office Circular [WOC 52/95]: *Protecting Children from Abuse: The Role of the Education Service*
- Welsh Office Circular [WOC 20/96]: *Children's Services Plans – Further Guidance*
- Home Office Code of Practice (July 96): *On the Record: The Government's Proposals for Access to Criminal Records for Employment and Related Purposes in England and Wales*
- Welsh Office Circular [WOC 35/96]: *'Child Care Procedures and Practice in North Wales' Implementation of the Report of Ms Adrianne Jones.*

Whilst guidance is one method by which government bodies can provide for child protection policies to be put into practice, another means of ensuring this is the use of inspection.

The role of inspection in policy

Increasingly the scrutiny of public services is achieved through the establishment of explicit, measurable standards (or indicators) and the measurement of attainment of those standards. There are five main bodies involved in the regulation through inspection of health, education, police and social services: the National Health Service Executive (NHSE), the Office for Standards in Education (OFSTED), Her Majesty's Inspectors of Constabulary (HMIC), the Social Services Inspectorate (SSI) and the Audit Commission.

The National Health Service Executive

The National Health Service Executive is responsible for the interpretation and implementation of government health policy in all sections (both 'purchaser' and 'provider' units) of the National Health Service. The NHS reforms were the flagship of the incorporation of market principles into public services. In her introduction to the White Paper, *Working for Patients* (Secretaries of State for Health, Wales, Northern Ireland and Scotland 1989), Margaret Thatcher observed, 'Taken together, the proposals represent the most far reaching reform of the National Health Service in its forty year history.' These proposals were subsequently enacted in the National Health Service and Community Care Act 1990 and implemented from 1 April 1991. Among the key changes introduced were:

1   Decentralisation of decision making (from Regions to Districts, from Districts to Hospitals).
2   A new self-governing status for hospitals – NHS Hospital Trusts (which was extended to include trust status for community health services).
3   The establishment of GP fundholding practices.
4   NHS management bodies to be streamlined – on business lines.
5   Greater emphasis on audit of service quality and value for money.

One significant effect of these changes was the realisation of a concept which had taken form in the 1980s: the internal market. As described by Robinson, 'an internal market has been created within the NHS in which the responsibility for purchasing, or commissioning services has been separated from the responsibility for providing them' (1994: 2). Thus the Health Authorities' role has become one of procurement; they may purchase the necessary services from a range of service providers, one being NHS Hospital Trusts. The required services are obtained through the use of contracts and service agreements.

At the same time as developing a decentralised market economy in the National Health Service, the government was anxious to retain a strong degree of central control. The formal machinery for achieving this was introduced in April 1994 through the operation of the National Health Service Executive (NHSE) (NHSE 1994). Through its national headquarters and its eight regional offices it controls the activities of the health authorities whose responsibilities are, through their purchasing of health services, to ensure the provision of comprehensive health care for their area. Another means of ensuring central government control over the operation of the NHS is established through the Secretary of State for Health being responsible for appointments of the chair of the various health authorities. The NHS Executive uses performance indicators, guidance and directives to achieve this high degree of central government control. This control is also achieved through financing, as it is responsible for the disbursement of central government funds to purchasing authorities and GP fundholders including capital expenditure. Health authorities are able to purchase health promotion and treatment services from predominantly three types of service providers: directly-provided health authority services, NHS Trusts, and private sector providers. This plurality of service providers is what creates the market economy within the NHS, creating competition (through tendering for contracts) between different providers. General practitioners have contracts directly with the NHS and through their fundholding capacity have contracts with service providers, again through competitive bidding processes, to supply the services that they are required under their contracts with the NHS to provide.

The National Health Service Executive promotes the establishment of Trusts and influences appointments of chief executives and Trust board members. It has a central strategic framework developed in accordance with health targets (for example, reducing the incidence and prevalence of specific illnesses, improving the general health of the population, and improving sexual and mental health) which are established by the Secretary of State and the Department of Health. The operations for achieving the objectives of the framework include the deployment of financial and human resources, information collection and management, performance management, the development and regulation of the market, and research and development. This creates a system where:

> Day-to-day management of the NHS consists of the relationship between the health authorities and general practitioners as purchasers of health treatments with their providers, within a hierarchical policy and management framework set mainly by the NHS Executive. (Flynn 1997: 208)

As a body, where interests are combined, the NHSE has worked with other government inspection bodies. For example, in 1995, jointly with the Social Services Inspectorate (SSI), it published findings on the implementation of the community care legislation (NHSE/SSI 1995).

NHSE guidance on child protection is contained in Part 18 of *Child Health in the Community: A Guide to Good Practice* (DoH 1996). It includes information on further government guidance on child protection (six sources), recent messages from research, information on Area Child Protection Committees, requirements concerning senior health staff designated for child protection purposes, and the necessity for child protection work to be included in contracts between purchasers and providers, which should include procedures and protocols to be followed. It also includes information on the legislative framework of child protection.

OFSTED and OHMCI (The Office for Standards in Education; the Office of Her Majesty's Chief Inspector of Schools in Wales)

Like the Social Services Inspectorate described below, OFSTED has responsibilities both to report to the public on standards in education and to the ministers responsible for the service as a means of regulation. As described by Midwinter within the central government management of the education services we can see the same type of concern to combine a high degree of central control over standards ('moves to gather enormous power into the bosom of the central authority', 1994: 160) with the introduction of the market place economy ('"privatism" and market style consumerism') as we have seen in the management of the health services. The role of OFSTED is crucial in this delicate balance.

The major changes to the education services were brought about by the Education Reform Act 1988 (with some subsequent modifications by the Education Act 1993). The 1988 Act 'laid the basis for the privatisation of the system and for creating the conditions for a market in education' (Simon and Chitty 1993). It has been described as 'seismic lawmaking in education' (Morris 1990: 2). First, the Act introduced the National Curriculum – three core subjects (maths, English and science), and seven 'foundation' subjects – which was received with some degree of consensus. More controversial however, was its emphasis on assessment and testing (at different age levels), and the consequent production of school 'league tables' of the results of those assessments and tests. Second, it introduced major changes in the management of schools. Notable among these are the local management of schools (LMS) and a new category of opted-out school, the 'grant-maintained school'. Under these provisions, schools operate on a cost-centre basis and are managed by a board of governors comprising both elected and appointed representatives. Grant-maintained schools are those which have chosen to opt out of local authority control altogether, and are funded directly by grants from central government. Whilst not politically feasible to go down the road of all schools being grant-maintained, the encouragement of central government for grant-maintained schools showed itself in the provision requiring the governors of all non-grant maintained schools to have an annual consideration as to whether or not to ballot the school's parents on becoming grant-maintained. The process was slower than had been hoped (all secondary schools grant-maintained by 1997), and by 1993 only about 800 schools had opted for grant-maintained status. There was even less enthusiasm by schools to adopt grant-maintained status in Wales.

A dramatic consequence of the Act has been the considerable downsizing of Local Education Authorities (LEAs) and a downgrading of their role. A number of writers have commented on the diminishing role of LEAs. Fallon (1991) has described the only functions remaining to LEAs as being responsible for school attendance, the provision of statements for pupils with severe learning difficulties, auditing and inspection of schools, and planning/ providing capital spending, (with further reduction in the role in relation to school inspection planned). Higgins (1993), concluded that 'advocacy/ arbitration is the residual role of the authority'. Brighouse (1991) has commented that 'in the management cycle ... the LEA has much diminished power in planning, organising, providing and maintaining.' Other writers are even more pessimistic about the future of LEAs. Brynin (1993: 177) notes that 'the purpose of LMS is negative: the elimination of LEAs.' Hutchinson (1993) considers that the end of LEAs is inevitable, although the timescale is uncertain, and advocates for the urgent development of other structures that will ensure that schools work together rather than against each other. Maden (1993) describes the impact of Education reforms as virtual dissolution of the LEAs.

As part of the dramatic overhaul of education services, a more independent inspection service was felt to be necessary. On 1 September 1992 the Offices for Standards in Education (OFSTED), which replaced Her Majesty's Inspectorate (HMI), was set up to implement the provisions of the Education (Schools) Act 1992, requiring a new independent system of school inspection. At the same time, the Office of Her Majesty's Chief Inspector of Schools in Wales – OHMCI (Wales) – was established. Whereas previously school inspections were undertaken by HMI directly, under the new system, in keeping with the political ideology previously described under role of the NHS Executive, OFSTED's role was primarily a commissioning role. Inspections are undertaken by teams of independent inspectors led by a Registered Inspector, working to a Framework of Inspection (OFSTED 1995). Similar provisions apply in Wales. The framework sets out four key elements which legislation required to be included in inspection:

- The quality of education provided by schools
- The educational standards achieved in schools
- The way in which financial resources are managed
- The spiritual, moral, social and cultural development of pupils.

The inspectors, who are not employees of OFSTED, are allocated to schools on the basis of competitive tender, and are paid by OFSTED for the work undertaken. When the report (with summary) of the inspection team is completed, the school is required to send a copy of the summary to the parent of every child at the school and to develop an action plan (which should also be made available to parents) based on the recommendations of the report. The full report should be made available by the school on request to parents, the local media, libraries and local employers.

Although OFSTED assumed the major part of the responsibilities of HMI, HMI continues to function primarily to offer advice on the regulation and monitoring of the school inspection system. They also inspect independent schools, teacher training, and LEA-funded further education. Again, a similar distinction applies in Wales. Despite the claims of OFSTED for independence, OFSTED has been criticised for its lack of independence from government, according to Flynn (1997). It was considered to be editing its reports at the request of ministers to highlight the responsibilities of schools, whilst at the same time, downplaying ministerial responsibility.

But what about child protection? The Framework for Inspection of Schools (OFSTED 1995) contains explicit standards relevant to the schools role, although the lack of detail supplied makes it difficult to know how those standards are assessed in the context of inspection. The relevant standard is *5.4 Support, guidance and pupil's welfare* which states: 'Inspectors must evaluate and report on ... the school's arrangement for child protection', and 'Judgements should be based on the extent to which the school ... has effective child protection procedures' (OFSTED 1995: 20).

Because of the lack of detail, it is impossible to know the extent to which inspections emphasise the role of the designated teachers, the accessibility of knowledge of child protection procedures to teachers, and whether they evaluate interagency working relationships in the context of child protection. With so much of the literature emphasising the difficulties of the role of the education service in child protection, it is tempting to consider that perhaps insufficient consideration to child protection in the inspection of schools is a contributing factor. This would be a very useful area to research.

Her Majesty's Inspectors of Constabulary

Thomas (1994) has described the history of police accountability as at times apolitical and at others a political 'hot potato'. The accountability for police has a long and in some ways troubled history of multiple responsibilities emerging out of the Victorian Watch Committees. Under the Police Act (1964), a formal tripartite structure of accountability was devised in which the local police forces were accountable to the local authorities, the chief constable and the Home Office. In London, the police force came under the direct control of the Home Secretary. This system has been criticised and discredited, and disguised an ever-increasing trend towards centralisation of the accountability of the police service under the chief constables and the Home Office, with the local authorities' role becoming marginalised. Thomas (1994) considers it a system in which chief constables acting individually and collectively through the Association of Chief Police Officers (ACPO) have been able to play the local authority police committee off against the Home Office to secure a greater degree of autonomy and independence. A series of court rulings have contributed to confirming the police in a role of public service that is different in some respects from all others by being accountable only to the law, leading to a construct of police discretion in law enforcement and a view that the police alone as public servants should not be accountable to democratically elected representatives of the public. During the 1980s, Her Majesty's Inspectors of Constabulary began looking more closely (along with the Audit Commission described below) at the effectiveness and efficiency of policing. In 1992 a Commission was set up under Sir Patrick Sheehy to look at police conditions of service and salaries. In 1993, the Home Office (Home Office et al. 1993) announced its intention to devolve the financial control of budgets considerably to local police services, developing a more localised system of managerialism and accountability described by Thomas (1994: 13) as 'more powerful and businesslike authorities which would give more leadership to the local police service and ensure that money is spent more effectively'. This was achieved through the implementation of the Police and Magistrates' Courts Act (1994) which made the local police force more independent from the local authority from April 1995. Thus we see a further example of the decentralisation of decision making and financial allocations which has characterised the government reforms in education, health and local government. However, as with those reforms, government retains a strong degree of centralised control over a decentralised administration, in the case of the police by several means. First, control is achieved by the nomination of more people with business and managerial experience by the Home Secretary to the local police authorities, and the retention by the Home Secretary of the final say over the appointment of chairs to the police local authority. Second, it is achieved by the introduction of Local Police Plans which are intended to conform to government target-setting, priorities and performance indicators (for example, detection rates for violent crimes and domestic burglaries, visibility of the force to the public, response times to emergencies, etc.). The role of Her Majesty's Inspector of Constabulary is to monitor these.

The Social Services Inspectorate

The Social Services Inspectorate (SSI) is the professional division of the Department of Health. Established in 1985, it replaced the Social Work Services of the Department of Health and Social Security, and is independent of the local authority and voluntary and private providers of social services. In 1992 the Inspectorate was restructured to create two divisions, one of which was devoted exclusively to the undertaking of inspecting social services departments. The head of the SSI is the Chief Inspector who is responsible for providing the Secretary of State with professional advice on government policy and on the quality of provision of social services. The Inspectorate's functions are to inspect the organisation, management and provision of social services; to promote quality, improve effectiveness and efficiency, and to promote the safety and well-being of people who use the services. It advises the Ministers and the Department of Health on making, implementing and reviewing health and social services policies, and on the effective and efficient delivery of those policies. It also aims to facilitate communications between the Department of Health and 'the field'.

It achieves this by undertaking and publishing research-based reports, inspecting social services departments, and organising conferences on current issues and dilemmas in practice. The following are some examples of SSI publications in the field of child care and child protection in recent years.

Table 3.1: Social Services Inspectorate Reports

Year	Report/Publication
1990	*Inspection of Child Protection Services in Rochdale* (North Western Region)
1992	*Alcohol Misuse and Child Mistreatment: Report of Second Training Initiative Developed from an Experimental Project published in April 1991* (Wales)
1993	*Evaluating Performance in Child Protection: A framework for the inspection of local authority social services practice and systems*
1994	*Evaluating Child Protection Services: Findings and Issues – Inspections of Six Local Authority Child Protection Services 1993: Overview Report*
1994	*Report on the National Survey of Children's Services Plans – Progress Made During 1993*
1995	*Domestic Violence and Social Care: A report on two conferences held by the Social Services Inspectorate*
1995	*Evaluating Child Protection Services: Child Inspections 1993/94 – Overview Report*
1996	*Area Child Protection Committees and Local Government Reorganisation* (Wales)

It is useful to look in more depth at three of these reports, the 1993 Framework for inspection, and the two overview reports in 1994 and 1995. The 1993 Framework document is a highly structured document setting out how inspections into child protection will be undertaken and the criteria that will be used. The first two chapters deal with the process of inspections and the third chapter deals with the content. The inspection is described as a six-stage process of planning, field work, analysing, judging, reporting, and evaluating. The content of the inspection is also highly structured, its framework containing three levels of indicators against which child protection services are to be evaluated. The three levels are dimensions, standards and criteria. Dimensions which are not defined are the broad categories which provide the context for standards and criteria. Each dimension has at least one standard relating to it, and one or more criteria for each standard. Both standards and criteria are defined. Standards are defined as the 'quality of performance which is required in the management and delivery of services, if service provision is to accord with Department of Health policy and practice guidance' (SSI 1993: 5). Criteria are described as 'specific and detailed statements of expectation about particular aspects of a generally stated standard'. Two distinct categories of dimensions are identified: dimensions of performance in case investigation and management, and dimensions of agency performance. The dimensions of case investigation and management are:

- common aspects of direct work with children and families
- recognition and referral
- immediate protection and identifying the nature of the concern
- investigation and initial assessment
- decision making about registration at child protection conferences
- comprehensive assessment
- formulation of child protection plan
- implementation of child protection plan
- review of child protection plan
- record keeping.

The dimensions of agency performance are:

- policy
- inter-agency working: policies and procedures
- resourcing
- management
- staff competence and deployment
- training
- supervision
- consultancy
- operation of the child protection register
- data protection and access to records
- complaints and representations.

Two examples of the hierarchy of dimensions, standards and criteria follow:

> **Dimension**: Review of Child Protection Plan
> > **Standard**: (one of two)
> > > Deregistration is the outcome of the child protection review conference only when all participants are satisfied that the abuse or risk of abuse is no longer present or sufficient to warrant continued registration.
> > > > **Criteria**: (two of five)
> > > > > – Arrangements are in place for differences of opinion between participants to be managed constructively, primarily by the Conference Chair.
> > > > > – Decisions to de-register the child's name are accompanied by consideration of the continuing need for services to the child and family.

And another example:

> **Dimension**: 'inter-agency working: policies and procedures'
> > **Standard**: (one of five)
> > > 'The SSD has a firm commitment to working with other agencies to ensure the planning, resourcing, implementation and review of child protection services.'
> > > > **Criteria**: (one of four)
> > > > > 'The SSD, along with other agencies on the ACPC, commits resources to inter-agency work and initiatives, particularly joint training.'

The report makes it clear that it is not expected that every criterion in every standard in every dimension will be used for each inspection: within the 21 dimensions there are 48 standards with 285 criteria against which to evaluate them. Rather, because inspections need to be tailored to the local circumstances, the statements of the standards 'provide a pool from which people planning an inspection can choose those that are appropriate to their inspection' (SSI 1993: 2).

The purpose of the inspections of six social services departments (Barnsley, Essex, Hereford and Worcester, Oldham, Surrey, and Wiltshire) in the 1994 overview report was to evaluate the extent to which local authority child protection services were being undertaken in accordance with *Working Together* (1991), and with the principles and regulations and guidance of the Children Act 1989 (SSI 1994b). Some of the concerns to emerge from that report were:

- 'a worrying number of cases where the child's welfare had ceased to be the primary concern' (p.3)
- 'Inspectors were extremely concerned about the number of cases where no keyworker had been allocated' (p.4)
- 'Authorities lacked quality control systems' (p.6)
- 'Inspectors seldom found comprehensive assessments' (p.6)
- '… in most authorities there were no child protection plans' (p.7)
- '… concerns about the way in which reviews under Part 8 of *Working Together* were being undertaken' (p.8) [these are interagency reviews when a child dies and abuse is suspected, or there are issues of public concern]
- 'Only one authority had a written policy on staff supervision' (p.10)
- 'The poor quality of records acted as a barrier to service user access to records' (p.11) (all SSI 1994b).

The 1995 Report summarised the inspections of eight social services departments completed between April 1993 and March 1994 (Greenwich, Hounslow, Islington, Leicestershire, North Tyneside, Wakefield, West Sussex, and Rochdale). The report is structured around nine key themes emerging from the inspections: Important Principles of the Children Act, Supervision, Quality Monitoring, Strategic Workforce Plans and Training, Procedures, Recording, Public Information, Management Information, ACPC Issues. The report is a bit more 'upbeat' than its predecessor, providing a somewhat more positive overview in the following:

> It was a very positive feature of the findings that the important principles of the Children Act – welfare paramountcy, wishes and feelings of children, partnership with parents, equal opportunities, and the keyworker role – all featured strongly in the performance of these services … (SSI 1995a: 4)

and

> Overall it was judged to be an encouraging picture, but not one which should permit complacency, and with some features that require a determined commitment if they are to be corrected. (SSI 1995a: 5)

Some of the concerns expressed were:

- 'All the reports comment on the need for systems that ensure regular, planned, recorded supervision' (p.8)
- 'All the reports comment on the need for a formal system to be established to monitor the quality of work' (p.11)

- 'All the reports comment on the lack of strategic workforce planning' (p.13)
- 'The majority of reports recommended that authorities should review their recording requirements and ensure they are implemented' (p.17)
- '... information to the public about child protection services is still a matter which is apparently a relatively low priority for SSDs' (p.18)
- '... authorities need to do more to improve the quality of management information in relation to referrals, time spent on work, outcomes and costs' (p.21) (all SSI 1995a).

This material however, only presents one side of the picture, that is, how the Social Services Inspectorate views the operations of the local social services departments. The reverse perspective is how departments view the Inspectorate. In research undertaken on behalf of the Welsh Office (Jackson et al. 1994) my colleagues and I asked Area Child Protection Committee chairs about their expectations on the Welsh Office in terms of policy and guidance. Before reporting on their observations, two points should be kept in mind. First, the relationship between the Welsh authorities (eight at the time of the study) and the Welsh Office is more direct than the relationship between the Department and Health and the English authorities because of the numbers involved, even allowing for the mediation of the English contact via regions. Secondly, the responses were as Area Child Protection Committee (ACPC) chairs, not as representatives of social services, although with one exception, all the chairs were senior managers of the social services departments. Whilst I would not want to equate social services with the Area Child Protection Committee, the role of social services as the lead agency in child protection (a role which is endorsed in the SSI framework for inspections), makes some of their concerns as an agency and their concerns as an ACPC member very similar.

ACPC chairs considered that they had minimal expectations of the Welsh Office. There was a 'sad lack of contact over policy issues in child protection on a regular basis'. It was speculated that geography might be a factor, and that those agencies which were physically closer might feel different. While the reactions of the Welsh Office were felt to be okay in consideration of a particular problem, it was felt that the agenda in the past had not been sufficiently proactive. Recent trends were addressing this to some extent at a collective level (meetings of ACPC chairs and inter-ACPC workshops were considered very useful). There was concern that the more individualised contact was about complaints – concerns about what others felt the ACPC was not doing right, than about what they were doing well or about what the ACPC considered to be problematical. For example, 'No one says, This is great. How you doing things? Are you doing it o.k.? What's the problems?

How can we help? Maybe that's not the role of the SSI, but I think it is, I don't think it's just to inspect.'

The two main, related, issues coming up for ACPC chairs where the SSI seemed unable to help were abuse of children by professionals and the role of education. In the following year however, the Welsh Office issued a circular, WOC 52/95, *Protecting Children from Abuse: The Role of the Education Service*.

The Audit Commission

The Audit Commission is an independent body which was established in 1982 under the Local Government Finance Act (1982), and began work in 1983. It is responsible for an overview of the external audit of local authorities and agencies within the National Health Service in England and Wales. Its original responsibilities were limited to the activities of local government, but in 1990 it assumed responsibility for external audit within the NHS as well. It carries out its responsibilities through the appointment of local auditors. It is concerned with the 'three Es' of service delivery: economy, efficiency and effectiveness. Flynn has defined these as follows, 'Economy is about the cost of the units used, and making economic use of them. Efficiency is concerned with the cost of producing outputs. Effectiveness is defined as producing results' (1997: 173). The Audit Commission can therefore be seen as the 'watchdog' of public services with a particular emphasis on value for money.

The Audit Commission has produced reports on various areas of local authority and health service activities such as the handling by local authorities of budgets transferred to them from health authorities (special transitional grants) for the purposes of funding care in the community under the 1990 National Health Service and Community Care Act (Audit Commission 1994a), the funding of police authorities under the new arrangements between them and the Home Office created by the 1994 Police and Magistrates' Courts Act, (Audit Commission 1994b), and variations in pay in local government (Audit Commission 1995). In relation to services for children, it has looked at provisions for children with special educational needs (Audit Commission 1992) and the provision of hospital services for children (Audit Commission 1993). For our purposes, the most relevant of the Audit Commission reports on children's services was the study of services for children in need, *Seen But Not Heard* (Audit Commission 1994c). That report broke new ground by looking at children's services across agency boundaries between community child health services and social services, which was a reflection of the heightened emphasis in legislation, regulations and guidance on interagency working. The preface makes clear that the report does not cover all children's services – only child health surveillance, the school health service, immunisation, family support and daycare, child protection and children looked after by social services.

The report, *Seen But Not Heard* (Audit Commission 1994c), drawing on surveys and on audits of eight health authorities and eight local authorities, identifies three key themes to achieve the most cost-effective provision of support to children in need. The first theme is that services must respond to and be focused on need. It distinguishes between those services which of necessity are provided on a universal basis (for example, education and health services), although even with the latter it considers that services are, and should be, becoming more focused or targeted. The task for services for children in need of protection however is to identify and provide highly focused services. A failure to target such services means both a waste of resources and a failure to ensure the well-being of children. A second theme is that services should only be offered where there is a likelihood of beneficial outcomes for the child and the family. This would include intermediate and long-term well-being of the child. Here the report considers that 'Inappropriate interventions are not only wasteful, they can also be detrimental to both child and parents' (Audit Commission 1994c: 7). Although it is not explicitly stated, it would seem clear that the phrase 'inappropriate interventions' refers to the application of child protection procedures in situations where the provision of family support, or even no intervention at all, would be more appropriate. The report was drawing on the findings from Gibbons et al. (1995a), unpublished at the time, that six out of seven children who entered the child protection system were filtered out without their names needing to be placed on the child protection register. The inference is drawn that too many children are being drawn into the child protection system who do not need the type of protection indicated when their name is added to the register (for example, the development of an interagency child protection plan). The third theme is that the provision of services must be jointly coordinated and based on a partnership between agencies and parents. After first acknowledging that the needs of a child for services to enhance his or her well-being are not likely to be the concern of just one agency, the report then draws attention to the two potential pitfalls of multiple agency provisions. First, there may be overlap and duplication of services. Secondly, there may be a failure to provide any necessary services at all: the child may slip through the net of services provided by different agencies. It considers that 'progress towards an inter-agency strategic approach to the full range of children's services has been disappointing except where it is mandatory' (Audit Commission 1994c: 18) presumably referring to child protection, where the Department of Health guidance on interagency working is described as 'firm'.

In terms of social services child protection work, the report is very clear that the optimal balance has not yet been found between providing proactive family support services and reactive, crisis-led, child protection services. For example, the report says 'Social services support is focused too narrowly at present' (p.19) and 'Because of the pressure of child protection work, field social workers have little spare time for work with other "children in need" who require support other than child protection' (p.23). The report considers that 'an initial response other than a full child protection investigation may be more appropriate in many cases. Guidelines for social workers on child protection referrals should be examined. What risk indicators are used and could assessment for another form of support be more appropriate in some cases' (p.58) (all Audit Commission 1994c).

It can be seen therefore, that the Report sets a clear agenda (explicitly set out in the report, agency by agency) for how services could and should change to be better coordinated and therefore more effectively provided. The report is not without its shortcomings. Parton (1994) has criticised the report as being at best 'superficial and naive' but at worst actually dangerous. It works from the premise that meeting needs is the only business of social services, whereas the legal context (relationships with police and courts) is a highly significant influence. Relationships with these bodies are not mentioned in the report. The understanding of risk as precise and quantifiable fails to get to grips with conceptual difficulties of risk and risk assessment. Finally, the report, while emphasising need, does not locate need in the context of increasing poverty and social deprivation. This is where Parton considers the report dangerous. Central policies are 'let off the hook' and local mechanisms (children's services plans and audits) are charged with the responsibility of solving problems that are not within their powers to address.

Research and policy

The commissioning and publishing of research is another means by which government can aim to influence practice at local level. There is a very close relationship between central government policy, research and local practice. Figure 3.2 illustrates some of the connections between the three.

Research can have a very direct influence on practice outside of the policy context by professional practitioners keeping abreast of developments in their field by reading books, academic journals and trade journals. It can also less directly influence practitioners by informing the training they receive both before and after qualifying in their fields. The figure is not meant to be comprehensive. For example, there may be policy developed

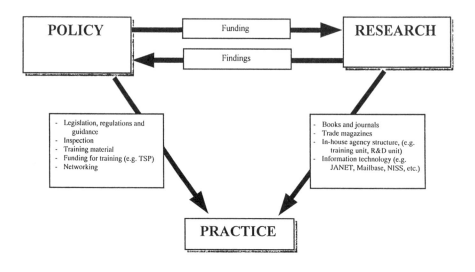

Figure 3.2   Policy, research and practice

which influences practice which is not research based (such as that derived from political agendas).

To keep the figure simple, it also does not highlight some of the reciprocal influences between practice, and policy/research. For example, practitioners presumably could and should influence the research undertaken in a number of ways. This is apart from the increasing emphasis on practitioner research described for example by Kahan, in her introduction to *Child Care Research, Policy and Practice* (Kahan 1989). As described by the Dartington Social Research Unit, referring to the customer-contractor relationships between the Department and Health and researchers, 'The lack of consultation and opportunity to influence research design meant that social workers had little ownership of the work and less commitment to its ideas, particularly if radical and uncomfortable changes were among its messages (1990: 61).

For our purposes, however, the indirect route is the more interesting. In this, the influence of research on practice is mediated by the central government policy-making process. Government commissions research directly; reciprocally, the findings of commissioned research are in turn reported to government, which then relies on a research dissemination strategy to ensure that practice becomes informed by the essential messages contained within the research. This route of research informing practice via government policy, is probably stronger for social workers (and perhaps teachers) than for professionals in the health service where there has traditionally been a greater emphasis on practitioners continuing to ensure their practice is up to date by keeping abreast of current research. For this reason, the following examples are drawn from government commissioned research influencing the practice of child welfare social workers.

As recently as 15 years ago, the connection between research and practice in child welfare was much more tenuous than it is today. When reporting on Children in Care in 1984, the House of Commons Social Services Committee stated: 'There is a lack of systematic research into children in care, and an even more noticeable absence of a co-ordinated approach to dissemination once completed' (House of Commons 1984: paragraph 258).

It was difficult to be clear whether the bigger problem was that research was not being done (although clearly the Department of Health had a long-standing child care research programme), or whether it was being done but simply not communicated to those people who needed to know about it.

Dartington reported, 'In the early 1980s, numerous criticisms were made of the poor relationship between research, policy and practice in social work' (Dartington Social Research Unit 1990: 61). But following this there was a drawing together of research commissioned by both the Department of Health and Social Security (DHSS) and by the Economic and Social Research Council (ESRC). Common themes from various research projects were identified and this was followed by the release of the first of three publications providing an overview of research in child care. The three were:

- *Social Work Decisions in Child Care: Recent Research Findings and their Implications* (DHSS 1985b)
- *Patterns and Outcomes in Child Placement: Messages from Current Research and their Implications* (DoH 1991a)
- *Child Protection: Messages from Research* (DoH 1995a).

Social Work Decisions in Child Care, or 'The Pink Book' as it came to be known, looked at nine studies concerning children in care; eight were funded by the DHSS, and one by the ESRC. Its publication had a tremendous impact on local authority child care social work and was accompanied by extensive training for social workers involved with children and families.

Partly its impact was so great because it was the first of its kind, but that is not to detract from the profound nature of many of the findings. For example, whilst it was clearly acknowledged as good practice that admissions of children to care should be meticulously planned with children being adequately prepared for the move, being given clear reasons, and being helped with the transition by meeting the carers beforehand, and being encouraged to bring toys from home, the research showed that most decisions were made rapidly and often in crisis. As a result admissions were not well planned. Even though practitioners were aware of best practice in arranging care episodes, they were not usually arranged in accordance with those principles. One of the reasons for this was the increasing use of compulsory care powers during the period (late 1970s to early 1980s). It was the period of time following the Children Act 1975, during which 'permanency planning' had become integrated into the day-to-day operations of social workers. In particular, Place of Safety orders were being used more and more frequently, and initiation of care proceedings by notice was relatively rare. Workers were in effect waiting for an incident, the proverbial 'straw that broke the camel's back' in situations where there were extreme concerns about the welfare of children, rather than planning to take measured action. The research held that the extensive use of Place of Safety orders was counterproductive. As we have seen earlier, although this message from research did not influence the practice in Cleveland where such orders were used at length, their overuse did appear in the Inquiry report (Butler-Sloss 1988) as a focus of concern, and informed the Children Act 1989 provisions regarding emergency protection of children.

A major theme highlighted by the 'Pink Book' was the lack of contact between children and the families during care episodes. There seemed to be little consideration given to the child's need for contact with his or her parents. In view of the finding that the families of children who were in care changed and reconstituted themselves with astonishing rapidity, often in a way that filled the niche in the family occupied by the child, such neglect of contact was seen as working against the child's eventual reunion with his or her family, even where that was planned.

The report found that workers seemed to lack skills in both work with parents and work with children. Parents of children in care may feel pushed aside and disillusioned when children are received into care. Social workers appeared to lack time and skills for direct work with children. Both of these findings had clear implications for the training needs of social workers. Finally, the report highlighted that reviews and case conferences were not central to the decision making process.

The 'Pink Book' set the style followed by later overview reports of including practical exercises with which practitioners could test some of the conclusions of the research against their own practice, and use as a means of structuring their practice in accordance with the research. These included ecomaps (a tool for highlighting the important social connections a child has), genograms (more commonly known as a family tree, depicting the structure of the immediate and extended family), planning tools and charts for plotting the number of moves a child in care has had. Following the publication, the DHSS implemented a programme of activity to disseminate the research messages.

Whilst the 'Pink Book' could be seen as scene-setting certain themes for the Children Act 1989, *Patterns and Outcomes* (DoH 1991a) was more like the coming on stage of the themes. It appeared at the same time as the implementation of the Act in October 1991. Unlike the 'Pink Book', it did not draw on a small number of specified Department of Health-funded projects (although some of these were included), but instead chose to explore the available research under three themes: 1) the promotion of the child's welfare, 2) partnership with parents and carers, and 3) planning, both strategically and for individual children.

Many of the themes drew on, and in some cases developed earlier themes highlighted by the 'Pink Book'. For example, it was found that children who remain in care after six weeks were destined for a long or very long stay in care, thus highlighting the need for concerted intensive action during the early stages of a child's care episode, if the objective of reunification of the child with his or her family was to be achieved. When Jane Rowe, who compiled the *Patterns and Outcomes* material for the Department of Health was discussing this theme at a conference, she suggested that it had always been known that the first few months of a child's career in care were crucial to determining the outcome – now it was understood that it was a matter of weeks rather than months. A related theme that was developed from previous research was the 'well established research finding that visiting is the key to discharge' (DoH 1991a: 36).

A major theme of *Patterns and Outcomes* was the role of family, and several sub-themes reinforce this. From the relatively good track record of placements with relatives, it was suggested that relatives should always be considered as a placement resource. More consideration in particular should be paid to sibling relationships, and placement with siblings is generally beneficial to the child's well-being. Attendance of parents at reviews, case conferences and planning meetings should become a normal part of policy and practice with written agreements, which are crucial for partnership, being used as much as possible. Not only agreements, but all plans should be written, and should specify what needs to be done, by whom, how and within what time span.

Several of the themes however appeared new, or at least to have a weaker connection with previous research themes. The health and education needs of children looked after merited greater attention. The Boarding Out Regulations, which preceded the Children Act by two years began to place a very positive emphasis on these two aspects of reviews. The educational disadvantage of children in the care system was seen as pronounced and disturbing even allowing for the disadvantage that children may experience before entering the care system.

Another new theme was that the gathering, testing, recording and weighing of evidence were seen as tasks basic to professional competence. Failure to obtain, handle and interpret evidence appeared to be a crucial factor in many of the continuing problems. Again, in a conference presentation, Jane Rowe drew attention to a concept highlighting a parallel between good practice and good research. The concept is 'Where is your evidence?'. Social workers are more and more called upon to state the evidence that justifies their conclusions. To do that, they may have to either show that they have been as rigorous in their gathering of information as a researcher or they may have to rely on the messages from research, or both. Once again, exercises (eight) were included at the end of the publication which were designed to help with developing understanding and implementation of the main messages. One of them, 'Where did the guidance go?', has been previously described. Others included were 'Ready to cope alone' (a tool for helping young people to assess their readiness for leaving care), 'Sibling Relationships: a check list' (a tool to assess the quality of sibling relationships) and 'How many barriers to parental contact?' (a tool to enable practitioners to overcome obstacles for parents to enable them to have contact with children looked after by the local authority).

The most recent, and for our purposes most relevant, of the commissioned research overviews however, is *Child Protection: Messages from Research* (DoH 1995a), commonly known as the 'Blue Book'. This did not have the restricted focus of the previous two research overviews in that it was not about the role of social workers, and was not about children being looked after. It was a compilation of 20 studies into various aspects of child protection work, the majority of which were commissioned by the Department of Health. Most of the studies were commissioned as a consequence of the Cleveland events and Inquiry (Butler-Sloss 1988).

In his foreword to the publication, John Bowis, Parliamentary Under Secretary of State described four predominant themes:

- The way we, as a society, define abuse
- The effects of the child protection process on children and families who experience it
- Side effects of interventions by child protection agencies
- The effectiveness of the process.

Let us consider these a bit more fully.

Definitions of abuse

Definitions of abuse are important because they influence thresholds of intervention. Definitions of various forms of abuse (neglect, physical injury, sexual abuse and emotional abuse) are contained in the categories of registration of *Working Together* (1991: 48), but within these categories there is considerable scope for variation between professionals on the types of incidents and concerns that would be considered abusive. Giovannoni and Bercera (1979) presented a wide range of abuse scenarios to over three hundred lawyers, social workers, police and paediatricians to explore the extent of agreement on definitions of abusive behaviour. They found that although there was considerable agreement within professional groups, there was little between them either on the type of behaviour or the severity of behaviour that would be considered as abusive. Trute et al. (1992) found gender amongst professionals to be an important determinant of attitudes towards child sexual abuse, as well as professional background. There are so many social factors that influence a professional's judgement as to whether an incident is defined as abusive, that Gibbons et al. comment 'child maltreatment is not the same sort of phenomenon as whooping cough … It is more like pornography, a socially constructed phenomenon which reflects values and opinions of particular cultures at particular times' (1995a: 12).

The impact of child protection on children and families

It is somewhat difficult to disentangle the main, or intended, effects of the investigation, from the side, or unintended, effects. Clearly, the outset of the investigation, when families first learn about the concerns or allegations can be extremely disruptive both to the family and to their relationship with professionals, so much so that future relationships may not recover. As regards the first awareness, Farmer and Owen (1995) in their study of 120 conferences over two years found that 'For over a third of the parents it was the first that they had heard of the allegation, and many experienced shock, confusion, anger and the onset of profound feelings of loss' (DoH 1995: 62). Sharland et al. (1995) also found shock to be a component in their study of 147 families referred because of allegations of sexual abuse: 'parent's response to an abuse allegation was commonly one of shock, guilt and a profound sense of loss' (DoH 1995a: 62). Cleaver and Freeman (1995) in a study of 583 child protection cases found the impact of suspicion worst when parents were unaware of gathering disquiet and had no previous dealings with social services. They found that professionals could easily lose sight of how violating a child protection investigation could be perceived to be by the family. Over time, the resulting 'cold hostility' of the family might improve, but a lingering suspicion of professionals was likely to endure. They also found a significant deterioration in intimate family relationships, especially between the adults. Nine of the 23 two-parent families broke up within two years of the accusation.

Professionals can take steps to reduce the impact of a child protection investigation. In the overview (DoH 1995a: 47) it suggests that 'In initial discussions with parents, the provision of information is helpful. At a protection meeting, preparation, understanding of procedures, physical layout and styles of interaction are important.' However, it is very important that professionals follow through on the child protection plan to provide support so that as a result of professionals working together closely, the families derive some benefit. Both of these were found to be problematical. For example, failure to follow through interventions with much-needed family support prevented professionals from meeting the needs of children and families (DoH 1995a: 55). 'In over half of cases, families received no services as the result of professionals' interest in their lives' (p.39). It appeared that preoccupation with risk in child protection conferences meant there was simply too little time, on average only nine minutes, to consider the development of a child protection plan that would provide support to the child and family (Farmer and Owen 1995).

Overall, in terms of impact on the children and families, Farmer and Owen (1995) looked at this most explicitly in terms of outcomes. Using three indicators of outcomes, whether the child was protected, whether the child's general welfare was enhanced and whether the needs of the parents or carers were met, they found that there was progress on all three in just 23 per cent of cases and progress on none of the three in eleven per cent of cases. The worst outcomes occurred where there were high levels of violence in families, parenting standards were poor, the children showed disturbed behaviour, and there was a lack of clarity amongst professionals about how the family should be handled resulting in little assistance for the social worker arising out of the case conference or review.

The effectiveness of child protection intervention

The big dilemma enmeshed in the 'Blue Book' is that many families are coming into the child protection system who are a) possibly better candidates for another form of intervention (that is, family support), b) having unhelpful consequences as a result of being involved in child protection, which causes them to struggle even more and c) perhaps being put off from receiving the help that they really need, either because the child protection system does not follow through on support or because at the end of the child protection intervention their relationship with professionals is so undermined that they are unable to work productively with them. The 'Blue Book' indicates that 'Families overwhelmed and depressed by social problems form the greatest proportion of those assessed and supported by child protection agencies' (DoH 1995a: 22) and '...child protection process works as well as it can with the most severe cases ... but it works less well with needy families who resent being brought into the "abuse" system' (p.34).

A very important question in this is 'What causes harm to children?' We are increasingly understanding that apart from fatality, the most serious harm done to children abused by their parents may be less directly attributable to the act(s) of physical abuse, and more to its emotional correlates – that is, the characteristics of the child's social environment within which abuse takes place. For example, in describing the consequences of physical abuse for children, Wolfe (1993: 155) notes 'the deficiencies in development among maltreated children are caused by a poor childrearing environment, of which physical injuries are only one aspect.' This is consistent with the conclusion of Gibbons et al. (1995b) in their ten-year follow-up of physically abused children; it was not the physical abuse that was the direct cause of developmental consequences, but rather the punitive, unreliable and coldly critical family styles, within which the physical abuse featured. As expressed in *Messages from Research*, 'the general family context is more important than any abusive event within it' (DoH 1995a: 54), and 'Protection issues are best viewed in the context of children's wider needs' (p.32).

The implications of this understanding are dramatic. Smith et al. (1995) in their study describe three per cent of children coming from families which are lacking in warmth, and a similar percentage coming from families which are high in criticism. Though the proportion of children physically abused by their parents are likely to be lower than these percentages, the developmental deficiencies, and the consequent need for intervention may be closer to that higher level than to the level of the numbers of children physically abused.

Thus substantiated abuse can be seen not only as a cause of harm to a child, but perhaps more importantly as a flag or marker indicating a type of worrying social environment within which a child is being raised. But many other children are growing up in similar environments, but without this flag that mandates intervention.

> A more effective approach in many situations where abuse is relatively minor is to tackle the causes of maltreatment by means of enquiry followed by family assessment, followed by, where appropriate, support services, rather than with heavy handed investigations which leave the family unassisted (DoH 1995a: 43).

Thus, the 'Blue Book' has come to be seen as endorsing a 'lighter touch' in child protection, although how that is to be implemented is still being worked out. But one problem is that it may be very difficult to determine what is meant by abuse that is 'relatively minor'.

The 'Blue Book' recommends that

> If policy and practice changes are to follow from this round of research, it should be to reconsider the balance of services and alter the way in which professionals are perceived by parents accused of abusing or neglecting their offspring (p.55).

In keeping with the pattern originally established in *Social Work Decisions in Child Care*, twelve 'True for Us' exercises are at the back of *Child Protection: Messages from Research*. They are designed to address criticisms that the research may be true for other times and other places, but not necessarily here and now. They can be used by individual practitioners, trainers or as part of a team exercise. The exercises include issues of definition, decision-making criteria, outcomes, partnership with parents, and the wider welfare of children.

Training and networking

Training

A most direct means for central government to exert influence over local child protection practice is through the provision of funding that is earmarked to be used in a specific way ('ring-fenced'). The Training Support Programme (TSP) is one such example, and is money provided for training. It is a supplement to training which the local authority has responsibility to provide, not a substitute for it. It does this by enabling the development of a training infrastructure and the extension of training to others who might not necessarily receive it (foster carers, members of the private and voluntary sector). It began in 1988/89 specifically in connection with local authority staff who work with elderly people, but after one year was extended to child care. In Wales the TSP was used to support child care from 1988/89. The extension to include child care was announced by the Minister for Health in July 1988 as part of the government's response to the Cleveland Inquiry report (Butler-Sloss 1988). The report recommended that there should be general continuing in-service education training for professionals concerning child care, urgent training to bring professionals up to date on child sexual abuse, and specialised training for experienced professionals involved in the investigation and management of cases where there is a suspicion of sexual abuse. As such the report makes explicit that there are very different levels of training outcomes needed by professionals by virtue of their different professional roles, or because of the different amount of experience they have. The report also recommended interagency training and recognition of the role of other disciplines. It endorsed joint training for police and social workers involved in interviewing children. Aspects of training for other disciplines were considered (police, medical staff, lawyers, judges and magistrates).

Although the substantial direct funding of child protection training can be seen as a consequence of the Cleveland Report recommendations, it can also be seen as part of a larger central government package on child care comprising *Working Together* (1991), The Children Bill (leading to the Children Act 1989), and *Protecting Children: A Guide for Social Workers undertaking a Comprehensive Assessment* (DoH 1988). Following consultation Local Authority Circular LAC (89) five set out the arrangements for the funding during the financial year 1989/90. The object of the TSP was to enhance the quality of services for children and families by providing, increasing and improving training provision for staff. During the first year of the programme, training in child protection, especially child sexual abuse was identified as a priority. Guidelines were produced (DoH, undated) which provided a framework within which bids for TSP money were to be made. The guidelines contained 13 sections addressing the following areas:

1 Emphasis on child's interests.
2 Balance between protecting children and supporting family.
3 A considered, measured approach to family intervention.
4 Broad theoretical base to training.
5 Training to relate to local policy and practice.
6 SSDs to take lead on establishment of 'joint training programmes on child abuse issues for all professional groups in direct contact with children'.
7 Training should be based upon levels of knowledge and skills of staff and upon individual training development plans.
8 All staff in contact with children should have foundation training (including ACPC guidelines and SSDs policies and procedures).
9 Staff involved in investigation, assessment and continuing work with abused children require specialist training.
10 Supervision and personal support is essential; training for supervisors.
11 Interagency management of child sexual abuse policy and practice should be seen as a training need for managers.
12 Training required for trainers.
13 Effectiveness of training should be monitored.

One of the impacts of the Training Support Programme was that social services training departments were able to become more differentiated and specialised in their deployment of staff to provide for training. In Wales, prior to the introduction of TSP there were very few child protection trainers. After several years of injection of TSP funding, and the need to develop highly coordinated and sophisticated training, most authorities had trainers with specific and exclusive responsibility for child protection. This continued until April 1996 when the introduction of local government re-organisation in Wales meant that such a specialised training force could no longer be sustained by the smaller authorities. At the time of writing the Training Support Programme continues to provide valuable ring-fenced money for child protection training.

Networking

Another means of government exerting influence on local practice is through the formal and informal machineries that it creates or utilises to get across its messages regarding child protection. There are a number of examples of this. The Michael Sieff Foundation stages an annual conference in a series entitled 'Working Together for Children's Welfare'. In recent years, conference themes have been on 'Child Protection and the Role of the Education System', 'Family Support in Protecting the Child', and 'Child Protection: Ten Years On' (a marking of the tenth anniversary of the conference series). At these, representatives from the Department of Health on occasion give insight into current Government thinking on child protection. For example, in 1994, Wendy Rose, Assistant Chief Inspector at the Department of Health presented a paper (Rose 1994) which anticipated the publication of the DoH-commissioned child protection studies (DoH 1995a). As described by Parton (1997), the essential message of this talk was that the heavy emphasis on investigation contained in *Working Together* (1991) was unintentional, and that the emphasis should be rather on the very strong messages of family support contained within the Children Act 1989. In 1996, after the publication of the DoH summary document, Wendy Rose delivered another presentation at a Michael Sieff Conference, again on the subject of the balance between child protection and family support, but on this occasion describing the elements of a strategy for refocusing child welfare services. In addition to government representatives, the participants at such conferences include senior managers, assistant directors and directors of voluntary and statutory agencies, practitioners, researchers and academics.

A more formalised mechanism for staff in the Department of Health and the Welsh Office to influence child protection practice is through the recently introduced ACPC forums. In England such forums have looked at issues such as ACPC Annual Reports (Armstrong 1994), and Part 8 Reviews (James 1994). In Wales they have looked at the effectiveness of Area Child Protection Committees (Jackson et al. 1994) and Part 8 Reviews (Colton et al. 1996). These may take the form of workshops, that is, presentations followed by opportunities for ACPC members from different committees to focus on some of the issues raised. Both of these means allow government representatives to engage agencies and individuals in a dialogue in a way that is much more informal and free-flowing than by using written guidance alone.

4 Area Child Protection Committees

I have explored the routes through which child protection policy is determined centrally and then communicated to local agencies to direct their practice. In addition to individual agencies having regulations and guidance to follow, the other route by which child protection is undertaken is through the local coordination of services. This is achieved by the operation of Area Child Protection Committees which ordinarily are geographically based on the local authority boundaries (although for some participants the area of the ACPC may only be a part of the catchment area for which they have responsibility). A variety of local agencies with an interest in child welfare send senior managers to this forum where interagency plans for the local operation of child protection systems are developed. The guidance on the composition, role and functions of Area Child Protection Committees is provided in Part 2 and Appendices 5 and 8 of *Working Together* (1991).

Executive authority of Area Child Protection Committees

As pointed out by Frost 'One could be forgiven for reading the DHSS circulars and reports on child abuse as arguing that "lack of coordination" is the *cause* of child abuse' (1990: 39) [original emphasis]. Hallett and Birchall describe the British system as one of 'mandated coordination' which entails agencies being 'directed or required to coordinate their activities by those in superordinate positions' (1992: 32). ACPCs are not executive bodies. They do not have the authority to require member agencies' compliance to their

117

decisions. *Working Together* (1991) makes it clear that 'ACPC members are accountable to the agencies which they represent. These agencies are jointly responsible for ACPC actions' (paragraph 2.7). For this reason, it is vital that the agencies take very seriously their child protection responsibilities and that representatives on ACPCs are sufficiently senior to implement decisions. For each constituent agency, the guidance requires that 'chief officers and authority members as appropriate must take responsibility for establishing and maintaining the inter-agency arrangements and should assure themselves from time to time that appropriate arrangements are in place' (paragraph 2.5). Additionally, representatives to the Committees should be individuals who 'have sufficient authority to allow them to speak on their agencies' behalf and to make decisions to an agreed level without referral to the appointees' agencies' (paragraph 2.8).

There are those who suggest that Area Child Protection Committees will never be fully effective until they have the authority to compel compliance on the part of their constituent agencies. Jackson et al. (1994), whilst not endorsing this view, note that several respondents (ACPC members) considered that ACPCs would not be truly effective until they had executive authority. Williams notes that ACPC members are accountable not to the ACPC but to the agencies they represent, and considers it 'questionable whether a representative body of this kind is the most effective way of developing policies and procedures which are independent of individual agency perspectives' (1992: 69). Stevenson expresses concern as to whether ACPCs '"have the clout" to influence their own organisations sufficiently' (1994: 132).

The composition of Area Child Protection Committees

The membership of ACPCs, which is covered in guidance, is drawn from senior managers of agencies who have a responsibility for, or an interest in, the protection of children from abuse. These would include social services, health, education, police and probation. These are listed in Appendix 5 (p.109) of *Working Together* (1991):

Social Service Agency

  – the local social services department
  – National Society for the Prevention of Cruelty to Children (NSPCC)

Health Authority

  – Management of District Health Authority(ies) in the local authority area

- Medical and psychiatric services professional representative(s)
- Nursing representative(s)

Family Health Services Authority

- Management of the FHSAs in the local authority area
- General practitioner representative(s) of the Local Medical Committee(s) in the local authority area

Education Service

- local authority education department
- teacher representative (normally a headteacher)

Police

Probation Services

Armed Services (where appropriate, for example if there is a large military presence in the locality).

In addition it is recommended that links are established between the Area Child Protection Committee and local authority housing departments, dental practitioner services, local social security offices, education establishments not maintained by the local authority, relevant voluntary agencies, and organisations representing religious and cultural interests.

There are a number of observations that can be made about the composition of ACPCs.

Size of ACPCs

ACPCs can be very variable in their size. Jackson et al. (1994) found the largest ACPCs to be three times the size of the smaller (31 members compared to ten with an average of 21). This variation was related to the finding that larger ACPCs included more agencies than those suggested in *Working Together* (1991), in many cases these are people listed under the category of 'establishing links'. It was also related to the finding that smaller ACPCs did not have representatives from one or more of the agencies suggested in the guidelines (for example, general practitioner representative, teacher representative), and also did not include people widely included by other ACPCs (even where not specifically included in the guidance, for example, the local authority solicitor). In one ACPC, a deliberate decision was taken to keep the size small in order to be more effective, a decision that appeared justified by the finding that there was an inverse correlation between size and attendance. The smaller committees had higher attendance percentages.

This is also consistent with the finding of the Social Services Inspectorate that 'failure to get things done is associated with an over-large membership of the Committee' (1994b: 39).

Gender

ACPCs tend to be very heavily gender-balanced towards men. In their study of ACPCs, Jackson et al. (1994) found the ratio of male to female of the sample was 2.45 to 1. As the sample size was fairly large in relation to the whole of the ACPC membership in Wales (the focus of the study), and as gender formed no part of the selection criteria for interview, they concluded that this closely reflected the actual overall gender balance. This finding is consistent with CCETSW (1992a) which found female staff to be less well-represented in the upper management of both voluntary and statutory welfare agencies.

In view of the very significant role of gender in child abuse, and the various findings of gender being a mediating variable in attitudes towards child abuse, this may be a very important consideration. After reviewing some of their concerns about the way gender is treated by some child protection writers, Frost and Stein (1989) conclude that 'the abuse of children has a gender dimension which is seriously underdeveloped both in terms of theory and practice' (1989: 51). Cloke and Naish (1992) in their examination of the health visiting and nursing role in child protection, combine the work of Parton (1985) highlighting the dominance of the medical model in child protection with observations on the male domination of medicine to contend a male domination in child protection.

It is not simply the sheer weight of numbers, but the actual differential status of decision making afforded to men and women in professional groups (McIntosh and Dingwall 1978; Pollock and West 1984; Pollock 1986) that contributes to the gender imbalance. Nevertheless, one can speculate on how different child protection services would be (and the process of managing them on an interagency basis) if women outnumbered men on Area Child Protection Committees by a factor of 2.5 to 1, or even if they were equally represented.

Member authority

We have seen that *Working Together* (1991) requires ACPC members to have sufficient authority to enable them to have a degree of autonomy of decision making. In addition to their concerns about ACPCs being too large to conduct business effectively, the Social Services Inspectorate were also concerned that failure to get things done was associated with agencies being 'represented by staff at too low a tier of management' (1994b: 39). ACPC members should be able to take some decisions without having to refer to their agencies. Just exactly which decisions these are is likely to vary from agency to agency, and to depend amongst other things on the degree of the centralisation of decision making. Jackson et al. (1994) for example found that in general, ACPC representatives thought they could agree or act upon decisions about matters of practice, training, and production of guidance or information leaflets, but did not feel that they could not commit their agencies to financial decisions or policy changes. Whilst representatives may be able to consult with more senior colleagues on matters coming up in the ACPC, there is frequently insufficient time after the agenda appears for such consultations to take place. One effect, therefore, of lack of authority of representatives may be to delay the process of decision making, with the risk that important issues will get lost.

Another concern is how contextual changes to the context of ACPCs affect decision making. Stevenson for example considers that ACPCs 'have an urgent and difficult role in addressing the implications of organizational change for the protection of children' (1994: 132). The reorganisation of local government (LGR) is one such change, and one of the implications of that has been that less senior members may be ACPC representatives. This is so for two reasons. First, the nature of the organisational bureaucracy involved has entailed less specialisation, and this will apply to senior managers as well as to practitioners. I have already commented on this trend in relation to child protection trainers, who became less specialised following local government reorganisation in Wales in April 1996. Second, representatives are likely to be less senior because there are more ACPCs to be serviced. This is especially true of geographically larger agencies whose boundaries supersede those of the ACPC. Even before LGR representatives from those agencies sat on multiple ACPCs (and as reported by Jackson et al. (1994) they had an interest in ensuring harmony across ACPC procedures). Where the number of ACPCs is larger, the time requirements for contributing to all the ACPCs may not allow for very senior managers.

Psychiatric representation

Working Together (1991) does not distinguish between child psychiatrists and adult psychiatrists in its inclusion of 'psychiatric services' in the list supplied in Appendix 5, but the guidance contained in paragraphs 4.27–4.29 makes it clear that in practice it is child psychiatric representation that is intended, although liaison with adult psychiatric services may need to be considered if they are already involved or to coordinate treatment services for sexual abusers or where there are parents with serious psychiatric

difficulties. Jackson et al. (1994) found that all Area Child Protection committees had a representative of child psychiatry, but few had one from adult
psychiatry, although one ACPC was reconsidering this because of the death
of two children involved in a mother's suicide. Similarly, two of the 21 Part 8
Reviews studied by Colton et al. (1996) involved a mother killing herself
and her child(ren) at the same time. In child abuse cases with the worst
outcomes (that is, fatality), Falkov (1996a, 1996b, 1997) found that mental
illness in parents featured very highly. We consider this study more fully when
we examine the role of Area Child Protection Committees in reviewing cases
of child abuse fatalities.

Area Child Protection Committees: roles and functions

The role and functions of Area Child Protection Committees are detailed in
Working Together (1991: paragraph 2.12):

a   to establish, maintain and review local inter-agency guidelines on
    procedures to be followed in individual cases;
b   to monitor the implementation of legal procedures;
c   to identify significant issues arising from the handling of cases and reports
    from inquiries;
d   to scrutinise arrangements to provide treatment, expert advice and
    inter-agency liaison and make recommendations to the responsible
    agencies;
e   to scrutinise progress on work to prevent child abuse and make recom-
    mendations to the responsible agencies;
f   to scrutinise work related to inter-agency training and make recom-
    mendations to the responsible agencies;
g   to conduct reviews required under Part 8 of this Guide;
h   to publish an annual report about local child protection matters.

Because Area Child Protection Committees are key to the interagency
coordination of child protection, it is useful to consider each of these
functions in greater detail.

To establish, maintain and review local inter-agency guidelines on procedures to be followed in individual cases

Working Together (1991) lays out the information required of a local procedural handbook. It must contain the following sections:

1 Law and Definitions.
2 Who is involved?
3 Referral and Recognition.
4 Immediate Protection and Planning the Investigation.
5 Investigation and Initial Assessment.
6 Child Protection Conference and Decision Making about the need for Registration.
7 Comprehensive Child Protection Assessment and Planning.
8 Implementation, Review and De-registration.
9 Other (special circumstances).
10 Local Agency Procedures.

Very little comparative study of interagency guidelines and procedures has been undertaken. Sanders et al. (1996a) undertook a comparative analysis of Area Child Protection Committee handbooks/manuals (they were described differently in different areas, and in some cases a distinction was drawn between handbooks and manuals). We considered four reasons why such a comparison is important. First, they are probably the most significant influence on the child protection practice of workers in different agencies. Although it could be argued that training is possibly an equally significant influence, there are some practitioners, (e.g. teachers, general practitioners) for whom access to training on child protection matters is problematic. Despite lack of training however, in most such cases they will have access to local child protection manuals. Second, to a limited extent, the manuals are an indicator of the degree to which practice conforms to policy, both local and governmental. In general, the less specific and comprehensive the interagency child protection guidance, the more ACPCs would appear to either tolerate wide variations in practice or else be prepared to find other means of ensuring consistency of practice. Third, by comparing the extent of consistency and inconsistency of local treatment of various topics/issues, the handbooks are an indicator of which aspects of governmental policy are considered more important at local level than others. Finally, the manuals demonstrate the ability of ACPCs to work closely together, often overcoming significant difficulties to do so. The very process of producing the handbooks was found to have promoted very positive working relationships in ACPCs. Some of their main findings of the analysis were:

- There was a high degree of clarity and consistency on criteria for registration and deregistration
- We found a surprising amount of variation in the involvement of children and parents in child protection investigations and child protection conferences; there was also variation in criteria for

exclusion of parents from all or some of the child protection conference proceedings
- Only half the handbooks addressed both appeals and complaints, some addressed one or the other; one addressed neither
- Abuse by foster carers was only addressed in half the handbooks
- There was a relative lack of emphasis on race, culture and language. (Sanders et al. 1996a)

In the main they concluded that the procedures handbooks were a very valuable tool to ensure that investigation of child abuse takes place within a policy context, thereby ensuring consistency of practice. However, they are imbalanced in that, like the government guidance they reflect, they say much about investigation, and little about prevention of abuse or treatment for victims of abuse. To be effective, a comprehensive child protection policy needs to address all three aspects of child protection. It may be possible to argue against the inclusion of prevention policy in the handbooks (on the basis that prevention is not primarily about work with individuals); it is certainly indefensible that the handbooks say so little about treatment. This is hardly surprising in view of the evidence from a number of sources that treatment is so significantly neglected in child protection services.

The inspections of child protection services (SSI 1994b, 1995a) have included consideration of the procedures in their findings. The 1994 report of six social services departments found that all of the ACPCs had produced interagency procedures. The inspectors were concerned about an inability to coordinate interagency activity, and an inability to establish the level of resources needed for child protection activity. The 1995 report of eight inspections included a checklist which specifically looked at whether procedures were clear in their requirements, up to date, known to staff, integrated into practice and regularly reviewed. The inspectors found that all ACPCs had procedures, three of which had recently been revised, while four were in need of revision. They were concerned that five of the procedures 'unhelpfully contained a mix of policy, procedures, practice guidance, and in one case, research' (SSI 1995a: 14). This concurs with Jackson and colleagues who found when looking at policy that:

> It is a matter of some concern if those who are responsible for the development of policy in relation to child protection are not clear about the nature of policy. Many of our respondents made little distinction between policy and procedures and for some the two were identical. In general we found that individuals closest to operational level were more likely to use 'policy' and 'procedures' interchangeably. More senior respondents tended to be clearer about the distinction between the two. (Jackson et al. 1994: 30)

When requesting child care policy documents from English authorities, Robbins also received a variety of material ranging from procedures to manifestos: 'Many authorities seemed themselves to be unclear about how precisely to distinguish between the types of documents they were working on' (1990: 6). Gibbons also notes, 'Policy aims in relation to child protection are not clear … the objectives the child protection procedures – the goals which they are intended to reach – are not formulated in a detailed way' (1997: 78).

To monitor the implementation of legal procedures

Armstrong (1994) notes that ACPCs appear from their annual reports to equate a relatively low level of legal activity with achieving partnership, a position about which she expresses reservations. The Social Services Inspectorate (1995a) in their inspection of eight social services departments found that information 'failed to meet some of the basic requirements, eg … information comparing different types of intervention:

- police protection order
- emergency protection order
- assessment order.' (SSI 1995a: 20)

Indicators of legal intervention are provided by the Department of Health and Welsh Office from returns supplied by local authorities. These have been summarised in annual Children Act Reports (DoH/WO 1993, 1994, 1995).

Table 4.1: Use of legal orders in relations to children

(children starting to be looked after during the period in question by status upon admission) (DoH/WO 1995: 7)

Type of Order	1.4.92 –31.3.93	1.4.93 –31.3.94
Emergency Protection Orders	1300	1600
Police Protection Orders	900	1200
Interim Care Orders	1000	1700
Full Care Orders	400	300

These figures show an increase in all orders made, except full care orders up to March 1994.

To identify significant issues arising from the handling of cases and reports from inquiries

First, it is important to be clear about the distinction between ACPC consideration of issues arising from cases and the interagency management of actual cases. Generally, apart from Part 8 Reviews, Area Child Protection Committees do not consider the handling of individual cases, a distinction that is missed by some writers in child protection. Williams (1992) and Lyon and de Cruz (1993: 147), for example, both appear to suggest that the ACPC directs the management of particular cases. A second observation about this particular function is that there is potential to confuse the line between issues arising from ordinary cases, and those that go very wrong (where there will inevitably be an internal review and possibly also an inquiry). Issues arising from inquiries will be considered when Part 8 Reviews are discussed below.

The two important issues for fulfilling this ACPC function are the operation of the ACPC subcommittee structure and the management systems for ensuring quality. As regards the first, nearly every ACPC has developed a subcommittee structure to enable it to deal with a larger volume of work than could adequately be addressed by the body of the Committee. These tend to be of two types: functional subcommittees, which concern themselves with particular subjects or issues, and district subcommittees, which are drawn on geographical boundaries, often based on social services departmental regions or local district council regions. Subcommittees may be either permanent ('standing') or time limited ('ad hoc'). Armstrong notes, '... for most ACPCs the system of organising sub-committees, or short term working parties, has become an effective way of handling issues' (1994: 31). Both functional subcommittees and district committees may address issues arising from the handling of cases.

In general the functional subcommittees address important issues on behalf of the whole ACPC. Most ACPCs have a training subcommittee; many will have a policy and procedures subcommittee; some will have a media subcommittee, a prevention subcommittee and/or a treatment subcommittee. There may be other functions allocated to subcommittees depending upon the nature of local issues which need to be addressed and whether or not they are able to be addressed within the main business of the ACPC. Jackson et al. (1994) found that three-quarters of the ACPCs they studied had a 'cases subcommittee' or a 'review committee'; however, their functions were quite different. In some their role was to review decisions of case conferences to register, not to register, or to deregister. In others they were ad hoc committees set up to coordinate the arrangements for a case review under Part 8 of

Working Together. Another function was to act as an appeal body for professionals, where there was dissension about a decision. In some cases, reviews are undertaken by district committees, thus obviating the need for a specific case review subcommittee.

District Committees (variously called 'district review committees' or 'district child protection committees') serve the purpose of keeping the policy development function informed by practice, as they often either have operational functions, or include as members individuals who have operational responsibilities. They are closer to the field and can, in some instances, take on work that the main committee would not be able to do as effectively, if at all; in that respect they may operate like an ad hoc functional subcommittee. Their two-way function linking practice and policy is very useful. They feed into the ACPC from practice, and contribute to the development of policy. Although it is clear that they are not responsible for the creation of policy, district committees are likely to be consulted about policy development. They coordinate operational child protection work, and ensure that ACPC policy is implemented at local level. Their ability to network at a local level can be very useful. They operate best where they have very clear terms of reference, and where they do not, problems about lack of clarity of function and confusion of role can arise. Where cases are not dealt with by a functional subcommittee of the whole ACPC, they are likely to be dealt with in a district subcommittee.

What is Quality?

The other main issue for fulfilling this ACPC function is the use of quality assurance systems. Virtually the whole of public service is governed by notions of defining quality and developing methods to achieve it. At a very basic level, the quality process can be described as 'say what you do, do what you say'. Quality assurance is an approach to quality which emphasises the importance of ensuring that all the processes and activities involved in producing services are working properly, from planning to delivery and feedback (Flynn 1997: 165). This implies a process in which there are clear specification of aims and objectives followed by the implementation of means to achieve them. The process can operate at many different levels within an organisation, from product manufacture, service delivery, management, marketing, recruitment, etc. Virtually any type of service or product can be subjected to quality assurance. The international standard for service quality assurance (ISO 9002, replacing the former BS 5750) assumes the role of a kite mark against which to measure services, and may be required by some agencies (for example, government bodies) when inviting tenders or contracting services.

Flynn (1997) offers two definitions of quality, one as a 'conformance to specifications', which is established through the operation of inspection and monitoring, and 'fitness for purpose', which he considers to be a consumer-defined quality control. The two types represent a top-down and a bottom-up process of ensuring quality respectively. Engel (1994) considers that it would extremely difficult to imagine how quality control in an interagency context could be achieved without a top-down approach based on protocols defining the tasks of workers. This is echoed by Biggs, who in his consideration of unifying tendencies in interprofessional collaboration, describes a clearly top-down model of quality control: 'It is about the control of, rather than servicing the work of, other professional groups' (1997: 195). Walsh (1991) has argued that welfare services quality control process need to become more sophisticated as a result of the entry of the market into professional activities, and notes that the bottom-up process of ensuring quality is difficult because it is closely allied to expectations of the service and consumer expectations are constantly changing. This is one of the difficulties of 'satisfaction' research. Davies and Dotchin lean towards the bottom-up model when they consider that 'the model of service quality which is now widely acknowledged is based on the notion that service quality as perceived by a consumer depends on the magnitude and direction of the gap between expected service and perceived service' (1995: 250).

Sinclair (1997) describes three methods of quality control in social work which broadly reflect the two approaches previously described (choice and market mechanisms; organisational approaches) plus a third which relies on the selection, training and professionalisation of individuals delivering the service. He is quite pessimistic about the current state of quality control when he describes current variations in practice and the failure of existing quality control mechanisms to have an impact on those variations in practice.

Unfortunately, it has to be acknowledged that to date the track record of ACPCs on quality systems has not been good. Armstrong (1994) in her appraisal of quality assurance derived from studying ACPC annual reports, is much more positive than Noyes (DoH 1991c), either of the SSI inspection reports (1994b, 1995a) or Jackson et al. (1994). She comments, '... many ACPCs have developed a more wide-ranging review procedure which may operate either very widely as a quality assurance technique, or more specifically on cases which raised concerns' (Armstrong 1994: 28). On the other hand, the 1989 overview of child abuse inquiries observed 'Inquiries describe the need for senior management to establish standards and monitor them, a process which effectively can fill the gap between a central policy and everyday practice' (DoH 1991c: 25). More recently, the SSI report of six authorities indicated:

Where there were inspection programmes there had been only a few 'one-off' evaluations and not a systematic inspection of cases to evaluate the quality of the work. If there had been a more systematic approach to quality control, some of the deficits identified by the SSI inspections would have been identified. (SSI 1994b: 43)

The later report on eight authorities (1995a) found that 'four authorities had no formal system beyond supervision to monitor the quality of child protection work' (SSI 1995a: 10). All eight of the reports comment on the need for a formal system to monitor the quality of work, and most recommended the implementation of a type of random audit whereby cases are routinely selected on a random basis for monitoring.

Jackson et al. found 'little evidence of the existence of any formal quality control systems and not much interest in developing them, one Chair going so far as to say "I wouldn't recognise quality control if it poked me in the eye"' (1994: 87). Another respondent in their study described the approach to quality control as 'somewhat relaxed'. The ACPC Chairs seemed unaware of what monitoring systems there were within the ACPC constituent agencies, perhaps because they were undeveloped. Drawing on the work of Mills and Vine (1990) and reflecting the at that time unpublished SSI report (SSI 1995a), Jackson et al. also advocated that work on non-fatal cases should be held up for scrutiny. They considered that the introduction of better management information systems augured well for the future and recommended that 'all ACPCs should develop quality control systems on an interagency basis, linked with agencies' internal systems' (1994: 91).

To scrutinise arrangements to provide treatment, expert advice and inter-agency liaison and make recommendations to the responsible agencies

The work of Area Child Protection Committees on arrangements to provide treatment is even less developed than their work on the development of formal quality control systems. In order to address this highly complex and controversial issue, it will be necessary to digress slightly into a consideration about the treatment needs of abused children. Dubowitz (1990), in his research, categorised interventions (not all strictly 'treatment' services) into five 'service models': individual counselling/social work; lay therapy (including crisis intervention, lay counselling, and Parents Anonymous – a self-help group); group treatment; children's programme (including child development programme, child therapy) and family treatment.

In this section it is proposed to restrict the consideration to the child's needs for a therapeutic service. Efforts to provide such services have been variable, uncoordinated and largely undeveloped. This is very surprising for two reasons. First, even a lay understanding of child abuse would suggest that abuse has harmful consequences for children which need to be addressed. Secondly, it is an indication of how far child protection services have abandoned a therapeutic orientation to child abuse in favour of a forensic one. Who would have been able to predict 35 years ago with the revelation of the battered baby syndrome that child welfare services would have gone down the road of accepting a policing role to the extent they have? Yet therapeutic services are very necessary. Bringing the abuse to an end and in very rare cases, punishing the abuser, is rarely sufficient to undo the harm that has been done to the child. This section will look at the consequences of abuse, the implications of knowledge of those consequences for treatment and services needed by children, a consideration of the therapeutic services available for children and how Area Child Protection Committees are addressing those needs for services.

The consequences of abuse

In the words of Summit (1988), abuse is 'developmentally toxic'. Although Agass and Simes (1992) consider that research confirms the common sense that 'the worse the abuse ... the greater the harm', in actuality there are a range of factors that affect how severe the consequences of abuse are, for example, the type of abuse, the duration of the abuse, the nature of the relationship to the abuser and the extent of the abuse. Some consequences may be short lived and some may be long term. Some writers, for example, draw a distinction between 'short-term' and 'initial' effects. Short-term effects are those that arise shortly after the abuse, and end shortly after the abuse. The term 'initial effects' is used to describe effects which whilst arising shortly after the abuse, may last for a short while, or may persist for a long period of time. Beitchman et al. (1992), in their review of the long-term consequences of sexual abuse, also describe 'sleeper' effects, those consequences of which both the child and others may be unaware, but which may arise with dramatic impact later in life.

The causes of the harm of child abuse are also complicated by the fact that multiple forms of abuse are often present in the same situation, and some combinations are worse for the child than others (Ney et al. 1994). Graziano and Mills (1992) note that 'in some important ways neglected children fare more poorly than do physically abused children'. I have already referred to the work of Wolfe (1993) and Gibbons et al. (1995b) in relation to the consequences of abuse and to Smith et al. (1995) about the harmful correlates of household lacking in warmth and high in criticism. Glaser considers that 'All forms of abuse are to some extent psychologically damaging. In that sense, all abuse is emotional abuse' (1992: 108). It is for this reason that *Working Together* (1991) points out that children should only be placed on the child protection under the category of 'Emotional Abuse' when it is the 'main or sole form of abuse' (paragraph 6.40). Combinations of various forms of abuse make it difficult for researchers to be precisely clear about the specific impacts and consequences of specific forms of abuse and also to be clear about what actually causes the harm when a child is abused.

Graziano and Mills (1992) summarising a number of reviews of the consequences of abuse identify the following in maltreated children, when compared with non-abused peers:

- Greater difficulty with self-control and aggression
- Less social sensitivity and empathy
- Poor cognitive skills and academic performance
- Poor social relationships, affective expression and moral development.

Brière (1992) describes seven major types of psychological disturbance frequently found in individuals abused in childhood: post-traumatic stress, cognitive distortions, altered emotionality, dissociation; impaired self-reference, disturbed relatedness, and avoidance. Beitchman et al. (1992) looking specifically at sexual abuse, consider some of the consequences for women to be sexual disturbance or dysfunction, homosexual experiences in adolescence or adulthood, depression and a tendency to be re-victimised, and for men a disturbance of adult sexual functioning.

The implications for treatment and services needed by children

Consideration of the consequences of abuse raises the questions: what services do children need arising from their experience of being abused and what services do they get? Clearly children need the abuse to stop: this is the primary focus of most of the intervention undertaken by child protection services. After the abuse has been stopped, children need more; they need help to undo, as far as possible, the effects of the abuse. It is equally true for children who have been physically abused as it is for children who have been sexually abused. This is where the child protection system appears to fall short in meeting the needs of children.

There are two ways the abuse can be brought to an end. First, work can be done with the child and family to change the parenting so that the abuse stops. Secondly, there can be a separation between the child and the abuser(s). Whether the child remains within the family whilst efforts are made to bring the abuse to an end or is removed depends largely upon the nature of the abuse. Keeping the child in the family, whilst working to prevent further abuse tends to be favoured for non-sexual forms of abuse.

Lie and McMurtry (1991) found that compared with children fostered for non-sexual forms of abuse, sexually abused children had fewer reunification attempts, spent a shorter period of time in out-of-home care, and were more likely to move to a permanent family placement. Hunter et al. (1990) considered several factors to explain the higher rate of removal of victims of sexual abuse in their findings:

- Sexual abuse may be more easily defined
- Sexual abuse may be seen as more addictive and less amenable to intervention
- Sexual molestation of children may give rise to a more negative emotional reaction
- Increased vulnerability causes social workers to over-intervene.

In a study of child protection plans, Hallett (1995) found that support for the family was the main plan developed (17 of 46), mostly for cases of physical abuse (13 of the 17). This was followed by removal of the abuser (13 of 46) which was used mostly for cases of sexual abuse (ten of the 13). In eight cases the child was removed from the home, although in some cases this was through agreement. In the remaining cases there were either issues of assessment, or the hostility of the family made it impossible to implement a family support programme, but the child still remained within the home.

The family remains intact   With the family remaining intact, when both the abuser and the child remain at home, the emphasis in therapeutic intervention, is on changing the parenting behaviour to reduce the future risk to the child (Graziano and Mills 1992). Some families, however, are potentially untreatable (Jones 1987), and whilst being clear that such families should nevertheless be given an opportunity to change, time limits may be needed so that alternative plans can be made for the child if the family prove not to be amenable to treatment. Jones also reviews the previous studies that have highlighted the incidence of re-abuse in families where abuse has already been identified, (from 16 per cent to 60 per cent in eight studies). This echoes the findings of Farmer and Parker (1991), who found that 25 per cent of children who had been removed to care because of abuse were re-abused when returned to parental care. This percentage is close to the finding of Dubowitz (1990) in his review of the cost effectiveness of intervention programmes, that 'of the 1,724 parents studied, 30 per cent were reported to have "severely" abused or neglected their child *during treatment*' [emphasis added].

It is hard to stop parents from abusing their children. Salter et al. (1985) in developing a model of treatment that accounts for the failure of 'insight oriented therapies', comment, 'Abusive parents are notoriously difficult to treat.' Corby, exploring the effectiveness of intervention and treatment, notes that several researchers have argued that 'non-recurrence of abuse is not an adequate measure because … the emotional quality of care for a child may continue to be low even though he or she is no longer subjected to physical violence' (1993: 130). It is perhaps for this reason that so much effort has gone into this endeavour, to the virtual exclusion of treatment for children themselves.

The child(ren) is/are separated from the abuser   Separation of the child from the family has traditionally meant removing the child to care. But even with the introduction of the Children Act 1989 there was speculation as to whether an opportunity had been lost to place more emphasis on the positive value of abusers being required to leave the home instead of the child. The provision in schedule 2 of the Act began the legal introduction of this principle by enabling local authorities to assist abusers to leave instead of the child: 'Where a child is suffering, or is likely to suffer, ill-treatment at the hands of another person who is living with him, and that other person proposes to move from the premises, the authority is em-powered to assist' (paragraph 5). It is very important here to note that this is a power, and not a duty on the local authority, thus making the pro-vision considerably diluted.

The provisions of the Family Law Act 1996, also further the legal basis for removing abusers rather than the child by changing the basis on which non-molestation orders may be made and by incorporating new exclusion requirements. A non-molestation order is an order which prohibits a named person (the 'respondent') from molesting another person who is associated with the respondent or who is a *relevant child* (this being a legal term for the child in question). A single order can be obtained in respect of both an adult partner and a child. Section 42(2)(b) allows such an order to be made without application 'in any family proceedings to which the respondent is already a party … if the court considers that the order should be made for the benefit of any other party to the proceedings or any relevant child'. By virtue of care proceedings being 'family proceedings' the court will be able on its own motion to make a non-molestation order.

The second means of separating the child from the abuser without removing the child is through the use of exclusion requirements. Exclusion require-ments are not however freestanding, and must be attached to either an interim care order or an emergency protection order although they do not have to last as long as either of those orders. Although those orders authorise the removal of the child, that removal will be obviated if the exclusion requirements are included. They are made on the grounds that if the person leaves, the child will cease to suffer, or to be likely to suffer, significant harm, and another person who is in the dwelling (who does not have to be a parent) is willing and able to care for the child, and agrees to the exclusion requirements. The effect of the requirements are to require the person to leave the dwelling where the child lives, to prohibit the person from entering the dwelling, and to exclude the person from a defined area in which is located the child's dwelling. Exclusion requirements may have a power of arrest attached to them.

Whilst in the past removing the child from the home situation may have been seen as the more effective means to eliminate the further abuse of the child, it may not lead to the best outcomes for the child in terms of enhancing the quality of the child's life. For example, the harm done to the child through removal, both in the short term and the long term, may outweigh the harm likely to follow from the abuse. Also, there is always a risk that children who have transformed themselves in such a way as to accommodate the abusive situations from their past will be at risk of inviting abuse in a future substitute care situation. There is now a considerable body of literature on the abuse of children in substitute care, both foster and residential care.

A significant discovery relating to the outcomes for children of the child protection intervention system is provided by Gibbons et al. (1995b) who could find

> ... no evidence that children who were legally protected (by care or other orders) did significantly better. Nor did those removed from their abusers, and placed in new permanent or long-term families, have significantly better outcomes than those who remained with their original carers. (p.176)

It could be argued that the treatment provided for children is ineffective in diminishing the impact of the abuse they experienced before they entered the child protection system. On the basis of the material below concerning the lack of emphasis within child protection systems on therapy, however, it is more likely that this equivalence of outcomes despite legal protection is a reflection of a loss of focus in child protection from helping the victim to punishing the offender. This is probably the most dramatic indictment of the failure of child protection services to benefit children, and could be a reflection that the entire process of child protection may have lost sight of what is at the centre – the child.

The therapeutic needs of children beyond ending the abuse   After abuse, children need help. Abused children need services that will help them make sense of what has happened to them; to come to terms with aggression; to develop self-control, social sensitivity and empathy, and to improve social relationships. They may need extra help to develop cognitive skills and improve academic ability.

Children who have experienced the trauma of sexual abuse, having learned to accommodate the abuse, may need to learn ways to prevent themselves from being victimised. Children who have become 'sexualised', for example, present great challenges for those around them, especially in substitute care situations (Sanders and McAllen 1995). They may need help to anticipate life events that are likely to trigger strong feelings associated with the abuse. They may need extra help to overcome the distorted perception of sexuality in relationships, so that they can begin to understand non-abusive sexuality in relationships. Issues of secrecy and power may need to be disentangled from their abusive context and put into a more appropriate perspective. For therapists working with such individuals the process is one of a voyage of transition from being a victim to becoming a survivor.

Children experience abuse in a variety of ways, and under a variety of conditions with varying degrees of impact: it follows that they don't all need the same kind and amount of help. A range of treatment services is required, provided by different agencies, having contact with the child in different contexts, designed to help the child undo as far as possible, or at least minimise, the impact of the abuse. It would be unhelpful, for example, to conceptualise the treatment needed by abused children as that provided by child psychiatric services alone. Pre-school settings and schools can provide environments in which children can begin to develop the cognitive and social skills left impaired by the maltreatment they have experienced. Haase and Kempe (1990) have described how schools can help children who have been abused through a nurturing role. Foster carers and residential social workers, if they are adequately prepared (through training and through involvement with a coordinated treatment plan for the child), can provide living-learning situations in which social learning can occur. Abuse-related learned behaviours can be addressed. Social workers have, in the last two decades, developed considerable skills in direct work to enter the inner worlds of children needing substitute families. Those skills are equally transferable to working with abused children.

If the therapeutic needs of children arising from abusive experience are extremely diverse, the one common component is that they all need a therapeutic service that is integrated and coordinated. That is the service they do not get.

Therapeutic services available for children   It would be fair to say that there is a sufficient body of knowledge of how to help abused children – the problem is not that we don't know how to do it, but that we don't do it. The available literature on treatment services tends to focus on methodology. Nevertheless, the question put by Graziano and Mills (1992), 'Who is treating the children, with what kinds of treatment, and for which psychological problems?' must be asked. They note that the literature on treatment contains very little controlled, empirical assessment of psychological treatment for children.

More significantly for our purposes, there is very little research on the *availability* of treatment services. A notable exception, in Florida, classified the types of families needing a therapeutic intervention service (for maltreated children) into live categories of level of functioning, with a similar rating of the types of services that were available for those families (Crittenden 1992). They found a complete mismatch of the types of services that were provided with the types of services that were needed.

One of the negative consequences of the emergence of sexual abuse in the late 1970s was the virtual dominance of interest in that form of abuse over other forms of abuse, both in research and practice. However, even with the predominant emphasis on treatment provided for children who have been sexually abused, Sharland et al. (1995), looking at 147 families over a nine-month period where there were suspicions of sexual abuse found 'persistent unmet need, deficient follow-through casework and an absence of adequate treatment and counselling services'. Thomas (1996) noted that in 1990, when the large voluntary childcare organisation NCH Action for Children, made a national offer to set up sexual abuse treatment centres, only one local authority accepted the offer. Farmer and Owen (1995) found that in their two-year study of two authorities, half of the children who had been sexually abused had received individual counselling and described it as highly valued; children who received no counselling or other direct help adjusted markedly less well. Another study, fairly large scale, looked at over 500 sexual abuse treatment programmes across all of the 50 American states and Puerto Rico (Keller et al. 1989). Although they obtained considerable information on the types of treatment services available (methods and clients), they did not explore the availability of treatment services. Bentovim (1992, 1993) whilst endorsing the work of the Interdepartmental Group on Child Abuse (DoH 1992a) in the development of work with offenders, notes the need for a similar comprehensive treatment which includes work with victims and parents who have a protective role to play. Although endorsing specialist units that will integrate protection and treatment, in the absence of such, he suggests an interagency treatment service which would be coordinated through a 'post-protection/treatment subcommittee' of the Area Child Protection Committee. This multidisciplinary, coordinated approach to the after-care of abused children is also endorsed by Baglow

(1990) who considers that agencies should liaise closely in the allocation of treatment responsibilities and simultaneous undertaking of treatment in respect of abused children and their families. The need for interagency coordination of treatment approaches is also supported by the work of Gibbons et al. (1995b) who noted that the kinds of resources that might make a difference for abused children were largely controlled by agencies such as Health and Education.

How Area Child Protection Committees address the need for therapeutic services

Important questions to ask in connection with treatment are: which children are getting a therapeutic service? which children are not? and why?. Unfortunately, the answers to these questions are not easily forthcoming as there has never been a national audit in England and Wales of such services. Armstrong (1994) describes several ACPCs undertaking or anticipating local audits of treatment services (for example, Barking and North Yorkshire generally, and Oxford in relation to treatment of juvenile sexual abusers), but overall observes, 'Many reports omit all mention of treatment or post-abuse work. Others explicitly note concern about the short-fall in this area' (1994: 30).

Jackson et al. (1994) looked at the emphasis on treatment in their review of the operations of eight ACPCs:

> Follow-up, after-care and harm reduction to children who have been abused, counselling for partners of abusers and a range of other issues which might broadly be described as treatment did not come up either under policy areas which had been addressed and run into difficulties or those which it was planned to tackle in the future ... Reasons given for the difficulties in developing policies around treatment are related both to attitudes of representatives and to resources. (Jackson et al. 1994: 71)

The following were some typical comments of members of ACPCs as regards the emphasis on treatment:

- 'Not very much on aftercare and treatment' (Social Services)
- 'Treatment – not that I've noticed' (Police)
- 'Very little treatment in regard to abuse' (Health)
- 'Lot of concentration on prevention and investigation without anybody much thinking what happens after' (General Practitioner)
- 'Treatment, not spending a lot of ... time looking at that' (Education).

Sanders et al. (1996b) considered the relative emphasis in the work of ACPCs in the development of preventive, investigative and treatment services and suggested:

> Few ACPCs are able to give serious consideration to issues of treatment. Where treatment was given specific consideration, it was limited in two ways. It tended to be about abusers rather than victims and it tended to focus on sexual abuse rather than other types. (Sanders et al. 1996b: 903)

Several measures would help to improve the situation:

1   A greater ACPC emphasis on treatment issues.
2   A greater appreciation of the contributions of various agencies to the treatment of abused children.
3   A greater awareness that consideration of the individual treatment needs of specific children, and the wider scale consideration of the availability of treatment services within a particular geographical area needs to be undertaken on an interagency basis.
4   A commitment by ACPCs to monitor the post-protection treatment plans that are being made for individual children, to establish if the range of treatment services available are meeting the needs of abused children.

As a fifth point, not specifically related to the work of ACPCs, they consider there is a need for research into the availability of therapeutic services.

A model for the interagency management of treatment services

The consequences for children of having been abused are varied, depending upon a range of factors; it follows that the therapeutic needs of children require a spectrum of after-care, counselling and skilled therapeutic and psychiatric services. No one agency has the exclusive role in the provision of therapeutic services, and thus treatment services, like those services designed to stop abuse recurring, require interagency coordination. Child psychiatric services could and should provide a lead role in that co-ordination. At the present time, the role of the child psychiatric input into ACPCs is much more limited than its potential would suggest.

The following are suggested as components of a renewed emphasis on treatment in the management of child protection services:

1   A standing interagency ACPC treatment subcommittee, chaired by the child psychiatrist, but not focused exclusively on child psychiatric services.
2   Specific arrangements for reviewing the treatment component of child protection plans.

3   An ongoing ACPC audit of the availability of treatment services provided by agencies.

To scrutinise progress on work to prevent child abuse and make recommendations to the responsible agencies

In the work of Area Child Protection Committees, prevention is also a neglected area when compared with the emphasis put on investigation, but not to the same extent as treatment. Armstrong, in her overview of 107 Annual Reports, notes, 'There were a great many reports where the section entitled Prevention was simply not about prevention activity' (1994: 41). On the other hand, she does consider that about 70 per cent of the reports contain information which can genuinely be regarded as preventative. Whether this is a high figure or a low figure must be considered in the context that guidance on Annual Reports specifically calls for ACPCs to set out the work they are doing to prevent child abuse. As an issue, prevention (unlike treatment and after-care services) is required to be addressed in the ACPC Annual Report (*Working Together* 1991, Appendix 8). In this context, 30 per cent of reports failing to get to grips with the issue of prevention must be seen as quite a high figure.

Renewed emphasis was given to prevention of child abuse by the establishment in Autumn 1994 of the National Commission of Inquiry into the Prevention of Child Abuse by the National Society for the Prevention of Cruelty to Children (NSPCC). It reported in 1996, indicating, in the Foreword that 'the weight of testimony has left the Commission in no doubt that most of the abuse children now suffer is preventable' (Williams of Mostyn 1996: ix).

Within the broader area of child welfare, the very concept of 'prevention', which began to gather support as the Children Act 1948 came into being, has come into a degree of disfavour with the advent of the Children Act 1989. It has been supplanted by the preferred terminology 'family support' because of the previously unhelpful association of prevention with the principle of avoiding children coming into care. Since the advent of the Act, 'care' (in the pre-Act sense of the word meaning both compulsory and voluntary arrangements for children to be looked after) is no longer something to be avoided, but rather, as well illustrated with respite care and family link schemes, a valuable service that may in the long term allow for children to experience a better quality of life.

Most managers and practitioners today are familiar with the primary, secondary and tertiary classification of prevention developed by Caplan (1964). Walker et al. (1988) translate these concepts into child abuse, and describe activities that would come within these three classifications.

Primary prevention aims to reduce the incidence of child abuse in the overall population, by action directed at the population at large. Secondary prevention entails identification of high-risk groups where child abuse is likely, and through the provision of targeted services aims to reduce the incidence of child abuse. Tertiary prevention is the provision of services to those children and families where abuse has already occurred to prevent the reoccurrence of abuse and reduce the harmful consequences. Gough (1993), drawing on the work of Parton (1985) and Hardiker et al. (1991), considers the tripartite division to be a medical model and describes other models of prevention applicable to child protection: legal and social welfare models, and residual, institutional, developmental and radical models. Armstrong (1994) in her overview of ACPC Annual Reports notes that most agencies use a tripartite division (and uses it herself for her own analysis). She notes that some agencies use a twofold classification of primary and secondary, dividing between 'pre-abuse' work (combining primary and secondary prevention in the tripartite model) and work following identified abuse (tertiary abuse in the tripartite model). Some examples she describes of preventative work in the agencies are health (health visiting and midwifery services), social services (family centres, Newpin and Homestart partnerships), and education (anti-bullying campaigns and school exclusion). She also noted efforts by agencies to stage events or launch campaigns ('don't shake the baby') designed to raise public awareness.

Primary prevention: targeting populations

MacMillan et al. (1994a, 1994b) have undertaken to review primary prevention in physical abuse, neglect and child sexual abuse. As regards physical abuse, they conclude that the evidence remains inconclusive, apart from home-visiting schemes. Sherman (1989) also endorses a home-visiting scheme as a model of prevention. As regards sexual abuse, Swan et al. (1985) provides one of the earlier attempts to evaluate child sexual abuse prevention, noting that such programmes had proliferated in the five years prior to their study, i.e. late 1970s/early 1980s. MacMillan et al. (1994a, 1994b) conclude that while education programmes can increase safety skills and knowledge about sexual abuse, no study has provided evidence that the programme actually reduces the occurrence of sexual abuse.

A major difficulty in primary prevention of child abuse and neglect is the question of how to use resources. This applies at both national and local level. The primary prevention of child abuse entails providing services across such a wide section of the population, and with such an impact that the circumstances that give rise to child abuse will not occur. Addressing the issue of resources and prevention (in the context of family placement services), the Short Report noted: 'If half the funds and the intellectual effort which has gone towards developing strategies for finding alternative families had been put into what we can only lamely call preventative work there would be unquestionable advantage to all concerned' (House of Commons 1984: xix).

But arguments about the cost-effectiveness of prevention (especially primary prevention) often ignore the numerical imbalance between the large number of children and families that have to be targeted to receive the service in order to avoid a numerically very small number of child abuse cases arising. One cannot compare the cost of providing a preventive service to a single child and family with the cost of providing an after-the-fact service to the same child and family. Broad-brush approaches to prevention are costly because many of the resources/services will be 'wasted' on those who are less in need of them. In the end, they may not be cheaper than providing services for a smaller group of the population deemed to be at risk. There are many good reasons for undertaking primary prevention, but cost effectiveness is not necessarily one of them. Broad-brush approaches to social welfare provision, (described as 'residual models of welfare' by Hardiker et al. 1991), have during the 1980s in both the US and the UK become politically unfavoured. Hardiker et al. outline some of the political context factors in opposition to such an approach. As previously noted, the Audit Commission (1994c) has been critical of the lack of targeting of resources in children's services.

These economic considerations will be very much at issue for those who are responsible for managing child protection services. For managers there are difficulties about the implementation of preventive strategies in child protection that do not arise when planning and coordinating policies around investigation, where until recently services have operated in a relatively cost-free, needs-led environment. This may to some extent account for the expansion of child protection services in recent years. Some of these difficulties would appear to be present in the US as well, as indicated by the following from the *American Journal of Public Health* policy statement: 'While prevention efforts are well documented in various segments of our society, they are not universally recognized or adequately supported by all public, private, and voluntary groups' (AJPH 1987: 111).

Secondary prevention: work with high-risk groups

Secondary prevention involves the identification of high-risk groups and as such depends upon the ability to predict abuse. One reason why primary prevention is important is because knowledge of the causes of child abuse is still not advanced sufficiently that it is possible to predict with a sufficient degree of accuracy which children will be abused (Rodwell and Chambers

1989). The reasons for this lie in the multi-causal nature of abuse. As stated by Egeland, 'abuse is a complex phenomenon and each case is unique. No one risk factor predicts with sufficient accuracy' (1988: 96). If the small number of children who are going to be abused cannot be extricated from the larger population of children who come from situations with factors associated with abuse with any degree of accuracy, then preventive strategies must of necessity be based on the larger groups.

Greenland (1987), a significant contributor to the Jasmine Beckford inquiry (London Borough of Brent and Brent Health Authority 1985), is noted for his substantial efforts to develop checklists of risk factors with predictive validity in the areas of physical abuse and neglect. The following are the factors he has identified:

- Previously abused or neglected as a child
- Age 20 years or less at birth of first child
- Single parent/separated; partner not biological parent
- History of abuse or neglect or deprivation
- Socially isolated or frequent moves or poor housing
- Poverty – unemployed/unskilled worker – inadequate education
- Abuse of alcohol or drugs
- History of assaultive behaviour and/or suicide attempts
- Pregnant/postpartum or chronic illness.

Wolfe (1993), in the process of trying to develop preventive targets, identifies risk factors associated with child abuse and neglect. The pragmatic difficulties of these checklists for practitioners (and for managers of child protection services) is that they often failed to distinguish service users referred for child abuse from those in receipt of child and family support services for other reasons. Parton and Parton (1989), looking at the work of Greenland, are somewhat sceptical of the ability of such checklists to predict abuse, although conceding that the risk factors identified, largely from retrospective studies, are *associated* with abuse. They are in agreement with Cohn who asserts 'At the moment we are unable to predict with accuracy who will or will not abuse' (1983: 171). Exploring the dilemmas and fallacies of prediction in child abuse, Dingwall also asserts that 'the value of any self-styled predictive checklist is small' (1989: 51). Browne and Saqi (1988) remind us that it is as important to understand why the majority of families subjected to stressful conditions do not abuse their children (94 per cent in their prospective study of over 14,000 births). The current concept of measuring risk, 'risk assessment' or 'risk analysis', is gaining in support amongst agencies. Nevertheless, such tools are not without their difficulties (Wald and Woolverton 1990; Caldwell et al. 1988). Channer and Parton (1990) in their discussion of the Greenland checklist draw attention to its lack of sensitivity to race and cultural issues, and potentially drawing on stereotypes about Black people that make them score more highly on such a risk tool.

Similar caveats about the predictability of risk factors would apply for child sexual abuse. Bergner et al. (1994), considering Finkelhor's Risk Factor Checklist (1979), note that although there would be undoubted preventive benefits of being able to predict child sexual abuse, they conclude, 'the eight factors comprising the Risk Factor Checklist ... did not strongly and significantly predict sexual victimization.'

The view of Wald and Woolverton (1990) as regards risk assessment in child abuse is that it should provide the basis of informed decision making for professionals (which would include service managers), but that it should not be taken in itself to be predictive – decisions about individuals should not be made on the basis of actuarial risk assessment. In the future, research may increase our ability to predict which children will and will not be abused, but that is of little help to those who must try to balance the resource allocations between prediction, investigation and treatment today.

Tertiary prevention: after-the-fact prevention of recurrence and reduction of harm

Exploration of the various levels of prevention highlights that the boundaries between the threefold classification of prevention, investigation and treatment are not so clearly defined as to completely avoid ambiguity. Tertiary prevention, the 'after-the-fact attempts to ensure that abuse will not recur' (Walker et al. 1988) is very similar to treatment, (which has been previously discussed) and is dealt with by them under that heading.

Area Child Protection Committees and prevention

In order to fulfil their functions listed in *Working Together* (1991), ACPCs must address prevention. It is tempting to argue that the more of all kinds of prevention there are, the better; however, there are difficulties with this. The cost-effectiveness arguments have already been considered. Another difficulty, cutting across all forms of prevention, and one which has been previously highlighted is the relative lack of emphasis on quality assurance mechanisms in child protection. Not only was their usage not in evidence, but there appeared to be no particular enthusiasm to develop them. In order for managers to take more of an interest in prevention, they would need to have available to them more sophisticated systems for assessing outcomes of preventive services. Poertner et al. (1991) have provided a model for this. At present, there are few attempts to audit outcomes. However, agencies are developing more sophisticated 'management information systems', which may in the future provide a better basis for input–output monitoring.

An ecological perspective on prevention

It is clear from ecological perspectives on child abuse (Belsky 1980; Garbarino 1981; Cicchetti and Lynch 1993) that the causes of child abuse extend beyond the psychological and family factors to causes that lie in the community and society. Hay and Jones suggest a framework for under-standing child abuse that relies on a network of complex and inter-acting factors from the individual to the societal level: 'Both risk factors and protective factors are present at the level of the individual, the family, the community and environment, the culture and the society, and can interact in myriad ways to result in different types and combinations of child mal-treatment' (1994: 380). They consider that such an understanding can help in the development of preventive services. At the extremes of this are forces within society which contribute to a social context within which abuse takes place. Several examples are:

- The feminist analysis of child sexual abuse (Driver and Droisen 1989) which emphasises the sexualisation of young girls and the power differentials between men and women in society
- The consideration of socioeconomic class status and child abuse undertaken by Pelton (1978)
- The links between societal acceptance of corporal punishment of children and child abuse described by Newell (1989) and criticism of the use of corporal punishment reported by the NSPCC Commission (Williams of Mostyn 1996)
- The consideration of poverty and material deprivation in relation to abuse (Parton 1985; Baldwin and Spencer 1993)
- The problem of violent individuals in a violent society (Strauss et al. 1980; Gil 1996).

Many of these factors are beyond the day-to-day operation of the Area Child Protection Committees, or present virtually insurmountable difficulties to address. However, to use the ecological model developed by Bronfenbrenner (1979), there are layers between the microsystem (containing the developing individual) and the macrosystem (the wider societal context) which may exert a powerful influence. These are the 'mesosystem' and the 'exosystem'. The 'mesosystem' comprises the interrelations among major settings containing the individual, for example, the various interactions between family, school and peer group. These interactions exert an influence beyond their separate individual influences. The 'exosystem' is seen by Bronfenbrenner as an extension of the mesosystem embracing other formal and informal social structures which, while not directly influencing the individual, impinge upon the immediate settings in which he or she is, thereby influencing those settings. The neighbourhood is given as an example of an exosystem.

The distinction between primary and secondary prevention has been described as that between targeting populations and targeting high-risk groups. There is a level at which these two can merge and which would appear to be a very legitimate focus for Area Child Protection Committees: targeting high-risk neighbourhoods. There is a body of literature which suggests that whilst it may be very difficult (because of high levels of false negatives and false positives) to target individuals through high-risk screening, certain geographical neighbourhoods, communities and vicinities are clearly more vulnerable to child abuse (especially certain types of abuse) than others. The large numbers of reservations about risk assessment inevitably raise the question of just how predictable child abuse is. The answer may be that whilst it is a very uncertain undertaking attempting to predict which child will be abused, it is less difficult to predict which neighbourhoods and communities will have high levels of child abuse. It may be that predictability is less certain at the micro level (predicting which particular child is going to be ill-treated on the basis of risk predisposing factors), but may increase as one goes from the microsystem to the wider and wider systems within which the child and the family live (community, culture, society, etc.). Some studies have focused on the identification of high-risk communities, using geographical mapping techniques, rather than high risk children and families (Garbarino 1981; Krishnan and Morrison 1995); there are potentially substantial benefits from this ecological/spatial orientation to risk. As described by Noble and Smith (1994) spatial mapping models ('Geographical Information Systems'), are not new. In both the US and the UK during the 1960s, poverty strategies were based on the identification of particularly disadvantaged areas. What is new however is the increasingly sophisticated tools for mapping the data and deriving conclusions for policy planning and strategy development. Derived from his own practice, Gill (1996) has described a fourfold connection between poverty and child abuse at a local level. First, poverty exacerbates difficulties that are already there within families (debts building up; feeling of loss of control; not being able to provide for children). Secondly, poverty emphasises the isolation within the community, (for example, housing markets tend to bring together people who are stressed). Thirdly, physical dangers for children are often greater in poor communities (dangerous stairwells; no secure play areas). Finally, poverty creates tensions within the neighbourhood.

Global strategies, whilst expensive, do work. A telling example of this is provided by Cunningham (1995) who looks at the decline in infant mortality in the twentieth century, 'the Century of the Child' as he describes it. He considers the reduction in infant mortality to be one of the most significant and dramatic changes in the lives of children and families during the whole of the period of childhood he examined (1500 to the present), and probably before. Whereas by the middle of the twentieth century the death of a child was a rare event and one which a parent would consider themselves unlucky to experience, in previous centuries a family would consider themselves very fortunate indeed if they did not experience the loss of a child in infancy. Whilst this period of time coincided with considerable 'social action' (which he uses in the sense of describing the actions of individual and group campaigners) to reduce infant mortality, he concludes that is 'likely that the decline in deaths from diarrhoea owed more to improved sanitation than to the activities of teachers, doctors, nurses and social workers' (Cunningham 1995: 166). There are times when global strategies are more effective than stop-gap measures that target interventions in an overly limited way, thereby addressing symptoms and not causes. To use again the whooping cough metaphor of child abuse by Gibbons et al. (1995a), described earlier, child abuse may be different from whooping cough in that it is socially con-structed (and whooping cough is not) but it is like whooping cough in that the measures to address it would be extremely limited indeed if they were restricted to dealing with symptoms, and were not backed up by an immunisation programme designed to prevent it occurring in the first place.

The link between community development, child abuse and child welfare

The NSPCC National Commission into the Prevention of Child Abuse indicated 'Community groups and neighbourhood initiatives can be effective in supporting families but their strength needs developing' (Williams of Mostyn 1996: 67). However, traditionally, the links between community development (or social action) and child welfare have been tense. Gill (1996) suggests that social work as a profession is not only perplexed about the connections between poverty, social deprivation and child abuse but also resistant, and considers that the reason for this is the nature of social work training which focuses on interpersonal qualities – structural issues take a back seat.

In the introduction to the first text explicitly linking community develop-ment and child welfare, Cannan and Warren write: 'Mainstream social work has, under pressure, too easily turned its back on the social action of new social movements ... and found a sense of purpose in clinical approaches and in the detailing of assessment and treatment procedures for children victimised in their families' (1997: 10). It is as if the diversity of approach has been the occasion for conflict and mutual distrust rather than for collaboration and mutual benefit. It could be caricatured as community workers believing caseworkers to be authoritarian, concerned with an individualistic approach, and not sufficiently concerned with the wider issues. Reciprocally one could caricature the perception of community workers held by case workers as being insufficiently pragmatic, not of benefit in the immediate situation and taking too long to see results, and being in the privileged position of not having to use authority. One way in which this conflict has been very real is in the influence that child protection has exerted on the nature of social work. I refer to its specific impact on the generic/specialist debate.

In 1982, the Barclay Committee (1982) reported entering into a debate about the generic/specialist nature of social work which had been going on since at least 1945 when Macadem (1945) was the first to suggest genericism in social work training. There has been a type of extended social work identity crisis since then with the familiar swings of the pendulum. Many aspects of this debate in the context of a postmodern theoretical framework, are listed in Table 4.2.

Table 4.2: Generic/specialist divisions in social work
(McBeath and Webb 1991)

postmodern	modernist
specialist	generic
decentred/dispersal	unity/unified

The furthest swing of the pendulum to the generic model of social work came with the introduction of reorganisation of social services in 1971 into a generic, 'one door' social services department (Seebohm 1968). By unifying the services provided by the previous Welfare Departments, Children's Departments and Mental Welfare Officers, clients were able to go to one place regardless of which of these services they required. The social work principles underlying the service were seen as essentially the same, regardless of the particular client group (Bartlett 1970). However, it was not required for the social worker providing the service to be fully genericised, and a generic service was frequently delivered by a team of practitioners specialising in work with various client groups. Further, the structure of the departments within which social workers operated was found to be variously organised along either functional or geographical divisions (Rowbottom et al. 1974). This model continued more or less without substantial changes throughout the 1970s, withstanding the impact of numerous child protection inquiries. Fundamentally, despite many inquiry recommendations concerning coordination, training and other aspects of interagency working, there was little criticism of the basic organisation of the way services were delivered. At the same time, most local authorities were, at least until the late 1970s, major employers of community workers.

The Barclay Report (Barclay Committee 1982), despite clear divisions within its constituency manifested by two dissenting reports (Pinker and Hadley), advocated a community social work approach (not to be confused with community development or community work approaches) in which practitioners were advised to embrace a neighbourhood model. Patch-based, generic work, in which the geographical areas covered by workers were so small that they could be expected to be locally known with good community links, was seen as the way forward. This method of working bridged the divide between individually oriented caseworkers and casework-phobic community workers. As a method of working, there was considerable value in it, and the social work press contained examples of some of the benefits arising from agencies which chose to adopt this model.

However, community social work died before it was born, or at least certainly before it had grown to maturity. The mid- to late-1980s saw a number of high-profile child abuse inquiries which were to raise once again the concerns about the abilities of social workers to address child protection issues:

- Jasmine Beckford (London Borough of Brent and Brent Health Authority 1985)
- Heidi Koseda (London Borough of Hillingdon 1986)
- Kimberley Carlile (London Borough of Greenwich 1987)
- Cleveland Inquiry (Butler-Sloss 1988).

Noyes, in his overview of child abuse fatality inquiries notes 'In addition, a number of inquiries discuss the decentralisations of Social Services Departments into neighbourhood or patch teams' (DoH 1991c: 26), giving as examples material from the inquiries into the deaths of Shirley Woodcock, Kimberley Carlile and Tyra Henry (respectively, London Borough of Hammersmith and Fulham 1984; London Borough of Greenwich 1987; London Borough of Lambeth 1987). It is arguable however, that the relevance for those cases was the extent of reorganisations and not its direction (i.e. decentralisation); several inquiries note the impact of the National Health Service reorganisation in 1982 – for example, Lucy Gates (London Borough of Bexley and Bexley Area Health Authority 1982) and Kimberley Carlile (London Borough of Greenwich 1987).

The response to these high-profile cases in the mid-1980s was a renewed emphasis on the development of workers with a high degree of specialism in dealing with child abuse. Depending upon the particular authority, there was a clear trend for workers to become more and more specialised. Whereas around the time of the introduction of the Seebohm social workers who undertook work with children and families may also have undertaken work with other client groups, within several years of Cleveland there were very few of those type of social workers, and even within child care social work there were the emerging specialisms of child and family work, child protection, and workers specialising in child sexual abuse, (in keeping with the Cleveland recommendation for Specialist Assessment Teams).

Community social work was dead. Likewise, community work as an enterprise was in decline. Very few people nowadays take community social work seriously; very few practitioners have probably even heard of it. Very few social work training programmes continue to offer community work/ community development as a serious option. Yet in view of our previous discussions about the relevance of local communities to child welfare in general, and child protection in particular, the abandonment of community social work may have been premature. However, if community social work is dead, community work and community development may be rising like the mythical phoenix from the ashes of its previous demise. According to Cannan and Warren, the need to develop new forms of social participation in view of the high levels of social exclusion of the 1980s 'have led to a re-emergence of community development methods in the social welfare field' (1997: 12). Furthermore, community social work as a methodology may be dead, but it still has supporters arguing for its relevance to child protection. Consider the following:

> The clustering of child protection cases, the research evidence, the role of support networks and the potential of local communities to protect their children all point to the necessity for a more broad-brush approach. This is not to argue that attention paid to what happens within families should be lessened, rather that community social work should be seen as complementary to family-based social work and should be properly resourced. (Gill 1995: 30)

This balance of intervention between casework with individuals and families and broader-based approaches through community work and community social work was more or less the position that existed in the early 1980s.

Family centres

A final and most significant consideration in the connection between communities and children, are family centres. Although family centres, in one form or another, have been around for several decades, the Children Act 1989 contained the first provision in law relating to them. It gave local authorities a duty 'to provide such family centres as they consider appropriate in relation to children within their area' (schedule 2, paragraph 9). Family centres are described as

> places where a child, his parents and anyone who has parental responsibility for or is looking after him may go for occupational, social, cultural, or recreational activities or advice, guidance or counselling or the person may be accommodated whilst he is receiving advice, guidance and counselling. (DoH 1991b: paragraph 3.18)

Interestingly whereas some of the provisions of schedule 2 refer explicitly to children in need, this provision does not, and therefore would apply as a general provision. In fact, the same guidance indicates 'Where local authorities are concerned about families with children who are living in a poor environment, it may be desirable to encourage the setting up of a neighbourhood facility for all local families to use, perhaps involving voluntary organisations' (paragraph 3.23).

From very early on, even before the introduction of the Children Act provision, there has been a wide variety of enterprises that came under the term 'family centre'. This has led to several attempts to classify them into typologies. As long ago as the early 1970s the term referred to agencies that were as disparate as

- A traditional day nursery that was changing its role to provide a more focused service for children and to involve parents more in the running of the nursery and in planning for their children
- A referral-only service, run by a voluntary organisation (for example, the Family Welfare Association), which provided an intensive assessment of family functioning (possibly with a view to assessing whether a child at risk should be returned to, or remain in, the care of his or her parents, or have plans for permanent placement elsewhere made, and
- A group of mothers in a very disadvantaged locality of South London, who undertook with advice from the local health visitor, to set up a scheme whereby they would look after each other's children collectively on a rota basis, thus providing parents with more time for themselves.

Walker (1991) identified three common characteristics of these diverse entities labelled as 'family centres', that they focus on the family as a whole, their function is to prevent family breakdown, and they are sited in neighbourhoods that particularly need them (for example, with high rates of local social disadvantage and children coming into care). They are provided by both the voluntary and the statutory sector. Different ways have been found of classifying family centres. Walker (1991) divides them into two categories, those with a service approach and those with a therapeutic orientation. Both Holman (1988) and the Department of Health (1991b) have developed threefold classifications with similarities, but not identical. Holman's classifications are client-focused models, neighbourhood models and community development models. Cannan (1992) has added a fourth to Holman's tertiary model, a service model. The Department of Health classification are therapeutic, community and self-help family centres:

- Therapeutic – In these, skilled workers carry out intensive casework with families experiencing severe difficulties with the aim of improving the ability to function as a family and relationships between parents and children or between siblings

- Community – Local voluntary groups including churches may provide a neighbourhood-based facility for parents to use as a meeting place and take part in particular activities. These may also offer such activities as playgroup sessions, parent/toddler groups, toy libraries, adult education classes

- Self-help – These may be run as a cooperative venture by a community group and are likely to offer various support services for families in an informal and unstructured way.

Although family centres can be considered a qualified success (at least in terms of popularity, involvement and beneficial outcomes), there are some difficulties. Because they serve different purposes, as pointed out by Holman (1992), they are differentially valued by the statutory agencies, the community and the voluntary services. The local authority is likely to favour the establishment of intensive/assessment/therapeutic family centres. The community and the voluntary organisations are likely to favour the establishment of open-access neighbourhood (or community development) models. Because of their concern to develop value-for-money services to achieve statutory objectives, local authorities are likely to want to do at least two things. First, they are likely to use their grant aiding relationships to voluntaries to achieve the types of services they require. As pointed out by Holman (1992), voluntary bodies may follow the wishes of the statutory bodies to gain funding. Sanders, in the description of Children Act training provided to voluntary organisations in Wales, points out the high degree of concern about the changing role of the voluntary sector:

But the use of local children in need definitions combined with the increasing dependency of voluntary organisations on statutory funding, means that voluntary organisations could become agents of local authorities in the provisions of services on their behalf, rather than independent providers of needed services. (Sanders 1993: 46)

Similar processes are described in the US by Gronbjerg et al. (1995: 583), who considers that 'market forces will favour those providers that match most closely the needs of the state agency for specific expertise.'

Secondly, they may choose, as many have done, to relabel and refocus previously existing day nurseries instead of developing a new family centre service. Family centres which are aggrandised nurseries appear to be less successful than newly established ones. The reasons for this are likely to be because of both staff and buildings. To change staff attitudes is a very difficult enterprise and one to which considerable attention was given in the implementation of the Children Act 1989. In any case, many nurseries were changing their ways of working with parents prior to the introduction of the Act. A second limitation is that buildings that are designed for very young children are not necessarily suitable for the types of activities that would suit groups of adults. It is interesting to note that Gibbons et al. (1990) found that more families got the type of help they needed when there was a broad range of local services available rather than conventional services solely provided by the local authority. Colton et al. in looking at the provision of local authority services for children in need consider that there should be a greater emphasis on family centres which they found to be 'one of the services least adequately provided' (1995: 58).

For our purposes, drawing on our previous consideration of the links between abusive families and the community, the family centres described as open-access, which are there for the whole community, not just for a small group of referred clients (but which may include those as well), are the link with communities that these families need. However, there are difficulties with this 'integrative' approach. First, they are expensive. To operate effectively, they must broadly be available to all (or at least all within a particular locality). In the language of cost-effectiveness previously considered with primary prevention, they will include those who are less in need of the service than some others, but for those others who are more in need (that is, abusive families), the process of inclusion is what is needed:

> ... in many areas the problems of young families are so acute and so many children are in urgent need that it is hard to justify allocating scarce places to families who seem to be coping relatively well. Even family centres with a commitment to offering a service to the neighbourhood and maintaining open

access find themselves under constant pressure to accept more and more families with serious difficulties. (Goldschmied and Jackson 1994: 216–17)

Second, there are tensions. The integrationist philosophy of the Children Act 1989, as pointed out by Sanders (1993), encompassed two types of integration: the integration of children in need into services for children who are not in need (the principle of 'normalisation'), and the integration into services for children in need regardless of the particular reason they are in need (whether because of disability, risk of abuse, or other). The intention of this is to de-stigmatise service delivery. However, there are difficulties, and it became clear in the period prior to the implementation of the Act that parents of children with disabilities had considerable reservations about receiving services alongside abusive parents. Instead of de-stigmatising the service to abusive parents, the parents of children with disabilities considered that they were being stigmatised.

To scrutinise work related to interagency training and make recommendations to the responsible agencies

We have already considered the impact on interagency child protection training of the child care component of the Training Support Programme, which arose from the recommendations of the Cleveland Inquiry (Butler-Sloss 1988) and which provided government ring-fenced money for the provision of training. To be truly comprehensive, a local child protection training strategy would need to undertake a full training-needs analysis of all staff, at whatever level, in all the ACPC constituent agencies, to ascertain in accordance with their particular roles and functions what they need to know about child abuse and child protection in order to operate effectively. It would need to explore how identified training needs could best be met, which training should be provided in-house by the agencies themselves, and which should be provided on an interagency basis. Where interagency training is provided by social services, consideration needs to be given to how much of the cost should be sought from Training Support Programme funding, how much, if any, it is reasonable to expect the social services, as lead agency to underwrite, and how much should be recharged to agencies. This can create difficulties. It is clear from Armstrong (1994), that in a number of cases at least, the shortfall from TSP for interagency training is provided by social services.

Virtually all the professions represented on ACPCs have arrangements for ongoing in-house training and development (although the emphasis put on child abuse and child protection in these is variable). Because of the very sensitive nature of the work, training in child protection tends to come after one has qualified and Rae (1992) has pointed out the range of post-qualifying courses available to social workers, paramedics, teachers, volunteers, nurses and other staff. The development of sophisticated and complex frameworks for post-qualifying awards, for example that developed by the Central Council for Education and Training in Social Work (CCETSW 1992b) could and should be linked into local training on child protection. Despite some of these programmes being interdisciplinary, they can be structured so as to conform to the necessary requirements for post-qualifying accreditation within different professions at the same time.

Difficulties can arise over the funding of interagency training. Agencies may have the expectation, (not always justified) that because of Training Support Programme funding, social services will supply and absorb the costs for all child protection training. There is an important distinction to be made between the social services responsibility for interagency training, funded by TSP grants, and the within-agency child abuse and child protection training which agencies should fund.

A training programme developed on that basis would then need to consider the rates of staff turnover within the respective agencies so that the frequency of the provision of various types of training could be estimated. That would address the training needs of particular staff at any one time in their individual careers, and over time for the agency. The strategy should also address the links between training and staff appraisal and development. This would entail the provision of training to individuals (particularly those with more extensive involvement in child protection) that goes from basic and broad to in-depth and focused.

In order to fulfil this function under *Working Together* (1991), most ACPCs find it useful to have a Training Subcommittee, and the Social Services Child Protection Trainer (or the training officer whose responsibility includes child protection) will be a member, if not the chair, of that particular forum. Some ACPCs have multidisciplinary trainers or training 'pools', a collection of trainers from different agencies who come together to coordinate child protection training. Whether a multidisciplinary trainer (the appointment of which is frequently a very high priority for ACPCs) or the social services trainer, he or she, after liaising with member agencies, will be responsible for submission of the TSP bid to secure funding for training. Whilst *Working Together* (1991) is very clear on the provision of internal training being outside of its remit on interagency working (paragraph 7.1), the trainer would need to be aware of how much training was provided within agencies, as a foundation for the development of interagency training:

> ACPC multidisciplinary training strategy must be located within the context of provision by agencies ... This kind of share in responsibilities appears to occur in

many ACPCs though it is often not stated as a strategy ... Some ACPCs give details of the way ACPC courses dove-tail into specific in-house agency training. (Armstrong 1994: 35)

We will consider within-agency training first before proceeding to explore interagency training.

Within-agency training

The overview of child abuse fatality inquiries provides a useful summary of the training needs of various professionals involved in child protection (DoH 1991c: 33–4), but interestingly, whilst it considers social work training, medical training, training for nurses and health visitors and training for police, it does not address training for staff in education.

Jackson et al. (1994) in their study of ACPC operations looked at four mechanisms through which ACPC policy informs practice: internal management systems, written material, training and delegate feedback arrangements. Because of different responsibilities and different degrees of decentralisation of decision making, agencies relied differentially on these four means, some placing significantly more emphasis on training than others. They looked at within-agency training for ACPC members from social services, health (with special consideration for general practitioners), police and education. Virtually all the professions represented on ACPCs have arrangements for ongoing training and development. Social Services Departments may have quite large training departments, with a high degree of training specialisation within the department. Teachers have two INSET (INService Education and Training) days per term, although these are rarely used for child protection purposes because of curriculum priorities. Police have their own training programmes. General Practitioners have a requirement to undertake certain amounts of postgraduate training.

Within Social Services Departments, training features significantly as a vehicle through which child protection policy and procedures are disseminated into practice. The Social Services Department Child Protection Trainer, usually being a member of the ACPC, is well placed to ensure that the training programme provides links with child protection policy and procedures. Training is also used as a way of informing staff of new procedures or changes in the child protection system, for example, the launch of a new local procedures manual will in most cases be accompanied by a programme of training. Some of the areas/targets for training might include: training for first-line managers, training in chairing child protection conferences, training in the law relating to child protection (including provisions for children to be looked after), the impact of bereavement, separation and loss, and an understanding of racism (DoH 1991c).

As regards health there is a wide range of representatives from the various health disciplines on Area Child Protection Committees. Representatives from health include paediatricians, psychiatrists (child and adult), nursing representatives, FHSA representatives, and other representatives from health authorities and trusts. Many of these will be involved in the provision of training to staff. Again, the provision of training is one way of ensuring that staff are kept informed of policy and procedures within child protection. Within health however, general practitioners (GPs) are a unique case. They often describe themselves and are described by others as 'self-employed', a status which creates difficulties for the interagency management of child protection. The role of GPs in child protection will be looked at more fully later. Considering the extent to which other agencies use training as one of the vehicles for disseminating policy, this may be a potentially useful area to explore in respect of GPs. Several child abuse fatality inquiries have commented on training issues for GPs, indicating that Family Practitioner Committees should include in GP training child abuse child protection procedures and training in regard to the role of health visitors and social workers (DoH 1991c). Child protection material can be included in courses on child health surveillance. It is surprising however, how little use is made of the Continuing Medical Education (CME) tutor, to promote training for general practitioners in child protection. The CME tutor is the individual with responsibility for organising postgraduate education for GPs. GPs are required to have a modest amount of continuing education, through attendance at approved courses. Course approval is undertaken by CME tutors, based on the educational content. Most CME tutors however, may be unaware of the importance and relevance of child protection training. Liaison between the CME tutor and the ACPC (most appropriately with the chair of the Training Subcommittee, or the Social Services Child Protection Trainer) would certainly appear to be indicated for the future.

For medical staff generally, areas for training might include: legal implications and evidential requirements of their work, emotional aspects of child abuse and neglect, recognition of child abuse (including junior hospital staff), and training in the roles of other agencies (see 'Interagency training' below) (DoH 1991c).

For nursing and health visiting staff, training could include: training for nurse managers in supervising child protection work, specific training for health visitors on their role in child protection cases, and the policy for child abuse (DoH 1991c). The need for supervision from both a qualified supervisor and increasingly through the use of peer supervision groups was pointed out in the Doreen Aston Inquiry (Lambeth, Lewisham and Southwark Area Review Committee 1989).

Because of the size of the police force, it is particularly important for them to make a distinction between what every officer needs to know, and knowledge and skills needed by those who are more involved in child protection (for example, officers working in family support units or their equivalent). Police training in child protection tends to be focused on those undertaking child protection investigations and this is easier to arrange in those police forces where there are specialist units dealing with child protection. The Cleveland Inquiry (Butler-Sloss 1988) was very clear that police training needed to be extended beyond the need to collect evidence for possible criminal proceedings.

In schools, child abuse and child protection training is predominantly aimed at designated teachers; other teachers get very little, if any, training in child protection. Even where training is provided free of charge, through social services-led multi-agency training, teachers are often (despite the example cited below), unable to take up opportunities because of the very high cost of paying supply teachers to provide cover. These costs come out of tightly controlled locally managed school budgets. The use of 'INSET' days, which would be second best to multi-agency training, is generally not possible because they are taken up with the demands of National Curriculum training. There are resource problems for child protection training, other than that supplied through social services (or the training 'pool'). In addition, Education Departments may not have sufficient staff equipped to deliver training in child protection. When compared with National Curriculum training, which is a high priority and obligatory, training in child protection, even in the basics such as recognition and identification of abuse, is low priority and optional.

Interagency training

According to *Working Together* (1991) 'Interagency training is essential if interagency procedures are to function satisfactorily' (paragraph 7.7). This statement reflects the very high emphasis accorded by government to joint training in child protection. The guidance provides information about the kinds and levels of training required by various staff, which may be summarised as in Table 4.3. The ability of training together with professionals from different disciplines to reduce barriers to understanding and thereby increase the effectiveness of joint working should not be underestimated: '... the mastering of the basic "cognitive maps" of other professionals is one of the hallmarks of the inter-disciplinary experience' (Clarke 1993). There is considerable potential for friction and conflict between professionals

Table 4.3: Staff child protection training needs (*Working Together* 1991)

Training in/for	Target group	Content
Joint Investigation	social services NSPCC health service police	joint investigation and subsequent intervention
Joint Interviewing	police social services	understanding each other's role; how to work together on interviewing team; how to interview children
Professional Staff	all professional groups in direct contact with children (including local authority lawyers)	involve trainers from different agencies; help staff to understand the role of other agencies; level and type of training dependent upon agency's child protection involvement, but all staff to be trained in recognition and immediate action
Other Staff	telephonists receptionists	what to do with reports of suspected child abuse

from different disciplines with different cultures and different value systems. However, after 25 years of different occupations working together in a structured way to protect children, there is evidence that the considerable ignorance as described by Hallett and Stevenson (1980) of the training, role and perspective of other professions continues. This is not to say that joint training is invariably beneficial, and there are variations in the quality of interagency training provided. There are pitfalls that need to be avoided in the provision of such training.

As pointed out by Armstrong and Riches (1988) training together cannot replace the need for basic professional competence training. It follows that whilst there are potential benefits of joint training at all levels of a professional career (Mathias and Thompson 1997), there is a need to be clear about the distinction between what training is best undertaken within the professional development and what is best undertaken jointly. This is of course an issue that is not restricted to child abuse and child protection training; there are many areas where working together between professions facilitates intervention, such as family support for children with disabilities, work with adults with a mental disorder, and adoption.

The Social Services Inspectorate report (1988) expressed concern over serious deficiencies in training. Stevenson (1994) notes, 'It is generally agreed that some of the events described as inter-professional did little more than bring together a mixed audience in one room and did little to enhance mutual understanding or give clarity to the concept of inter-professional work' (1994: 133).

Another potential hazard that interagency training must address is that different professional groups have different preferred methods of learning. The work of Kolb (1984) on individual learning styles (learning by feeling, learning by watching, learning by thinking and learning by doing) has demonstrated that various occupational groups are located all over the semi-Cartesian space formed by setting out the learning styles as orthogonal axes. This suggests that in terms of the preference for those four learning modes, occupation is a very powerful influence. This is not to deny that people may choose occupations on the basis of the way they like to learn, or that they come to rely on different ways of learning because their particular occupation requires it. Either and both may be true. The point is that individuals in different occupations have preferred learning styles according to their occupations. Hallett and Birchall (1992) note for example that the training doctors receive, with the emphasis on technical skills and autonomy, prepares them poorly for cooperative working. Stevenson highlights the 'differences between professions in their approach to training, notably the balance between the didactic and the experiential' (1994: 133). One can easily imagine the types of difficulties training programmes might get into if they did not address this particular issue. Some preparatory work for an interagency programme could usefully be devoted to negotiating a preparedness on the part of participants to experiment with forms of learning with which they may be less familiar.

Hallett and Birchall (1992) provide a very useful overview of the literature on interagency training. Just a few of their numerous observations are:

- There was a lack of training and skills in managing role blurring between paediatrician, nurse and social worker (Kauffman and Neill 1977)
- Role play and gender awareness are essential ingredients of inter-agency training (Attias and Goodwin 1985)
- Interdisciplinary training can alleviate role confusion and overlap between health visitors and social work (Robinson 1979)
- It is important that training emphasises collaboration and not usurpation of other's skills and roles (Urzi 1977; Kane 1980)
- It is necessary for doctors and other professionals to acquire social science perspectives and skills (Newberger and Bourne 1979).

Training together, by allowing opportunities for sharing of fundamentals (for example, professional values), helps to reduce potential for unhelpful dialogue and conflict, and lessens suspicion and wariness. McFarlane (1993) describes some of the principles underlying interagency child protection training, and supplies several examples of training exercises designed to create opportunities to explore perspective differences between professionals from different agencies. He considers that although it has an important role to play in facilitating interagency communication, it does not provide 'the answer'. In that sense, because other steps are needed to overcome the structural barriers to interagency working, interagency training could be described as a necessary, but not sufficient, requirement for positive collaborative multidisciplinary work. Ideally, the training should mirror the interagency working by being led by trainers from different disciplines wherever possible. The key message for McFarlane is 'that while different professionals have greater or lesser levels of responsibility there is collective ownership of the concern (1993: 126).

To conduct reviews required under Part 8 of *Working Together*

Although there are a range of adverse developmental consequences that can befall children as a result of being abused, the worst consequence is death. The consequences of a child abuse fatality are so dire, in a variety of ways, and for a variety of people and agencies, that my colleague Nigel Thomas and I have argued that:

> ... the particular risk of fatality has come to dominate the child protection system to the extent that it is often not balanced against other risks. Instead the system has been driven towards zero tolerance for the risk of fatality. In that sense the system could be described as 'death avoidant'. In the terminology of risk theory, child abuse fatality is a high consequence, low frequency risk which in the construction of child protection systems has not been balanced against high frequency, 'low' consequence risks. (Sanders and Thomas 1997: 111)

It is almost impossible to overestimate the impact that the series of inquiries into child abuse fatalities has had on the current arrangements for child protection. The most significant work on this, best described as discourse analysis, is that by Parton (1985). He examines the social reaction to the death and subsequent inquiry in relation to Maria Colwell, and the media coverage of several other inquiries to illustrate how certain models and priorities have come to dominate the child protection agenda. Sanders et al. (1996b) and Jackson et al. (1995) have described the impact of inquiries, and the concern of the media with them, on the perception of risk in child protection. One consequence, which is very topical in terms of the current 'refocusing' debate is that fatalities have been a powerful 'net' adjusting force (to use the metaphor of net widening in *Child Protection: Messages from Research*). They have had the combined effect of both widening the net (so that more families come into the system) and reducing the net mesh size, so that fewer exit the system once they are in it.

ACPCs have been required to undertake case reviews since the introduction of *Working Together* (1988) after the Cleveland Inquiry (Butler-Sloss 1988) and these arrangements were brought forward when the guidance was reissued in 1991. According to paragraph 8.1 of the latter guidance, the circumstances that should trigger such a review are:

> Whenever a case involves an incident leading to the death of a child where child abuse is confirmed or suspected, or a child protection issue likely to be of major public concern arises, there should be an individual review by each agency and a composite review by the ACPC.

These reviews have two main objectives – to ensure that all the necessary lessons are learned, and to allay public concern about the nature of the service. Hallet (1989) suggests that in addition to those two functions they also serve to establish the facts of the case, and to establish accountability (from errors of omission or commission). James (1994) considers that they also inform government about the need to review national policies and amend guidance. As all Part 8 reviews are required to be submitted to the Social Services Inspectorate, this function is potentially very valuable, Jackson et al. (1994) recommended that the Welsh Office should consider how to coordinate the lessons learned from all case reviews and disseminate that information.

There are seven general principles to be observed when undertaking Part 8 Reviews: urgency, impartiality, thoroughness, openness, confidentiality, cooperation and resolution (paragraph 8.4). The local authority should inform the Department of Health (or in Wales, the Welsh Office) as soon as information comes to light in which a Part 8 Review may be required. Written records (case files and notes) concerning the child and family should be secured by agencies. The chair of the ACPC and the custodian for the child protection register are meant to be notified as soon as possible. The chair will undertake to ensure that all relevant agencies are informed. Each agency should carry out an urgent internal review to ascertain:

a)   if the agency child protection procedures have been followed;
b)   if the case suggests that there is an urgent need to review those procedures;
c)   if any other action is needed within the agency.

Staff involved in the case should be informed of the review process. The review should be separate from any possible disciplinary proceedings which may arise. There should be a designated senior manager in each agency who has the designated responsibility for undertaking the review. As part of the agency's review, a chronological history of the agency's contact and involvement with the child and family should be developed. The agency should establish if its practice conformed to agency policy and procedures. Part of the review should involve a consideration of which services were provided, and recommendations arising from the internal review. Because relationships with the media are very strained at the time of reviews, it is helpful for agencies to have a clear policy on dealings with the media. This is particularly difficult, and therefore especially important, where organised abuse is involved.

The whole process should take about eight weeks; one month for the agency to undertake an internal review, a further week for it to go to the Area Child Protection Committee, and three weeks for the ACPC to produce a composite overview report which is forwarded to the Department of Health, or in Wales the Welsh Office, via the Social Services Inspectorate. Having made recommendations for changes, the ACPC should put arrangements in place to monitor agreed changes (which should be published).

There have been three studies to date of Part 8 reviews, but before considering those, it is useful to look at inquiries undertaken over the last 25 years. Inquiries can be seen as predecessors to Part 8 Reviews, and chronologically that would be accurate, although inquiries are still able to be arranged, and indeed one of the issues arising from the Part 8 Review should be a consideration as to whether or not a further inquiry is indicated.

Overviews: Child Abuse Inquiries

There have been more than 40 child abuse inquiries over the last 25 years. As Figure 4.1 illustrates, the inquiries appear to have come in three waves during the period 1973 to 1989, although it is more difficult to speculate on whether this reflects heightened concerns during certain periods of time, or diminished concern at others. There have been two government summaries of these inquiries, (DHSS 1982; DoH 1991c), and several other useful summaries (Hallett 1989; Reder et al. 1993). Let us now consider briefly these four studies.

Child Abuse: A Study of Inquiry Reports 1973–1981   The first government report (DHSS 1982) examined 18 inquiries into child abuse fatalities. It looked at agency functions, professional practice and the context of professional practice. As regards relationships between agencies it highlighted separate viewpoints and duplicate functions as two areas that can cause tensions, and noted some of the difficulties around child protection

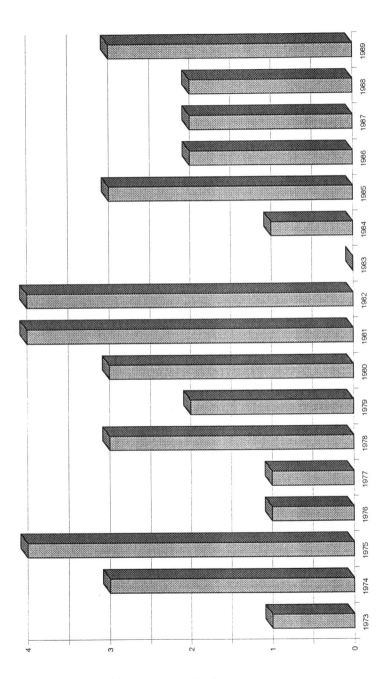

Figure 4.1   Child abuse inquiries by year

conferences. Some interagency difficulties are attributable to the mechanics of communications: 'Effective communication and records are integral to good practice. Inadequate professional responses often stem from communicating and recording inaccurately or not at all ...' (p.69). The report summarises professional practice as follows: 'The overall impression of practice given by the reports is one of much good work interspersed with numerous omissions, mistakes and misjudgments by different workers at different times' (p.69).

Child Abuse: A Study of Inquiry Reports 1980–1989   The second government report (DoH 1991c) was undertaken by Phillip Noyes of the NSPCC, and examined 19 further reports beyond the 18 studied in the earlier study (DHSS 1982). In comparing the two, he noted the degree of coherence of the themes arising from the earlier study compared with his own, in which there was a more complex picture. The study reported on the functions of the various agencies (social services, NSPCC, health agencies, education authorities, police and probation services), issues for management (including training which we have discussed previously), interagency working, and the management of individual cases. Whilst there is much material in the overview about issues to do with child protection practice, the following is some of the material that is more directly relevant to the management of the services.

Lack of clarity of senior management's role and of the ACPCs' function – A somewhat surprising finding is that the inquiries do not appear to focus on senior management, and yet as we have shown, that level is a clear link in the chain of policy coming from central government to practice. The 'inquiries do not make clear what they believe to be the responsibilities of senior management' (DoH 1991c: 23). It is suggested that 'membership of these committees should include those who have the authority and responsibility to bind their agency to implementing the recommendations of the Committee' (p.52). The role of the Area Child Protection Committee is also found in a number of inquiries to be somewhat equivocal. The 'ACPC has no budget, no delegated responsibilities, no secretariat' (p.51), and 'to be effective ACPCs need resourcing, strategic planning, and commitment' (p.54). Though there appears to be considerable emphasis and even improvement in the latter two, resourcing of ACPCs continues to be a problem (Jackson et al. 1994). Armstrong however, describes 52 per cent of ACPC reports giving information on budgets, although there are regional variations contributing to this picture. On the lack of information about budgets in many reports, she conjectures 'One reason for this may be that in many ACPCs there is no budget to talk about' (1994: 10). She notes that 'Debates over budgets can be fierce' (p.10) which reflects some of the difficulties described by Jackson et al. (1994). When considering the ability of ACPC representatives to commit their agencies, finances were generally excluded. ACPCs appear to face tensions in two directions. As described in the overview, 'Some proposals for the role of the ACPC would seem to pitch it into headlong confusion with the responsibilities of individual agencies' (DoH 1991c: 52). But facing the other way, 'there is a need too for ACPCs to feel a closer relationship to central Government' (p.54).

Ability of ACPCs to address ongoing/future issues – One of the points to emerge from the Cleveland inquiry (Butler-Sloss 1988) was that prior ability to effectively coordinate interagency arrangements for the protection of children was no guarantee of future success. The Cleveland ACPC was considered to have been very successful in the guidelines it established for the interagency coordination of protecting children from physical abuse. However this did not help when diagnoses of sexual abuse began to be made on a large scale. It appears to follow from this that ACPCs need not only to develop arrangements for current child protection, but need to anticipate, and possibly have mechanisms for addressing new issues as they emerge. In Cleveland we witnessed the emergence of a 'new' form of abuse children were experiencing. Since that time however, there have been numerous examples of new issues in the field of child abuse that ACPCs have had to address, for example:

- Organised abuse – defined in *Working Together* (1991) as 'abuse which may involve a number of abusers, a number of abused children and young people and often encompasses different forms of abuse. It involves, to a greater or lesser extent, an element of organisation' (paragraph 5.26.1)
- Abuse carried out by children or young people (paragraph 5.24.1)
- Abuse of children in foster care; abuse of children in residential care
- Abuse of children by people using professional roles to gain access to children ('professional abuse')
- Abuse of children by females.

No doubt there will be more. It is vital that Area Child Protection Committees have the flexibility and the goodwill to tackle new issues as they emerge.

Impact of inquiries – Many of the issues raised in the report were addressed in *Working Together* (1991) and other subsequent guidance. For example, in response to 'What is needed is an integrated standard of practice for child protection' (DoH 1991c: 111) there is the Social Services Inspectorate document (1993) of dimensions, standards, criteria in the inspection of child protection agencies, previously described.

The report looks at some of the influences that the inquiries have had on child protection. One of the great disappointments of the succession of child abuse inquiries (and we will see the same when we consider the work of Colton et al. 1996 on Part 8 Reviews), is that the 'quest for understanding about why children are killed by some people and not others is scarcely taken forward' (DoH 1991c: 109). This seems to be one of the most dramatic statements of the distortion of priorities within child protection. Sizeable resources are allocated to consider very fully the circumstances of children that come to be killed by their parents. Whilst the Cleveland Inquiry cost several million pounds (estimates vary between £2–4 million), most inquiries are more likely to cost around £250,000, estimated by the Beckford inquiry. The inquiries tend to focus on child abuse almost exclusively in terms of individual pathology with very little consideration given to wider issues of disadvantage within society.

They have also contributed to the development of the role of the caring professionals as agencies of social control or, as described in the report, in terms of 'social policing': 'In order for police and social workers to develop closer working relationships, social workers have had to become more like police, (at least in terms of attitudes underlying child protection work), and police have had to become more like social workers' (Sanders et al. 1996c: 89). Serious consideration should be given as to whether this is the role we want for our 'caring' agencies. Interestingly, the theme of developing a separate child protection agency, employing a range of staff from different disciplines was considered, and rejected, by the Kimberley Carlile inquiry, in favour of a model of a 'thorough-going shared responsibility' (DoH 1991c: 53) of the type we now have. The inquiry commented poignantly, 'it is unclear what kind of child protection service society wants' (London Borough of Greenwich 1987: 140–1).

Another influence described is that inquiries, operating in the climate of a 'moral panic' about child abuse (Cohen 1972; Parton 1985), provide for the community a sense that something is being done. But in light of our previous consideration of the lack of emphasis on understanding causes, this is a largely palliative effect. The inquiries have resulted in a polarisation of interests of the various parties who have a stake in child protection, that is, the child, the parents, the public and the professionals. And finally, the report, anticipating the debate caused by the publication of *Child Protection: Messages from Research* (DoH 1995a) considers that a further influence of the inquiries has been the fragmentation, even isolation, of child protection from the rest of the services in child care.

Hallett: 'Child-Abuse Inquiries and Public Policy' Hallett (1989), reviewing the major inquiries up to the time of the Carlile Report (December 1987), notes that there are generally three types of inquiries: internal inquiries, locally commissioned external inquiries, and external inquiries commissioned by the Secretary of State. In general, local inquiries are to be preferred to inquiries commissioned by the Secretary of State. Local inquiries, however, have less powers by virtue of being non-statutory. A particular difficulty here is the lack of ability to compel witnesses to give evidence; this is also a difficulty with the arrangements for Part 8 Reviews. As described by Hallett, there was considerable trust and naiveté on the part of professionals giving evidence to the Colwell Inquiry. Since then, with the very dramatic consequences of inquiries both for individuals (loss of job, change of career) and for agencies (low morale, difficulty recruiting), professionals are understandably much more resistant to providing evidence to inquiries.

There are no standard procedures for the operation of inquiries, and the way they conduct their business is determined by the chair of the panel of inquiry, influenced, to varying degrees, by members of the panel. Inquiries can be classified according to whether they adopt inquisitorial or adversarial methods for fulfilling their terms of reference, although Hallett considers this distinction perhaps misleading as all inquiries have inquisitorial functions. Of the 34 she examined, only ten had adopted an adversarial, or as she describes it, a 'quasi-litigious' approach. But among those are inquiries which have had the highest public profiles, for example, Maria Colwell, Jasmine Beckford, Tyra Henry, Kimberley Carlile and Cleveland. These ten adversarial cases include all seven of the inquiries which were conducted in public, another factor which may have contributed to their very high public profile. Hallett argues in favour of inquisitorial methods as they are 'cheaper and quieter, less stressful for participants and perhaps, better suited to situations where complex issues of policy, practice and professional judgement are for determination' (1989: 122).

The origins of inquiries are rooted in local campaigns, usually involving the media (for example as described previously with Stuart Bell MP, in Cleveland). The criminal trials of the abusers are also closely related to these local campaigns and media interest. In a number of instances, during trials, judges have felt it necessary to comment on the action or inaction of agencies, remarks which may have contributed to, or even sparked off, the local concern and campaign. Although these types of comments could be seen as outside the remit, and even the expertise, of judges in criminal trials, they are very rarely (the Beckford case being an exception) criticised in the inquiry reports for making them.

In evaluating the impact of inquiries, Hallett considers that they have undoubtedly had an impact on local policy and practices, and describes examples where the responses to the issues raised by the inquiry are being put into effect even before the inquiry has concluded. However, she also notes that 'similar and repeated failings were being revealed in successive inquiries' (1989: 138), and one must question the extent to which this is because the lessons learned from inquiries, other than the most high-profile ones, were not being effectively disseminated. Of course there are resource issues as well, as described so vividly by Ambache (1988) included in Hallett's consideration. This letter to Community Care highlights the intolerable dilemma in practice in which one is clearly aware of the parameters of good practice, but restrained from putting them into effect because of the lack of resources.

However, any consideration of resources in child protection, in the *current* debate about refocusing of child protection services would have to question the extent to which, had extra resources been made available, they would have resulted in benefit to the children. Hallett considers that the tendency to focus on individuals in the inquiries has diverted attention away from the need to address resource issues. One could argue that this may have been an occasion when had extra resources been allocated, they may have done as much harm as good. Extra resources, allocated to child protection services at a time of expanding definitions of child protection, could lead to better resources for subjecting more children and families to child protection while still not addressing the need to divert resources to address the needs of children more holistically. Extra resources are probably best argued for in the context of absolute clarity about the objectives of child protection intervention, and consequently, the priorities for intervention and associated costs derived from those objectives. It would be fair to say that we still do not have that absolute clarity about how best to enhance the overall welfare of children and families.

Like Noyes (DoH 1991c), Hallett comments on the tendency of inquiries to individualise, both in focusing on the individual pathologies of the families and on the actions and inactions of the professionals. She notes the absence of questioning the wider context, for example, the kinds of social processes which lead adults to harm children (such as the socialisation of men's violence and sexuality).

Finally, Hallett notes the tendency of inquiries to be used to allay public anxieties. She anticipates the emphasis in future policy on the use of 'routine-ised, low-key internal review within agencies', brought in by the use of Case Reviews, and appears to regard them positively in that they will 'regularise the acceptance of a degree of error in complex service-delivery systems and attempt to improve practice without seeking scape-goats' (1989: 142).

Reder, Duncan and Gray: Beyond Blame Judging from references to Reder et al. (1993) in material produced by Area Child Protection Committees, this may be one of the most influential non-government texts for the management of child protection services. Unlike Hallett (1989), their focus is much closer to practice, both in terms of work with children in families, and in terms of interagency coordination at the level of networks in contact with the child and family (that is, those professionals likely to be represented at a child protection conference). They used a systemic approach, described as a process in which 'human groupings come together, interact, develop and transform over time' (p.20) to analyse 35 inquiry reports into child abuse fatalities undertaken between 1973 and 1989. Like Hallett (1989), they noted the lack of a framework for undertaking inquiries. They found their analysis to be hampered by the lack of basic information on the families, the type of information that would help to understand the background of the circumstances leading to the fatality (reflecting my earlier discussion of the lack of inquiry into causes). They note for example, 'many reports began their account with the birth of the fatally abused child, as though previous history had no relevance for what followed' (Reder et al. 1993: 31). They look very closely at the circumstances of the families of the relevant child, and the meaning that the child has for the families. A majority of the inquiries contain references to serious difficulties in interagency communication (a finding reflected in other reports) and related that to the impact on professional communications of different patterns of professional networks at different levels within the agencies. The assessment process was flawed by a number of difficulties amongst which were the selective interpretation of information (related to the 'rule of optimism', Dingwall et al. 1983), and pervasive belief systems, in which a fixed view dominates a worker's thinking. They also considered, as noted, that fundamental information about the child and family were often missing. To address this, they provided genograms (family trees) of all of the families they studied.

Some of their notions of the links between families and the professionals seem to have been particularly taken up. For example they describe the following which will probably sound very familiar to any experienced child protection practitioner:

- Care and control imbalances in the family–professional relationships
- Dependence
- Closure (family reduce their contact with external world; few people able to meet and talk with them)
- Flight
- Disguised compliance

- The 'not-exist' double bind (in which efforts of worker to see child frustrated by so-called 'Catch-22' thinking').

They follow this up with the application of the concepts to a particular inquiry (Doreen Aston: Lambeth, Lewisham and Southwark Area Review Committee 1989).

As we have indicated, the value of this book comes from its very close connection with practice. It examines networks of child protection agencies in the context of their closeness to the family, looking at how working with families can influence the professional networks as well as the other way round. In that sense, it has parallels with the work of Fürniss (1991) who in his work on child sexual abuse theorised a mirroring process between the family network and the professional network, so that the professional network, through the process of identifications with different family members, comes to reflect and experience similar dynamics (for example, conflict patterns) between themselves as operate within the family. In both cases, a number of issues of interagency working are largely derived from a practice dynamic, rather than from the policy context of delivering an interagency child protection service.

Part 8 Reviews   As we have seen from paragraph 8.1 of *Working Together* (1991), Part 8 Reviews are not necessarily restricted to cases ending in fatality, and this is highlighted in the study undertaken by Colton et al. (1996 discussed below) where it was found that of the 21 Part 8 Reviews received from the Welsh Office, seven were not because of a child being killed by parents. Like inquiries, there have been a number of overview reports of Part 8 Reviews. James (1994) produced a study for the National Conference of Area Child Protection Committees in 1994. Dr Adrian Falkov (1996a) undertook a study for the Department of Health which explored the connection between fatal child abuse and parental psychiatric disorders. Colton et al. (1996) undertook a study of all Part 8 reports presented to the Welsh Office since the implementation of the Children Act 1989. These three reports are briefly summarised here.

James: Study of Working Together Part '8' Reports (1994)   This study looked at 30 case reviews completed during the period October 1991 to December 1993. The sample was selected across English Social Services Inspectorate (SSI) regions and across age bands according to the age of the child at the time of the death or serious incident.

The figures indicate the number of cases; figures in brackets indicate the number of children where this is different. Because of the way the sample was selected the tables should not be interpreted to imply geographical or age patterns.

Table 4.4: Regions for Part 8 Study (James 1994)

Region	Number
North of England	8
Central	6
South of England	8(11)
London	8(9)

Table 4.5: Age at death (James 1994)

Age	Number
less than 6 months	7
6–11 months	3
1–4 years	13
5–12 years	5(9)
over 12 years	2
Totals	30(34)

James found that of the 30 cases, 26 had previous involvement with the social services department; 17 cases involved children known to be at risk, and twelve had been the focus of a child protection conference, which in ten cases had resulted in the child's name being added to the child protection register.

The reports were very variable in size (from 2000–40,000 words) with between four and 99 individual recommendations. This appeared to indicate a difficulty getting the report size and depth just right as two reports were felt to lack important details, and others had so many recommendations that it was very difficult to distinguish the significant ones

It will be recalled that the inquiries (previously discussed) lacked a framework. James considered that the Part 8 Review reports as well lacked a structure – although *Working Together* (1991) does provide some specification as to how the Review should be undertaken. James therefore provides a recommended structure for future reviews comprising:

1   Introduction.
2   The Inter-Agency Review Process (including a list of agencies and dates agency reports received).
3   Family composition.
4   Chronology of events.
5   Overview of the family.
6   Commentary on events.

7   Issues for individual agencies.
8   Issues for ACPC procedures.
9   Action already taken.
10   Reasons whether or not an Independent Review is needed.
11   Summary and recommendations.

Like Reder et al. (1993), James endorsed the use of genograms as a helpful tool to better understand family dynamics, and provided several examples. James was also concerned about the absence of detail in the Reviews of the men in the children's lives, and considered this might be a reflection of lack of effort on the part of the agencies to collect this information. An important finding was that most reports concluded that existing local interagency procedures were satisfactory; it was non-compliance with the procedures which was criticised in the reports. This suggests that it was probably the right strategy at the right time to move away from costly inquiries, which continued to raise the temperature of the fatality review process, and which probably began to yield very limited returns in terms of how systems should be modified, towards a system of internal reviews. These, whilst having the ability to continue to point out lessons to be learned, focused largely on the internal quality assurance process.

Another theme to emerge from James's study was that it is easier to identify the risks to children in such families than it is to ensure their safety. Partly this may be seen as a consequence of 'as repeated episodes of worrying but not fatal harm come and go it is easy for professionals to come to believe that really serious harm is unlikely to occur' (para. 3.13b).

This has parallels with 'the rule of optimism' first described by Dingwall et al. (1983) and the concepts of 'selective interpretations' and 'pervasive belief systems' described by Reder et al. (1993). A parallel process may be operating within the family. Tom, a parent who had killed his partner's child, suggests from his interview in prison (Open University Audiotape material: Stainton Rogers et al. 1989) that there are thresholds, and each time one was crossed, it was easier to repeat the abuse afterwards. Thus over time, the abuse of the child became progressively more severe. James used a ten-category indicator to consider the 'chaotic' nature of the families from which the children came:

1   Multiple relationships of the adults.
2   Frequent changes of addresses.
3   Numbers of young (pre-school) children close in age.
4   Health problems.
5   Children (and some adults) with learning difficulties.
6   Special educational needs (in addition to learning difficulties above).

7 Poverty or financial mismanagement.
8 'Domestic' incidents involving police action, for example, children left unattended, violence between spouses.
9 Records of offenses committed.
10 Long-term involvement of many caring organisations.

In a majority of the cases (16 of 30), children were living in families where most of these ten features were present. On the other hand, he also found reports noting that families living in the most disadvantaged areas may appear to be indistinguishable from neighbouring families, or even less harmful. This may be one of the difficulties confounding worker's efforts to predict which parents will abuse (and fatally so), and which will not. This is a particularly poignant issue for professionals who work in areas of extreme social disadvantage where there are few economic opportunities and high unemployment.

Finally, he noted that the increased risk when long-term key workers leave, through moving away or through some reorganisation of responsibilities, may be underestimated. In addition to these consequences he identified a number of issues arising from the study, and suggested changes to the referral and investigation processes.

As a result of his study, James made a number of recommendations as to how *Working Together* (1991) might be amended to take the findings into consideration. The main findings concern the process of referral and recognition, and that of investigation and initial assessment. As regards the referral process, among other recommendations is suggested, that 'on receipt of a referral check should be made *at once* with the keeper of the Child Protection Register ... the child should be seen on the same day by staff from one of the statutory agencies' (James 1994: para. 4.1, original emphasis).

As regards the investigation and initial assessment process, the study suggests that 'visits to family homes should ensure that all children in the family are safe, not merely the child who may have been named in the referral' (James 1994: para. 4.1). He describes some excellent work with the police on joint investigation.

It is arguable that this emphasis on the urgency of the referral process, especially without any distinction as to whether some referrals may be more urgent than others, does little to bring into child protection the 'lighter touch' described in the media when *Child Protection: Messages from Research* was launched in June 1995.

Falkov: Study of Working Together Part '8' Reports Dr Adrian Falkov studied the significance of parental mental disorder in fatally abused children. He examined 105 Part 8 Reviews received at the Department of Health during 1993 and 1994. Five were excluded from the sample because they did not meet the criteria. Of the 100 remaining cases, 32 contained clear indication of parental psychiatric difficulty. The rest of the cases were either insufficiently documented or indicated no details of psychiatric difficulties. In one-quarter of the cases (25), the perpetrator was the parent affected by mental illness, in ten cases it was the partner. These figures add to more than 32 because in some cases both the perpetrator and the partner were affected by psychiatric difficulty.

A key finding was:

> ... not the absence of agency input, (adult mental health services in particular), but rather an absence of effective intra and inter agency coordination, collaboration and communication ... In general a parental mental health perspective amongst child agencies was lacking and there was little emphasis on child protection and the nature of children's experiences prior to their premature deaths amongst adult services. (Falkov 1996a: 20)

It is reassuring that his approach to this analysis is not to focus on individual pathology as the sole, or even the main, etiological factor in child abuse, and he acknowledges the difficulties of predicting the individual actions which led to the deaths of the children. His conclusion that there should be better integration between adult psychiatric and child protection services is based more on the need to understand the impact of being a parent on an individual who has a mental disorder, and the reciprocal impact on the child (in terms of development) of having a parent who is mentally disordered than on the need to avoid child deaths attributable to a parent's mental disorder. He calls for more research into the 'bidirectionality of influences between psychiatric symptoms and parenting capacity' (p.23), and argues for a much stronger coordination of services and better reciprocal understanding between adult mental health and child protection.

Colton, Roberts and Sanders (1996)   Colton, Roberts and Sanders undertook a study of Part 8 Reviews carried out in Wales since the implementation of the Children Act 1989 (from 1991–1996). Of the 21 Part 8 Reviews they received from the Welsh Office, 14 were concerned with a parent killing a child (involving 15 children). Of the remaining Reviews two were undertaken in respect of adolescent suicides (not involving parental abuse) and two were undertaken to address concerns about paedophiles having access to children through their professional roles (in both cases, teachers). In one a Review was undertaken because of concerns about a child whose older sibling had died in suspicious circumstances but where the child himself (born after the death of his sibling) had not come into surveillance as a consequence. Another Review was undertaken in relation to a very young child where there were very substantial, but non-fatal, injuries during a time of high professional scrutiny. A final non-fatality Review concerned a young person who was physically and sexually abused whilst in foster care.

Of the 14 cases (including 15 children) where there had been a death resulting from abuse by a parent, the children were of the following ages:

Table 4.6: Part 8 Reviews: Death by parent – ages (Colton, Roberts and Sanders 1996)

Age	Number
less than 6 months	6
6–11 months	3
1–4 years	3
5–12 years	3
over 12 years	–
Totals	**15**

This study selected all cases which had been subject to a Part 8 Review, unlike James' sample which was deliberately selected to have different ages represented. Therefore the pattern of very high representation of very young children (within the general reservation about small sample size) may be significant.

The authors looked at the family and background characteristics of the 19 cases in which children were the focus (excluding the two adult sexual abusers). They found material problems such as financial and housing concerns to be the most common characteristic of family background (eight cases). Problems in the relationship between parents, usually accompanied by parental violence in the relationship also featured frequently (seven cases). After those two factors, other factors were parental mental health problems (five cases), which makes an interesting comparison with the material of Falkov, 1996a, parental delinquency and/or criminality (five cases), and behavioural difficulties of the child (five cases). Six of the children had been previously placed on the child protection register.

Using James's ten-category list of 'chaotic' family structures, they found long-term involvement of a number of welfare agencies in eight of the cases, and police involvement because of domestic difficulties in six cases. Four children had learning difficulties, and a further four had additional special educational needs. The recommendations of the report are divided into two groups, those to do with the undertaking of Part 8 Reviews and those concerned with suggestions for improving practice in working with families, a management/practice division. The main management concerns were with the generally very inconsistent approach to undertaking reviews and the need for an independent element in the review process. These two points have both been previously addressed in our discussion concerning inquiries. As regards the inconsistent approach to undertaking Part 8 Reviews, Colton et al. (1996) endorsed, and developed, the framework suggested by James. As regards the lack of independent component to the review process, this may be one of the disadvantages about the tendency to move from inquiries to Part 8 Reviews, although as we saw, only a small number of the inquiries were open to the public. However it may be provided, there needs to be an independent element to the reviewing process, or there is a danger, even with interagency checks and balances, that common agendas and interests may come to dominate the process.

The practice, or casework, concerns were about the lack of assessment, the large numbers of professionals involved with families which tended to undermine continuity of involvement, the sometimes peripheral involvement of medical practitioners especially general practitioners, the lack of clear plans to monitor the implementation of recommendations, and the lack of consideration of staff needs.

Limitations of Part 8 Reviews

Although Part 8 Reviews highlight lessons that need to be learned in order to improve interagency practice, there are limitations to what they can achieve and constraints that prevent them from being more effective. We have highlighted a number of these including the lack of attention given to the causes of fatalities, difficulties in interagency cooperation, insufficient emphasis on monitoring, lack of comparison, and insufficient consideration given to the impact on staff of the fatality and the subsequent review process. We have limited our attention to the management issues; much more could be said about the shortcomings in practice identified by the Reviews (for example, unstructured approach to assessment, failure of individuals and agencies to accept responsibility, the involvement of large numbers of professionals, the role of general practitioners, etc).

Lack of attempt to understand causes   First, and perhaps most importantly, Part 8 Reviews do not attempt to address the causes of abuse or of fatality. Noyes (DoH 1991c) commented on this in connection with inquiries, and Colton et al. (1996) in connection with Part 8 Reviews. The question 'why?' appears to be less important than whether or not procedures were followed. The restrictive nature for the terms of the Review as outlined in *Working Together* (1991) makes it hardly surprising that there is often very little information that might be helpful to understand why a child was fatally abused; there is generally only a description of what the agencies did, and considerations of what could have been done better. In many cases this may be regardless of whether those actions were seen as playing a role in the fatality. It is surprising to find the extent to which important basic information about the children and their families was either completely missing, or could only be put together to form an overall picture by assembling components from the reports of the different agencies. The use of genograms and other structured assessment tools is very rare, which is surprising considering their value in understanding such families (Reder et al. 1993) and the role that they can play in assessment of families in the child protection system (DoH 1988).

Whilst not addressing causality, most Reviews do attempt to assess how predictable was the abusive incident or fatality. In many cases reviews have concluded that despite practice which may have been good or poor, the actual incident was unavoidable or unforeseeable. Understanding the causes of abuse and fatality can lead to better efforts to prevent them, but as we have already indicated, prevention of abuse is not a high priority for Area Child Protection Committees.

Lack of interagency cooperation   The usefulness of Part 8 Reviews in deriving valid lessons for future practice may be severely impaired by the unwillingness of agencies to take part in the Review process. We have already commented on difficulties for inquiries when they do not have power to compel individuals to give evidence, for example, by subpoena. Part 8 Reviews, by virtue of being the result of government guidance, also do not have direct powers to compel individuals to give evidence. At the best of times, interagency relationships in child protection are fraught with difficulty. Hallett and Birchall (1992) describe a range of facilitators and inhibitors to interagency coordination. Some inhibitors to good interagency coordination include incompatible values and goals, lack of clarity as to how to achieve the objectives of coordination, differences in style of operation, discrepant planning and financial cycles, differences in styles of operation and fears of loss of autonomy. Jackson et al. (1994) however, found interagency relationships on the whole very good, especially between social services agencies and police, although relationships involving education agencies appeared to be generally less strong. Sanders et al. (1997) identified two factors which influenced the nature of interagency relationships between ACPC members. One was the extent of fragmentation or decentralisation of the agency (usually as a result of professional roles or government reforms within the caring services). The other was the extent to which the objectives of the agency were in accord with the main policy emphasis within child protection. This means, for example, that those agencies whose objectives were more in line with the emphasis in policy on the investigation of suspected child abuse (for example police, social services, and some health agencies) had closer relationships with each other than they did with agencies who had different child protection concerns such as prevention and treatment (other health agencies and education services).

It can be seen that relationships between agencies are influenced by a wide range of factors and can vary considerably. Even when they are positive, this may be precarious. They can become much more strained at the time of a fatality when there is a high likelihood of unfavourable media coverage. Felicity Leenders, Nursing Officer at the Department of Health has described the relative lack of support and solidarity (and therefore the risk of scape-goating) experienced by health workers at such times. One can expect that at such times there is an even greater likelihood of a 'cover-your-back' approach, and participation in the review process may become strained, even if it is not refused outright (although I have learned of an ACPC where the paediatrician representative had indicated that he would refuse to participate in future Part 8 Reviews because of his concerns about how past ones had been dealt with). The differential input of medical represen-tatives was highlighted in the example of two mothers, in two different authorities, committing suicide along with their children described by Colton et al. (1996). In one of the case reviews there was a very full account of the role of the psychiatric services prior to the event. In the other, there was no input at all into the review concerning the adult psychiatric ser-vices, even though it was known that the mother used the service prior to her suicide.

Lack of detail on monitoring   From the reading of the Review reports it is very difficult, if not impossible, to establish whether Reviews have actually improved practice, and what evidence there is of this. The lack of emphasis on quality control processes that we have previously considered in relation to ACPC operations also extends to Part 8 Reviews. All Reviews will have recommendations, the number of which may vary considerably. However, what is less clear are the arrangements agencies have made to monitor the implementation of the recommendations. To complete the review process there needs to be internal and external monitoring systems to ensure all of the recommendations are implemented and evaluated in terms of impact and effectiveness. This process should be undertaken at different levels. Agencies need procedures to ensure that recommendations relating to their practice and management are implemented and evaluated. ACPCs should have procedures to ensure that the interagency recommendations are im-plemented and evaluated. And finally, it would be most useful, as all Part 8

Review reports are forwarded to the Social Services Inspectorate, if as a result they had arrangements, apart from inspection, to monitor the implementation and recommendations arising from all Part 8 Reviews.

Lack of comparison in Part 8 Reviews Whilst there are considerable benefits to the undertaking of Part 8 Reviews, it is often difficult to know how extensive are the issues identified within agencies. In one Review examined by Colton et al. (1996) a particular district was identified as needing significant changes to its child protection practice in order to conform with the expectations of the ACPC. The authors however could only speculate on the extent to which other districts had significantly superior practice. If one were to draw an analogy with research methods, it would be like comparing differences between research that draws on a comparison group to establish that found differences are genuine and one which relies solely on retrospective analysis (with all the limitations that imposes).

A difficulty with the conclusions derived from Part 8 Reviews is that they rest on the assumption that any bad practice identified has contributed to the fatality; this may be true, but equally it may not. There are measures that ACPCs could adopt to address this when undertaking Reviews. One way would be for a matched case or cases to be identified at the same time as the case under review, which would provide a basis for comparison. To be useful, the case or cases should be matched on as many relevant factors as possible, such as age, family composition, family circumstances, etc. In such cases important differences and similarities of practice could be observed, as well as being assessed against a reasonable standard of practice. These comparisons should help to identify which differences in practice appear to be significant.

A second, and probably more effective, means to address the lack of comparability would be through using a system of random audit. Under such a system, child protection cases within agencies are randomly selected for review. The audit is based on previously identified standards and the practice is compared with what is expected according to those standards similar to those we considered previously (SSI 1993). Using random audit over time ACPCs would be able to build up a picture of the practice in their agencies and an area profile highlighting geographical variations. Part 8 Reviews which were conducted against this background of information would be much more illuminating, and would also be better able to inform the process of developing standards.

Support to staff There has been virtually no research into the impact for the worker of a death of a child on their caseload, and even less on that impact when the cause of it is due to child abuse. Clearly, there are likely to be similarities and differences between circumstances when the death is due to abuse and when it is due to other causes. In the past, it has been virtually impossible for workers to avoid the stigma and media vilification in high-profile inquiries, but that may be lessened by the trend towards lower-profile internal reviews. Nevertheless, workers frequently experience considerable levels of stress and anxiety associated with both the fatality and the ensuing review. As described in one Review:

> There is no formal arrangement or mechanism through which members of staff involved in traumatic cases can have access to a personal counsellor ... staff involved in cases where events like the death of a child occur are bound to have deep feelings of self-doubt, guilt, remorse and grief.

It is likely as well that these effects are not only profound, but also long term. Although we know that the impact can be traumatic and perhaps even traumagenic, agencies appear not to have introduced measures designed to support staff after a fatality, and during and beyond the review process. In another example, 'One final concern was that staff who were interviewed clearly remained distressed by the child's death and also did not appear to understand the need for, or the purpose of, the enquiry.'

This lack of consideration to the needs of staff undertaking very difficult work, which becomes particularly stressful at times of a child abuse fatality, almost appears to reflect a degree of indifference. Considering that child protection services are substantially dependent on the quality of staff in the field, the general lack of consideration is of some concern, not only for the individual worker, but in terms of the impact it must have on the morale of staff. For this reason, because of the impact it will have on the future of the child protection service, Part 8 Reviews should consider the needs of staff for counselling and support arising from the incidents leading to the Review, and the extent to which those needs have been addressed.

To publish an annual report about local child protection matters

Working Together (1991) requires that

> ... each ACPC should reappraise annually the work which has been done locally to protect children from harm in its area and plan for the year ahead. The annual report of the ACPC, which should be made by the ACPC to the head of each agency, should underline that the accountability for the work of the ACPC rests with its constituent members. (paragraph 2.21)

In addition, the report should be sent to the Social Services Inspectorate (who in turn will arrange for copies to be forwarded to other government bodies), the Regional Health Authority, and local Joint Commissioning Councils (JCC). The report should be structured along lines provided in Appendix 8 of *Working Together* (1991) and should be produced by the end of July each year. The format for the Annual Report is:

Section I: Prevention
Section II: Protection
Section III: Policy and Procedures
Section IV: Training

Each section has further details of material to be included.

The most substantial overview analysis of ACPC Annual Reports was that undertaken by Armstrong (1994) as a discussion report for the ACPC National Conference on 8 March 1994. That study examined 107 Annual Reports completed in respect of the period April 1992 to April 1993. The reports were very varied, both in style and content almost to the extent of making it impossible to make comparisons. Armstrong considered this diversity to reflect the changing nature of Area Child Protection Committees. A number of the reports were over 60 pages in length; many were under ten pages. Unfortunately, the brevity of some documents was not achieved by a tight, focused organisation, but rather by leaving out fundamental material. Some were presented to a commercial standard; others were very short of this standard, and appeared as an unedited collection of various components, in different typefaces and without page numbering (a factor which limits their usefulness). Armstrong looked at the arrangement of the contents of the reports and suggested they fell into five categories:

- 'The view from the bridge' (the work of one person)
- The centralised report (integrating material from agencies into a single style and format)
- The mix (centralised section(s) plus direct contributions from agencies)
- The muddle (guidance ignored; information missing)
- The mosaic (ACPC reports plus district reports).

Armstrong considers that the diversity of content and style of ACPC Annual Reports derives from a lack of clarity about their purpose, and specifically about who the audience is meant to be. She extrapolates four different groups that could be seen from the reports as target audiences:

1   ACPC member agencies (some of the reports designed as a basis for ACPC development, others to inform members of ACPC progress).
2   Department of Health (in Wales, the Welsh Office).

3   Those with a responsibility for children (local children's services).
4   The general public.

It would appear however, that these reports are intended by guidance to be targeted at the first group, ACPC members, for both purposes outlined above. The requirement to provide copies for the Department of Health and Welsh Office is not meant to indicate that the report is for that purpose (and indeed Armstrong appears to indicate that a lesser standard applies when agencies see the drafting of the report as simply for the purpose of fulfilling requirements under guidance). The guidance (*Working Together* 1991: paragraph 2.22) appears clear that extracts from the Annual Report may be used in the compilation of information for the public, which suggests therefore that this should not be its primary target.

Some of the issues to emerge for Armstrong (1994) from her analysis of the Reports are the various partnerships (between agencies, with families, with children), the funding of ACPC activity, and the operation of ACPCs, (addressing the roles of the police, health agencies and social services).

This chapter has explored the operation of Area Child Protection Committees, a vital link in England and Wales in the transmission of child protection policy from government to practitioner. I have described briefly what they are and their composition, but the bulk of the chapter has been devoted to a consideration of the eight functions of ACPCs described in *Working Together* (1991). Not only are they links between government and practitioner, however; they are also a forum where people from different professional disciplines come together to manage the child protection services, thus providing an interagency context for practitioners from different disciplines to jointly intervene in situations where children need to be protected. They operate therefore as a stage upon which many of the conflicts between different professional perspectives are addressed, and hopefully resolved. The next chapter explores issues in the management of child protection services from the perspectives of the various agencies and disciplines involved.

5 The professional/agency context of child protection

This chapter looks at child protection in England and Wales from the perspective of the different agencies involved. It does not address practice as that has already been well covered. Instead, in keeping with the emphasis in this book, I intend to address child protection issues from a management perspective. The agencies that will be considered are social services, police and crown prosecution service, health (health visitors, community child health doctor, child psychiatrist and general practitioner) and education. In the section on health I also consider briefly the case for the inclusion of adult psychiatry in child protection. Each section will look at:

a)   The main responsibilities of the agency/profession
b)   The main responsibilities of the agency in relation to child protection
c)   The child protection role(s) of the senior agency managers (that is, those likely to be on Area Child Protection Committees)
d)   Issues and dilemmas in child protection for that agency.

Social services

Social services role (general)

Since the reorganisation of services in accordance with the recommendations of Seebohm (1968), social services have had very broad responsibilities for a wide range of client groups. In the period immediately following the reorganisation, it appeared that given the nature of statutory responsibilities in relation to children and young people, elderly persons, people with disabilities and people with a mental disorder, there were indeed very few people left in the community for whom social services might not potentially have some responsibility, should their circumstances warrant it (basically at that time such a group would have consisted of fit and healthy adults between the ages if 18 and 65 who did not have children). This is clearly not to imply that all, or even most, of these people receive a service from social services. Two decades of increasingly tight fiscal control on public expenditure have meant that services have become increasingly focused on those in greatest need, arguably ignoring those who may have considerable needs not sufficient to attract the necessary services.

In the context of children's services, conflict between doing more and doing less manifested itself in the Children Act 1989 provisions regarding children in need. The intention of the Act in defining a 'child in need' was to provide a means to target limited resources at those children who are most in need, by providing criteria upon which to base the allocation of resources. Under section 17(10) of the Act, a child is taken to be in need if,

> a) he is unlikely to achieve or maintain, or to have the opportunity of achieving or maintaining, a reasonable standard of health or development without the provision for him of services by a local authority under this Part;
> b) his health or development is likely to be significantly impaired, or further impaired, without the provision for him of such services; or
> c) he is disabled.

The definitions of terms accompanying this indicated that development is intended to be construed broadly to include intellectual, emotional, social or behavioural development and 'health' refers to both physical and mental health.

I have argued elsewhere (Sanders 1993) that the Act's concept of a child in need is both restrictive and expansive: It is restrictive in the sense that the definition (while fairly vague and open to interpretation) is intended to specify a group of children who are *entitled* to help from local authority social services departments. This replaces the fairly discretionary application of the previous principle for allocation of resources to support families, that of avoiding the need for children to come into care. The concept is expansive, however, in that at both the individual level and at the level of services for all children who are in need within a particular authority's area, there is a range of specified duties in relation to those children that was not there before the Act.

The second component of the 'in need' definition refers to children who might be in need of protection, and the Act therefore clearly signals the principle that children at risk of abuse should be regarded as children in need, and all the services the authority provides for children in need should be available to them. In conjunction with other principles of the Act it signals the intent that work with abusing families should, where possible, be on a voluntary basis, utilising principles of working in partnership with parents, except where this will expose the child to increased risk. Paragraphs 2.29 of Volume 2 of the Children Act Regulation and Guidance series (DoH 1991b) and the more recent publication *The Challenge of Partnership in Child Protection: Practice Guide* (DoH/SSI 1995) address this issue.

The social services role in child protection

The role of social services in child protection is described in *Working Together* (1991, paragraphs 4.2–4.7). Whilst other agencies may or may not be involved in a child protection case, there are very few situations where social services will not be involved. The social services therefore is likely to be involved at every stage in the process as described in *Working Together* (1991), paragraph 5.10.

(i) referral and recognition   Although referrals may originate from a wide variety of sources, they end up at a common point, the local social services department. The police and/or the NSPCC may be intermediaries along the process of referral, or in some cases, the NSPCC may be the agency undertaking the investigation, by arrangement with the local authority.

(ii) immediate protection and planning the investigation   Where there is an immediate risk of harm to the child the social services must consider the necessity to take steps to protect the child. They may arrange for the child to be removed under voluntary arrangements, to persuade the person causing the risk to the child to leave voluntarily, or perhaps to secure an Emergency Protection Order which lasts for eight days and which can either authorise the child to be removed, or, where the child is already in a safe place (for example, a hospital), the detention of the child in that place. Whether or not such action is necessary, the social services will need to plan how to undertake the investigation. This will take the form of a strategy discussion (which does not have to be a meeting), between the police and the social services. Local procedures will advise on the circumstances calling for a strategy discussion and joint investigations (see below).

(iii) investigation and initial assessment   The responsibility to undertake investigations is placed on the local authority by section 47 of the Children Act 1989:

> Where a local authority –
>> (a)   are informed that a child who lives, or is found, in their area –

(i)   is the subject of an emergency protection order; or

(ii)   is in police protection; or

(b)   have reasonable cause to suspect that a child who lives, or is found, in their area is suffering, or is likely to suffer significant harm,

the authority shall make, or cause to be made, such enquiries as they consider necessary to enable them to decide whether they should take any action to safeguard or promote the child's welfare.

One decision to be made by the strategy discussion/meeting is how far the investigation should be undertaken jointly between the police and social services. Some situations may not require joint investigation, after the initial police/social services consultation. An example might be abuse of a child by a stranger (although *Working Together* (1991: paragraph 5.23) suggests that such cases should be treated the same as intrafamilial abuse). Extrafamilial abuse is more likely to be pursued by the police. On the other hand, there are other examples, where, after the initial consultation between police and social services, the investigation will be undertaken solely by the social services, without the police playing a role. This is most likely for example where emotional abuse, not combined with other forms of abuse, is the source of the concern. In the practice of

... joint interviewing on a selective basis only ... differences can lie in the type of abuse which is included, the extent to which investigators (whether police or social workers) specialise in child protection work, the proportion and type of case subject to joint procedures, and the point at which both the police and social workers cease to be involved in the case. (Brown and Fuller 1991: 233)

(iv)   child protection conference and decision making about the need for registration   Social services have a lead role in the organisation of child protection conferences. The conference is the major forum for interagency sharing of information and concerns. It is also the forum for the consideration of risk(s) – often using a structured risk analysis format – and for making child protection plans. There is considerable potential for lack of clarity about the decision-making functions of the child protection conference, as it is sometimes mistakenly believed to be a forum for establishing whether or not abuse has taken place (a matter for the courts), deciding on whether or not care proceedings should be initiated (that is for social services to decide) or whether a prosecution should be sought (a matter for the police in consultation with the Crown Prosecution Service). Of course, those latter agency decisions are influenced by views expressed at conferences, but the decisions remain formally with the agencies and not the child protection conference. The only decision the conference makes is whether or not to add

the name of the child(ren) to the child protection register. The keyworker will normally be the social services department social worker (although it could also be the NSPCC worker). In the past it was common practice for workers other than the social worker to be named as the key worker, usually on the basis of having more extensive contact with the family. This practice is discouraged, as being based on an unclear conception of the essentially coordinating role of the key worker. In recent years, concerns have been expressed at the high number of unallocated child protection cases. Part of the social worker's role would also be to prepare children and parents for participation in the child protection conference, a practice which has become much more common in the last decade.

(v) comprehensive assessment and planning Where the child's name is added to the register, there should be a comprehensive assessment of the child's and family's situation. It will need to be undertaken in accordance with the Department of Health's guide to comprehensive assessments, the 'Orange Book', and will need to consider who is to undertake the assessment, where it will be undertaken, during what timescale, how it should be recorded and the means to involve the family in the assessment (DoH 1988). Although consideration is given as to who should undertake the assessment, it almost invariably falls to the social worker to arrange (and in fact, the guide is subtitled *A Guide for Social Workers Undertaking a Comprehensive Assessment*). The assessment should be multi-agency in that it includes contributions from all relevant agencies. It should involve the child's parents and/or carers so that it is something that is done with them, not to them.

Assessment is clearly vital in child protection. We have already described how inspections by the Social Services Inspectorate had highlighted their absence and Colton et al. (1996) noticed their absence was among the concerns expressed in Part 8 Reviews. A major difficulty is the time taken to undertake them. Before the Orange Book appeared, the SSI (1986) considered that the problem was not that insufficient time was given to the work of assessment, but that there was the need for a more structured and systematic approach. This appears to skirt the issue, especially in view of the size of a full comprehensive assessment (167 questions laid out over 35 pages). The DoH's approach is that it is not a question of more time being allocated for assessment, but that existing time spent with families could profitably be used going through the process. Pragmatically, agencies have tried to cope with these conflicting demands on them by rationing the use of comprehensive assessments in some ways that appears to make sense (for example, by having different levels of assessments for different levels and kinds of risks).

(vi) implementation, review and, where appropriate, de-registration   The main vehicle adopted for the implementation and review of child protection plans are the multi-agency core groups. Core groups appear in *Working Together* (1991) almost as an oversight or an afterthought. It is possible that this is because they were a fairly recent development at the time *Working Together* (1991) was produced. They are described in paragraph 6.26 (though not labelled 'core group' as such) as 'a group led by the key worker (which) has been identified to work with the family'. Details of the core group should be included on the child protection register details (*Working Together*, 1991: Appendix 4). Core groups are also referred to in the standards set out in *Inspecting for Quality: Evaluating Performance in Child Protection*, (SSI/DoH 1993), for example in relation to decisions at case conferences (standard 5), implementing child protection plans (standard 8) and reviewing child protection plans (standard 9). Colton et al. (1996), in looking at Part 8 Reviews, found the use of core groups in only half the cases where children's names had been added to the child protection register. Horwarth and Calder (1997) in their national study of core groups found that 24 per cent of respondents had neither policy, procedures nor practice guidance relating to core groups.

The social services role in Area Child Protection Committees

Staff from social services play three main roles in child protection: the ACPC chair, the Child Protection Coordinator (or equivalent senior child protection manager) and the Child Protection Trainer. For social services staff, because of the lead responsibility of that agency for child protection, there is a need to be particularly clear on the distinction between that part of their role which is on behalf of social services and that part which is more of an interagency role on behalf of the entire ACPC.

The ACPC chair   The main role of the chair, obviously enough, will be to chair meetings of the Area Child Protection Committee, which usually meet between four and six times per year, but may meet more or less frequently. He or she will liaise closely with the child protection coordinator over the preparation of the agenda for meetings. In fact, they are the individual likely to put most issues on the agenda for consideration. The responsibility for the appointment of the chair and the secretariat for the ACPC rests with the social services department. Although it is not expressly required that the chair is from that department, this is usually the case. The social services can however appoint a senior person from one of the other agencies, or even an independent person with the requisite experience to be chair. This is very rare. Jackson et al. (1994) found that of the eight Welsh ACPCs, only one had a chair that was not from the social services department (from Health), and that was for a temporary period because of worrying circumstances concerning recent allegations of abuse in children's homes. The chair should ordinarily be a very senior manager of social services, at least assistant director (AD). In fact, because of the hierarchical nature of most social services department, the AD is usually the highest level of responsibility exclusively for children and family services, and therefore most likely to be ACPC chair, although it is not unknown for the ACPC to be chaired by the social services director (who has a broader remit of responsibility for the entire range of social services provisions, not just children). Nevertheless, even for the AD, unlike the child protection coordinator, child protection is only one of many responsibilities that he or she will have within the broader range of child welfare.

Having the chair exclusively occupied by social services can cause difficulties. Stevenson (1989) points out that the Department of Health failed to follow the suggestion in the Cleveland Report that 'One way of ensuring a greater commitment would be for the chairmanship to rotate on a biennial basis between senior staff of the agencies involved reporting direct to each authority' (Butler-Sloss 1988: 54; cited in Stevenson 1989: 180). She questions why the chair has to come from one of the member agencies at all, and suggests an independent chair would ensure that the chair was not from an agency with vested interests if conflicts should arise. In our findings (Jackson et al. 1994; Sanders et al. 1997), it was noted that there was an imbalance in the sense of ownership by ACPC members which could possibly have been offset by a process of rotating the chair. We also noted that for district committees there seems to be much more willingness to allow other agencies to assume the Chair role. We conclude therefore that it is because of the external constraint of guidance rather than internal politics that ACPCs almost invariably have social services chairs, and that if they were given a free hand, there might be a more shared approach to chairing ACPCs. It is surely important to avoid child protection coming to be seen as an exclusively social services responsibility.

The Child Protection Coordinator   The Child Protection Coordinator (or equivalent title) will be the only person on the ACPC whose entire role is devoted to the management of child protection services. Curiously, there is very little written about the role which is very much at the centre of, and vital to, the success of local interagency coordination of child protection services. This may be the reason why although virtually every social services department has someone in the role, they are frequently given different titles. In meeting with child protection coordinators during the work on the Welsh Office Review (Jackson et al. 1994), there was variation in the degree of role clarity encountered. In some cases the clarity allowed for very forward thinking on the interagency development of local child protection services; in other cases, the inherent role conflict and confusion caused impediments to such work. Sometimes this role confusion is because of internal difficulties and transitions, sometimes because of emerging awareness of how different the role one carries is from the 'same' role in other agencies. The coordinators are likely to have formal and informal contact, either individually or in groups, with coordinators from other areas to derive support for a role that is unique within the agency and the ACPC.

It was in response to a question put to all ACPC members about whether they were the right person (role) to represent their agency on the ACPC that issues of role confusion and the need for role clarity emerged. Also, it was rare, but did occur, that the child protection coordinator was also the individual who chaired child protection conferences. Although this has changed with the introduction of independent chairs, it highlighted the diversity at the time of the role. In some agencies, child protection managers carry line-management responsibility for child protection work; in others they do not. *Working Together* (1991) says virtually nothing about the role, although the role of nearly every other professional involved in child protection is given some consideration. Hallett and Birchall (1992) in their literature review of coordination and child protection emphasise practitioner collaboration rather than managerial aspects, and say very little about the role of the child protection coordinator. Likewise, Hallett (1995) in her chapter on 'The machinery of interagency collaboration in child protection' says nothing about the role, although she does refer to the issue of role clarity in inter-agency collaboration (for practitioners). As indicated, the role is not totally on behalf of the ACPC, and the postholder may need to be clear about the proportion of their time spent on ACPC business and that on social services child protection matters (for example, the development of in-house child protection procedures apart from the interagency procedures, and contributions to training for social services staff).

It has been a very difficult decade for child protection coordinators. One of the difficulties that arose in relation to why ACPCs have made so little progress on treatment and prevention is that the ground-rules keep changing with regard to investigation. As pointed out by Hallett and Birchall (1992), 'One of the key tasks of Area Child Protection Committees has been to produce local procedural guidance which structures professional discretion and decision making ...' (1992: 49). Child protection coordinators are at the centre of this process. The local interagency procedures needed to be changed in 1988 in connection with the Cleveland Report (Butler-Sloss 1988) and the *Working Together* guidance (1988) emerging from that, again in 1991 following the implementation of the Children Act 1989 and the reissue of *Working Together* (1991). In the latter case, some of the ACPCs we encountered in the 1994 Review were only just completing their revision of the local procedures that year. The *Memorandum of Good Practice* (Home Office and DoH 1992) required considerable revision of the procedures although perhaps not as extensively as previously. At the current time, with the Department of Health announcing in 1996 that *Working Together* (1991) will be revised to take into consideration the messages from research (DoH 1995a), and the appearance of the most recent consultation document (DoH 1998), the deadline for which was 30 June 1998, child protection coordinators can look forward to yet another period of intensive work to revise local procedures. In the past it has taken about two years to produce revisions to government guidance on child protection. To this ever-changing policy context, add the changes brought about by local government reorganisation, the reforms in health and education, and it is remarkable that child protection coordinators and the ACPCs they work with are able to achieve so much.

Virtually all of the work of the Area Child Protection Committee lands on the desk of the child protection coordinator. He or she is the person who has operational responsibility for progressing the work of the ACPC and thus is very involved in setting the agendas for issues discussed, and in ensuring that decisions are acted upon. Consequently, he or she needs to keep informed of the views of members in the agencies; methods used to do this vary. There will ordinarily be regular liaison with the Chair over issues coming up in the ACPC, and perhaps debriefings on post-meeting business. Some may have a policy of ensuring that they are available to practitioners, from whichever agency, when needed ('open door'). Others may have involvement in the more localised forums for consideration of child protection (for example District Child Protection Committee meetings and Review Committees), described earlier. Involvement in training (in-house and interagency) and in local in-house children's services management fora are other ways of keeping informed.

The Child Protection Trainer   Training issues have been addressed under the functions of the Area Child Protection Committee, and so will not be considered in depth here. As previously indicated, the other work that the child protection trainer does is important. They may be exclusively a child protection trainer, a child welfare trainer, or a social services trainer, with a broad remit for staff development and training across all client groups. Hendry (1995) describes the role as one of emerging specialism; however, this trend has not been uniform, and local government reorganisation has in some cases reversed this. Hendry also points out that a social services-employed trainer is not the only way of doing things (and does bring with it certain difficulties of professional loyalties and perspective), and she describes two additional models that agencies are currently using. In one model, a person is specifically recruited to take on the task of coordinating interagency training (not the social services trainer). In the other, the ACPCs Training subcommittee takes on the role of developing interagency training initiatives, and each project is headed by an ad hoc type working group. Myers and Cooper (1996) describe the development of an interagency training pool with 30 members, which they consider to be both innovative and cost-effective. The pool is defined as 'a range of professionals working with children and families who are involved in planning, design and delivery of interagency child protection in addition to their specific agency role' (Myers and Cooper 1996: 290). They consider the importance of the scheme being supported by the ACPC to establish 'ownership', and of it coming under the Training subcommittee. Where the trainer is a social services employee, there is potential for role confusion similar to that described for child protection coordinators: 'In training, more perhaps than in other field within child protection, there are difficulties in drawing a line between the Social Services Department and the ACPC' (Armstrong 1994: 34).

Some social services child protection issues and dilemmas

In terms of their lead role, all of the issues for all of the agencies become issues for the social services representatives on Area Child Protection Committees. However, there are child protection issues which by their nature have implications for social services, which we consider briefly here. Several of these are the abuse of children in residential and foster care and the development of joint budgets for child protection.

Abuse of children in substitute care   The abuse of children in substitute care has been a concern for some considerable period of time. Indeed, if one revisits the material on the historical context of child protection, it would appear that early child protection concerns focused on the protection of children who were living with people other than their biological parent. At least one non-parent featured in the cases of Mary Ellen Wilson, Denis O'Neil and Maria Colwell.

Working Together (1991 paragraphs 5.20.4–7) provides guidance on the abuse of children by staff in residential settings: children and staff should be enabled to report their concerns; referrals for such abuse should be dealt with as any other referrals for abuse; the investigation should include an independent element, and if abuse is pervasive within the culture of the establishment(s) then it may be necessary to invoke some degree of secrecy in planning the investigation. Berridge and Brodie (1996) review the recent history of concerns and inquiries in residential child care in the UK and consider that if it is not actually in crisis, then it is at least certainly a crisis of confidence. They identify common themes in the management, policy and practice of residential care within three particular inquiries: Pindown (Staffordshire), Ty Mawr (Gwent) and the Frank Beck case (Leicestershire). At the time of writing, one of the largest UK inquiries is about to report in relation to abuse of a large number of children at a number of establishments by a large number of individuals taking place over years in North Wales. It looks likely to set the record for being the most expensive child abuse inquiry to date, with an estimated projected cost of around £10 million.

Recommendations that have been arising during the inquiry include:

- A guardian *ad litem* for every looked-after child
- An independent visitor scheme
- Independent oversight of local authority decision making for individual children
- Three-year training for social work and special accreditation to work with children
- Better information sharing between social services and police (by protocol).

Bloom (1992) in the US looks at three concurrent actions needing to be taken: a) protecting the child-victim and other children, (b) supporting the alleged perpetrator and all other staff members, and (c) maintaining the reputation and integrity of the agency. Suggestions are made on how to achieve these.

Guidance on foster care is contained in *Working Together*, paragraphs 5.19.2–4. Here the guidance is essentially that local authorities are required to terminate unsatisfactory placements which could lead to the removal of the child forthwith, that the section 47 duty to investigate applies equally to foster-care children as it does to any other children in the community, that this applies to children placed by a voluntary organisation (an exceedingly rare occurrence nowadays), and that the voluntary organisations procedures should reflect how such allegations should be handled. A considerable body of literature has also developed around the abuse of children in foster care and how such allegations should be addressed. Carbino (1991, 1992) in the US considers that it is in the nature of family foster care that allegations of abuse and/or neglect in foster homes will arise, and notes that most agency policies and procedures reflect little awareness or understanding of the issue. Sanders and McAllen (1995), Thomas (1995), Nixon and Hicks (1987) and Nixon et al. (1986) have all noted the vulnerability of foster carers to allegations of abuse. Verity and Nixon (1995) and Nixon and Verity (1996) have undertaken an international survey of foster carers and agency workers into allegations against foster carers. Of 519 returns, 177 foster carers had experienced an allegation. Dobson (1996) has also looked at social work attitudes to allegations against foster carers. Whilst it is clear that many foster carers do abuse children in their care (and there are various explanations for this), it is also true that foster carers are likely to have a very high proportion of untrue allegations made against them as well. Finally, it would be fair to say that insufficient consideration has been given to the impact of both fostering, and of allegations against the foster parents, on the foster carer's own children.

Lack of an ACPC budget   Since the advent of the NHS Reforms, with the creation of internal markets, public bodies have become even more cost-conscious than they already were. Those changes were introduced under the ideological aegis of introducing the market into public services, with the intention of reducing public expenditure (which, according to Flynn (1997), did not succeed as public expenditure continued at 40 per cent of GDP). As a result, ACPC member-agencies have become even more conscious of costs associated with all activities. The reason this is described here as a social services issue (though in reality more of an ACPC issue), is because without a budget, social services have traditionally attempted to subsume ACPC activities into their own budgets. This of necessity has meant that they could not do as much proactive planning as they might have wished had there been a larger budget to which agencies contributed. It also means that they are perhaps more eager than others to secure a budget to which all parties contribute.

One way the heightened concern with finances became clear was in the Review undertaken by Jackson et al. (1994) – in order to study levels of delegated authority, they asked ACPC members what kinds of decisions they would be able to take on their own, and commit their agencies to, and what kinds of decisions they would feel compelled to refer back to their agencies. The most frequent response was that all ACPC decisions that would involve committing agencies to expenditure would need to be referred back to the agency.

They also looked specifically at the issue of financial arrangements for Area Child Protection Committee activities. *Working Together* indicates that

> It will be the duty of the agencies represented on an ACPC to reach agreements on the budget the ACPC requires to accomplish the tasks which have been identified, and in order to support the work of the secretariat. Agencies should allocate funds to the ACPC in accordance with agreed arrangements at the beginning of each financial year so that the ACPC has an annual budget. (1991: paragraph 2.16)

It should be clear that this budget is limited solely to ACPC activities and is not meant to encompass the entire cost of providing child protection services within the ACPC area. In practice however, it can be very difficult to draw the line between what is an individual agency's child protection responsibility, and what services come under the interagency umbrella of child protection. At least one agency in Wales considered it useful to attempt to undertake such an audit of all expenditure and services that could broadly be classified as child protection (including, for example, prevention and treatment services).

Jackson et al. (1994) found very large variations and inconsistencies between and within ACPCs concerning arrangements for funding. Only three of the eight ACPCs were able to supply written information about budgets and of the three, one had no budget, one had a budget of £3,000 and the third had a budget of £62,000. They found it difficult to understand how such large variations could be explained. These inconsistencies were also confirmed in interviews. Police contributions to an ACPC budget were particularly difficult to understand. In one ACPC, the police explained that the reason they could not contribute to a joint budget was because they are not able to contribute to budgets over which they have no control. In another ACPC however, a different police force made a contribution. In other areas distinctions were made between contributions in services and facilities as opposed to cash contributions (for example, furnishing video suites, supplying interviewing equipment). In this respect, police were seen as substantial contributors.

Securing budgets is not easy and in some cases it may not be agreed on the first go; several attempts may be necessary. Resistance may occur because of a lack of clarity about funding considerations – it is absolutely vital for these to be addressed. Matters such as how the funds would be raised, the basis for the relative contributions from agencies, how the funds would be used, who would authorise expenditure and how expenditure would be monitored are all issues that need to be considered in the development of an ACPC budget. Unless for example, all are agreed about what constitutes 'fair shares', there may be difficulty actually collecting the funds even if a budget is agreed in principle. Furthermore, tensions can be created in what might otherwise be reasonable interagency working relationships if the financial issues cannot be resolved. In one area, there was a difficulty supplying copies of the local procedures handbooks to general practitioners: no funding could be secured from the Family Health Services Authority (FHSA), because it was considered that they do not employ general practitioners. As a result, general practitioners were written to, and asked if they wished to buy a handbook. One can anticipate the coolness, and also the variation in the response. In the end, a pragmatic solution was found to ensure that all GPs' surgeries had a copy of the local procedures handbook. In their present form, arrangements for securing a joint budget are full of hazards, and in many areas simply do not work, have not been able to be developed, or just don't exist. However, these difficulties will not go away unless they are tackled in a different manner. One might argue that in the present financial climate joint financing problems are going to get worse rather than better.

On a more positive note, it might be useful to reflect on what ACPCs could do if they have a proper budget. Clearly there would be benefits, depending upon how the funds were used, in developing the role of the secretariat, financing small research projects, and contributing to the development of joint training on a more equal basis than perhaps has been the case in the past. However, proper funding could probably only be achieved if there were more commitment from central government to finance it directly through providing 'ring-fenced' money. This certainly would have been the preferred solution up until recently. In the context of the current refocusing debates however, it seems likely that new policies will need to be developed in advance of deciding how to most effectively fund the child protection component of child welfare.

Police and Crown Prosecution Service

The Police

The role of the police (general)

The primary functions of the police are to protect the community and to bring offenders to justice. The retributive component of their role is undertaken in conjunction with the Crown Prosecution Service. The current focus of policing has been a continual process of refinement from a much broader role which originally included responsibilities for traffic control, employment regulation, weights and measures, street lighting (Thomas 1994), most of which are now functions undertaken by local authorities.

In recent years, the police have become much more involved in social issues traditionally addressed by the caring professions. We see an increasing integration of 'caring' functions into the 'care and control' role. Stephens (1994) highlights the emergence of a policing role in relation to specific groups of people, for example, women who are victims of assault, cases of child sexual abuse, mentally ill persons and juvenile offenders. In their consideration of the joint working of police and social workers in child sexual abuse, Conroy et al. (1990) have observed that the simplistic equation of police as controllers and social workers as carers no longer portrays the complexity of the work; the police have had to become more aware of welfare considerations and social workers to accept the need for control.

The police role in child protection

Whilst the overriding consideration of the police will be the welfare of the child, the focus of police involvement in child protection will be to ascertain whether or not a criminal offence has been committed, to establish which person or persons is responsible, and to gather evidence in the most effective manner so as to determine whether or not a conviction should be sought, and if so to maximise the likelihood of obtaining a conviction. As pointed out in *Working Together* (1991), 'Failure to conduct child abuse investigations in the most effective manner may mean that the best possible protection cannot be provided for a child victim' (paragraph 4.12).

The police are likely to have an eye towards possible civil proceedings involving the child, where they may be called to give evidence as well as possible criminal prosecutions, and the information they gather (either individually, or jointly with social services) will be relevant for both. For our purposes we will consider here the police role primarily from the standpoint of possible civil proceedings, and address issues to do more specifically with the criminal prosecution when we consider the role of the Crown Prosecution Service. The primacy of the police role in child protection as it has emerged over the last 20 years, is based on their involvement in both civil and criminal proceedings arising out of abuse. It is worth stating here though some of the primary differences between criminal proceedings and civil proceedings, which are described most adequately in *Working Together* (1991):

> The evidential requirement of the criminal courts is proof beyond reasonable doubt that the defendant committed the offence of which he/she stands indicted. The burden of proof rests with the prosecution, i.e. the defendant does not have to prove his innocence. Proceedings for the protection of children under the Children Act take place in the civil courts which work to a lesser standard of proof, that of the balance of probabilities. It is not unusual for the police or the Crown Prosecution Service to decide that criminal proceedings cannot be instigated against a person suspected of child abuse on the grounds that there is insufficient evidence to meet the higher standard of proof and for the civil courts to decide that the child needs protection from the same individual. The criminal courts focus on the behaviour of the *defendant*; the civil courts on the interest of the *child*. (paragraph 4.13, original emphasis)

In the early stages of child protection (the 1970s), the relationship between the police and other agencies involved in child protection was, to put it mildly, strained. This was true both in terms of their participation in case conferences and their involvement in Area Review Committees (the predecessors of ACPCs). There was a polarity between the police on the one hand, and social services and health on the other, which was reflected in the extreme events in

Cleveland a decade later. This dichotomy can be constructed as a polarity between therapeutic/treatment objectives and investigative/legal objectives. The debate on these objectives continues to the present time, especially over the extent to which they are in conflict or whether they can each be equally pursued vigorously without detriment to the other. The following two extracts indicate the two ends of the dichotomy. Government guidance would appear to indicate that welfare and justice objectives are not in conflict: 'The interests of justice and the interests of the child are not alternatives. The children have a right to justice and their evidence is essential if society is to protect their interests and deal effectively with those who would harm them' (Home Office and DoH 1992: Foreword).

Hallett and Birchall however observe, '... in general, the police may feel they have little need of the other services in relation to their crime control functions and the therapeutic professionals have mixed views about the utility of police investigations' (1992: 139). Waterhouse and Carnie (1991) found competing professional objectives (that is, criminal investigation or assessment of child protection risk) to be one of five factors which created the kinds of difficulties in interagency communication they found in 25 per cent of 51 cases of intrafamilial child sexual abuse. Looking at professional attitudes towards child sexual abuse in Canada, Trute et al. (1992) found:

> Greatest difference in attitude between service sectors was tied to emphasis placed on treatment versus punishment as a primary aspect of professional intervention. Significant differences were found between child welfare and police, the two service sectors most needing a coordinated approach during the 'investigative phase' of professional intervention. (Trute et al. 1992: 359)

These ideological tensions were manifested in practice tensions. Parton notes that police complained that 'social services departments (and indirectly paediatricians) ... (were) keeping cases of "battered children" from the attention of the police' (1985: 108). Hebenton and Thomas (1992) provide further examples of tensions between police and other professions, most notably social workers, around this time. One of these was fear of police domination of conferences. Guidance issued by the DHSS (1976) advised that senior police representatives should be invited to both case conferences and Area Review Committees. It could be argued that this document, which came only several years after the Colwell Inquiry, was pivotal in establishing the nature of child protection as a forensic as well as a therapeutic undertaking, leading to a much greater emphasis on the investigation of abuse.

This uneasy alliance between police and other professionals continued until 1987, when a number of occurrences resulted in contrasting effects on the nature of cooperation between police and other agencies. One was the incidents in Cleveland, which highlighted and exacerbated tensions in police relations with other agencies. One of the recommendations to come out of the Cleveland Inquiry to facilitate potentially difficult relationships between the police and social workers, was the establishment of Special Assessment Teams so that

> ... the completion of a medical examination, a social work assessment, and appropriate inquiries by the police, carried out in a planned and co-ordinated way, should allow the Specialist Assessment Team to present their joint assessment and conclusions to the referring agency or a case conference. (Butler-Sloss 1988: 249)

Not many authorities took up this suggestion but most attempted to develop new ways of working together in child sexual abuse.

The other event, with a contrasting effect, was the Bexley 'Experiment' – a scheme for the joint investigation of sexual abuse by police and social workers (Metropolitan Police and London Borough of Bexley 1987). The scheme was considered to be so successful that by 1990, joint investigation (of sexual abuse) was considered to be the norm around the country.

Another landmark in the police child protection role was the Home Office circular which was very clear about the criteria for success in police involvement in child protection, 'The success of the police intervention ... is not to be measured in terms of the prosecutions which are brought, but of the protection which their actions bring to children at risk' (Home Office 1988). It also recommended that every police force set up joint investigation schemes with the social services, and establish procedures to videotape children's evidence.

The 1990s have been characterised by increasingly smoother working relationships between police and other professionals involved in child abuse and child protection, especially with social workers. The main concerns facing both professions have been issues around the collection of evidence in child abuse cases, especially sexual abuse (see Dennett and Bekerian 1991; Waterhouse and Carnie 1991; Fielding and Conroy 1992; Smith 1992; Kirby 1994; McQuillan 1994; Munns 1994). How should such evidence be collected? How much reliance can, or should be given to children's allegations? How should organised abuse in general, and ritual abuse in particular, be tackled? What approach should be adopted with juvenile sexual abusers? Considerable impetus was given to this trend of closer collaboration, by the publication of the *Memorandum of Good Practice* (Home Office and DoH 1992).

This has raised the question for some of whether the investigation of child abuse should involve social workers at all. There have been suggestions that perhaps the trend of the police having increasingly more involvement, which began in the 1970s and continued during the 1980s and 1990s, should be encouraged to go all the way, so that police take over the role of child protection investigation altogether. This would free social work to return to a therapeutic role in working with victims of abuse, which some would argue is the proper role of social work, not social policing. One of the debates featuring in Gambrill and Stein (1994) is 'Should the Police have Greater Authority in Investigating Cases of Suspected Abuse?' Lindsey and Hawkins (1994) argue that the boundary between neglect and abuse has become blurred, and severe physical abuse, which is a criminal matter, should be left to the police. They say nothing about sexual abuse. McDonald (1994) however argues that the police are already significantly involved, and contends rather that the 'YES' position as put forward by Lindsey and Hawkins is really arguing that the social work role in child protection should be eliminated. He observes in his argument that the police and judiciary are oriented towards the past, whereas issues concerning removal, parental rights, etc. are oriented towards the future.

I have argued elsewhere (Sanders et al. 1996b) that the current emphasis in British child protection policy is skewed in favour of investigation at the expense of both prevention and treatment. The involvement of police in child protection mirrors a process in which, before Colwell, local authority child protection was essentially a therapeutic endeavour; after Colwell, it began to become more of a balanced forensic/therapeutic undertaking, and in recent years, it has become primarily a forensic activity. In order for the two agencies (police and social services) to come together from fairly diverse polarised positions in the 1970s to joint investigations in the 1990s, two things needed to happen. First, considerable attitude change was required on the part of both social workers and police. Second, this attitude change had to be supported by the context within which child protection work is undertaken. In order for police and social workers to develop closer working relationships, social workers have had to become more like police (at least in terms of attitudes underlying child protection work), and police have had to become more like social workers.

We have already referred to the police getting more involved in the protection of vulnerable people in a 'caring' capacity in recent years. At the same time, there is evidence that the social work role was changing in such a way that the use of authority, compulsion, control and coercion featured more prominently. During this period for example, we see the rise of 'permanency planning', a concept imported from the US (see Maluccio et al. 1986). This is an approach to child care planning in which social workers became much more proactive in securing a stable future for a child, often, if need be, achieving it through the means of contested adoptions. Also at this time social workers were increasingly using compulsory interventions (Packman et al. 1986). As pointed out by Cooper (1993) these were more pronounced around the times incorporating major child fatality enquiries, for example, Colwell (DHSS 1974), and Beckford (London Borough of Brent and Brent Health Authority 1985). Before and after Colwell, the numbers of place of safety orders obtained rose from 204 (1972) to 759 (1976). Before and after Beckford and Cleveland (Butler-Sloss 1988), they rose by 42 per cent from 1978 to 1988. Clearly social workers were reading from inquiries that they should be more willing to use compulsory measures to secure a child's protection. This fitted in well with being able to work much more closely with the police.

It is important however not to overstate this increased harmony, and the reader should not believe that everything is rosy in the garden. There have been and continue to be serious difficulties in working relationships between social workers and police based on different objectives, values and training. Thomas (1994) describes some of these difficulties very well in his consideration of the police and social workers working together in child protection. Lardner (1992), who concluded that the degree of honesty and openness in the relationship between social workers and the police was 'suboptimal', found the factors influencing the nature of the relations to be related to management structure and style, timescale, training, communication quality and organisational decision making. Nevertheless, the overall situation is a far cry from the kinds of stresses and strains in the relationship there were in the mid-1970s.

The role of the senior police on Area Child Protection Committees

Of the four main groups on Area Child Protection Committees, (Social Services, Education, Health and Police), the police are likely to be numerically the smallest (and this applies to the District Child Protection Committees). They are likely to have two types of representatives, one from a specialist child protection unit (for example, 'Family Support Unit' or equivalent), where one exists and one from the senior management.

It may be useful to clarify the role of specialist police child protection units at this point. These units highlight the local emphasis provided on joint investigation, by fielding a small group of specially trained police officers to work with social workers (often child protection specialists themselves) on new referrals of abuse. They often have special facilities made available (for example, video interview suites) and ideally are located in buildings which are not conspicuously identifiable as police premises. Lloyd and Burman (1996) provide an overview of how these units have developed in Scotland, but little has been written about their development in England and Wales. They note that whereas in England and Wales the use of joint investigations tends to be restricted to investigation of sexual abuse, in Scotland they are used as well for physical abuse and in some cases are extended to neglect. The roots of specialist units can be traced to the Cleveland Inquiry (Butler-Sloss 1988), the Bexley Experiment (Metropolitan Police and London Borough of Bexley 1987) and a 1988 Home Office circular (in Scotland, Scottish Office Social Work Services Group 1988).

There are a number of ways of focusing police child protection interventions into specialists, and these different means may be reflected in different titles. In some cases they are exclusively concerned with child abuse; in others they may include responsibility for domestic violence (i.e. spouse abuse) or all forms of violence against women (for example, including rape). They do not usually include responsibility for the prosecution of abusers, which is normally passed to the CID.

The police are more likely than other agencies to be represented on more than one ACPC, because the ACPC boundaries tend to be smaller than police force areas, For example, in Wales, at the time of the Review (Jackson et al. 1994), there was only one ACPC that was coterminous with a police region (which brought with it considerable advantages). In one case there was one police region covering three ACPC areas, and in two cases one police region covering two ACPC areas.

This geographical consideration raises difficulty for the police, not so much for the representative from the specialist child protection unit, who usually will only relate to one ACPC, but for the senior manager, who may be required to sit on a number of ACPCs going over very similar material. This raises at least three issues for the police. First, whether the considerable degree of duplication of effort by senior police managers across ACPCs is necessary or avoidable in terms of being cost effective. Second, suggestions may be raised as to whether government guidance should be sufficiently detailed to guide practice, so that ACPCs do not have to work on developing the same or very similar material in different places. Certainly in the context of local government reorganisation, it was of great concern to the police representatives that they may be called upon to sit upon even more ACPCs than previously – a clearly untenable suggestion. Finally, the police have a very strong interest in the procedures developed on different ACPCs being similar. They would not be able to have several different sets of force procedures for each of the ACPCs on which they were represented. That would cause considerable confusion and difficulty for the police practitioner who would be obliged to work in one way in ACPC A, but follow a different and perhaps conflicting set of procedures in ACPC B. As expressed by one ACPC police representative, 'Why are we all sitting around in all the different groups around the country talking about the same things? Not a reflection on ACPCs but a reflection on the Government.'

However, this multiple representation also gives the police a unique insight into how different ACPCs can be, a strong position from which to evaluate strengths and weakness.

Some child protection issues and dilemmas for the police

The issues for police tend to centre around the investigative process and the way child protection services are managed. We have already referred to the discontent concerning duplication, but there are more difficulties concerning relationships with other agencies. Largely, these concerns are around agencies other than social services.

Investigative issues   The police do not appear to have any reservations about the forensic nature of child protection. As stated by one police representative on an Area Child Protection Committee, 'Criminal prosecutions are an important part of the child protection plan, for a number of reasons – punishment of the offender, a statement to the child that he/she is believed.'

Videotaping interviews was considered to be a major asset for interviewing abused children. The removal of the necessity for children's evidence to be corroborated was welcomed. The Criminal Justice Act 1991 was seen as a dramatic and welcome change which changed the whole police approach to child protection. Whilst acknowledging the improvements, concerns were expressed about the fact that even though children can give evidence via live video link that they still have to give it at all and the video is not accepted as evidence on its own. The role of barristers caused concern as well. Concern was expressed that some still cross-examine the children as if they were adults.

The Children Act 1989 was also welcomed as a useful piece of legislation because it promoted liaison between the police and other agencies involved in child protection, gave children a choice and regarded their welfare as paramount, and introduced police protection powers which were considered helpful. Prior to the introduction of the police protection provisions of the Act, police had to contact the emergency duty team if they encountered a child who needed immediate protection.

Management issues   One of the difficulties for police is working with agencies who have such different conceptions of managerial authority, which may lead them to adopt a view that other agencies are not sufficiently able to make decisions, and that other agencies do not have sufficiently clear managerial structures. The inability of other agencies to make decisions was particularly concerning. In some cases this was because in the new de-centralised structures, it was difficult, and time-consuming, simply to locate where the decision-making authority lay. Some concern was expressed about the very different communication styles, compared with the crispness of decision making and the clarity of authority structures found within the police. As expressed by one ACPC police representative:

> In the police we communicate very directly. But other people are much more protracted in their communications; take longer to get to the point. If we have to say something unpleasant, etc., just say it. Whilst we expect that members of the public would not understand our role, we expect a better understanding of our role from other professionals.

A common theme for the police is the role and use of authority both within the ACPC and within its constituent agencies. They would like the ACPC to have more teeth and were particularly concerned about the fragmentation of member agencies brought about by the reforms in Education and Health. Though this is not unique to the police, because of the large size of their establishment, they are particularly sensitive to the need to distinguish between what every police officer needs to know ('standing orders') and what those specialising in work with abused children need to know. For example, all officers need to know about the police protection provisions and about the necessity to check the child protection register (contained in the routine orders) if they encounter a worrying situation. As one manager expressed it, 'If I went to a domestic dispute, and there were children in the house, it's the most important thing I would want to know.' Officers on the beat however do not need to be familiar with the *Memorandum of Good Practice*, which is required by police in the child abuse specialist units. Different levels of training and different written material help to achieve this.

Training of police officers to be able to undertake 'Memorandum' interviews is another issue. In one case the force was finding that despite intensive training they were encountering situations in which there was no one available to do such an interview. A pilot specialist unit proved successful and so the force was switching over to the establishment of a specialist unit for the whole of the area. Specialist units can provide for workers gaining experience and wanting to stay longer. Working against that was the Home Office decision that police officers should rotate through different posts at different time intervals; four years was mentioned in connection with specialist abuse units. There was concern that this would not allow people time to build up, and use, the necessary expertise.

The Crown Prosecution Service (CPS)

The Crown Prosecution Service (whose acronym should not be confused with the Child Protection Service in the US) is at the centre of the criminal justice system in relation to prosecuting abusers. As such, virtually all of the issues relevant to children's experiences in the criminal courts are relevant.

The role of the Crown Prosecution Service (general)

The Crown Prosecution Service was set up in 1986 under the Prosecution of Offences Act 1985, modelled to some extent, but with important differences, on the procurator fiscal system in Scotland. Before 1986, all prosecutions were begun and followed through by the police. With the introduction of the CPS, the system changed so that the police decide whether or not to begin a prosecution but the CPS actually undertakes the prosecution (or they may decide not to proceed). To do this they may either use their own lawyers or brief counsel. Should the police or the CPS decide not to proceed with a prosecution, it is an unusual feature of the British criminal justice system that citizens have a right to bring a private prosecution. As one might anticipate, relationships between the CPS and the police can get tense at times particularly when the CPS decides not to proceed with a prosecution of a case brought by the police.

The CPS is an independent body headed by the Director of Public Prosecutions who in turn is responsible to the Attorney-General. It does not deal with all court prosecutions, only those originating with the police; other bodies (HM Customs and Excise, Inland Revenue, Post Office) also have prosecuting powers. Neither, as indicated, does it bring all cases put before it to court. It applies two filters to decide if cases should go to court or not. The first is an assessment of the nature of the evidence. Only cases where there is a realistic prospect of conviction are brought. The second filter is a consideration of whether prosecution is in the public interest, and criteria are set out to help the CPS determine this. As pointed out by Ashworth (1995) the two are related, and in general the emphasis is on diverting the less serious offences and prosecuting the more serious ones.

This is not the end of the application of discretion in the prosecution, as the CPS also has to consider the most appropriate charge to bring. In most cases the police bring the initial charge, but the CPS has power of review. The police and the CPS have been developing 'Charging Standards' to help produce consistency of practice in this area. It should help to alleviate the difficulties of undercharging and overcharging. The CPS are also involved in any subsequent discussion about how the defendant will plead.

The Role of the Crown Prosecution Service in Child Protection

Working Together (1991: paragraph 4.12) describes the role of the CPS as follows:

... it is the responsibility of the Crown Prosecution Service to review and, where appropriate, conduct all criminal proceedings instigated on behalf of a police service. In some cases advice from the Crown Prosecution Service will be sought prior to proceedings being instituted.

The CPS role is limited to criminal proceedings and does not extend to the possible civil case ('Care Proceedings') which may arise as a consequence of abuse. The merging of interests however, is in the ability of evidence established for the purposes of criminal proceedings to be used in civil proceedings. As described in the *Memorandum of Good Practice*:

> In such circumstances the interview might need to serve objectives [civil] which are additional to, and no less important than, those with which this Memorandum is primary concerned [criminal] ... The rules of evidence which apply to civil proceedings are generally less stringent, and so is the burden of proof. From those perspectives a video recording prepared according to the standards recommended in this Memorandum is likely to be suitable for civil cases. (Home Office and DoH 1992: 3–4)

Therefore, the *Memorandum of Good Practice* requires that every child abuse case should be prepared (in terms of evidence gathering) to the standard required for a criminal prosecution.

Before looking at the CPS role in child protection it is necessary to consider some of the features of the court system in relation to children. A beginning of the reforming process came in the form of the Pigot proposals (Home Office 1989). The experience of children giving evidence in court, especially in cases where they were giving evidence as a victim of sexual abuse, was not a happy one. It would be fair to say that up until the late 1980s and before the implementation of the Criminal Justice Act 1991, the situation for children was very harsh indeed, almost to the point of legitimately being described as 'system abuse'. Tales of barristers being delighted to have succeeded in confusing a frightened and anxious child, in order to undermine the credibility of her testimony, created a sense of outrage in the media and the public.

The situation in the UK was reflected in the US as pointed out by Spencer and Flin:

> In the USA, the increasing number of child abuse cases going through the courts focused public attention on the unsatisfactory way in which the legal system then treated the evidence of children: in particular that it made the experience of giving evidence a frightening and distressing one, and that the law worked on the assumption that children who complain of sexual abuse ought not to be believed. (1993: 11)

In the UK, the position was summarised in the Pigot Report:

In cases which involve children existing committal proceedings are irredeemably flawed. They enable defendants to subject child witnesses to all of the burdens which we have already discussed: delay, appearance in open court, cross-examination in open court, face-to-face confrontation with an alleged perpetrator and repeated and unnecessary worry about matters which may be extremely distressing or even traumatic. (Home Office 1989: paragraph 6.6)

So what did Pigot recommend? Let us consider three of the main issues raised in the report, and the action that followed: competency, method of giving evidence and corroboration.

Competency   First the report recommended that the competency requirement which was applied to potential child witnesses should be dispensed with. It was based on the 'archaic belief that children below a certain age or level of understanding are either too senseless or too morally delinquent to be worth listening to at all' (Home Office 1989: paragraph 5.12). The report also recommended that children under the age of 14 should give evidence unsworn. The Criminal Justice Act 1991 contained the following:

– a child's evidence in criminal proceedings shall be given unsworn
– a deposition of a child's unsworn evidence may be taken for the purposes of criminal proceedings as if that evidence had been given on oath
– ... the power of the court in any criminal proceedings to determine that a particular person is not competent to give evidence shall apply to children of tender years as it applies to other persons.

This appears to be everything Pigot could have wanted, but Spencer and Flin (1993) have reservations about whether the legislation actually achieves its objectives or has simply made things more complicated, thereby creating legal loopholes.

Method of giving evidence: Live evidence or evidence in advance of trial?   The report made radical proposals that children under 14 (or 17 in a sex case) are examined in advance and a videotape of the examination is shown in court in lieu of the child attending court. Children 'ought never to be required to appear in public as witnesses in the Crown Court, whether in open court or protected by screens or closed-circuit television, unless they wish to do so' (Home Office 1989: paragraph 2.26).

A framework was suggested in which the child gave evidence which was videotaped, was cross-examined by defence (in chambers before a judge) after they had seen the tape, the cross-examination being videotaped, and at the trial both videotapes would be submitted as evidence, the first as evidence in chief, the second as cross-examination. The child would however have the right to choose to give evidence in the traditional method.

This framework was too radical for the Home Office, and the government framed alternative proposals in the Bill which became the Criminal Justice Act 1991. The provisions in the Act which came into effect on 1 October 1992 did not eliminate the requirement for the child to attend court, but instead expanded on the already existing arrangements in some circumstances where videotaped evidence was already accepted. The child's evidence could be submitted on videotape provided that the child was available to be cross-examined on the evidence contained within the video. This cross-examination could be by means of a live video link. To soften the blow of not entirely eliminating the need for the child to attend court, several other provisions were also introduced to make it easier for the child. First, the child would no longer be required to be produced for committal proceedings as well as the trial. Of course the child may have to come to court on two occasions in any case if there are both care and criminal proceedings. Second, the provisions eliminated the right of unrepresented defendants to cross-examine the child.

Corroboration   The corroboration of children's evidence requirement was introduced by the Criminal Law Amendment Act 1885 as a means of defusing parliamentary opposition to the introduction of permitting children to give unsworn evidence in cases of sexual intercourse with a girl under the age of 16. Therefore, it provides a necessity for corroboration in two circumstances – where the offence is of a sexual nature, and where the complainant is a child – and these have been separately addressed in recent changes. English law also contained a provision that the unsworn evidence of one child could not corroborate the unsworn evidence of another. This provision allowed for the abuse of multiple children (something we have become more aware of in recent years), and therefore, even in situations where several children were able to give a clear and credible account, a conviction could not be made. In recent times the corroboration requirements have been vigorously opposed as containing an implicit statement that women and children are more prone to telling lies than anyone else. The corroboration requirement was backed up by a duty to warn, in which the judge is required to inform the jury that it is dangerous to convict on certain evidence unless it is corroborated, (and similar provisions applied to magistrates in a self-warning requirement). The duty to corroborate in connection with children's evidence, the duty to warn, and the inability of children to corroborate each other had already been largely abolished by section 34 of the Criminal Justice Act 1988, but many technical issues concerning corroboration remained (see Spencer and Flin 1993: 212–18), including corroboration in sexual matters. The Pigot Committee strongly condemned what was left of the corroboration requirements and the warning duty, and was unequivocal in its recommendations that the residual corroboration requirements in cases concerning sexual offences be abandoned. It considered that the basis of such corroboration, that sexual complainants are more likely to lie than others, was unsound, and that the duty to warn was confusing, 'impenetratable', to members of the jury. In abandoning the corroboration requirements, English law was following precedents set by other English-speaking countries: most US jurisdictions during the 1970s, some Australian jurisdictions during the 1980s, Canada in 1987, New Zealand in 1989.

Although the above changes represented a substantial improvement for children giving evidence in the 1990s compared with the suffering endured by many children in the 1980s and before, there is clearly more that can be done. Courts have become more child-friendly, but they are still an ordeal for the child. It is probably only a matter of time before children are kept out of courts altogether as per the recommendations of the Pigot report, but one wonders whether it will be a long time or a short time. Many of the changes described above were incorporated into the *Memorandum of Good Practice* (Home Office and DoH 1992), along with a considerable body of advice and guidance on how interviews should be undertaken to maximise the likelihood of their being accepted in court.

The role of the Crown Prosecution Service on Area Child Protection Committees

Despite Masson's (1997) assertion that by virtue of being an independent agency the CPS cannot formally participate in ACPCs, they are occasionally represented on ACPCs, and where they are, their contribution is generally valued, especially if there are local difficulties with the judiciary. They are not an agency included in Appendix 5 of *Working Together* (1991) which lists the agencies to be included on ACPCs. They are also sometimes represented on District Child Protection Committees, and this may be either instead of or in addition to their membership of the ACPC. In some cases, rather than being a member, they may on occasion be invited along to join in the consideration of a judicial or forensic issue. Their role is not to inform of reasons for lack of prosecution on individual cases, but to keep ACPCs informed of criteria for prosecution, and to keep themselves informed of ACPC thinking on the role of prosecution in child protection intervention. In another case, also highlighting the avoidance of using the ACPC as a forum to consider individual decisions, an issue arose where a child had been abused, and the CPS, who was a member of the ACPC, came to explain why a decision had been taken that the child should not be counselled prior to giving evidence. As a result, the protocol for arranging such counselling was established. They would probably expect to communicate to ACPCs their approach of getting away from a 'conviction-at-all-costs' approach to one which emphasises the child's welfare in the judicial context. The 'user-friendliness' or 'child-centredness' of the local judicial facilities and procedures will probably feature highly.

Like the police and social services, in order to provide a more sophisticated service, the CPS are getting more involved in specialisation, and the emergence of CPS solicitors for children's cases has become more common. The CPS are likely to be involved in the establishment of the police specialist child protection units, and to take an active interest in the sufficiency of medical evidence in child protection, perhaps through liaison with the police surgeon or with local paediatricians, especially those with particular expertise in child abuse. They would be involved in making an appropriate choice of counsel, where counsel is to be instructed, in making special provisions for vulnerable witnesses, in the 'fast-tracking of cases' as a means of avoiding delay and in ensuring that all members of the Area Child Protection Committee understand that they take child abuse cases very seriously.

Child protection issues and dilemmas for the Crown Prosecution Service

The following issues are likely to be of concern for the Crown Prosecution Service: delay, the application of discretion for the benefit for the child, beginning counselling/therapy, witness care programmes, and allegations made after a long period of time.

Delay   Delay in judicial matters of child abuse is a very long-standing concern. Plotnikoff and Wooflson (1995) note the recommendation over 30 years ago by the Magistrates Association that there should be a system of fast-tracking for cases involving assaults on children. A period of three months' delay which caused so much concern at that time, would nowadays, when delays in cases coming to trial may be as long as a year, be considered an outstanding achievement. Children's experience of time differs from that of adults. What feels like a relatively short period of time for an adult may feel like a very long time for a child, especially if they are experiencing anxiety and stress. This principle was acknowledged in the 'no delay' provisions of the Children Act 1989. Section 1(2) says, 'the court shall have regard to the general principle that any delay in determining the question is likely to prejudice the welfare of the child.' This section applies to 'any proceedings in which any question with respect to the upbringing of the child arises'.

In connection with children giving evidence, there are two ways that the Criminal Justice Act 1991 addresses this. First, where a child witness is involved, it allows the CPS to bypass committal proceedings to move a case directly to Crown Court by issuing a notice of transfer. Second, it places a statutory duty on courts to 'have regard to the desirability of avoiding prejudice to the welfare of any relevant child witness that may be occasioned by unnecessary delay in bringing the case to trial' (schedule 6, paragraph 7). This would include children who are witnesses to certain types of offences as well as children who are victims. In 1994, the CPS issued guidance to staff on child witnesses in the form of a code and explanatory memorandum: 'The CPS fully supports the notion that children are a class of victims and witnesses to whom special care should be paid. Delay should be avoided in all cases involving a child victim or witness' (Crown Prosecution Service 1994a, 1994b).

The application of discretion for the benefit of the child   There are regional variations in the application of principles of videotaping children's evidence. Whilst this is clearly of concern from the point of view of the entire national judicial system, it is also an indication of the necessity to raise standards locally to provide the best possible judicial system for children. The following extract highlights the concern:

> ... the exercise of judicial discretion has operated to undermine the broad purpose of legislative intent because many judges have interpreted the new provisions rigidly and restrictively. The project came across a number of examples of what the Director of Public Prosecutions has condemned as 'justice by geography' ... courts where the legal culture inhibited the use of discretionary procedures on behalf of the children. We were told of areas in which the videotaping of interviews with children had almost stopped because of the response of local judges. In a court outside our study, the CPS reported that the resident judge has instituted a policy concerning the use of videotaped evidence, in which tapes involving children under 10 will probably be accepted but 'he would need a great deal of convincing' to admit the tapes of children over 12. (Plotnikoff and Woolfson 1995: 96–7)

The age of ten is not cited in the legislation as a cut-off of the kind imposed by the judge of question, and it is clearly an idiosyncratic judgment of the kind leading to inconsistency across the country. The authors go on to give other examples of inconsistent and discretionary practice.

Beginning counselling/therapy   The important issue of when to begin treatment for young children in relation to the timing of giving evidence is something the CPS are often asked for their views on. One of the reasons for the no-delay principles involving child witnesses who are victims, described above, is to enable children to begin the process of healing as soon as possible. This kind of therapeutic process may not operate well in the kind of restrictive questioning methodology described in the *Memorandum of Good Practice* (Home Office and DoH 1992). Plotnikoff and Woolfson (1995) describe the belief that therapy cannot begin until after the trial as a 'common though mistaken view'. It is a view held particularly by police and social workers. Two of the dangers of pre-trial therapy are that it may be seen as 'coaching' the child (that is, helping the child to prepare what he or she should say in court), and that it may involve leading questions leading to further disclosures, requiring additional statements to be taken.

However, the guidance to Crown Prosecutors is that the CPS cannot and should not prevent therapy from taking place but to be aware of how it may taint evidence and therefore they need to be informed if it takes place, its nature, and require individuals providing therapy to keep a written record. *Working Together* (1991) is very clear on the question:

> There will be occasions when the child's need for immediate therapy overrides the need for the child to appear as a credible witness in a criminal case. This needs to be weighted up and a decision made on the basis of available knowledge. There should always be discussions with the CPS on the particular needs of the child, and the needs of the child are of prime importance. (paragraph 5.26.9)

Another commonly held, but mistaken, view is that not having a videotaped interview will stop therapy from being allowed.

Witness care programmes   The Crown Prosecution Service is also involved in programmes designed to reduce the child's stress level about appearing, and giving evidence, in court. Witness preparation or witness care programmes help with this and generally entail providing information to the child (in age-appropriate form) about the process and circumstances of the judicial proceedings. This may be through locally developed or national child witness packs, but in either case would need to include information about the local courts. There may be special arrangements for local agencies (for example, the NSPCC) to work with children as witnesses to help them to prepare for court. The process of preparation may involve court familiarisation visits for the child prior to their appearance to give evidence. There may be arrangements for someone who the child knows and trusts to accompany the child to court and to be with them while the evidence is given.

Allegations made after a long period of time   It is generally accepted that one of the factors leading to the emergence of awareness of child sexual abuse in the 1970s was through adult survivors beginning to share with others their experience of abuse suffered as children. This kind of disclosure has in the past presented difficulties for the Crown Prosecution Service because of both its criteria described previously, the sufficiency of the evidence, and whether such prosecutions continued to be in the public interest after such a long time. It was common for there to be considerable variation of practice.

In one area, the CPS may have a policy of not prosecuting after too long a period has passed (in one case this was described to me as being anything over three years); in another it may be the policy to bring prosecutions, regardless of how long ago the offences are alleged to have taken place.

Potential harm of videotaping interviews An issue which does not appear to be a concern for the police or the Crown Prosecution System, is whether or not too many children are being subjected to videotape interview procedures which may possibly be further damaging to the child, may be unreliable in the sense of not revealing the whole story (the process of children disclosing is understood to be one of progressively increasing details shared with others, not a blurting of it all at once) and finally, may be very unlikely to secure a conviction. We must ask the question 'why is such a different approach taken to child sexual abuse in the 1980s than was taken in relation to physical abuse in the 1970s?'. This question needs to be asked because in many ways child sexual abuse has come to drive the child protection system. Many of the procedures developed during the 1980s and 1990s as a response to child sexual abuse have been implemented in such a way as to bring into the same arena all forms of abuse, for example, the variation in practice on whether other forms of abuse (in particular physical abuse) are subjected to *Memorandum* videotaped interviews. Strategy discussions are largely a device to plan the process of evidence gathering, because of the difficulties inherent in establishing guilt of sexual abusers. There was no need to introduce them before in relation to physical abuse. One of the reasons for this emphasis within child protection on sexual abuse is the more sophisticated understanding of sexual abusers that has developed in recent years. We have come to see them as predatory individuals who, manifesting an addiction to children as sexual objects, are very intractable and difficult to work with effectively. The work of Finkelhor (1984) on the preconditions of child sexual abuse (motivation to abuse, overcoming internal inhibitors, overcoming external inhibitors, overcoming child's resistance) in the US, and the work of Ray Wyre (drawing on the work of Ryan and Lane 1991, on the sexual assault cycle) in the UK, have been influential in developing an understanding of perpetrators of sexual abuse that is very different from perpetrators of physical abuse. In comparison with physical abuse, there is a much greater need to protect other children in the community. The knowledge of the large number of children a single abuser may abuse in a lifetime has lent renewed urgency to increasing the effectiveness of prosecution. There are no similar concerns with physical abusers.

Thus it is clear that the use of videotaped interviews was primarily introduced to advance practice in working with sexual abuse, but how far has this been successful? There is evidence to suggest that their use in court is actually quite limited. Plotnikoff and Woolfson (1995: 79) for example, describe a small-scale study in which 36 interviews were videotaped. Nine of those cases proceeded to trial, and the videotapes were used in three. In all three cases the defendants were acquitted. Masson notes the 'large number of investigations being geared to the production of a video of the child even though only a tiny proportion (currently about 1.5 per cent) are likely to lead to a prosecution' (1997: 94).

Finally, there appears to be within the Crown Prosecution Service, as perhaps within the police, little questioning of the fundamentals of the involvement of children in forensically driven processes. The aims of both the police and the Crown Prosecution Service, laudable as they may be, are to refine the system within which the child finds him or herself so that the experience is less damaging to the child, and does not compound the abusive experience they have already had into multiply abusive experiences. This is really very important for the children. On the other hand, there does not appear to be any evidence of questioning towards the premises of prosecution. Are basic assumptions about whether or not prosecution in child abuse cases is a good thing challenged or are they implicit values which remain untested?

The health agencies

Government policy in relation to child health services emphasises a more focused delivery of services in the future. Consider for example this extract from *Seen But Not Heard*:

> Traditionally, the health service has provided services universally available to all, while local authority social services have provided more highly targeted support. Although this broad distinction remains, in future community health agencies will need to focus more of their scarce resources, while local authorities will need to broaden their remit to provide a wider range of initiatives that provide families with support. (Audit Commission 1994c: 2)

More recent NHS guidance (NHS Executive 1996) has emphasised this point as well as highlighting the need for clearly defined relationships between the different sectors of the health services (hospital, community and primary care), and developing closer collaboration with other agencies that have a responsibility for the welfare of children (for example, social services departments, local education authorities and voluntary agencies). The document also describes five related themes of child health services, children with disabilities, impact of 'socio-economic variations' on child health, the vulnerability of children to violence and emotional abuse, partnership principles, and equity in service provision.

As part of a locally coordinated and comprehensive service for children and families, local authorities are required to develop and publish children's services plans. This process requires consultation with other service purchasers and service providers amongst which are the health authorities and trusts. In addition, there may be joint commissioned undertakings, the following of which are described by the NHS Executive (1996): school health services, child protection, respite care services, child and adolescent mental health services, services for children with disabilities, services for children deemed to be in need under the Children Act 1989, children with special educational needs, looked-after children, adoption services, and education services for sick children in the community.

I have already discussed the impact of reforms in both health and education on the process of managing child protection services. Despite the dispersion of health influence created by the fragmentation of the structure, health agencies continue to exert a powerful influence in child protection, in part attributable to the very large numbers of health agencies represented in the management of child protection services. Table 5.1 illustrates the agency representatives on eight child Area Child Protection Committees.

Table 5.1: Agency representation on eight Area Child Protection Committees
(Jackson et al. 1994)

Agency	Number (n = 171)
Health	60
Social Services	41
Education	21
Police	14
Probation	11
Other	24

They considered that there were two reasons for the particularly large numbers from health agencies, one being the need to represent both purchasers and providers of services, the other being the different health roles which were relevant in child protection. Health agencies (along with other agencies) are required to help the social services fulfil its responsibilities to children who are in need in its locality, and as we have indicated, children at risk of abuse are defined to be 'in need'. Section 27 of the Children Act 1989 indicates that 'Where it appears to a local authority that any authority or other person ... could, by taking any specified action, help in the exercise of any of their functions under this Part, they may request the help of that other authority or person, specifying the action in question.'

Where such a request is made, then the authority whose help is requested, 'shall comply with the request if it is compatible with their own statutory or other duties and obligations and does not unduly prejudice the discharge of any of their functions.' Health authorities are amongst those included. In order to help health authorities fulfil their child protection responsibilities, *Working Together* (1991) advises that they should,

> ... identify a senior doctor, a senior nurse with a health visiting qualification and a senior midwife (designated senior professional) as the co-ordinator of all aspects of child protection work within their district. This will include the provision of advice to social services departments and to health professionals. (paragraph 4.20)

These roles are described more fully below. However, there have been general difficulties in the involvement of health agencies in child protection. Some of these are related to the impact of health reforms; some are related to differences of views on the part of health staff as to how they see their professional responsibilities in child protection, requiring further clarification and elaboration.

Since *Working Together* (1991), there have been at least three subsequent publications of official guidance addressing the role of medical and nursing staff in child protection: *Child Protection: Guidance for Senior Nurses, Health Visitors and Midwives* (DoH 1992b), *Child Protection: Medical Responsibilities* (DoH/BMA/Conference of Medical Royal Colleges 1994), and *Child Protection: Clarification of Arrangements between the NHS and Other Agencies* (DoH/WO 1996). The guidance for nurses was basically an update and elaboration of the responsibilities as detailed in *Working Together* (1991) to take into consideration the new organisational and legislative framework within which health professionals were operating. It is likely to be revised again in the near future. *Medical Responsibilities*, however, was produced because of concerns expressed by doctors about participating fully in child protection work, specifically concerns about confidentiality. Consequently, the General Medical Council (GMC) twice revised its guidance to doctors about the circumstances under which they should divulge confidential information in cases of child abuse in the period between the issuing of *Working Together* (1991) and the appearance of *Medical Responsibilities* (1994). This highlights the continuing controversial nature of the involvement of medical practitioners in the child protection system. The advice concerning confidentiality and child protection issued by the GMC as it appears in *Medical Responsibilities* is: 'where a doctor believes that a patient may be the victim of abuse or neglect the patient's interests are paramount and will usually require a doctor to disclose information to an appropriate, responsible person or officer of a statutory agency' (DoH/BMA/Conference of Medical Royal Colleges 1994: 2).

The statutory agencies are social services, NSPCC, or the police. A significant departure from the previous government guidance is the distinction between concerns that are very clear (for example, if there is clear evidence of abuse or an allegation), and those in which there is uncertainty. In the case of clear concerns, there is no discretion; the matter should be reported. In cases where there is uncertainty, the matter should be discussed with a senior or more experienced colleague to ascertain if the concerns are such as to reach a 'critical threshold of professional concern'. If the matter does reach the threshold, then again it should be referred to the statutory agencies. The threshold is considered to be a matter for the professional judgement of the more experienced medical colleague. The net effect of this two-tier system is to retain the control for the decision making in the hands of the medical profession. This compromise is intended to address the concerns of the medical profession that information that may be ambiguous should not be shared with non-medical people. It seems fairly clear from the process and content of medical responsibilities that the result is as much about preserving vested professional interests as it is about the most effective ways of protecting children. Indeed it could be argued that it is not the interests of the child that are being balanced against professional autonomy, but the interests of others in the situation. What, after all, one might ask, is the connection between confidentiality and the abuser's emphasis on maintaining secrecy? It could be argued, for example, that confidentiality, although intended to be a protective device in the power imbalance between a professional and a client, could itself become a collusive tool of abuse, when it serves to maintain the secrecy that is vital to the abuser to perpetuate and maintain the abuse.

The rest of the guidance deals with referral issues and matters to do with participation of doctors at child protection conferences (a very difficult area to address). The third document, *Child Protection: Clarification of Arrangements between the NHS and Other Agencies* (DoH/WO 1996), is the substantive revision to *Working Together* (1991) arising from reorganisation of health services into purchasers (health authorities) and providers (health trusts).

The new structure of medical and nursing child protection

The new structure provides three categories of health staff with responsibilities for local child protection. There are senior officers, 'designated' professionals and 'named' professionals. Three individuals are identified from each Health Authority to sit on each ACPC to which it relates, the senior officer (who should be at executive director level or above), a senior doctor (with child protection experience) and a senior nurse (who should have a health visiting qualification). The senior nurse and the senior doctor are the 'designated' professionals and they sit on the ACPC as 'representatives of the District Health Authority and not as representatives of the Trusts which employ them' (p.2). The senior nurse should preferably also have a midwifery qualification and access to midwifery advice. The senior doctor will either be a consultant community paediatrician or the lead senior clinical medical officer (paragraph 2.47). The role of the two designated professionals should be clarified in all contracts between the Health Authority and the service-providing Trusts, including time commitments. For their parts, each Trust providing obstetric and child health services should have a 'named' child protection doctor and a 'named' child protection nurse (who have appropriate experience) to carry more local responsibility, within their Trust role, for child protection.

A positive feature of this arrangement is that it addresses, in the case of nursing at least, the confusion that previously surrounded the role of the designated nurse. Several reports (CANO 1993; Royal College of Nursing 1994) looked at nursing and child protection and found that the role of the designated nursing officer (as it was under *Working Together*, 1991) varied from area to area. In some areas, the role is very much as indicated in *Working Together*, that is, concerned with managerial functions (for example, policy dissemination, communication and monitoring). In other areas, however, it was found to be much more of a practitioner post, described as a clinical nurse specialist (child protection). In those areas the role involved 'attending case conferences, assisting with preparation of court statements, attendance at court, training and day to day management of child protection issues' (CANO 1993, 4th draft). A similar point was made in *Nursing and Child Protection* (Royal College of Nursing 1994), which highlighted difficulties when designated nurses carry other, non-child protection, responsibilities. These two reports highlighted that the role was being interpreted in two very different ways, both of which are legitimate needs in a child protection service. Difficulty was caused by attempting to combine the two functions into the same role. Professionals who are too close to practice may not have the managerial overview and authority necessary for involvement in ACPC considerations of policy and planning. By separating out the roles into designated professionals (senior managers) and named professionals (specialist practitioners), the new structure appears to be attempting to address this previous difficulty. A less positive feature of the new arrangements is that the designated health individual (for the Health Authority) and the named health individual (employed by one of several Health Trusts) can be one and the same person, which is logical enough because the individual representing the Health Authority on the ACPC may also be the individual employed by the Trust who has the most experience of child protection matters. It does however create the potential for role confusion for the individual, who will need to be clear about which hat they are wearing in different circumstances.

The Health Authority representatives are not the only health representatives on Area Child Protection Committees. In addition to the senior officer and the two designated professionals, there should also be a representative from the Family Health Services Authority and a Local Medical Committee GP representative. Special arrangements need to be made concerning local fundholding GPs, who may or may not choose to be represented by the Local Medical Committee representative. However, the guidance recommends that there should only be a single GP representative on the ACPC, and representation of other GP interests should be by liaison between general practitioners, fundholding general practitioners, the Local Medical Committee and the Health Authority. Traditionally, although not specified in either Appendix 5 of *Working Together* (1991) or in *Child Protection: Clarification of Arrangements between the NHS and other Agencies* (DoH/WO 1996), there are also child psychiatrists on the ACPC. Thus a list of health professionals on ACPCs would comprise:

1 Senior Officer.
2 Designated Doctor (paediatrician or SCMO).
3 Designated Nurse.
4 Family Health Services Authority.
5 Local Medical Committee GP.
6 Fundholding GP representative (optional).
7 Child Psychiatrist.

In the next sections I consider four different health roles represented on Area Child Protection Committees: health visitor, community child health doctor, child psychiatrist and general practitioner. I also consider the case for adult psychiatrists to be members of ACPCs.

Health visiting

The health visiting role (general)

The role of the health visitor is defined in the National Health Service Regulations (1972) as

> ... the person employed by a local authority to visit people in their homes or elsewhere for the purpose of giving advice to the care of young children, the person suffering from illness and expectant or nursing mothers, and as to the measures necessary to prevent the spread of infection, and includes the person so employed by a voluntary organisation with a local health authority.

Health visitors have duties to visit children in the community but are not vested with statutory powers in relation to those duties. Their practice will be guided by principles and targets set for community child health by the National Health Service Executive, as contained for example in *Child Health in the Community: A Guide to Good Practice* (1996).

Health visiting has recently celebrated its 100th anniversary. Its origins can be traced back to the ravages of a succession of cholera epidemics during the middle to late nineteenth century. Considerable work was done by the medical officers of health, regional officers responsible for public health provisions set up under the Public Health Act (1872) which followed from a two-year Royal Commission into public health (1869–71). In Manchester and Salford in 1882, voluntary programmes were set up to supervise paid home visitors who would go into people's home with health education messages. They came to be described as 'health missioners' or 'sanitary visitors'.

By the turn of the century however, the situation was still not much better, at least in terms of infant mortality and the health of the citizens who survived to adulthood. The very high rates of infant mortality gave rise to the infant welfare movement. Mother and baby clinics were set up where mothers could learn about their babies and the care they required. The sudden realisation that nearly half of the recruits for the Boer War were considered unfit for military service provided another picture of the health of British subjects – a very poor picture indeed.

Table 5.2 notes the trend in public health over the period from the middle of the nineteenth century to the present day as going through various stages.

Table 5.2: Trends in public health (Robertson 1991)

Time Period	Public Health Service Provision
Mid-nineteenth century	Prevention of acute fatal diseases
Turn of century	Teaching to prevent disease in the very young
Post-Second World War	Social advice and health education for the whole family
1960s to 1970s	Specialisation and screening programmes
Present day	More group work, community projects; health statistics used for analysis and action on priorities

Robertson describes two models to facilitate the understanding of the health visiting role, the prevention model and the family health needs model. Using the prevention model she summarises the three main roles within health visiting:

In their educational role, they attempt to promote positive health and to prevent the occurrence of disease by increasing people's understanding of healthy ways of living and their knowledge of health hazards ... Health Visitors undertake health surveillance, aiming to discover difficulties at an early stage and, through prompt attention, to prevent irreparable damage ... Where established conditions or situations already exist, health visitors can help to prevent further deterioration at an individual family level by giving supportive care. (Robertson 1991: 2)

No doubt the reader will recognise in the above the three-fold division of prevention into primary, secondary and tertiary described by Caplan (1964) which has previously been considered. But it also represents a tripartite division of methodology used. Health visiting aims are mainly achieved through teaching, surveillance and support.

The second model, the family health needs model, has the potential to enlarge the focus of health visiting to include the wider community within which the family are based. Robertson describes four areas of health needs:

General environment
> local area; accommodation; standard of living

Physical health
> nutrition; home safety; hygiene; developmental attainments (screening); medication

Mental/emotional health
> Parent: knowledge and attitudes; psychological illness; postnatal depression; emotional stability
> Child: play needs; normal discipline; affection

Social aspects of health
> Mother support from: family, friends, community; group activities
> Family Unit: emotional support; housing
> Child: play with other children; stimulation

A family health needs approach has been described by Orr (1992a) and the community orientation to health visiting has also been described by Orr (1992b). Health visiting is not just about working with children and families, although clearly owing to its origins that still tends to form the bulk of the work. Increasingly, however, health visitors are providing a service for elderly persons, utilising broadly the same methods and principles as in working with children – promoting a healthier lifestyle. It is increasingly common for health visitors to have specialisms which may form part or all of their responsibilities, for example with homeless families, diabetics, families with a handicapped member or hospital liaison.

As indicated, the role of the health visitor is a broad preventive role. The Audit Commission has appeared not to recognise the value of this kind of role, and instead has recommended:

Regular routine contacts not resulting from an assessment of need should be discouraged. After a universal first visit from a health visitor to each family with a new baby, all further routine visiting, apart from the agreed surveillance programme, should be based on assessed needs against agreed priorities in order to release resources for situations where there are clear needs. (Audit Commission 1994c: 39)

This is tantamount to saying there is no role for primary prevention and all efforts should be channelled into secondary prevention. It also ignores the children's needs post-natal, which are constantly changing right up until the time they go to school (when most health visiting responsibility ends) and after.

Nevertheless, even with the greater emphasis on more targeted focusing in health visiting in recent years, the availability of health visiting to all still makes it quite conspicuous in the world as a truly comprehensive primary prevention programme.

The health visiting role in child protection

There are two features of health visiting in relation to child protection that are worth noting. First, because of the nature of their role they see a cross-section of the community. As described in Government guidance:

The health visitor's role is unique, in the main, because she offers an unsolicited service. Her work is largely with the 'well' population, with visits to families being made over a long period of time and is concerned with the family as a whole as well as each individual within it. She is trained to recognise deviation from the normal ... (DoH 1992b: 4)

Health visitors see the well-functioning families as well as those that are on the edge. They see the rich and the poor, the happy and the wretched. Because of this they are likely to get a very good overview of the nature of the community within which their work is based. They are less prone to the type of distortion that is a danger for those who work exclusively with families on the edge. For social workers, there may be the danger of making unconscious comparisons of the values and standards of families being worked with, not against the childrearing standards and values in the wider community, but against the standards and values within the rest of the group of families being visited. Although the practitioner may be aware of the need to use an objective standard to assess parenting (Adcock and White's *Good-enough Parenting* (1985) was very much in vogue when it appeared), there is also the necessity to avoid the class imperialism of imposing middle-class values on working-class families and communities. Although social workers will indeed have contact with non-client families and children in their private lives, nevertheless, in their working lives they will have considerably more contact with families in difficulty than with ordinarily functioning families. Social workers who operate in local areas of particularly high deprivation (for example, in post-industrial mining communities) may find the task of establishing benchmarks particularly difficult. They may have their work cut out for them trying to distinguish neglect in a particular family, who may be surrounded by so many families in poverty that it is difficult to define where the boundary is between neglect and deprivation. Health visitors, however, by virtue of their responsibilities for all children within the community are able to have a broad perspective against which to evaluate family dysfunction or problematic child-rearing.

Second, perhaps deriving from the medical model of child abuse as it emerged during the 1960s, and by virtue of their medical training, health visitors are likely to approach child abuse as any other health difficulty in the community which needs to be prevented: what is its epidemiology? What causes it? How can the root causes of it be addressed? What can be achieved by health education and promotion? Robertson (1991), in her consideration of the health visiting role in child abuse, adapts the previous principles from the preventive model to the particular circumstances of the child abuse situation.

The working party which produced the document *Child Protection: Guidance for Senior Nurses, Health Visitors and Midwives* (DoH 1992b), considered that every senior staff who was responsible for the provision of professional advice and supervision to staff working with children and families should have their own copy of the guidance. It emphasised a 'paramount need for nurses, midwives and health visitors to have ready access to a senior nurse, or midwife, who is knowledgeable and experienced in the subject of child abuse' (DoH 1992b: viii). It also indicated how important it is for staff to be aware of Health Authority policy on child abuse, to be confident in the use of guidelines, and to receive regular updating of knowledge of child abuse. It highlights the key activities of 'senior nurses' (a term used to signify both health visitors and midwives). These are

- Proactive and reactive approach to child abuse
- Provide leadership and supervision
- Keep senior managers informed
- Introduce new staff to local policies and procedures (induction programme); ensure they are understood
- Assess training needs
- Set up communications between managers and practitioners and between agencies
- Keep informed about arrangements for child protection conferences

- Ensure there is a system for records transfer
- Assist in Part 8 Reviews
- Set up small-scale local research projects.

The document *Child Protection: Clarification of Arrangements between the NHS and other Agencies* (DoH/WO 1996) says very little about the role of the health visitor. Paragraphs 2.44–2.46 highlight the centrality of the role in child protection which must be acknowledged by the employing Trust, and the need for ongoing training, support and clinical supervision. Health visitors are expected to attend child protection conferences. Historically, supervision has not played a significant role in health visiting, but there are indications that this may be changing. The process of engaging in reciprocal supervision (peer supervision) appears to be gaining favour and may be a resource-effective way of providing ongoing clinical supervision for health visitors. Jackson et al. (1994) found that it was beginning to be more widely used at the time of their review.

In terms of their working relationships with other professions, there have been some tensions for health visitors. Taylor and Tilley (1990) found negative stereotypes and role conflicts contributed to deep-rooted tensions and areas of conflicts between health visitors and social workers. Fox and Dingwall (1985) on the other hand found that definitions of maltreatment by social workers and health visitors (by means of rating maltreatment vignettes) were quite close, with only one example being significantly different. It may be that social workers and health visitors can agree on what is abuse, but not necessarily on how best to tackle it. This may be consistent with the finding in the Republic of Ireland by Butler (1996) which showed that attitudes of public health nurses (the health visitor equivalent) were considerably at variance with official policy of commitment to collaboration and coordination. Iskander (1989) considers that health visitors need assertiveness training to counteract their frequent experience of not being heard by doctors, a theme developed by Tattersall (1992) in his consideration of the need for health visitors to be able to communicate assertively in child protection work. He gives an example of the kind of difficulties that can arise for a health visitor who is not able to do this. In their extensive overview of interagency working, Birchall and Hallett (1995) found that the need for cooperation, especially information exchange was widely accepted, but co-working was more problematical. They also found (1996) that health visitors were rated highly as co-workers.

The most recent debate within health visiting is the status of the profession. Although training to become a health visitor has always entailed being qualified as a nurse in the first instance, and then undertaking subsequent specialist training to become a health visitor, the current debate is whether for the purposes of regulation, health visiting should be regarded as an independent profession within its own right, or as a specialism within nursing.

Health visiting and nursing representation on the ACPC

Under the new regulations (DoH/WO 1996), the role of both designated professionals is the same, whereas under *Working Together* there were different roles ascribed to the designated nurse and the designated doctor. To start with, they need to liaise with the named professionals in each of the Trusts, and the responsibilities that they have may be carried out via the named professionals. The guidance describes five broad roles of the designated health professional, an advisory role, a policy and procedures role, a training role, a coordination and communication role and a monitoring role. They should provide advice to other agencies, NHS trusts, GPs, health authorities, Family Health Services Authorities (FHSAs), health visitors, school nurses and other health professionals. They should work with other agencies on the development of interagency policies procedures (and the handbook) and ensure that there are 'robust' internal procedures. They should organise training for all health staff (including GPs). One of the two designated professionals should be on the ACPC training subcommittee. They should be helping Trusts to identify training needs. They also need to attend to their own training needs and professional development. They need to ensure that obligations relating to children are met by arrangements between purchasers and providers. They should monitor contracts, and be involved in a child protection audit.

As indicated, the designated professionals will be liaising with the named professionals in the Trusts to ensure optimal communication. The responsibilities of the named professionals include: clinical child protection supervision; training; quality/audit/monitoring; the development of practice; advice on legal matters; conducting internal reviews and contributions to Part 8 Reviews.

Child protection issues and dilemmas for health visitors

Prevention As has already been indicated, a perennial difficulty for health visiting will be the lack of emphasis on prevention within government policy. We have already seen how the Audit Commission (1994c) has attacked the principle of ongoing health surveillance beyond the first visit. *Working Together* (1991) as I have already indicated places insufficient emphasis on both prevention and treatment, and as a consequence Area Child Protection Committees place little emphasis on them. For a worker, such as a health visitor, whose role is entirely preventive and for managers of such services, it must be very frustrating trying to put prevention on the agenda. In addition, it may produce tensions when other agencies (for example, social services and police) try to get health visitors to come away from their preventative health promotion role and take on roles (for example, surveillance not of health but of abuse) which are not legitimately theirs. Noyes (DoH 1991c) notes the extensive consideration given to the health visiting role in the Doreen Aston inquiry (Lambeth, Lewisham and Southwark Area Review Committee 1989). He writes

> The inquiry notes some conflict in philosophy and expectation of the health visitor, on the one hand facilitating and supporting individuals and families requiring an open, honest and direct relationship with parents whilst ensuring other professionals were kept fully informed. On the other hand, because a health visitor is usually afforded easy access to the home there is a social policing role in relation to early identification of abuse with a view to protecting the child. This can lead to loss of parental confidence and trust. A balance must therefore be maintained between these two approaches (DoH 1991c: 12)

It could be argued that we have police who have a role in child protection, we have social workers who over the last years have accepted a policing role in their work which was not there previously, and now we want to introduce a policing role into health visiting ... the last place it should be. It could be argued that before we try introducing balance into the role of the health visitor between open, honest involvement and policing, we should be addressing the issue of the need for balance within child protection. It may be that we will achieve better balance by having interagency cooperation between agencies, some of which have a policing role and some who do not, rather than by having all of the statutory agencies absorbing a policing role into their work.

Health visitors and their managers will get on very well with social services and the police while they work to the agenda of those agencies and look at their role in investigation (and clearly there is a legitimate role in this). They will get on less well if they rock the boat and begin saying more forcefully 'why is prevention not on the agenda?' (both literally and metaphorically). One nursing manager noted that for nearly two years during her time on an Area Child Protection Committee, the virtually sole issue was the development of the interagency investigative procedures. She considered this to be an extremely cost-*ineffective* means of using managerial time (which she estimated as approaching £30,000). Whilst appreciating the work that was being done in the voluntary sector on prevention (notably the establishment of a number of 'open access' family centres), she was very critical of the lack of emphasis that was able to be given to this by the statutory sector (referring in this case to the social services).

I may be in danger of overstating this, and on the other hand, the child protection prevention role of health visitors is valued by other agencies. Smith observes sardonically, 'The health visiting profession is valued highly, not only within child protection. It is regarded by all agencies, *other than health*, as a potentially major contributor to the support-versus-protection debate in child protection' (1998: 99, emphasis added).

Quality control/monitoring/auditing   The health services generally appear to have developed quality control procedures before social services departments. One of the sources of frustration for senior nursing managers is that of trying to incorporate into the management of child protection services, systems that were developed internally within health agencies (for example, random audit). Issues around the lack of quality control in child protection have previously been considered.

GP control of health visiting   In recent years there has been a proposal that all health visiting services should be removed from the Community Health services to come under the direct control of fundholding General Practitioners. Whilst there is concurrently a trend for more and more health visitors to be based in GP surgeries, they continue to be accountable to the Community Health Trusts directly and not to the GPs. The Audit Commission report (1994c) addressed the issue of health visiting services being based both in GP surgeries providing a GP list service and in community health facilities providing a patch-based service. It noted three factors to be taken into consideration when deciding what type of service is most appropriate: the size of the practice population, the distribution of needs within the child population, and the degree of interest of GPs in preventive work. Factors favouring a patch-based service (either in addition to, or instead of, a GP surgery service) would include larger GP surgeries, ethnically mixed population, high levels of deprivation, and lack of interest on the part of GPs. One of the drawbacks of health visitors being based in GP surgeries is the isolation from colleagues which can lead to concerns about supervision of child protection issues (Nash 1997). One way to address this is through the development of child protection advisors (CPAs) described by Bass (1995) who are specially trained health visitors and school nurses and able to advise colleagues on child protection matters.

Although the general benefits of health visitors being practice-based is accepted, there was substantial opposition to the proposal to have health visitors directly accountable to GPs by the Health Visitor's Association (now the Community Practitioner's and Health Visitor's Association), and to date there has been no change in the line of accountability of health visiting services. One GP (from the sample used in Jackson et al. 1994) commented on a potentially bleak future for the health visiting profession, should GPs become the employers of health visitors.

Community Child Health Doctor (Community Paediatrician or lead Senior Clinical Medical Officer)

The Community Child Health Doctor's role

Consultant paediatricians operate in both hospital-based (acute) services and the community health services. Both the Audit Commission (1994c) and the British Paediatric Association endorse the general principle that child health services should be led by a consultant paediatrician overseeing a 'seamless' service for children and families across the community and acute sectors:

> In community health services, a consultant community paediatrician can bring the benefits of increased status for the service and added drive towards quality and evaluation. Most children rarely need acute in-patient care but virtually all children use community child health services. (Audit Commission 1994c: 54)

The document also considers agendas for both health commissioning and health providers in child health. As regards the commissioning of child health services, child health surveillance and immunisation, child health clinics, the involvement of GP fundholders, the provision of school health services and arrangements for monitoring and evaluating child health services all need consideration. In relation to community child health service providers, the agenda should include consideration of the health needs of the population, of priorities and criteria being adopted, staff skills, service information needs and the organisation of the service.

The Community Child Health Doctor's role in child protection

When considering the medical role in child protection, it is important to remember that the rediscovery of abuse in the late 1950s and early 1960s began with it being defined as a paediatric problem (the 'battered baby' *syndrome*). Paediatricians (Hobbs and Wynne 1986, 1987) could also be said to have contributed to defining sexual abuse as a problem in Britain, an issue about which, despite some level of awareness, no real action had been taken.

Child Protection: Clarification of Arrangements between the NHS and other Agencies indicates that part of the role of the Community Child Health Medical Staff is to provide direction to community child health staff towards the development of a 'high level of expertise in the examination, diagnosis, assessment and ongoing care of children who are considered to be suffering, or at risk of, significant harm' (DoH/WO 1996: paragraph 2.47).

Let us consider these four aspects of child health doctors roles sequentially.

Examination and Diagnosis Community child health doctors will be responsible for providing medical opinion on bruises, vaginal and/or rectal abnormalities, and other indications of physical or sexual abuse. They may also carry out examinations when requested in cases of severe neglect. They are the only professionals whose evidence will be accepted. Whilst other professionals may have some knowledge of the significance of different types of physical indicators arising from their basic training, many physical conditions (for example, Mongolian blue spot, bleeding disorder bruising, strawberry naevus and more described by Rose 1985) can be very difficult to distinguish from non-accidental injury. I can recall as a practising social worker with some years of experience in child protection being shown a number of slides containing non-accidental, accidental and medical condition images and getting more than I would care to admit wrong. It was a humbling experience, and one that emphasises the uniqueness of the medical experience for ascertaining causes of marks. It is also useful to note that medical colleagues with less experience may also misdiagnose physical signs (both false positives and false negatives), which is why the level of expertise of the person undertaking the medical examination is important. Even so, such evidence may be challenged, which I will discuss below. Within the medical framework, examination leads to a formal diagnosis on what the physical findings are and their origin (and in terms of the medical/physical findings at least, lead to a recommended treatment and prognosis). Difficulties may arise over who is to carry out some examinations: in general, parents (on the basis of familiarity) are more likely to prefer their family doctor, whereas the child protection agencies (on the basis of more substantial experience and expertise) are likely to prefer a paediatrician. Information in the form of leaflets may be useful to provide information to both young people and parents about the role of medical examination in child protection cases. These can provide jargon-free, user-friendly information on why the medical examination is necessary, the ability of the young person to refuse consent, where the examination will take place, who will undertake it, what it will entail and what will happen afterwards.

The findings from a medical examination may be used as evidence in court. Before the introduction of the Children Act 1989, there was some confusion over the right of a doctor to undertake a medical examination of a child who was the subject of a place of safety order, as it was unclear what extent of parental status was afforded by the order. This was likely to be especially contentious where the parent refused consent or the child was reluctant. This was clarified in the Children Act, and the application for an Emergency Protection Order (part 6c) contains explicit provisions for the court to make directions regarding a medical (or psychiatric) examination of the child. This can be in the form of expressly authorising, forbidding or defining the circumstances surrounding such an examination. The Act is also unequivocal that a child may refuse consent to be medically (or psychiatrically) examined even where a court has made an authorisation: 'Where any direction is given ... the child may, if he is of sufficient understanding to make an informed decision, refuse to submit to the examination or other assessment' (Children Act 1989: section 44(7)). A very important principle to come out of the Cleveland Inquiry (Butler-Sloss 1988) is that children should not be subjected to repeated medical examinations for evidential purposes (although clearly there may be a need for a child to be examined on a number of occasions for purposes of medical treatment).

A medical examination, where it happens, will take place before the video-taped interview (if one is being undertaken). They do not occur in all cases, and indeed in one study (Wattam 1992) of 106 children, medical examinations were recorded for 28 per cent (of which 20 per cent were either negative or inconclusive, and the remaining eight per cent were positive). Wattam advances the position that the assumption underlying medical examinations of abused children (which she describes as an 'intrinsic feature' of cases of assault) is that an act with physical consequences will be detectable because of the recency of the act or its severity, and she argues this may not always be the case. Spencer and Flin (1993) appear to confirm this view in respect of child sexual abuse, but appear to see no difficulties in terms of physical abuse:

> Nor are there problems of admissibility about expert evidence from paediatricians about the nature and possible causes of injuries suffered by the child. In cases of sexual abuse, however, medical evidence is of limited value, and lawyers, psychologists and other professionals need to be aware of this. In the first place, the absence of medical evidence cannot be taken as 'negative proof'. (1993: 237)

Assessment   Although the emphasis when considering medical examinations was on neglect and physical and sexual abuse, psychological or emotional abuse, and perhaps less severe forms of neglect being longer-term processes and not necessarily accompanied by physical trauma, may require a longer-term assessment. This is not to discount the significance of a longer-term medical assessment for children who have been sexually or physically abused as part of the ongoing treatment plan for the child (which can form part of a comprehensive social work assessment undertaken in accordance with the 'Orange Book' (DoH 1988). Medical assessment, for the purposes of establishing the extent of longer-term harm can be undertaken voluntarily with parents (and if old enough, the child), or if need be, under a Child Assessment Order. One of the medical concerns expressed about the introduction of the Child Assessment Order was that the seven days provided for the assessment did not provide the long-term overview necessary to get a full picture of the factors associated with the child's development, or lack of development. This can most clearly be seen for example in cases of failure to thrive, where centile charts are used. These charts show the child's height, weight and head circumference as a comparison with the rest of the same gender and age population in terms of percent above and below that particular measurement. Using weight as an example, a measurement below the third centile (indicating that 97 per cent of children the same age weigh more) can be taken as worrying, but the extent of concern depends upon a number of factors (size of parents, other children in the family with a similar pattern, the establishment of a medical cause for the low weight). Patterns of weight gain or loss can best be established over a longer period of time (seven days would clearly be inadequate), and can be connected with variations in the care of children (for example, weight gain during periods of time living with relatives or looked after by the local authority). Centile charts are not however, without their problems, and a survey of community growth screening showed that a wide range of charts were in use throughout the UK (Hulse 1995). Some years ago as well, there were concerns that centile charts were not picking up children of ethnic minority backgrounds who were below the third centile because the charts had been standardised on all-white populations.

As with Emergency Protection Orders, a child can refuse to submit to a Child Assessment Order on the same basis, that is, being of sufficient understanding (Children Act 1989: section 43(8)).

Ongoing care　In addition to providing knowledge about the significance of medical findings as a contribution to planning the child protection intervention (case conferences, child protection register, interagency child protection plan), child health doctors may also have to provide evidence. In court they may function in several different capacities. They may simply be providing evidence of the medical findings and informing the court of the significance of the findings. More senior and experienced community child health doctors may be requested to act in the role of 'expert witness', in which case they are expected as an expert to shed light on the significance of findings (in which they actually played no earlier role), and in this capacity they may be able to offer opinions, and not just facts.

Despite my earlier account of paediatrics taking the lead in the early definitions of forms of abuse, early accounts of the role of paediatricians in child protection find examples of them being unwilling to become involved:

> [in relation to a paediatrician] ... He found the whole battered baby subject most anxiety provoking and apparently had always tried to avoid being involved in such cases ... After unwillingly telling the parents of the nature of the child's injuries,

the consultant was reluctant to have anything more to do with the case, refused to participate in any case conferences and refused to communicate directly with the worker. (Baher et al. 1976: 101)

and in relation to providing court evidence:

Paediatricians were unwilling to give this evidence, and some pressure had to be applied to persuade them to do so. They appeared to feel that they had played their role in identifying abuse and involving a social agency and did not wish to feel responsible for the outcome of their action: the removal of the child. (Baher et al. 1976: 110)

Lynch (1996) considers that fear about involvement in child protection work may be contributing to under-recruitment to the profession. This reluctance may be related to fears of litigation. Considering the potential repercussions for paediatricians (for example, following Cleveland), there may be some justification for this. Hoyte (1996) of the Medical Defence Union, describes a number of ways and arenas in which parents may challenge paediatricians over child abuse decisions (complaints procedures, public inquiries, litigation, disciplinary actions and defamation actions) and the means to protect paediatricians from vulnerability in those situations.

But beyond providing evidence to court and contributing to the assessment of the child's ongoing medical treatment needs, child health doctors will also play a significant role if, as a result of the abuse, children come to be looked after. Not all, but many, perhaps even a majority, of the children who are looked after have experienced some form of abuse leading to their accommodation by the local authority. In quite a few cases, a history of abuse will only emerge after the child has entered the care system. Macaskill (1991) in her consideration of family care for sexually abused children notes that in some cases children who, despite years of therapy had never disclosed being abused, did so in placement to the foster carers.

The Children Act 1989 (and the Boarding Out Regulations 1988, before that) provided a framework for a much more proactive involvement of health agencies with looked-after children because of their extreme vulnerability to poor health. This emphasis on the health of looked-after children can be seen in the following requirements:

- When children are placed, notifications must be sent to health agencies and general practitioner; children are required to have a medical examination (unless examined within the preceding three months)
- When placing a child, agencies are required to give consideration to the child's state of health, health history, the impact on his or her development of the health and health history, existing arrangements for medical

and dental treatment and surveillance, and health screening (immunisations, vision and hearing tests)

- Health is one of seven areas given extensive consideration in the *Looking After Children* material now being used by most local authorities (DoH 1995b)
- Medical examinations are required for looked-after children (once every six months if the child is less than two years old; once every year for older children).

Despite this there is evidence that a large number (over 70 per cent) of looked-after children are not having medical examinations while they are looked after, and that the quality of the examinations is poor (Cleaver 1996; Butler and Payne 1997; Mather et al. 1997). No doubt a substantial proportion of these are older children who have a right to refuse medical examinations, even in the context of being looked after, but the low percentage of actual examinations suggests that new strategies (for example, moving away from the concept of 'examination' to that of 'health' thus making the process more relevant for the young person) are needed.

Community Child Health Doctors on the Area Child Protection Committee

The designated professional role of community child health doctors is the same as that for the senior nurse on the ACPC, previously described. The role is essentially concerned with liaising with the named professionals in each of the Trusts, advising other professionals on child protection, contributing to the development of policy and procedures, and contributing to training (for which they would need to ensure that they are regularly updated). As part of their training and professional development role they would wish to address the development of professional support networks and peer supervision. The role is concerned with facilitating communication and coordination, and with monitoring the outcomes of intervention. They would need to ensure that health staff receive information about which concerns need to be referred on, to whom, how and when.

Designated doctors are most likely to be paediatricians. In their study of ACPCs, Jackson et al. (1994) noted that the provision of service across community/hospital boundaries was perceived as a difficulty by health staff:

> Some respondents identified differences in patterns between community health services and hospital services, indicating a more structured approach within the community health services, and difficulty in getting information into the hospital systems. As described by one respondent, hospital workers don't have the same

'level of input' on child protection matters as community health workers. Child protection was seen as 'not their problem'. A different ethos towards child protection within hospitals was also seen as the source of some of the difficulties arising, for example health visitors not being informed of children who attend casualty. (Jackson et al. 1994: 45)

From the point of view of children's services, (and the role of child protection within that), there were seen to be clear advantages where services were unified across community and hospital provision. This theme of integrating child health services (whether across long-term acute services, or across hospital/community boundaries) has been a long-running theme in the delivery of health care services since the publication of the Court Committee report (1976).

Child protection issues and dilemmas for Community Child Health Doctors

Medical expert witness role   As well as the potential discomfort of appearing in court and the potential for recrimination on the part of the parents, to which I have already referred, other difficulties can emerge for paediatricians giving evidence in court. One of these is the practice, increasingly common, of different parties in the proceedings calling in expert medical witnesses (usually another paediatrician) to provide testimony to discredit the evidence given. Substantial financial incentives may be involved for the professionals giving expert testimony. At least two factors contributing to this dilemma can be identified. First, we are looking to medical colleagues for certainty in an endeavour which as I have already indicated (referring to Wattam 1992 and Spencer and Flin 1993) may be more uncertain than we would like. It may be a bit like the emperor's new clothes to say that medical professionals do not have all the answers; they have more or less expertise in their particular role within child protection, the same as other professionals. This was one of the very clear messages to come out of the Cleveland Inquiry (Butler-Sloss 1988), where there was too much uncritical reliance on the medical evidence (the reflex anal dilatation) as a conclusive indicator of abuse. Child abuse is not exclusively a medical diagnosis, although a medical diagnosis contributes to its identification. And of course, medical professionals may not necessarily agree, again referring in Cleveland to the dispute between the paediatricians and the police surgeon over the significance of the medical findings. Disagreement is more likely over newer medical indicators until there is a more substantial body of evidence upon which to base judgements. Another example of medical disagreement was the controversial eponymous 'Paterson' factor (Sharron 1987), in which a Scottish bone specialist, C. Paterson, maintained that fractures in the bones of young children could be the result of copper deficiency rather than abuse, calling for a much more thorough investigation before pressing for care orders. Other medical colleagues agreed on the existence of a tendency to fracturing due to copper deficiency in young children, but they disagreed that there was a potential for confusing that with fractures caused by abuse because of the absence of other associated symptoms. Nevertheless, this medical dispute was called upon in child protection court cases to invalidate, or attempt to diminish, the weight of medical opinion when considering suspicious fractures to children.

A second factor in this dilemma is that it highlights the drawbacks of a system which relies on the opinions of expert witnesses in the context of an adversarial judicial system. This is not peculiar to paediatricians, but perhaps affects them more than most. As described by Spencer and Flin (1993) in their very full consideration of expert assistance to the court to establish the veracity of a child's evidence, any party to civil or criminal proceedings may call upon experts to give testimony that is outside of the knowledge or experience of the judge or jury. They consider that there are five ways in which expertise can be made available to the court of which calling expert witnesses is only one. Interestingly they also note the little-used provision of courts in both England and Scotland for the court to obtain 'neutral' expert opinion, neutral in the sense of not being on behalf of the parties, but on behalf of the court. Nevertheless, they consider that this neutral expertise may be made available to the court through indirect means. It strikes me as peculiarly odd that we can have some professionals (that is guardians *ad litem*), whose responsibility is to act on behalf of the court, and other professionals (medical experts) whose testimony is solicited on behalf of the contesting parties in the proceedings. In such cases there is an interest that is perhaps quite divisive of professional interests and antagonistic to the interests of the child, in undermining the findings of colleagues and discrediting their conclusions when considering the need of a child for protection. It is perhaps a reflection of the fact that the courts are still not sufficiently child-centred, that the determination of civil and criminal proceedings in relation to child protection rest upon adversarial premises rather than inquisitorial ones.

Part 8 Reviews   One of the seven principles underlying Part 8 Reviews described in *Working Together* (1991: paragraph 8.4) is 'Co-operation: The local ACPC should provide a framework to ensure close collaboration between all the agencies involved'. And yet, when the death of a child through abuse or neglect comes to light, there can be considerably heightened tensions between agencies as they begin to unravel their involvement with the child and the family, even where the previously existing relationships were quite harmonious. This is not helped by the intense media interest in finding out who is to blame. I have previously referred to the position of one paediatrician who had decided on the basis of dissatisfaction with a previous Part 8 Review to discontinue future involvement. Part 8 Reviews are not judicial bodies; they do not have the power to compel individuals by subpoena to provide information. The undertaking of a Part 8 Review needs to be undertaken in a spirit of mutual learning, with a positive agenda of promoting more effective means to protect children and avoiding recriminations. Paediatricians, and others, may have potential litigation in mind, or the difficulties for their agencies if they are found blameworthy.

Medical examination of children   The medical examination of children can also raise issues for community child health doctors. To begin with, there are the issues of good practice. For example, the principle of not undertaking repeated examinations (to which I have previously referred) can become intermingled with the necessity for having examinations for therapeutic assessment purposes, and can be attacked in the context of court proceedings as multiple examinations for evidential purposes. Developing best practice in the undertaking of examinations is also an issue. It is clearly established, for example, that a good principle (not always observed in practice) in the undertaking of the medical examination, is that the examination of the particular areas of concern should take place in the context of a full medical examination, beginning with the less sensitive (for the child) aspects of an examination. This is partly to provide a more general context for the findings, but also to put the child at ease so that he or she comes to see it as an overall examination, and not an uncomfortable focusing on the skin marks or the damage to genital and/or rectal areas. As described by Lynch, 'The medical examination should be a thorough one, not just focusing on injuries and other overt evidence of recent abuse' (1996: 53). Another good practice component of medical examinations is to emphasise the purpose of the examination being that of providing the child with reassurance (for example that no permanent damage has been done). Prior et al. (1994) for example ascertained children's views on the investigative process, and found that they wanted to be given explanations and information and wanted to know the results of the medical examination and investigations.

I have already referred to the older child's consent being necessary. Where such consent is forthcoming, and with younger children who may not have the necessary understanding to provide informed consent, there are still issues of empowering the child or young person. Being sensitive to gender preferences for the examining physician and providing the child with opportunities to ask questions are several examples.

There are also issues about who undertakes the examination. It is still common for police surgeons to undertake medical examinations of children as well as paediatricians, and there will need to be some guidelines as to when it is appropriate for one and when the other to examine the child. A final difficulty is where children are not referred for medical examination because penetration did not feature as part of the disclosure.

Finally, it is important to remember the other children in the family. Lynch suggests that 'full assessments of the health and development of all the children in the family should take place' (1996: 54). For her, this is presumably related to her earlier study with Roberts (Lynch and Roberts 1982) studying 69 children from 40 families where abuse had occurred. They looked at the sibling group and found that although there were no physical injuries, there had been a history of concern about the emotional care of some of the siblings. They also found that lack of physical injury did not necessarily protect siblings of abused children against developmental and behaviour problems. The difference between the abused and sibling groups for the occurrence of developmental delay was not statistically significant.

Covert Video Surveillance (CVS)   A recent controversial issue in paediatrics is the use of covert video cameras in hospital wards. In November 1997, paediatricians at Staffordshire NHS Trust published the results of their covert video surveillance of 39 children who were suspected of being in a life-threatening situation at the hands of their parent or step-parent (Southall 1997). The presenting symptoms in most cases were a recurrent loss of consciousness, going blue or stopping breathing. The decision to undertake CVS was taken by a multidisciplinary team when there were suspicions that the problems were caused by the parents. The videotaped recording revealed 30 attempts at deliberate suffocation, and other cases of poisoning, fractures and deliberate forms of abuse. Alarmingly high rates of sudden and unexpected death were found in siblings (twelve out of 41) of the target sample children, and four of these parents subsequently admitted suffocating eight of the siblings. This puts into context, perhaps, the findings of Newlands and Emery (1991) that sudden infant death syndrome is significantly higher (15.6 per thousand) for siblings of children on the child protection register, than it is in the local population (3.1 per thousand). A very interesting finding of the research is that the parents are extremely plausible and may appear very kindly and caring to their children in the presence of professionals, only to dramatically alter, showing a more sinister and sadistic side to their character, when alone with their child. The majority of the parents in the study (23 of 39) were found to be suffering from a serious personality disorder.

This advance in child protection however, has not been without its critics and has caused some unease for health professionals (Sadler 1997). There is considerable controversy on the practice of CVS, not least because of ethical considerations. When the use of such surveillance becomes more well-known and widespread, then parents (including those who do not pose such a threat to their children) may become understandably reluctant to use the facilities.

Family planning/sexual health clinics for young people   More and more, young people are being targeted for specialist sexual health services as part of the effort to reduce pregnancies in young women. The government target is to halve the number of pregnancies to young women under the age of 16 by the year 2000 (DoH 1992c). Family planning services on offer from GPs have been less successful for young people because a) the general practitioner is likely to be the family doctor as well, and this may act as a disincentive for the young person seeking contraception, and b) many general practitioners are apparently unaware of the Gillick provisions allowing them to treat a person under 16 without informing the parents (as many as a third reported by Francome (1993)). There are a range of policy issues that could be considered in connection with young people and sexual activity (see Selman and Glendinning 1996), but my primary objective is to consider this in connection with the child protection service.

It could be argued that the conceptual framework protecting children from sexual abuse on the one hand, while providing more developed services for the sexual activity of an increasingly younger population, contains potential for ideological conflict and professional tensions that may perhaps eventually come to a head. In 1992, 6000 young people under the age of 16 sought emergency ('post-coital') contraceptive protection. The provisions of the Gillick principle are such that not only is the service entitled to maintain confidentiality in respect of young people using the clinic, but it could be interpreted as being required. It is interesting to compare this with Sweden, where doctors are expressly forbidden to correspond with parents about a young person's request for contraception (Jones 1986). In the UK, under section 6 of the Sexual Offences Act (1956) it is an offence to have sexual intercourse with a girl under the age of 16 years (although a person under 24 can use belief that the girl was 16 or over as a defence). Below the age of 16, whether or not the sexual act is considered to be abusive will depend upon a number of factors weighed up by professionals, for example, the nature of the relationship, whether there was any degree of coercion, etc. But the professionals involved with the young person, probably in accordance with locally agreed protocols about how to deal with such situations, will be making the decision as to whether the situation is abusive and requires a referral to the statutory child protection agencies. The establishment of this protocol, and adherence or lack of adherence, to it once established, can contribute to significant tensions within the medical profession between doctors providing family planning ('sexual health') services for young people and doctors providing paediatric services to a child protection system. One way out of this dilemma is for the doctor to simply avoid asking questions about the nature of the relationship (that is, who the sexual partner is) and simply to focus on the request for the contraceptive service.

However, to highlight the tendency towards inconsistency, imagine the following scenario. A young person (14) discloses to a professional that she is having a sexual relationship with her stepfather and is not sure about how to seek protection, but she does not want to go to the family doctor. She does not use the term 'abuse' nor does she suggest that there is coercion in the relationship. How does the professional respond? One might suggest that the professional would respond very differently if they were a) a school teacher, b) a medical person providing sex education in the school, and c) a 'sexual health' clinic doctor or nurse. I have already referred to the tensions arising between child protection professionals and teachers over issues of non-referral of abuse situations. But where would the teacher stand if for example after telling this young person about her responsibility to report the matter to the social services, this 14-year-old were to say:

> I have told you this in confidence. I appreciate what you say that you have to refer to the child protection services. However, I am a Gillick competent person, and I do not give my consent for you to breach my confidentiality, having told you this in your role as a professional.

Fortunately, the young person is not likely to say something as sophisticated as that. She will probably not know about Gillick. If one-third of GPs do not, then why should she? But it does highlight that the advice given to young people that professionals must disclose abuse that they learn about is predicated on the assumption that the young person does not have the right herself to tell someone something in confidence. If one is considering children's rights, should children not have the right to a confidential service? Of course there are many further complexities to this argument. As a reply, one could argue for example that the child would be treated the same as any adult that reported a case of child abuse – the confidentiality would be limited by the need to protect a vulnerable child. But the fact that this is in relation to the service that the child herself receives would make the situation different than it would be for a third-party reporter. I would suggest that the differences between how a health professional and a teacher would deal with the same information leads to the conclusion that the Gillick principles seem to apply in terms of young people and health services, but not otherwise, for example in terms of young people and child protection services. This may be a reflection of the nature of the issue leading to the Gillick decision (prescribing contraception). In addition of course, it may also be a reflection of the different power bases of the two professions.

And of course in the context of this section on paediatric issues, the dilemma may be even more poignant when considering the difficulties between two different medical professions, one with an orientation towards protecting children from unwanted sexual experiences, the other towards protecting the child from the unwanted consequences of sexual activity.

Child psychiatrist

The child psychiatrist's role (general)

The child psychiatrist will in all likelihood be heading up a multidisciplinary child and adolescent mental health services (CAMHS) team at a community- or hospital-based child (and adolescent) centre. The core of the team is likely to consist of a clinical psychologist, social worker, community nurse, occupational therapist, specialist teacher and non-medical psychotherapist (Nicol 1989). In some areas nurse therapists or nurse counsellors and play therapists may form part of the team as well. In facilities that provide a residential service with education on the premises, the specialist teaching role is likely to be particularly significant. As a 'great deal of work which focuses on the emotional well being of children and their behaviour is undertaken within wider children's health services, primary health care, social services, education and the voluntary sector' (NHS Executive 1996: 58), very close links may be established with community agencies as well (for example, educational psychologists, education welfare officers and social services).

There are a number of different models of providing a local child and family psychiatric service. Several teams may be working together under the same roof, with either functional/methodological or geographical divisions. The differences between teams adopting different methodologies may be very wide indeed, along the lines of family therapy teams, teams that focus on behavioural approaches, and teams adopting a traditional child psychiatric orientation which involves individual work with members of the family (usually the child psychiatrist works directly with the child and the social worker with the parent or parents). How closely these teams operate together and the nature of the relationships between teams may vary from region to region. In more remote areas, the service may be provided by a single team operating from the basis of one of the methodologies described. A more recent operating style within teams is to adopt an interchangeability model in which the genericism of the team is emphasised despite it comprising different professions with different professional perspectives and backgrounds. Thus all the members of the team would be described as 'therapists', and would be allocated and undertake similar work. This model may be seen to reduce unnecessary hierarchical and status differentials within the team.

The Health Advisory Service has recommended the adoption of a four-tier approach to child and adolescent mental health services, entailing input by non-specialists (GPs, social workers, etc.), input by specialist CAMHS workers operating in the community, a team approach for more difficult situations requiring a more coordinated and multidisciplinary approach, and finally highly specialist, inpatient, provision for those with very severe disorders.

The child psychiatrist's role in child protection

It could be argued that the failure of child psychiatric services to influence child protection in such a way as to put the needs of children for post-abuse help higher on the agenda is another bit of evidence indicating the imbalance in child protection. *Child Protection: Clarification of Arrangements between the NHS and other Agencies* (DoH/WO 1996) provides the following guidance to staff working in child and adolescent mental health services. Staff in these services may recognise or come to suspect that a child is being abused or is at risk of abuse, in which case they need to be familiar with the local procedures. They will require training, updating and clinical supervision for their role in child protection. Children who have been (or may have been abused) should only be assessed by staff with appropriate skills. Whilst the service needs to focus on both the needs of the child and those of the parents, the welfare of the child, and any other child in the family is paramount at all times. If the abuser is him or herself a juvenile, there may be an assessment role for the service and it is important to liaise with other appropriate bodies (for example, probation) which may provide a treatment service for abusers. Finally,

> Mental health professionals assessing actual or suspected abusers should ensure that any report produced, particularly for another agency or child protection conference, makes a clear statement of assessment of risk to any child with whom the abuser has contact regardless of diagnosis or treatability. (DoH/WO 1996: 12)

Like the community child health doctor, another role played by the child psychiatrist is to give evidence in care proceedings (or perhaps related proceedings, for example a child assessment order). This is especially likely to be the case where an attempt is being made to satisfy the significant harm threshold on the basis of emotionally damaging experiences alone. As pointed out by O'Hagan (1993) in a fictionalised account of a social worker giving evidence related to emotional abuse, it can be very difficult to establish emotional abuse to the satisfaction of a court. Other forms of abuse are more obvious, and also may have a more compelling impact on judges. In the case of court proceedings for emotional abuse however it is very likely that a child psychiatrist's assessment and evidence will be required.

The child psychiatrist's role on the ACPC

It is really quite remarkable how little *Working Together* (1991) or *Child Protection: Clarification of Arrangements between the NHS and other Agencies* (DoH/WO 1996) say about the role of the child psychiatrist in ACPCs. The role is so conspicuously absent in the considerations that one feels compelled to check that it really does specify that a child psychiatrist should be included ... and indeed it does. In Appendix 5, which lists who should be included on the ACPC, item (b)ii is 'Medical and psychiatric services professional representatives'. As we have already indicated, because of the lack of treatment emphasis within child protection services, the treatment needs of abused children gets marginal consideration within ACPCs, and therefore the child psychiatric role is less than it should be. In my view, the current role is restricted to a) meeting the most extreme treatment needs of children who have been abused, b) being clear about the responsibilities to report abuse when suspicions arise, and c) participating when required in the process of investigating abuse. This latter is less common, but is more likely to feature in cases where emotional or psychological abuse is the only form of abuse causing concern.

The role however, could be, and arguably should be, about coordinating the provisions of the type of post-therapeutic help of varying types that virtually all abused children need in varying degrees.

Child protection issues and dilemmas for child psychiatrists

Resource constraints   All forms of abuse entail some degree of emotional abuse. As we pointed out earlier, if children survive the abuse, and the vast majority do, then there will be developmental consequences for the child, in many cases quite serious, but overall reflecting a broad range of severity. In the words of one ACPC child psychiatrist, 'Whatever form of abuse occurs, it is never free of emotional abuse'. This may confront the child psychiatrist with the very difficult question of how much input to have into cases of child abuse. Because of resource constraints, it would certainly not be tenable for the child psychiatrist to attempt to attend every child protection conference. Indeed very few are likely to have a child psychiatrist (or even a team-member from the local child and family psychiatric service) in attendance.

Keeping the teams intact   Child and family psychiatric teams have been another arena in which the tensions within child protection have been played out. A good example of this has been the role of social work input into the teams. Since 1974, hospital social work has come under the management of the local authority social services department, being removed from the administration of health authorities who employed them previously. With the subsequent rise in child protection activity undertaken by local authority social services departments, one method of deploying more staff for child protection work attempted over the last two decades (sometimes successfully, sometimes not) has been to redeploy social workers based in child and family psychiatric teams into the social services departments. In the SSD teams they would either undertake child protection work as part of their generic child care social work role or more general social work with children and families, releasing others to specialise in child protection work. One of the early conflicts arising from this managerial approach was between the Maudsley Hospital and the London Borough of Southwark, but the issue continues and in Wales several agencies have more recently removed social work staff from child and family psychiatric facilities in order to redeploy them in social services departments. In some cases, because the social work role is considered vital to the operation of child and family psychiatric services, social work posts are being bought in privately.

There can hardly be a more stark manifestation of the imbalance within child protection policy between prevention, treatment and investigation, as I have described in this book, than this managerial approach to the need for more staff in child protection. Many of the difficulties experienced by children involved in the child and family psychiatric services will have arisen from experiences of parenting that may be described as abusive. And yet, the need for therapeutic input for such children is being subjected to the need to investigate child abuse allegations in a way that may ultimately lead to civil and criminal proceedings.

General practitioner

The role of the general practitioner

General practitioners are responsible for the primary health care of people in the community. Because of their relatively easy access, general practitioners are likely to have extensive contact over longer periods with children and their families than perhaps most other professionals. As a result, they have considerable knowledge of their patients, the patient's families, and of the communities within which their patients live. They provide temporal and geographical stability and continuity in the professional contact with the child and family. They also act as the vital referral link between people and other parts of the health service.

There are now two types of GP, fundholding and non-fundholding. The original proposal for fundholding general practitioners can be traced back to Maynard (1986) who proposed that GPs could be given the powers to purchase services from hospitals on behalf of their patients. The proposal was incorporated into the White Paper, *Working for Patients* (Secretaries of State for Health, Wales, Northern Ireland and Scotland 1989), and subsequently incorporated into the NHS and Community Care Act 1990. Not all GP practices were able to opt for fundholding status, some practices were too small for fundholding to be tenable. Of those who were eligible, many did not; the take-up was very patchy. In central London for example, the take-up was fairly low both because many of the practices were too small and because a good number of those practices that were eligible chose not to. Fitzgerald and Fitzgerald (1995), speaking from the perspective of general practitioners, highlight what they consider to be the advantages and disadvantages of non-fundholding. Advantages of non-fundholding are: less bureaucracy, less stress, less friction within the partnership (with a concomitant better patient–doctor relationship). Among the disadvantages suggested are: patients get a second-rate service in relation to outpatient appointments and hospital waiting lists, the practice receives less money per patient than fundholders; there is little help in upgrading facilities, and no money is available for ancillary services like physiotherapy or counselling.

General practitioners' surgeries have increasingly become the site of more community health services that in the past may have been located in community health clinics. The trend in recent years has been for services like family planning and child health screening to be based there. However, there are some hints of competition between GPs and the community paediatric service for child health surveillance work. Health visitors, as was indicated, are increasingly based in GP surgeries.

The GP's role in child protection

General practitioners as a group appear to have expressed more reservations about their involvement in child protection than most other professional groups. It is possible that the changes brought about by Medical Responsibilities (DoH/BMA/Conference of Medical Royal Colleges 1994), arose from the concerns of GPs in response to concerns about their resistance to involvement in child protection. Certainly there appeared to be much less concern on the part of paediatricians, and this may reflect the historical origins of child abuse originally being seen as a medical issue: Kempe was a paediatrician. It would be interesting to speculate on other reasons why there are differences between paediatricians and GPs on the need to balance protecting children against confidentiality. General practitioners are seen as reluctant to get involved, and unaccountable within the child protection process. Although there may be a tendency to attribute these to the impact of the health reforms, these difficulties preceded those reforms, and were arguably only made slightly more difficult by the creation of fundholding status. As regards the lack of accountability, it is striking how often GPs are described in terms that implied a complete autonomy. For example, one ACPC member said: 'Where they don't follow ACPC policy, the ability to ensure they do in future is extremely questionable.'

As with all professions involved in child protection there are likely to be individual variations. With GPs as well, there are some who work well in the child protection field and others who do not. The difficulty is that there is no way to improve the practice of the latter.

This autonomy has been seen to lead to difficulties, for example, lack of GP attendance at case conferences, GPs not reporting serious sexual abuse cases, and difficulties getting GP representation onto ACPCs. Problems of poor GP attendance at case conferences have been well documented (McMurray 1989; Harris 1991; Lea-Cox and Hall 1991). A study undertaken by Simpson et al. (1994) in Stirling found that out of a possible 190 case conferences, GPs attended just over 10.5 per cent, a very low figure in any case, but particularly so when compared with the level of attendance of health visitors (nearly 80 per cent).

Another concern about the lack of accountability of general practitioners is the higher degree of protection their professional status appears to afford them in the context of public anxiety about child abuse. Social workers (as we indicated earlier) and health visitors feel very vulnerable to accusations of not protecting children, particularly in cases resulting in a child abuse fatality. Though GPs have been criticised in inquiries (for example, the Reuben Carthy tragedy hinged around the non-reporting of injuries by a GP to Social Services – Nottingham Area Review Committee 1985), the impact on GP professional practice has been minimal, compared to the impact on developments within social services departments and social work. Noyes observes the following from his observations of the general practitioner role in inquiries:

> A theme running through the inquiries is the isolation of the GP and the non-involvement in the interagency system ... substantial evidence to suggest that many general practitioners do not operate within a co-operative philosophy and are isolated from the efforts which other professionals concerned with child welfare are making to ensure good liaison and common action to protect children from abuse ... it is rare for a general practitioner to attend a case conference ... concern that general practitioners may fail to diagnose abuse because of the relative rarity of presentation ... much evidence suggesting that the general practitioners isolate themselves ... isolation may be two way and so that general practitioners were not always invited to case conferences. (DoH 1991c: 13)

Bury and Elston as well have commented on the 'isolation' of GPs described above. They observed '... general practitioners and hospital doctors operate separately, both from each other and from the social services' (1987: 59). The

Audit Commission, in their overview of child welfare services provided by health and social services, comment in relation to child protection 'greater efforts are needed to secure the co-operation of ... GPs perhaps through individual approaches to ... GPs' (1994c: 45).

The GP's role on the ACPC

Prior to *Child Protection: Clarification of Arrangements between the NHS and Other Agencies* (DoH/WO 1996), there were considerable difficulties with the representation of general practitioners on Area Child Protection Committees, and it remains to be seen to what extent the new guidance will resolve them. Certainly it attempts to address some of the issues which have caused difficulties in the past, and which we describe briefly here. Under the new arrangements, both fundholding and non-fundholding GPs are to be represented on the ACPC. There is a GP who is there as a representative of the Local Medical Committee. The fundholding GPs may be represented by a number of means, by arrangement through the Health Authority representative, by a representative of a multi-fund or consortium, or by the GP representative from the Local Medical Committee.

Let us now look at some of the concerns about GP involvement in ACPCs. Jackson et al. (1994) commented extensively on this role. The same types of concerns about lack of accountability and autonomy in practice are reflected in ACPCs. They found that several committees experienced difficulty in recruiting GP representatives. Different reasons were given: lack of commitment to the process of managing child protection, lack of funding for attendance at meetings, and a feeling of inability to represent other general practitioners. Where GPs were able to be recruited, their attendance level of 38 per cent was the lowest of all the professional groups represented on ACPCs. Once there, they encountered difficulties in deriving mandates from, and feeding back to, colleagues. Unlike more formalised and structured agencies, for GP representatives, the approach to representing views is not to know how colleagues will think on every issue that comes up, but rather that their colleagues know who to contact if they have anxieties about a child protection issue. There is concern to get it right, so that representatives do not find themselves agreeing to something that colleagues would find untenable. In some cases a representative might take an issue to the Local Medical Committee to seek a representative view (bearing in mind that the LMC may be a small committee representing the interests of a much larger community of general practitioners). The GP representative is a channel into the ACPC for GP concerns. However, the effectiveness of this approach is open to question, as GP representatives (along with headteachers) are the least active contributors to ACPC agendas. This may reflect only a lack of proactive role in the agenda;

they may possibly feel a better mandate from colleagues in connection with issues that are already on the agenda. This seems unlikely. Rather it appears to confirm that the GP representative is in difficulty trying to represent a colleague group who simply have no interest in issues of child protection.

Another manifestation of the difficulty surrounding the involvement in general practitioners in child protection is in the local handbook for interagency procedures. In examining the guidance for general practitioners contained in eight handbooks:

> All except one of the handbooks incorporated guidance for general practitioners ... Of the seven handbooks that offered advice to general practitioners, no two mechanisms for referring concerns were identical, despite all being loosely based on the guidance in *Working Together*. The differences largely come from applying different procedures to different situations. In one handbook, there is a different/ additional procedure for sexual abuse from that for other forms of abuse. In another handbook, there are four circumstances described (emergency, non-emergency, sexual abuse, and worrying background), all of which have a different set of requirements for the general practitioner. In some cases the general practitioner is advised to refer to the Social Services Department at the same time as referring to the paediatrician. In others, the referral to the paediatrician can come before (as a consultation), or even instead (passing to the paediatrician the responsibility to make the referral) of a referral to the Social Services ... conclude that the variation reflects the results of different locally negotiated agreements. It is more difficult to determine the extent to which these divergent solutions are manifestations of communication difficulties and unresolved issues between general practitioners and Area Child Protection Committees. It is known for example, that the ACPC producing the handbook which contains no reference to general practitioners has experienced other difficulties in its relationships with this group of professionals. (Jackson et al. 1994: 113–14)

Finally, it is surprising how little use is made of the Continuing Medical Education (CME) tutor, to promote training for general practitioners in child protection. The CME tutor is the person with responsibility for organising postgraduate education for GPs. There are requirements for GPs to have a modest amount of continuing education, through attendance at approved courses. One way of increasing the profile of child protection for GPs would be for the topic to be incorporated into CME training programmes. One way of beginning this would be to consider the nature of the connection between CME tutors and the ACPC training subcommittee.

Child protection issues and dilemmas for GPs

Parent–child conflict A very real difficulty for GPs is the role conflict for them in trying to balance their patient responsibilities with the child-as-patient and parent-as-patient dichotomy. The system of medical ethics which has evolved has apparently not equipped them to address these kinds of conflicting interests in such a way as will allow them, as it has for others, to make a priority of the interests of the child-as-patient. That being said, this does appear to conflict with the Gillick principle, where, at least with older children, in relation to consent to treatment, the interests (and wishes) of the child are able to take precedence.

Continuity of involvement   I have briefly referred to the GP's continuity with the child and family over a longer period of time. After the child is removed from the home (which albeit happens in a very few cases, but may appear in the minds of many to be a more frequent occurrence than it actually is), the general practitioner will still have ongoing contact with the family. This may produce some discomfort for him or her.

Contracts   GPs work to service contracts. If it's in the contract, they do it; if it's not in the contract, they don't do it. In the past, health representatives on ACPCs have commented on the lack of child protection responsibilities in contracts as being a factor contributing to a lack of emphasis and priority within practice. The new guidance is very clear on the need to include child protection in contracts: 'Comprehensive service specifications for services for children, of which child protection is a key component, should be drawn up ... Child protection should be specifically addressed within service specifications' (DoH/WO 1996: paragraph 2.25–2.27). It remains to be seen what impact this will have on the clarity of health professional responsibilities in child protection.

Local issue/national dilemma   I have already referred to the difficulty of ACPCs trying to resolve locally issues that are essentially national in character. The involvement of GPs in child protection is a particular issue. It seems that we will have to wait until there is a real national commitment to children before some of these issues can be resolved. This is not to suggest that it will be resolved simply by getting more GPs to attend child protection conferences (for example, by setting that as a specific target to be achieved, which can be monitored). As I have indicated previously, a fundamental difficulty in British child protection is the balance of priorities. In order to get GPs more involved in child protection, it may be necessary to a) ensure that the national agenda for child protection is open to dialogue (as it has the potential to become in the 'refocusing' debate), and b) find out what is on GPs' agenda for child protection. How would they imagine a child protection system should operate? The research does not shed much light on what positive expectations general practitioners would have of a child protection system, and how they would see their role in that system.

Making a referral to child protection   One of the big stumbling blocks for GPs has been the issue of dealing with uncertainty about suspicions of abuse. If a bruise or a disclosure is clear-cut then GPs are able to deal with the situation by referring the matter to an agency who will investigate the abuse. On the other hand, in many cases the evidence may be very border-line, and there is a need for sharing with another individual. Under previous guidance, any suspicion, no matter how slight, was to be referred to the investigating agencies. This may involve the matter eventually being referred to a medical professional with more experience of child abuse (paediatrician), but after the matter has been shared with non-medical professionals, a process seen as violating confidentiality, particularly if the judgement is that the matter would not warrant a referral to child protection. This would constitute a violation of medical confidentiality. The revised arrangements allow for an internal medical dialogue between GPs and more experienced colleagues before referring to child protection. That being the case, there is still no guarantee that after receiving advice from a paediatrician that a matter should be referred to the child protection system, that the GP will still do it, but it seems arguable, that more of the doubtful cases will be referred to the system than previously.

The Case for Adult Psychiatrists on Area Child Protection Committees

Falkov (1996b, 1997) reviewed the context and historical overview, as well as the extent and nature of the association between parental psychiatric disorder and child maltreatment in a two-part Highlight series for the National Children's Bureau. He observes that the literature on the association is pre-dominantly based on studies exploring the presence of a mental disorder in maltreating parents, rather than on developmental outcomes for children of parents with a mental disorder. I have already referred to Falkov's material on the link between parental psychiatric disorders and child abuse fatalities (1996a), where a rather high level of parental disorder was found. I also referred to the significance of parental psychiatric disorder in the Colton et al. (1996) study of Part 8 Reviews. Two of the issues considered by Cassell and Coleman in their discussion are parents with depression (which they consider to be the more substantially researched area) and psychotic parents. In connection with depression they note that children are more likely to be adversely affected, perhaps to the point of significant harm, when the depression 'affects all aspects of family life, when relationships are unreliable or when the parent's hopelessness and lack of energy lead to neglect' (1995: 171). In the case of psychosis, there is more risk to children if the child is somehow involved in the parent's delusional system. They also look at the impact on children of a range of neurotic disorders.

One must consider whether the involvement of adult psychiatrists in ACPCs would address some of these issues. However, one of the dangers in child protection has been the tendency (more pronounced in the US) to pathologise the causes of child abuse as mental disorder, as if to say 'children are abused because their parents are mentally ill', or 'a person would have to be mentally ill to abuse a child'. Zigler and Hall (1989) for example, in their consideration of the aetiology of child abuse, describe the psychiatric orientation as being the earliest model, but nevertheless still widely used. In their criticisms of the approach, the empirical justification for which they consider to be equivocal, they include: '... by believing abusers to be "crazies", remedial and preventive efforts are directed away from the general population where abuse is most likely to occur' (Zigler and Hall 1989: 60).

With that caveat, there could be at least three roles for adult psychiatrists in Area Child Protection Committees, (whilst still avoiding the trap of 'pathologising' all child abuse aetiology):

- To coordinate services between child welfare agencies and adult psychiatric services to ensure a focus on children's welfare when a parent is suffering from a mental disorder, and the impact of being a parent on an individual's mental health
- To consider risks of unpredictable and dangerous behaviour on the part of parents towards their child(ren)
- To consider, in conjunction with probation services, the extent and range of services for sexual abusers.

This might help to address the difficulties raised by Falkov (1996a) in which child protection services were not sufficiently oriented towards adult psychiatric services, and the latter were not sufficiently in tune with the vulnerability and heightened risk to children of parents with a severe mental disorder.

Education

The role of education professionals (general)

One way of looking at schools and schooling is as the main vehicle through which the societal construction of childhood is worked out. Education has changed dramatically over the centuries: 'Since the Second World War, school has become an increasingly important part of a child's life, dominating evenings with homework and effectively ending the old habits of juvenile contributions to domestic management' (Hardyment 1992: 92). Schooling has gone from being a provision made for an elite few, males, by predominantly religious bodies for purposes of 'enlightening' to something that is provided free for all on a compulsory basis (in many countries) for purposes related to the roles that people will take in society. Whereas in medieval times and earlier, people's social status in life was fixed at birth, in contemporary times in societies where there is greater social mobility (for example as manifested by differences between one's own socio-economic status and one's parents), such mobility is related to the provision of education within society and the educational attainment of the individual. There are variations throughout the world. Provisions within the UN Convention specify the right of the child to education, making 'primary education compulsory and available free to all' (Article 28(1)). The Convention further specifies that countries should provide secondary and higher education, ensuring a range of provision in secondary education, and should make efforts to encourage attendance and reduce dropping out. As we saw when we looked at the work of Hetherington et al. (1997) all of the European countries they examined provided universal education from the age of five or six.

Within the UK there are a range of issues concerning the provision of education that serve as a background to looking at the role of education in child protection services. I have already referred to issues arising from the education reforms undertaken during the last ten years beginning with the 'seismic' Education Reform Act (1988). In addition, the Children Act (1989) contained numerous provisions pertaining to schools and their relationship with the local authority, specifically the social services. For example, the 1989 Act provides that in the case of children in need, children who need assessments for the purpose of educational statementing may have the assessment combined with that necessary for the purposes of establishing the services needing to be arranged by the social services department. Whilst this does not appear to have yet been undertaken on a large scale (probably because it is a power rather than a duty), it does provide opportunities for education authorities, schools and social services to work closely together. The Act contains a provision that other agencies must help social services departments fulfil their responsibilities to children in need (unless incompatible with their other responsibilities), and education is one of those other authorities listed. For the first time with the Act, a duty to review the local provision of day care (section 19) was established, and this duty is undertaken in conjunction between the social services and the education authority. In some places, social services will take the lead in coordinating the review, in other places education, but the emphasis is that it must be a joint undertaking. There are also new provisions pertaining to the liaison between education/schools and social services when children are looked after. Some of the other issues that have taxed teachers are bullying in schools, school exclusions and teacher overload.

Bullying has been an issue within schools for centuries, but it is only in the last two decades that it has begun to be the subject of serious study, and only within the last five years that it has begun to be defined as an issue about which action needed to be taken. In recent times many, but by no means all, schools have begun to reframe the concept of bullying from an accepted evil ('something that happens') about which individual children have to learn how to develop individualised strategies to avoid becoming, or continuing to be, the victim of a bully. 'You've got to stand up to them' was the advice most commonly given, along with meaningless aphorisms, such as 'They're all cowards really'. It has been reframed as a social difficulty in which some young people have learned (for a variety of reasons) to abuse power in their social dealings with others. It is no longer seen as an accepted evil, but rather as a social ill which can, and should, be addressed. With some schools beginning to develop very proactive approaches to the problem, it also becomes an issue about which there are wide variations in practice between schools.

About 25 per cent of primary school children have been the victims of bullying whilst the figure drops to about ten per cent for secondary schools. The period of transition from primary into secondary school is a time of particular vulnerability for pupils. The more positive responses from schools tend to begin with a policy which acknowledges that bullying is a form of inter-personal abusive behaviour that must be challenged by the school taking a very strong stance to show all pupils that it is not to be tolerated. The policy, developed by the school governors, perhaps with advice from the local education authority, may encourage pupils to inform if they are victims, know of people being bullied or indeed if students engaged in bullying behaviour are wanting to seek help for themselves to address the difficulty. The policy will ordinarily contain specific action to be taken in relation to all parties involved in the bullying, and will need to be very clear in particular as to how to empower the victim in bullying situations. In some cases it may lead to exclusion from school for the bully.

School exclusion is another difficulty faced by schools. The numbers of school exclusions have increased in recent years. As pointed out by Brodie (1995), boys are three or four times more likely to be excluded than girls; children from ethnic minorities are excluded more than their white counter-parts (a study in Nottingham suggested five times more likely), and children who are looked after by the local authority have a very high risk of school

Table 5.3: Trends in school exclusions (Brodie 1995)

Year	Exclusions
1990–91	2,910
1991–92	3,833
1992–93	8,000 (900 permanently)
1993–94	11,000

exclusion. The reasons for increase have been attributed to the education reforms. The competition between schools may be making schools less committed to having difficult pupils on the books; the national curriculum demands may limit the strategies and time available for staff to deal with disaffected pupils, and finally, the budgets being managed by schools may suggest that for pupils within two years of school leaving, excluding may be financially more attractive than the process of statementing.

Finally, teachers have experienced considerable professional strain in implementing the national curriculum and the other changes brought about by the education reforms. Much of the administrative work associated with increased testing in primary and secondary school, leading to the establishment of 'league tables' has been undertaken by teachers who already consider themselves overloaded in the provision of extra teaching to enable students to do well in exams.

The main responsibilities of education in relation to child protection

The education role within the management of child protection is not an easy one and is probably best described as potentially, if not actually, tense. And yet, the role of education in child protection services is extremely important. As an agency, they will have most contact with an individual child (of school age). Schools are an important source of information in cases of suspected abuse (Cleaver and Freeman 1995). Briggs (1997) summarises three main reasons why schools are important in child protection: the majority of children aged 5–16 are enrolled in school, teachers have extensive contact with children who have been abused, and teachers are (or should be) trained in child development.

There are three main functions that education provides in relation to the child protection system (apart from developing effective strategies for dealing with bullying, which many would define as a form of abuse). The first is to act as a referral agent for school-age children. The second is to contribute to child abuse prevention, in two ways, a) through the provision of 'keep safe' programmes which are intended to help prevent children being sexually abused, and b) through teaching designed to develop parenting skills in young people so that they are better prepared for parenthood when it comes. In some cases this latter point may be combined with strategies designed to encourage students to put off having children until they are more mature, part of a national strategy designed to reduce teenage pregnancies. The third function is to contribute to interagency discussions and planning for children who have been abused. These functions are described in both *Working Together* (1991) and the new Working Together consultation document (DoH 1998) and have been further developed by government guidance issued in 1995. *Working Together* (1991) states: 'The education service does not constitute an investigation or intervention agency, but has an important role to play at the recognition and referral stage' (paragraph 4.35) and 'Schools and further education colleges have a role in preventing abuse not only by adopting sound policies and procedures on the management of situations where there is suspected abuse, but also through the curriculum' (paragraph 4.39). In relation to child protection conferences, *Working Together* (1991) notes: 'All the agencies which have specific responsibilities in the child protection process should be invited to send representatives. These include: ... education (when the child is of school age)' (paragraph 6.25). The main points of the 1995 guidance (Welsh Office Circular 52/95) concern staff awareness of indicators of abuse, the need for a designated teacher, staff awareness of local child protection procedures, school procedures in cases of child abuse or abuse of a child by a member of staff, training for designated staff, and the need for a local education authority senior officer to have responsibility for child protection.

The ability of teachers and others in schools to act as a referral agent of children who may have been abused, or likely to be at risk of being abused, are related to a number of factors – the ability to recognise abuse and its indicators (overcoming perhaps internal predispositions *not* to see), an understanding of the responsibilities when children are abused, and finally an inclination to act in accordance with those responsibilities. All of these are potentially problematical.

As noted by David (1993) in a chapter entitled 'It doesn't happen here: schools and child protection', the failure of teachers to actually see the occurrence of child sexual abuse may be based on their belief in childhood innocence. This belief has had to be challenged by many professionals in their training on child sexual abuse (but especially those involved in investigating abuse); it may be that teachers continue to find this difficult because they receive less training in abuse than these other professionals. If they are able to overcome this predisposition not to see, then teachers have to recognise the indicators of abuse, and this too, in the context of a lack of training for teachers is problematical. Finally, and perhaps most significantly from an investigative perspective of child abuse, when teachers are aware that a child is being abused, they may not report it. Two reasons for this are lack of knowledge of the reporting procedures, (the importance of which is emphasised in *Working Together* (1991)) and an unwillingness to report despite knowledge of it being required. David (1993) notes that teachers may be unwilling because of their fears of overintrusive intervention on the part of the social services (removal of the child from his or her home *and* from the school). Crenshaw et al. (1995) in the US found that the factors that were related to whether educators (who overall had a high level of awareness of mandatory reporting requirements) reported child abuse or not were the type of abuse, the 'quality of suspicion' (in other words how certain they were) and the educators' belief that schools should be the first line of defence against child abuse and neglect. Abrahams et al. (1992), also in the US, undertook a survey of 568 teachers and found that 74 per cent had encountered a potential case of child abuse and neglect and 90 per cent reported it. That seems a rather high rate of non-reporting in the context of mandatory reporting requirements. Teachers in that study also considered that they had insufficient education on addressing child abuse. Webster (1991) also highlights the need for teacher training to enable them to respond to child sexual abuse. Despite these concerns about barriers to reporting, it should be noted that education is a main avenue of referral to the child protection system. Gibbons et al. (1995a), for example, noted that teachers, school nurses and education welfare provided 23 per cent of referrals whereas health staff provided 17 per cent, household members and other lay people 17 per cent, social services professionals 13 per cent, and police or probation twelve per cent. They also found that schools provide the kinds of resources that might make a difference in the lives of abused children (Gibbons et al. 1995a).

Using schools as a means of preventing abuse has a strong appeal because it emphasises primary prevention, which I have already indicated is a relatively neglected area of child protection. Most of the literature on keeping children protected from abuse by school programmes is in relation to sexual abuse. In the US, Kohl (1993) surveyed 126 school-based sexual abuse prevention programmes and found that they reached hundreds of thousands of students, parents, teachers and other school staff. She also noted that most were well established (since early to mid-1980s) and operated a prescribed curriculum and resource materials, although there were differences in format, duration and materials used. It is also useful to note that such programmes have been developed around the world – Canada and New Zealand both have launched exciting and innovative programmes designed to help children explore issues of keeping themselves safe, distinguishing between good touches and bad touches, taking early action to mobilise protective services, etc.

One of the difficulties with school-based sexual abuse prevention programmes is the lack of outcome measures on their effectiveness. Outcomes tend to be measured by pre- and post-test comparisons of knowledge of sexual abuse (not just necessarily students). However, I referred earlier to the work of MacMillan (1994b) whose overview concluded that whilst such programmes do increase safety skills and knowledge about sexual abuse, no study has provided evidence that the programme actually reduces the occurrence of sexual abuse. This is a serious shortcoming, especially if one considers the view of Webster that many school-based child sexual abuse prevention programmes are 'seriously flawed, have not been scientifically evaluated, and contain unintended negative consequences for both children and teachers' (1991: 146). Johnson (1997) in his evaluation of the impact of personal safety education in Australia found some children to be reluctant to use the measures they had been taught; they concluded that over-reliance on one preventive strategy was dangerous.

The child protection role(s) of the senior agency managers (those likely to be on Area Child Protection Committees)

The child protection responsibilities within schools and local education authorities are described in *Working Together* (1991). Apart from that, there is little reference to child protection responsibilities in the education statutes. It is not surprising therefore that manuals for school governors say very little about it (Mahoney 1988; Sallis 1988; Leonard 1989; Baher 1990). In fact, they say little or nothing even about liaison with social services, which would suggest that other than issues of exclusion and suspension, school governors are not being made aware of their responsibilities for groups of children with difficulties. I have referred previously to the child protection content of school inspections.

Area Child Protection Committees are likely to have several representatives from education. There should be a senior representative from the local education authority and in addition, there should be at least one representative from the schools. Frequently there will be a separate representative for primary schools and for secondary schools. *Working Together* (1991) has guidance for the local education authority representatives and for the 'designated' teachers within schools (which all schools are required to have, p.120), but does not address the role of the headteacher representative on ACPCs. The headteacher representative will most likely be one of the local 'designated teachers'. A 'designated teacher' is a person within the school who ensures 'that locally established procedures are followed' and who acts 'as the channel for communicating to the social services department relevant concerns expressed by any member of the school staff about individual children'. They are not particularly meant to be experts in child abuse (although they should be knowledgeable about signs and indicators of abuse), and the guidance emphasises that 'Investigation of cases must be left to the social services department or other appropriate agencies.' Thus they are meant to be knowledgeable about what procedures are to be followed when concerns arise about a child who may be being abused, but should not undertake other actions. In primary schools, the 'designated teacher' is ordinarily the headmaster. In secondary schools, however, the 'designated teacher' is less frequently the headmaster, and more often is a deputy head of the school (probably one with pastoral responsibilities). Likewise, for the youth service a senior officer should have the same responsibilities as a designated teacher. As regards the role of the designated officer within the local education authority, *Working Together* (1991) says that he or she should have 'responsibility for co-ordinating education service – including youth service – policy and action on child protection' (p.120). This should include ensuring that 'arrangements for designated teachers are in place'. The person should also be the normal point of contact between the education service and the social services, and would normally be the representative on the ACPC.

Child protection issues and dilemmas for schools and the education service

Lack of training I have mentioned in this section the fact that teachers may not refer situations that should be referred partly because they receive less training than perhaps they should. Because of the large numbers of teachers, a distinction could be made, as was done in the case of the police, between what those who are specialising in child abuse and child protection need to know (for example, the designated teachers) and what every teacher needs to know. Unlike the police however, there is a much reduced emphasis on this. Jackson et al. (1994) found one authority who were producing two levels of guidance for professionals along these lines – one that would be distributed to all staff containing basic information about what to do if concerned, the other giving much more detailed information about roles of those with specific responsibility for child protection. In the case of teachers especially, written guidance, rather than training, appears to be the managerial means whereby staff are informed of their responsibilities. However, simply having access to guidelines is frequently not enough to help a teacher decide what action to take when confronted with a very uncertain situation in which the possibility of abuse may be one consideration.

Providing child protection training for teachers is problematical, especially since the decentralisation of education authorities. Braun (1988, 1994), David (1993) and Wonnacott (1995) have described the content that would need to be included in training teachers about child abuse and child protection, so there is no shortage of material. However curriculum pressures and decentralised budgets do not allow for many teachers to take part. As noted previously, INSET days are devoted almost exclusively to curriculum matters. In cases where training is provided free of charge to participating agencies, teachers often have difficulty attending because of the high cost of supply teachers to cover whilst they are away. Braun (1994) described the cost to the school of a teacher being away for a day as being about £100 at that time. This must come from a very tightly managed local budget. It may not be a priority, even for designated teachers, as described by David (1993: 79) where a 'young teacher colleague who volunteered to go on a course and to act as the named contact was refused permission because of National Curriculum work'. Interestingly, Tite (1994) in Canada found similar conflicts between child protection and the main activity of teaching (concerns about academic learning) which we can take as similar to national curriculum preoccupations in the UK), and also commented on 'haphazard' exposure of teachers to child abuse information.

Doing too little; doing too much   Unless teachers are very clear about their role, there is a danger that they can do either too little or too much. Doing too little would entail not reporting concerns to the appropriate individual in order for procedures to be followed. I have pointed to a number of reasons this might occur. At the other extreme, doing too much could entail teachers undertaking unauthorised investigative work, asking too many detailed questions prior to the matter being properly investigated (if investigation is warranted). To start with, it is now known that children object strongly to being interviewed at school, and this is particularly true if they are taken out of class for the purpose (Thoburn et al. 1995). Further, although it is not the primary objective of the child protection system, a potential criminal prosecution, and even necessary care proceedings could be undermined if a child is questioned before a proper investigation in a way which might influence how that child responds to the investigation. Doing too much can be seen to arise from two difficulties: not being clear about the need to refer on, and trying to fit the concern into a pastoral model of addressing a child's difficulties. It is quite understandable that, in other circumstances, a teacher on learning of the distress a child was experiencing would seek to question the child so as to ensure the child knew that he or she was interested, and to gain as full a picture as possible so as to be able to advise the child. But this is just what must not happen when the concern is abuse. Both social services and the police, (and no doubt the Crown Prosecution Service) get very worried about people who are not trained investigators contaminating evidence by leading questions, planting ideas in the child's mind, obtaining statements in circumstances that cannot be tested, etc.

A further difficulty is the tendency to want to respect a child's request that the matter is disclosed in confidence. It is accepted good practice that children should be told as early as possible, as soon as there is an indication of what might be forthcoming, that concerns about the child's welfare must be reported to the appropriate agency. Ideally, a child would know this before even making the decision to approach a teacher, but it is unlikely that children's awareness of child abuse and child protection, even with 'Keep Safe' school-based prevention programmes, would entail that awareness.

Peripheral role of schools in child protection   A very disturbing aspect of child protection is the extent to which education is on the periphery of child protection. David (1993: 78) notes: 'Most documents about child abuse and protection ... appear to have had little or no input from classroom teachers or even heads of schools'. I referred earlier to my work with colleagues (Sanders et al. 1997) which looked at how two factors in particular seemed to account for the 'levels of involvement' in the management of child protection services, found by several researchers (Evans and Miller 1992; Jackson et al. 1994) as manifested through the operation of Area Child Protection Committees. Those two factors were the extent of the fragmentation of the agency (and we have seen the decentralising impact of the education reforms since 1988), and the extent to which the policy objectives of the agency are in accord with those of child protection. By policy emphasis I was referring to the extent to which the agency is involved in investigation, prevention or treatment of abuse. In effect this means that agencies such as the police and social services which are both strongly centralised (or at least not fragmented to the same extent) *and* have a strong emphasis on investigation (which in the current child protection ethos drives the child protection system) are at the centre of child protection. Agencies such as education and general practitioners which are both highly decentralised and do not have a significant role in investigation are at the very fringe. Other agencies which may be high on one and low on the other are somewhere in between. Jackson et al. (1994) found a number of indicators that education was indeed on the periphery of the interagency management of child protection.

When they compared all of the interagency relationships between social services, health, police and education (ten dyadic comparisons) at both field level (as rated by managers) and at Area Child Protection Committee level, they found that all agency relationships with education were rated as the least strong. Headteachers were very poor attenders of ACPC meetings (attending on average 47 per cent of meetings) and very rarely contributed to the ACPC agendas. Like their GP colleagues on Area Child Protection Committees which

I discussed earlier, headteacher representatives also have considerable difficulty representing their profession on the ACPC. One secondary school headteacher I interviewed in connection with the Welsh Office Review (Jackson et al. 1994) indicated that although being on the ACPC had benefited him considerably in that he became much better informed about child abuse and child protection matters, and benefited his school because of his greater awareness, he did not consider that the other secondary schools in the ACPC area had benefited from his representation on the Committee. He did not feel that he had an understanding of the variations between schools in child protection practice, nor did he feel that he had means to influence that practice. Although there were meetings of the local heads in the area, child protection matters were not on the agenda. There was no forum for designated teachers to meet.

Abuse by teachers and allegations of abuse against teachers   One of the most pressing concerns within child protection for teachers is that they will be the subject of an allegation of abuse; a very pressing child protection concern of social services and the police is that teachers will abuse students. Physical punishment as a form of school discipline is something about which there has been a gradually changing attitude from one of it being necessary for the child's character to one where it is construed as a form of publicly condoned institutional child abuse. The practice is becoming increasingly unacceptable throughout the world. Benthall (1991) notes that the ritual corporal punishment practised in English boarding schools must be seen as both physical and sexual ('psychosexual dynamics'). It is interesting to speculate therefore on the extent to which the vulnerability of school children to sexual abuse can be seen as an outgrowth of this practice.

Sloan (1989) describes the 1986 case of a head teacher in Cornwall investigated for child abuse, highlighting the need for joint intervention by police and social services and more training for teaching staff. Jones (1994) looked at the power relations within an English special residential school setting where the principal was able to sexually (and physically) abuse a number of boys. The legitimation of his authority derived from parents, local authorities and the community is seen as contributing to the abuse. There are parallels to be drawn with the social services concerns of abuse of children in residential care establishments which I have previously described. Jackson et al. (1994) when collecting data for their study of the operation of Area Child Protection Committees found a number of the ACPCs to be grappling with the complex interagency dynamics involved in attempting to develop policies about abuse by professionals because of the concerns of education representatives. Dolmage (1995) in Ontario examined the prevalence of accusations, charges and convictions of teacher sexual abuse of students and found that the numbers were low, given the size of the population of the public school system, and that the acquittal rate for teachers appeared to be higher than one would expect. This gives some credence to the concern by teachers that they are more likely to be falsely accused than others because of their close contact with children. Colton et al. (1996) found that two of the 21 Part 8 Reviews they examined were undertaken because of a teacher (in one case a head-teacher) systematically sexually abusing children over a number of years.

Hodgkins (1994) speaking at the Michael Sieff Conference in 1994, described the fear of false allegations experienced by teachers as 'profound'. He describes the three distinct sets of proceedings arising from allegations (criminal proceedings, child-care proceedings and disciplinary proceedings), and noted the potential for confusion amongst participants between them. In response to the concern about false allegations, managers and teachers have attempted to adopt practices that will minimise the risk of false allegations being made (not being alone with a child, or alternatively keeping the door open at all times; not touching a child, even for the purposes of comforting when distressed or upset). It has been observed however, that these practices detract from the kind of ordinary caring and warm environment that one would hope to create within a school. Other actions are more a matter of clarification, for example, 'clearly defining inappropriate professional contact' and 'defining and drawing up guidelines concerning restraint' (Hodgkins 1994). There were also some recommendations made concerning how such allegations should be handled, including ensuring that the individual is informed about the outcome of an investigation of an allegation, enabling the individual to attend case conferences in the way that a parent can (a rather controversial proposal which was questioned at the time), and looking at levels and kinds of support for accused individuals. Many of these are the same issues that arise in connection with foster carers and residential workers accused of abusing children in their care. Eric Forth MP, speaking at the same conference, indicated appreciation of the fears about false allegations against teachers, and awareness of the very serious consequences of such an allegation on both the accused and his family. The annex to the 1995 government guidance (Welsh Office 1995), provides guidelines on action to take upon learning of an allegation, situations that may or may not require a referral to the child protection agencies, the investigations that may arise, the follow-up action after the matter has been referred to the child protection system, the involvement of the police, who should be notified, considering whether suspension is appropriate, support for the teacher during the period of suspension, and other matters. It would seem that many of the issues considered at the Michael Sieff Conference were integrated into the government guidance.

It is clear that children are sexually abused by teachers (who may have used their entry into the profession as a means to gain access to children), and that teachers are at risk (perhaps even more so than other professionals) of false allegations of sexual abuse being made against them. Attempting to develop policies on the basis of denying, or even minimising, either of these aspects runs the risk of generating conflict rather than creating solutions, and so both must be firmly acknowledged when ACPCs are trying to develop policies on 'professional abuse'.

Providing a sensitive and supportive service for abused children   Compared to other children, abused children are more likely to show behaviour problems at school and have difficulties with friendships (Gibbons et al. 1995b), difficulties which may present challenges for schools. Can schools help by providing a 'therapeutic environment' for children known to have been abused; will the national curriculum demands allow for that? Many abused children can quickly be absorbed into the 'emotionally and behaviourally disturbed' (EBD) stream, which can all too quickly lead to exclusion and education provision in separate (and severely limited) establishments. Sexual 'acting out' of children who have been sexually abused, and who have become 'sexualised', is very likely to happen in the school context where children have considerable unsupervised peer group contact, and this can present major difficulties for schools. It may take the form of children being sexually provocative, because that has been part of their socialisation experience, or it may take the form of children being sexually predatory, seeking to create opportunities to involve others in the sexual activities they have previously experienced. Ideally, teachers would be involved in a comprehensive inter-agency child abuse treatment planning programme for each child devised as a consequence of the child protection intervention, but as I have noted, treatment in child protection is given the lowest priority. The role of teachers as defined in guidance is about making sure they know how, when, and to whom to report suspicions of abuse.

6 Conclusions

The government proposes to revise *Working Together* (1991) to take account of the need to refocus child protection services. The consultation document (DoH 1998) contains much that is familiar in terms of the previous two versions of *Working Together* (1988, 1991), for example, the structure of the consultation document is modelled very closely on the two previous versions. The main message according to the document is that 'child protection work must be placed firmly within the context of wider services for children in need' (paragraph 1.2). The revised guidance will provide clearer guidelines on how children enter and leave the child protection system, and on the interface between child protection systems and systems for children in need. In considering the causes of stress on families, it is welcome to see consideration of social exclusion, but the focus (emphasising domestic violence, mental illness of a parent or carer, and misuse of drugs or alcohol) still appears to favour a pathological model of understanding child abuse that is based on aberrant parents, or at the broadest level, dysfunctioning families. However, the summary of the list of eleven proposals (DoH 1998: 6–7) and the translation of those proposals into ten specific objectives of the child protection system is welcome and contains some very useful items, relevant to some of the themes I have discussed in this book. The proposals, for example, contain the following provisions which suggest that the child protection system should:

- Be owned by all agencies not just social services
- Promote access to services for children in need without triggering child protection

- Encourage agencies to provide treatment and therapy for children who have been abused
- Promote a stronger message about community responsibility for protecting children.

Among the ten objectives are the following which suggest that child protection should:

- Give clear routes in and out of the child protection system so that children and families are not drawn into the net unnecessarily
- Recognise the significance of ethnic and cultural diversity
- Promote community responsibility for the welfare of children.

By selecting these seven, I do not mean to imply that the others are less important, but they are perhaps less novel, containing, for example, an emphasis on cost-effectiveness, involving parents, listening to the views of the child, protecting children at risk of significant harm. Some of these are messages that were contained in the Children Act 1989 and in *Working Together* (1991). After this statement of proposals and objectives, the document proceeds to offer questions on the functioning of Area Child Protection Committees, legal and ethical considerations, the roles of the various agencies involved in child protection, the arrangements for working together in individual cases, the child protection conference and the register, joint training and case reviews.

At one and the same time, change is not easy, and yet it is impossible to avoid because change is happening all around us, and the systems within which we operate – families, workplaces, communities, child protection systems – continually adapt to the ongoing changes around them. As I stated at the beginning, this book is about the operation of systems within systems. In order for the internal system to operate, it must adapt to the changing environment created by the external system. In this metaphor, we can talk about the ACPC as the coordinating body of the local child protection system being the internal system, operating within the external 'system' of government child protection policy. That system can be seen as dynamic (changing over time, historically) and as located within the wider system of international efforts to protect children from abuse (cross-culturally). Jackson et al. (1994) noted that though many representatives on ACPCs wanted to move in certain specific directions, they felt that the operation of the ACPC was constrained to operate in accordance with government policy, and government policy was about the forensic process of investigating abuse. One of the peculiar ironies about the attempt to change the direction of the child protection system is, as a colleague once remarked to me, that many of the messages to come out of the research upon which the new proposals are based were well known to practitioners. It was well known, certainly in the early days of child protection, that there are disadvantages, in terms of harm to family functioning, in bringing families into the child protection system. That's no surprise to any practitioner. It was well known that for many families, the stress of surviving under very adverse circumstances was a contributing factor to child abuse. That's no surprise either. Nor it is a surprise that children who have been abused need help. Practitioners may have learned more and more about the particular difficulties that may arise from the experience of being abused, but the general principle that abuse is 'developmentally toxic' (to use the phrase by Summit) was well accepted, and it was appreciated that as a result children needed something to help them unravel the abuse – not necessarily a child psychiatrist, but someone capable of helping them make sense, in a positive way that builds esteem, of the damaging experiences they have had. What is perhaps a surprise for practitioners is that after years, building on commissioned research, the government appears to be set to change child protection policy in a direction that will address some of these long-standing difficulties.

However, before being seduced by the potential benefits of a child protection system overhaul, it may be useful to consider the extent to which the proposals are prepared to truly examine the fundamentals that have come to be accepted bedrock principles in child protection. My unease on this point comes, for example, from my earlier consideration of family group conferences. There I noted that the consultation document indicates that whilst family group conferences may be a good thing, the decision as to whether a child's name is added to the child protection register is a matter for professionals alone. This suggests to me a lack of imagination in the government proposals regarding how different a child protection system could be, and that the proposals are modifications to the existing system rather than a true and fundamental re-think of what the objectives of child protection should be. The evidence we have so far about the position of children within their wider family context (success of placements of children within the extended family, the potential support provided by grandparents and siblings, evaluative studies of family group conferences) suggest that it is a potential that has been untapped in an age of decreasing emphasis on the extended family. The emphasis on main-taining the professional autonomy over the register suggests a continued emphasis of the existing policy priorities in child protection. The consultative document contains proposals that also appear to confirm this, for example: 'continue to keep safe children who are in need of protection, and provide clear objectives for the child protection system, with a focus on good out-comes' (DoH 1998: 6). The inclusion of the word 'continue' suggests the need to acknowledge the undoubtedly good work that has gone on over the last 30 years to protect children from serious abuse at the hands of their parents and carers. However, it also suggests that there is an awareness of resistance to any proposed diversion of the resources allocated to protect children from harm into systems designed to promote their welfare more generally.

Those who were in practice during the time the Children Act 1989 came into being will be aware of how important two factors were to its success or failure. Those two factors were attitudes and resources. Let us consider each of these.

The sea-change necessitated by the Children Act on so many principles required a massive commitment to training to become familiar with the provisions of the Act and to begin to develop commitment to them on the part of practising professionals. I was a trainer then, and I recall the wall of resistance to the new principles, such as partnership with parents and accommodation as a totally voluntary service, that I encountered around the country. Much of the resistance was based on previously accepted, but now re-evaluated, principles of intervention such as permanency planning and the use of authority in intervention. The irony is that the difficulty of changing attitudes is often because of the transformation of attitudes and fundamental beliefs that were required in the first place to get to the starting point. A religious conversion metaphor might explain this better. It is not too difficult to bring an individual up in a particular religion, say Christianity or Judaism. It may not be too difficult to bring about a conversion from one religion to another, say from Christianity to Judaism, or the other way around. But how likely is it to convert a convert? How difficult would it be to take a person who has converted away from say Christianity to Judaism, and to attempt to convert him or her back to Christianity. That to me is the task that for many was involved in the Children Act attitude change required, and I believe that is the task ahead for changing child protection.

I was a non-child welfare specialist when I entered social work with all of the preconceptions and attitudes about children in families that were probably held by many lay people (the sanctity of the family, the significance of the blood tie). It was exposure to child welfare specialists and my own developing experience of working with children and families that made me examine very critically, *in the light of government legislation and guidance*, my own attitudes on these issues, and come to accept the necessity, in the best interests of children, to intervene positively, implementing a fairly aggressive child care policy on behalf of one of the authorities that was leading the permanency planning movement in child care in the 1970s. It was a difficult transition to accept the principles of the Children Act 1989, moving in some ways back towards a position close to the starting point. It is small wonder that many people see the prevailing beliefs in child welfare as resembling the to-ing and fro-ing of a pendulum.

The 'lighter touch' in child protection, as it is sometimes described, may have very similar parallels, and present similar challenges, not only for social workers but for all the professionals involved in child protection. We have managed to get education representatives to say 'We're all child protection professionals now' (no mean achievement), but now we will be asking them to reconsider what that means. They will have had to overcome initial reservations about the intrusiveness of child protection into the lives of families in order to make that statement. What will they make of the need to adopt a 'lighter touch' in child protection? There is a sense in which practitioners and managers might feel 'please make up your mind', in the context of a policy that swings back and forth. People who have travelled the road to Damascus may not want to go back.

The other difficulty for implementing the changes is resources, and there are only two points I would want to make in connection with this. First, it didn't work with the Children Act 1989. Second, it will not work with child protection unless new resources are put in. As I have indicated, I was providing Children Act training in the two-year period between the passing of the Act and its implementation. No new resources were made available specifically for the implementation of support services for children in need under section 17 of the Act. In Chapter 5, in my description of the role of social services in child protection, I have described the definition of a 'child in need' as being both expansive and restrictive at the same time in that it defined more duties and powers to be undertaken in relation to a more targeted and focused group of children. Presumably as part of the political context of targeting services for those most in need, the government at the time saw no need for extra funding: it was going to be a more cost-effective use of existing funds (cost-effectiveness being a key element of the current child protection consultation document as well). However, managers in child and family social services sections were already anticipating how they were going to address this. In some cases, they planned to take all of the children receiving services before the implementation of the Act and redefine those children as 'in need' for the purposes of the Act. In other cases local authorities tried to say, but were overruled by the Department of Health, that they could not define any children other than those in need of protection as being 'in need' (this little bit of history is very important in light of the current child protection proposals). Consequently, in part owing to a lack of resources, evaluations of the implementation of children-in-need provisions have been very critical of the extent to which needed family support services have been provided.

A very early discussion of the role of resources in the child protection refocusing debate was broadcast by BBC radio on 4 July 1994. Taking part in the discussion were June Thoburn (University of East Anglia) and Denise Platt (then director of Hammersmith Social Services). Both agreed on the necessity for there to be more resources for support services for children in need;

however, the division appeared to be whether or not those services could be funded by diverting money from the child protection system (Thoburn) or whether they required new funding, leaving the resources available for child protection intact (Platt). As was argued, it may be that better family support services *now* may provide less need for child protection services *in the future*, but that is no justification for leaving children less protected now. It is likely that provisions relating to the refocusing debate will go the same way as the children-in-need provisions under the Children Act 1989 unless they are properly resourced.

There has emerged a degree of consensus in child protection between professionals in child abuse. 'Child abuse is everybody's business' and 'We're all child protection agencies now', though said with a certain degree of pride about overcoming barriers to interagency working, can also hide an ideological hegemony, in which the attempt to get others to see child protection matters and issues in certain ways appears to have been successful. We have effectively silenced the voices of those who might say 'child protection is about prevention; child protection is about treatment.' What goes along with this is perhaps a tendency to give up looking at the fundamentals of child protection. The question must be asked 'How far are those who are in a position to shape child protection policy, both nationally and locally, really prepared to re-examine the very fundamentals of child protection?' To do this one has to try to strip away all one's notions of preconceptions and assumptions. By their very nature, preconceptions and assumptions are not easy to make conscious. They tend to surface most readily in the process of dialogue, when one learns that the sources of disagreements are not about current issues, but about the understandings preceding the consideration of the issues.

It is a little too easy for senior managers in child protection to perhaps explain away the criticisms of the child protection system as being based on a lack of understanding of the nature of child protection work, or an insufficient apprehension of the dilemmas faced by child protection managers and practitioners, or even that the critics do not have a child-centred focus. What is harder is for managers to accept that the critics have a different, but equally legitimate understanding of child protection, that they understand the dilemmas in practice as an obstacle to moving in certain directions and an incentive to move in others, and *that they too are concerned about the welfare of children.*

I am reminded of the local BASPCAN presentation by an Assistant Director (formerly child protection coordinator) in 1996 reviewing the impact of local government reorganisation on child protection services. In it, using a positive reframing approach so characteristic of people who have been able to rise in local government politics, he referred to the opportunity that had been created by local government reorganisation to rationalise the service. By that he meant that there were difficulties that had been identified, but which were so fundamentally integrated into the operation of the system that they could not be addressed. They were there, people knew they were there, and yet they could not be addressed. Local government reorganisation presented the opportunity to address them. In like manner, the refocusing debate can present opportunities to rethink fundamentally what child protection is about, not simply how to make it more effective at doing what it is already doing. This calls perhaps for a considerable amount of reflection on the nature of child protection.

The picture I have tried to present in this book is of a spider's web of connectedness of themes and issues in child protection. I have explored different perspectives on the development of child protection services – historical, cross-cultural, structural, Area Child Protection Committees, and professional/agency. There are others one could have chosen. An ecological perspective could have examined child abuse from its microsystem context to a macrosystem context. Likewise an aetiological perspective could have examined the multiplicity of causes of abuse, at all different levels, weighing up current knowledge of the balance between predisposing factors, protective factors and notions of resilience. I have not focused on these two perspectives simply because they are too close to the operational practice level, and I wished to focus on the systems in place to protect children. In that sense the book has been about child protection and not about child abuse.

In the historical context I have tried to map out where the models of child protection that we currently use have come from, highlighting the link with the US, and more specifically with the polarity of approaches that emerged there at the end of the nineteenth century. In the cross-cultural context, I have looked at the need to find a balance between ethnocentric and culturally relative positions in considering definitions of child abuse and highlighted on an international basis the power dimension of who defines what is a child abuse issue and where. I also considered the powerful role of language in determining from where our models of child protection come. In the structural context, I have attempted to illustrate the policy context of child protection, illustrating the mechanisms within each of the different agencies for ensuring that government policies are translated into field level practice. I have also tried to highlight here and in the following section on Area Child Protection Committees some of the dynamics of the different agendas of the different agencies, and how those are played out. The final part considered the perspectives of the different professionals/agencies. They all have different problems and dilemmas that they are addressing and these can be played out in the process of attempting to manage child protection on a joint basis.

We might think that 'refocusing' is the solution, but the kinds of concerns raised in the debate are the current manifestations of very complex governmental systems and priorities that have developed over a long period of time derived from complex interactions with values and fears in society.

If one looks at the powerful forces *driving* the child protection system in certain directions then it may be that it is not new plugs and points that are required, but a whole new engine. I am concerned however that we are simply stopping to do a routine service ... and a 3000-mile one at that!

References

Abrahams, N., Casey, K. and Daro, D. (1992) 'Teachers' knowledge, attitudes, and beliefs about child abuse and its prevention', *Child Abuse & Neglect*, 16(2): 229–38.

Adcock, M. and White, R. (1985) *Good-enough parenting: a framework for assessment*, London: British Agencies for Adoption and Fostering.

ADSS (Association of Directors of Social Services)/NCH Action for Children (1966) *Childen Still in Need: Refocusing child protection in the context of children in need*, London: NCH Action for Children.

Agass, D. and Simes, M. (1992) 'The Adult Legacy of Childhood Sexual Abuse: Individual Therapy with Adult Mental Health Referrals where CSA is the Key Factor', *Practice*, 6(1): 41–59.

Ainsworth, M., Blehar, M., Waters, E. and Wall, S. (1978) *Patterns of Attachment: A Psychological Study of the Strange Situation*, NJ, USA: Lawrence Erlbaum.

AJPH (*American Journal of Public Health*) (1987) Policy Statement 8614 (PP): Prevention of Child Abuse, *AJPH*, 77(1): 111–113.

Ambache, J. (1988) 'The very harsh realities of tackling child abuse', *Community Care*, 705, 31 March: 13.

Amdi, V. (1990) 'The cause of child abuse and neglect and their effects on the development of children in Samaru Zaria, Nigeria', *Early Child Development and Care*, 58: 31–43.

Ariès, P. (1962) *Centuries of Childhood*, London; Jonathan Cape.

Armstrong, H. (1994) *Discussion Report: The Annual Reports of Area Child Protection Committees 1992/93*, Paper presented at Area Child Protection Committees National Conference, 8 March 1994, London: Department of Health.

Armstrong, H. and Hollows, A. (1991) 'Responses to Child Abuse in the EC', in Hill, M. (1991).

Armstrong, H. and Riches, P. (1988) 'Back to the child', *Insight*, 16 Aug.: 18–19.

Ashworth, A. (1995) *Sentencing & Criminal Justice*, London: Butterworths.

Attias, R. and Goodwin, J. (1985) 'Knowledge and management strategies in incest cases: a survey of physicians, psychologists and family counsellors', *Child Abuse & Neglect*, 9: 523–33.

Audit Commission (1992) *Getting in on the Act: Provision for pupils with special educational needs – the national picture*, London: HMSO.

Audit Commission (1993) *Children first: A study of hospital services*, London: HMSO.

Audit Commission (1994a) *Taking Stock: Progress with Community Care*, Community Care Bulletin No. 2, December, London: HMSO.

Audit Commission (1994b) *Cheques and Balances: A Framework for Improving Police Accountability*, London: HMSO.

Audit Commission (1994c), *Seen But Not Heard: Co-ordinating Community Child Health and Social Services for Children in Need*, London: HMSO.

Audit Commission (1995), *Paying the Piper: People and Pay Management in Local Government*, London: HMSO.

Baglow, L. (1990) 'A Multidimensional Model for Treatment of Child Abuse: A Framework for Cooperation', *Child Abuse & Neglect*, 14: 387–95.

Baher, E., Hyman, C., Jones, C., Jones, R., Kerr, A. and Mitchell, R. (1976) *At Risk: An Account of the Work of the Battered Child Research Department, NSPCC.*, London: Routledge and Kegan Paul.

Baher, L. (1990) *The School Governors and Parents Handbook*, Oxford: Basil Blackwell.

Baines, M. (*c.* 1865) *A Few Thoughts Concerning Infanticide* (p. 197 in Rose, L. (1986) *The massacre of the innocents: Infanticide in Britain 1800–1939*, London: Routledge and Kegan Paul).

Bakan, D. (1971) *Slaughter of the innocents: A study of the battered child phenomenon*, San Francisco: Jossey-Bass.

Baldwin, N. and Spencer, N. (1993) 'Deprivation and Child Abuse: Implications for strategic planning in children's services', *Children & Society*, 7(4): 357–75.

Barclay Committee (1982) *Social Workers: Their roles and tasks*. The Barclay Report, London: Bedford Square Press.

Barnes, P. (1995) *Personal, Social and Emotional Development of Children*, Oxford/Milton Keynes: Blackwell/Open University.

Barrett, D. (1994) 'Social Work on the Streets: Responding to Juvenile Prostitution in Amsterdam, London and Paris', *Social Work in Europe*, 1(1): 29–32.

Barth, R.P., Duerr Berrick, J., Needell, B. and Jonson-Reid, M. (1995) *Child welfare services for very young children interim report*, Berkeley, University of California: Child Welfare Research Centre.

Bartlett, H. (1970) *The Common Base of Social Work Practice*, Washington, DC: NASW.

Bass, A. (1995) 'Supporting health visitors in child protection', *Health Visitor*, 68(10): 410–11.

Beitchman, J., Zucker, K., Hood, J., DaCosta, G., Akman, D. and Cassavia, E. (1992) 'A Review of the Long-term Effects of Child Sexual Abuse', *Child Abuse & Neglect*, 16: 101–18.

Bell, L. and Tooman, P. (1994) 'Mandatory reporting laws: a critical overview', *International Journal of Law and the Family*, 8(3): 337–56.

Belsey, M. (1996) 'Does Mandatory Reporting Help to Protect Children? – Against', *Abstracts of ISPCAN Eleventh International Congress on Child Abuse & Neglect*, 43.

Belsky, J. (1980) 'The Ecological Integration Model', *American Psychologist*, 35(4): 320–35.

Belsky, J. (1988) 'Child Maltreatment and the Emergent Family System', Chapter 17, in Browne et al. (1988).

Benthall, J. (1991) 'Invisible wounds: Corporal punishment in British schools as a form of ritual', *Child Abuse & Neglect*, 15(4): 377–88.

Bentovim, A. (1992) 'The Role of Mental Health Professionals in Relation to the Children Act 1989', *Child Abuse Review*, 1: 126–30.

Bentovim, A. (1993) 'Treatment Services for Sexually Abused Children and Families: Forwards, Backwards and Standing Still', *Child Abuse Review*, 2: 196–202.

Bergner, R.M., Delgado, L.K. and Graybill, D. (1994) 'Finkelhor's Risk Factor Checklist: A Cross-Validation Study', *Child Abuse & Neglect*, 18(4): 331–40.

Berridge, D. and Brodie, I. (1996) 'Residential Child Care in England and Wales: The Inquiries and After', Chapter 13 in Hill, M. and Aldgate, J. (eds) *Child Welfare Services: Developments in Law, Policy, Practice and Research*, London: Jessica Kingsley.

Besharov, D. (1990) *Recognizing Child Abuse: A Guide for the Concerned*, New York: The Free Press (Macmillan).

Biggs, S. (1997) 'Interprofessional collaboration: problems and prospects', Chapter 9 in Øvretveit, J., Mathias, P. and Thompson, T. (eds) *Interprofessional working for health and social care*, London: Macmillan.

Birchall, E. and Hallett, C. (1996) 'Working together: inter-professional relations in child protection', *Health Visitor*, 69(2): 59–62.

Birchall, E. and Hallett, C. (1995) 'Working together in child protection', *Health Visitor*, 68(10): 406–9.

Black, J.A. and Debelle, G.D. (1995) 'Female genital mutilation in Britain', *British Medical Journal*, 310 (6994): 1590–4.

Bloom, R.B. (1992) 'When staff members sexually abuse children in residential care', *Child Welfare*, 71: 131–45.

Bowen, R. and Hamblin, A. (1981) 'Sexual Abuse of Children', *Spare Rib*, Vol. 106, May.

Boushel, M. (1994) 'The Protective Environment of Children: Towards a framework for anti-oppressive, cross-cultural and cross-national understanding', *British Journal of Social Work*, 24: 173–90.

Boykin, A. and Toms, F. (1985) 'Black child socialization: A conceptual framework', in McAdoo, H. and McAdoo, J. (eds) *Black children: Social, educational, and parental environments*, Newbury Park, CA: Sage.

Braun, D. (1988) *Responding to Child Abuse*, London: Bedford Square Press.

Braun, D. (1994) 'Teachers in the Community: Setting the Scene', Presentation at the 8th Annual Michael Sieff Conference: Child Protection and the Role of the Education System, March 1994, Surrey, UK: Michael Sieff Foundation.

Breiner, S.J. (1992) 'Sexuality in traditional China: its relationship to child abuse', *Child Psychiatry & Human Development*, 23(2): 53–67.

Bremner, R.H. (ed) (1970) *Children and youth in America: A documentary history, 1600–1865*, (Vol. 1), Cambridge, MA: Harvard University Press.

Brière, J. (1992) *Child Abuse Trauma: Theory and Treatment of the Long Lasting Effects*, London: Sage.

Brighouse, T. (1991) 'The Uncertain Future of Local Education Authorities', *Local Government Policy Making*, 18(1): 8–13.

Briggs, F. (1997) 'The Importance of Schools and Early Childhood Centres in Child Protection', *Journal of Child Centred Practice*, 4(1): 11–23.

Briggs, F. and Hawkins, R. (1997) *Child Protection: A guide for teachers and child care professionals*, New South Wales, Australia: Allen & Unwin.

Brodie, I. (1995) *Exclusion from School* (Highlight no. 136), London: National Children's Bureau.

Bronfenbrenner, U. (1979) *The Ecology of Human Development*, Cambridge, MA: Harvard University Press.

Brown, L. and Fuller, R. (1991) 'Central Scotland's joint police and social work initiative in child abuse: an evaluation', *Children & Society*, 5(3): 232–40.

Browne, K., Davies, C. and Stratton, P. (eds) (1988) *Early Prediction and Prevention of Child Abuse*, Chichester: John Wiley & Sons.

Browne, K. and Saqi, S. (1988) 'Approaches to Screening for Child Abuse and Neglect', Chapter 5 in Browne, K., Davies, C. and Stratton, P. (eds) *Early Prediction and Prevention of Child Abuse*, Chichester: John Wiley & Sons.

Brynin, M. (1993) *Pressure on Education*, Aldershot: Avebury.

Bury, M. and Elston, M. (1987), 'Professional Collaboration and the Abuse of Children', in *After Beckford: essays on themes related to child abuse*, Department of Social Policy and Social Science, Royal Holloway and Bedford New College.

Butler, I. (1998) *Child Prostitution*, presentation at BASPCAN (South Wales) Seminar, 19.1.98, Cardiff, UK.

Butler, I. and Payne, H. (1997) 'The health of children looked after by the local authority', *Adoption & Fostering*, 21(2): 28–35.

Butler, S. (1996) 'Child protection or professional self-preservation by the baby nurses? Public health nurses and child protection in Ireland', *Social Science & Medicine*, 43(3): 303–14.

Butler-Sloss, E. (1988) *Report of the inquiry into child abuse in Cleveland 1987*, Cmnd 412, London: HMSO.

Butt, J. (1996) 'Race equality', *Research Matters*, 1: 50–52.

Caldwell, R.A., Bogat, G.A. and Davidson, W.S. (1988) 'The Assessment of Child Abuse Potential and the Prevention of Child Abuse and Neglect: A Policy Analysis', *American Journal of Community Psychology*, 16: 609–24.

Caffey, J. (1946) 'Multiple fractures in the long bones of infants suffering from chronic subdural haematoma', *American Journal of Roentgenology*, 56: 163–73.

Cannan, C. (1992) *Changing Families, Changing Welfare: Family Centres and the Welfare State*, Hemel Hempstead: Harvester Wheatsheaf.

Cannan, C. and Warren, C. (1997) *Social Action with Children and Families: A community development approach to child and family welfare*, London: Routledge.

CANO Community Care and Paediatric Network Group (1993) *The Role of the Designated Senior Nurse Child Protection* (4th draft).

Caplan, G. (ed.) (1964) *Principles of Preventive Psychiatry*, New York: Basic Books.

Carbino, R. (1991) 'Advocacy for foster families in the United States facing child abuse allegations: how social agencies and foster parents are responding to the problem', *Child Welfare*, 70: 131–49.

Carbino, R. (1992) 'Policy and practice for response to foster families when child abuse or neglect is reported', *Child Welfare*, 71(6): 497–509.

Cassell, D. and Coleman, R. (1995) 'Parents with psychiatric problems', Chapter 11 in Reder, P. and Lucey, C. (eds) *Assessment of parenting: psychiatric and psychological contributions*, London: Routledge.

Caudill, W. and Weinstein, H. (1969) 'Maternal care and infant behaviour in Japan and America', *Psychiatry*, 32: 12–43.

CCETSW (Central Council for Education and Training in Social Work) (1992a) *Practising Equality: Women, Men and Social Work*, London: CCETSW.

CCETSW (Central Council for Education and Training in Social Work) (1992b) *The Requirements for Post Qualifying Education and Training in the Personal Social Services: A Framework for Continuing Professional Development* (Paper 31, revised edition), London: CCETSW.

Channer, Y. and Parton, N. (1990) 'Racism, cultural relativism and child protection', Chapter 6 in The Violence Against Children Study Group (eds), *Taking Child Abuse Seriously*, London: Routledge.

Cicchetti, D. and Lynch, M. (1993) 'Toward an ecological/transactional model of community violence and child maltreatment: consequences for children's development', *Psychiatry: Interpersonal and Biological Processes*, 56(1): 96–118.

Clarke, P.G. (1993) 'A typology of interdisciplinary education in gerontology and geriatrics: "are we really doing what we say we are"', *Journal of Interprofessional Care*, 7(3): 217–27.

Cleaver, H. and Freeman, P. (1995) *Parental Perspectives in Cases of Suspected Abuse*, London: HMSO.

Cleaver, H. (1996) *Focus on Teenagers*, London: HMSO.

Cloke, C. and Naish, J. (1992) *Key Issues in Child Protection for Health Visitors and Nurses*, Harlow: Longman.

Cohen, S. (1972) *Folk Devils and Moral Panics*, London: McGibbon and Kee.

Cohn, A.H. (1983) 'The prevention of child abuse: what do we know about what works?', in Leavitt, J. (ed.) *Child Abuse & Neglect: Research and Innovation*, The Hague: Martinus Nijhoff.

Colton, M., Drury, C. and Williams, M. (1993) *Final Report on Stage 1 of Research Project on Children in Need in Wales under the Children Act 1989*, Department of Social Policy and Applied Social Studies, University of Wales, Swansea.

Colton, M., Drury, C. and Williams, M. (1995) *Staying Together: Supporting families under the Children Act*, Aldershot: Arena.

Colton, M., Roberts, S. and Sanders, R. (1996) *An Analysis of Area Child Protection Committee Reviews on Child Deaths and Other Cases of Public Concern in Wales: A Report for Welsh Office*, Welsh Office: Cardiff.

Conroy, S., Fielding, N. and Tunstill, J. (1990) *Investigating Child Sexual Abuse*, London: Police Foundation.

Conte, J. and Shore, D. (1982) *Social Work and Sexual Abuse*, New York: Haworth Press.

Cooper, A., Hetherington, R., Baistow, K., Pitts, J. and Spriggs, A. (1995) *Positive Child Protection: A View from Abroad*, Lyme Regis: Russell House Publishing.

Cooper, D. (1993) *Child Abuse Revisited: Children, Society and Social Work*, Milton Keynes: Open University Press.

Corby, B. (1993) *Child Abuse: Towards a Knowledge Base*, Buckingham: Open University Press.

Costin, L. (1991) 'Unraveling the Mary Ellen Legend: Origins of the "Cruelty" Movement', *Social Service Review*, 65: 203–23.

Costin, L. (1992) 'Cruelty to Children: A Dormant Issue and Its Rediscovery, 1920–1960', *Social Service Review*, 66: 177–98.

Council of Europe (1991) *Sexual Exploitation, Pornography and Prostitution of, and Trafficking in, Children and Young Adults,* Committee of Ministers of the Council of Europe.

Court Committee (1976) *Fit for the Future – Report of the Court Committee on Child Health Services,* London: HMSO.

Crain, W. (1992) *Theories of Development: Concepts and Applications* (3rd edn), NJ, US: Prentice Hall.

Crenshaw, W., Crenshaw, L., and Lichtenberg, J. (1995) 'When educators confront child abuse: An analysis of the decision to report', *Child Abuse & Neglect,* 19(9): 1095–113.

Crittenden, P. (1992) 'The Social Ecology of Treatment: Case Study of a Service System for Maltreated Children', *American Journal of Orthopsychiatry,* 62(1): 22–34.

Crown Prosecution Service (1994a) *The Code for Crown Prosecutors,* London: Crown Prosecution Service.

Crown Prosecution Service (1994b) *Explanatory Memorandum for use in connection with the Code for Crown Prosecutors,* London: Crown Prosecution Service.

Cunningham, H. (1995) *Children & Childhood in Western Society since 1500,* Harlow, Essex: Longman.

Cunningham, J. (1988) 'Contributions to the history of psychology: L. French historical views on the acceptability of evidence regarding child sexual abuse', *Psychological Reports,* 63(2): 343–53.

Daro, D., Migley, G., Wiese, D. and Salmon-Cox, S. (1996) *World Perspectives on Child Abuse: The Second International Resource Book,* Chicago, IL: National Committee to Prevent Child Abuse.

Dartington Social Research Unit (1990) 'The Dissemination of Research Findings in Social Work', in Department of Health (1990) *DH Yearbook of Research and Development,* London: HMSO.

David, T. (1993) *Child Protection and Early Years Teacher,* Buckingham: Open University Press.

Davis, L. (1994) *Children of the East,* London: Janus.

Davies, M. and Dotchin, J. (1995) 'Improving quality through participation: an approach to measuring children's expectations and perceptions of services', Chapter 13 in Cloke, C. and Davies, M. (eds) *Participation and Empowerment in Child Protection,* Chichester: John Wiley & Sons.

DeChesnay, M. (1989) 'Child sexual abuse as an international health problem', *International Nursing Review,* 36: 149–53.

DeMause, L. (1976) *The History of Childhood,* London: Souvenir Press.

Dennett, J. and Bekerian, D. (1991) 'Interviewing Abused Children', *Policing,* 7(4): 355–60.

DeSilva, D.G. (1997) 'Sexual Abuse in Childhood in Southern Sri Lanka', paper presented at BASPCAN 3rd National Congress 'Approaching the Millennium: The Future Shape of Child Protection', Edinburgh, 8–11 July.

DHSS (Department of Health and Social Security) (1974) *Report of the committee of inquiry into the care and supervision provided in relation to Maria Colwell*, London: HMSO.

DHSS (Department of Health and Social Security) (1976) *Non-Accidental Injury to Children: The Police and Case Conferences*, LASSL (76)(26).

DHSS (Department of Health and Social Security) (1982), *Child Abuse: A Study of Inquiry Reports 1973 – 1981*, London: HMSO.

DHSS (Department of Health and Social Security) (1985a) *Review of Child Care Law: report to ministers of an interdepartmental working party*, London: HMSO.

DHSS (Department of Health and Social Security) (1985b) *Social Work Decisions in Child Care: Recent Research Findings and their Implications*, London: HMSO.

DHSS (Department of Health and Social Security) (1988) *Working Together: A guide to arrangements for interagency co-operation for the protection of children from abuse*, London: HMSO.

Dingwall, R., Eekelaar, J.M. and Murray, T. (1983) *The Protection of Children: State Intervention and Family Life*, Oxford: Blackwell.

Dingwall, R. (1989) 'Some problems about predicting child abuse and neglect', in Stevenson, O. (ed.) *Child Abuse: Public Policy and Professional Practice*, New York: Harvester Wheatsheaf.

Dobson, R. (1996) 'Fostering torment', *Community Care*, 25–31 Jan.: 28–9.

Doek, J. (1991) 'Management of child abuse and neglect at the international level: trends and perspectives', *Child Abuse & Neglect*, 15 (supp. 1): 51–6.

DoH (Department of Health) (undated) *Working with Child Sexual Abuse: Guidelines for Training Social Services Staff*, London: DoH Training Support Programme (Child Care).

DoH (Department of Health) (1988) *Protecting Children: A Guide for Social Workers undertaking a Comprehensive Assessment*, London: HMSO.

DoH (Department of Health) (1989) *The Care of Children: Principles and Practice in Regulations and Guidance*, London: HMSO.

DoH (Department of Health) (1991a) *Patterns and Outcomes in Child Placement*, London: HMSO.

DoH (Department of Health) (1991b) *The Children Act 1989 Guidance and Regulations: Volume 2 – Family Support, Day Care and Educational Provision for Young Children*, London: HMSO.

DoH (Department of Health) (1991c), *Child Abuse: A Study of Inquiry Reports 1980–1989*, London: HMSO.

DoH (Department of Health) (1992a) *Strategic Statement on Working with Sex Offenders*, London: HMSO.

DoH (Department of Health) (1992b) *Child Protection: Guidance for Senior Nurses, Health Visitors and Midwives*, London: HMSO.

DoH (Department of Health) (1992c) *The Health of the Nation: A Strategy for Health in England*, Cmnd. 1986, London: HMSO.

DoH (Department of Health) (1995a) *Child Protection: Messages from Research*, London: HMSO.

DoH (Department of Health) (1995b) *Looking After Children: Trial Pack of Planning and Review Forms and Action Records (revised)*, London: HMSO.

DoH (Department of Health) (1996) *Child Health in the Community: A Guide to Good Practice*, Leeds: Department of Health.

DoH (Department of Health) (1998) *Working Together to Safeguard Children: New Government Proposals for Interagency Co-operation*, London: Department of Health.

DoH/BMA/Conference of Medical Royal Colleges (1994) *Child Protection: Medical Responsibilities*, London: HMSO.

DoH/SSI (Department of Health/Social Services Inspectorate) (1995) *The Challenge of Partnership in Child Protection: Practice Guide*, London: HMSO.

DoH/WO (Department of Health/Welsh Office) (1993) *Children Act Report 1992*, London: HMSO.

DoH/WO (Department of Health/Welsh Office (1994) *Children Act Report 1993*, London: HMSO.

DoH/WO (Department of Health/Welsh Office (1995) *Children Act Report 1994*, London: HMSO.

DoH/WO (Department of Health/Welsh Office (1996) *Child Protection: Clarification of Arrangements between the NHS and OtherAgencies*, London: HMSO.

Dolmage, W. (1995) 'Accusations of teacher sexual abuse of students in Ontario schools: Some preliminary findings', *Alberta Journal of Educational Research*, 41(2): 127–44.

Doxiadis, S.A. (1989) 'Kempe Memorial Lecture: Children, Society and Ethics', *Child Abuse & Neglect*, 13: 11-17.

Driver, E. and Droisen, A. (1989) *Child Sexual Abuse: Feminist Perspectives*, Basingstoke: Macmillan.

Dubowitz, H. (1990) 'Costs and Effectiveness of Interventions in Child Maltreatment', *Child Abuse & Neglect*, 14: 177–86.

Dunn, P. (1976) '"That Enemy Is the Baby": Childhood in Imperial Russia', Chapter 9 in DeMause, L. (ed.) *The History of Childhood*, London: Souvenir Press.

Edwards, S. and Soetenhorst-de Savornin Lohman, J. (1994) 'The impact of "moral panic" on professional behaviour in cases of child sexual abuse: an international perspective', *Journal of Child Sexual Abuse*, 3(1): 103.

Egeland, B. (1988) 'Breaking the Cycle of Abuse: Implications for Prediction and Intervention', Chapter 6 in Browne, K., Davies, C. and Stratton, P. (eds) *Early Prediction and Prevention of Child Abuse*, Chichester, John Wiley & Sons.

Engel, C. (1994) 'A functional anatomy of teamwork', Chapter 3 in Leathard, A. (ed.) *Going Inter-Professional: Working Together for Health and Welfare*, London: Routledge.

Erikson, E. (1963) *Childhood and Society*, Norton: New York.

Evans, M. and Miller, C. (1992) *Partnership in Child Protection: The Strategic Management Response*, London: National Institute for Social Work/Office for Public Management.

Falkov, A. (1996a) *Study of Working Together 'Part 8' Reports: Fatal Child Abuse and Parental Psychiatric Disorder*, London: HMSO.

Falkov, A. (1996b) *Parental psychiatric disorder and child maltreatment, Part I: Context and historical overview*, National Children's Bureau Highlight No. 148, London: NCB.

Falkov, A. (1997) *Parental psychiatric disorder and child maltreatment, Part II: Extent and nature of the association*, National Children's Bureau Highlight No. 148, London: NCB.

Fallon, M. (1991) *Education*, 26/4/91 cited in Simon, B. (1992) *What Future for Education*, London: Lawrence & Wishart.

Farmer, E. and Owen, M. (1995) *Child Protection Practice: Private Risks and Public Remedies – Decision Making, Intervention and Outcome in Child Protection Work*, London: HMSO.

Farmer, E. and Parker, R. (1991) *Trials and Tribulations: Returning Children from Local Authority Care to their Families*, London: HMSO.

Ferguson, H. (1990) 'Rethinking child protection practices: a case for history', Chapter 7 in The Violence Against Children Study Group (eds) *Taking Child Abuse Seriously: Contemporary issues in child protection theory and practice*, London: Routledge.

Fergusson, D.M., Fleming, J. and O'Neill, D.P. (1972) *Child Abuse in New Zealand*, Wellington: Government Printer.

Ferrier, P.E. (1986) 'The International Society for Prevention of Child Abuse and Neglect: presidential address', *Child Abuse & Neglect*, 10(3): 279–81.

Fielding, N. and Conroy, S. (1992) 'Interviewing Child Victims: Police and Social Work Investigations of Child Sexual Abuse', *Sociology*, 26(1): 103–24.

Findlay, C. (1987) 'Child Abuse – The Dutch Response', *Practice*, 4: 374–81.

Finkelhor, D. (1979) *Sexually victimized children*, New York: The Free Press.

Finkelhor, D. (1984) *Child Sexual Abuse: New Theories and Research*, New York: Free Press.

Finkelhor, D. (1994) 'The International Epidemiology of Child Sexual Abuse', *Child Abuse & Neglect*, 18(5): 409–17.

Finkelhor, D. and Korbin, J. (1988) 'Child abuse as an international issue', *Child Abuse & Neglect*, 12: 3–23.

FitzGerald, G. and FitzGerald, G. (1995) 'To Budget or Not To Budget? The

Experience of a Non-Budgeting General Practice', in Murley, R. (ed.) *Patients or Customers? Are the NHS Reforms Working?*, London: Institute of Economic Affairs.

Flynn, N. (1997) *Public Sector Management* (3rd edn), Hemel Hempstead: Prentice Hall/Harvester Wheatsheaf.

Folks, H. (1902) *Care of destitute, neglected, and delinquent children*, New York: Macmillan.

Forbes, C. (1989) 'The sexual exploitation of children: The Philippines', Chapter 10 in Moorehead, C. (ed.) *Betrayal: Child Exploitation in Today's World*, London: Barrie & Jenkins.

Fox, S. and Dingwall, R. (1985) 'An Exploratory Study of Variations in Social Workers' and Health Visitors' Definitions of Child Mistreatment', *British Journal of Social Work*, 15: 467–77.

Fox-Harding, L. (1991) *Perspectives in Child Care Policy*, Harlow: Longman.

Francome (1993) *Children Who Have Children*, London: FPA.

Freud, S. (1966) *The Complete Introductory Letters of Psychoanalysis*, New York: Norton.

Frost, N. (1990) 'Official intervention and child protection: the relationship between state and family in contemporary Britain', Chapter 2 in The Violence Against Children Study Group (eds) *Taking Child Abuse Seriously: Contemporary issues in child protection theory and practice*, London: Routledge.

Frost, N. and Stein, M. (1989) *The Politics of Child Welfare: Inequality, Power and Change*, Hemel Hempstead: Harvester Wheatsheaf.

Fürniss, T. (1991) *The Multi-professional Handbook of Child Sexual Abuse*, London: Routledge.

Fürniss, T. (1996) 'Does Mandatory Reporting Help to Protect Children? – In Support', *Abstracts of ISPCAN Eleventh International Congress on Child Abuse and Neglect*, 40–41.

Gambe, D., Gomes, J., Kapur, V., Rangel, M. and Stubbs, P. (1992) *Antiracist Social Work Education: Improving Practice with Children and Families – A Training Manual*, London: Central Council for Education and Training in Social Work (CCETSW).

Gambrill, E. and Stein, T. (eds) (1994) *Controversial Issues in Child Welfare*, London: Allyn and Bacon.

Garbarino, J. (1981) 'An Ecological Approach to Child Maltreatment', Chapter 7 in Pelton, L. (ed.) *The Social Context of Child Abuse and Neglect*, London: Human Sciences Press.

Gerry, E. (1913) 'The Relations of the Society for the Prevention of Cruelty to Children to Child-saving Work' in *Proceedings of the National Conference of Charities and Correction 1882*, Fort Worth, Indiana: Fort Worth Printing Co.

Gibbons, J. (1997) 'Relating outcomes to objectives in child protection policy', Chapter 5 in Parton, N. (ed.) *Child Protection and Family Support: Tensions, contradictions and possibilities*, London: Routledge.

Gibbons, J., Conroy, S. and Bell, C. (1995a) *Operating the Child Protection System: A Study of Child Protection Practices in English Local Authorities*, London: HMSO.

Gibbons, J., Gallagher, B., Bell, C. and Gordon, D. (1995b) *Development after Physical Abuse in Early Childhood: A Follow-up Study of Children on Child Protection Registers*, London: HMSO.

Gibbons, J., Thorpe, S. and Wilkinson, P. (1990) *Family Support and Prevention: Studies in Local Areas*, London: NISW/HMSO.

Gilbert, N. (1997) *Combatting Child Abuse: International Perspectives and Trends*, Oxford: Oxford University Press.

Gil, D. (1970) *Violence against Children: Physical Child Abuse in the United States*, Cambridge, MA: Harvard University Press.

Gil, D. (1996) 'Preventing Violence in a Structurally Violent Society: Mission Impossible', *American Journal of Orthopsychiatry*, 66(1): 77–84.

Gill, O. (1995), 'Neighbourhood Watch', *Community Care*, 8–14 June: 30–31.

Gill, O. (1996) *Poverty and Child Abuse: Practice Perspectives*, paper presented at British Association for the Study and Prevention of Child Abuse and Neglect (BASPCAN) Conference, Cardiff, 6 June 1996.

Giovannoni, J. and Bercera, R. (1979) *Defining child abuse*, New York: The Free Press.

Glaser, D. (1992) 'Abuse of Children', Chapter 5 in Lane, D. and Miller, A., *Child and Adolescent Therapy: A Handbook*, Buckingham: Open University Press.

Goddard, C. (1995) 'Tenth International Congress on child abuse and neglect: "creating a caring society for children: a world-wide challenge"', *Child Abuse Review*, 4(2): 146–8.

Goddard, C. (1996) 'Read all about it! The News about Child Abuse', *Child Abuse Review*, 5(5): 301–309.

Golding, P. and Middleton, S. (1982) *Images of Welfare: Press and Public Attitudes to Poverty*, Martin Robertson.

Goldschmied, E. and Jackson, S. (1994) *People Under Three: Young children in day care*, London: Routledge.

Gordon, L. (1988a) *Heroes of Their Own Lives: The Politics and History of Family Violence*, New York: Russell Sage.

Gordon, L. (1988b) 'The Politics of Child Sexual Abuse: Notes from American History', *Feminist Review*, 28: 57–64.

Gough, D. (1993) 'The Case For and Against Prevention' in Waterhouse, L. (ed.) *Child Abuse and Child Abusers: Protection and Prevention*, London: Jessica Kingsley.

Gough, D. (1996) 'The Literature on Child Abuse and the Media', *Child Abuse Review*, 5(5): 363–76.

Graziano, A. and Mills, J. (1992) 'Treatment for Abuse Children: When is a Partial Solution Acceptable?', *Child Abuse & Neglect*, 16: 217–28.

Greenland, C. (1987) *Preventing Child Abuse and Neglect Deaths: An International Study of Deaths due to Child Abuse and Neglect*, London and New York: Tavistock.

Greenwood, D. and Stini, W. (1977) *Nature, Culture and Human History*, New York: Harper and Row.

Gronbjerg, K.A., Stagner, M.W. and Chen, T.H. (1995) 'Child welfare contracting: market forces and leverage', *Social Service Review*, 69(4): 583–613.

H.M. Government (1985) *The Prohibition of Female Circumcision Act 1985*, London: HMSO.

H.M. Government (1989) *The Children Act 1989*, Chapter 41, London: HMSO.

H.M. Government (1996) *The Family Law Act 1996*, Chapter 27, London: HMSO.

H.M. Government (1997) *The Sex Offenders Act 1997*, Chapter 51, London: HMSO.

Haase, C.C. and Kempe, R.S. (1990) 'The School and Protective Services', *Education and Urban Society*, 22: 258–69.

Haj-Yahia, Mhmd M., and Shor, R. (1995) 'Child Maltreatment as Perceived by Arab Students of Social Science in the West Bank', *Child Abuse & Neglect*, 19(10): 1209–19.

Hallett, C. (1989) 'Child-abuse inquiries and public policy', Chapter 6 in Stevenson, O. (ed.) *Child Abuse: Public Policy and Professional Practice*, Hemel Hempstead: Harvester Wheatsheaf.

Hallett, C. (1993) 'Working Together in Child Protection', Chapter 7 in Waterhouse, L. (ed.) *Child Abuse and Child Abusers: Protection and Prevention*, London: Jessica Kingsley.

Hallett, C. (1995) *Interagency Coordination in Child Protection*, London: HMSO.

Hallett, C. and Stevenson, O. (1980) *Child Abuse: Aspects of inter-professional cooperation*, London: George Allen and Unwin.

Hallett, C. and Birchall, E. (1992) *Coordination and Child Protection: A Review of the Literature*, London: HMSO.

Hampton, R., Gelles, R. and Harrop, J. (1989) 'Is violence in black families increasing? A comparison of 1975 and 1985 national survey rates', *Journal of Marriage and the Family*, 89: 969–80.

Hardiker, P., Exton, K. and Barker, M. (1991) *Policies and Practices in Preventive Child Care*, Aldershot: Avebury.

Hardyment, C. (1992) 'Looking at children: a history of childhood 1600 to the present', in Holdsworth, S. and Crossley, J. (eds) *Innocence and Experience: images of children in British art from 1600 to the present*, Manchester: Pale Green Press.

Harris, J. and Melichercik, J. (1986) 'Age and stage-related programs', in Turner, J. and Turner, F. (eds), *Canadian Social Welfare*, Ontario, Canada: Collier Macmillan.

Harris, A. (1991) 'General practitioners and child protection case conferences', *British Medical Journal*, 302: 1354.

Harrison, A., Wilson, M., Pine, C., Chan, S. and Buriel, R. (1990) 'Family ecologies of ethnic minority children', *Child Development*, 61: 347–62.

Hay, T. and Jones, L. (1994) 'Societal Interventions to Prevent Child Abuse and Neglect', *Child Welfare*, 73(5): 379–403.

Hebenton, B. and Thomas, T. (1992) 'Police Attendance at Child Protection Conferences: A Reappraisal', *Children & Society*, 6(4): 364–76.

Hendrick, H. (1994) *Child Welfare: England 1872–1989*, London: Routledge.

Hendry, E. (1995) 'The inter-agency child protection trainer – a developing role', *Child Abuse Review*, 4 (3): 227–9.

Heras, P. (1992) 'Cultural considerations in the assessment and treatment of child sexual abuse', *Journal of Child Sexual Abuse*, 1(3): 119–24.

Hetherington, R., Cooper, A., Smith, P. and Wilford, G. (1997) *Protecting Children: Messages from Europe*, Lyme Regis: Russell House Publishing.

Higgins, K. (1993) 'The Local Education Authority: a disappearing phenomenon?', *Local Government Policy Making*, 19(5): 15–20.

Hill, M. (ed.) (1991) *Social Work and the European Community: The Social Policy and Practice Contexts*, London: Jessica Kingsley.

Hobbs, C. and Wynne, J. (1986) 'Buggery in childhood – a common syndrome of child abuse', *Lancet*, 4 October, 792–6.

Hobbs, C. and Wynne, J. (1987) 'Child sexual abuse – an increasing rate of diagnosis', *Lancet*, 837–41.

Hodgkins, P. (1994) 'The Education Support Service', presentation at the 8th Annual Michael Sieff Conference: Child Protection and the Role of the Education System, March 1994, Surrey: Michael Sieff Foundation.

Holman, B. (1992) *National Children's Bureau Highlight No. 111: Family Centres*, London: NCB.

Holman, B. (1988) *Putting Families First: prevention and child care*, London: Macmillan.

Home Office (1988) *The Investigation of Child Abuse*, Circular 52/1988, London: Home Office.

Home Office (1989) *Report of the Advisory Group on Video Evidence* (Chairman Judge Thomas Pigot QC), London: Home Office.

Home Office, Department of Health, Department of Education and Science, and Welsh Office (1991) *Working Together Under the Children Act 1989: A guide to inter-agency co-operation for the protection of children from abuse*, London: HMSO.

Home Office, Northern Ireland Office and Scottish Office (1993) *Inquiry into Police Responsibilities and Rewards,* (the Sheehy Report), London: HMSO.

Home Office and Department of Health (1992) *Memorandum of Good Practice on Video Recorded Interviews with Child Witnesses for Criminal Proceedings,* London: HMSO.

Horejsi, C., Craig, B. and Pablo, J. (1992) 'Reactions by Native American parents to child protection agencies: Cultural and community factors', *Child Welfare,* 71(4): 329–42.

Horwarth, J. and Calder, M. (1997) 'Core Groups: Modelling Inter-Agency Practice in the Late 1990s', presentation at BASPCAN 3rd National Congress, 8–11 July, Heriot Watt University, Edinburgh.

House of Commons (1984) Second Report from the Social Services Committee Session 1983–84, *Children in Care, Vol. 1* together with proceedings of the committee (the 'Short Report'), 28 March 1984, London: HMSO.

Howitt, D. (1992) *Child Abuse Errors: When Good Intentions Go Wrong,* London: Harvester Wheatsheaf.

Hoyte, P. (1996) 'Protecting the Paediatrician: Responding to Recrimination', *Child Abuse Review,* 5(2): 103–12.

Hughes, R. (1996) 'The Department of Health research studies in child protection: a response to Parton', *Child & Family Social Work,* 1(2): 115–18.

Hulse, T. (1995) 'Growth monitoring and the new growth charts', *Health visitor,* 68(10): 424–5.

Hunter, W., Coulter, M., Runyan, D. and Eversor, M. (1990) 'Determinants of Placement for Sexually Abused Children', *Child Abuse & Neglect,* 14: 407–17.

Hutchinson, G. (1993) 'To boldly go: Shaping the future without the LEA', *Local Government Policy Making,* 19(5): 9–14.

Hutchison, E. (1993) 'Mandatory Reporting Laws: Child Protective Case Finding Gone Awry?', *Social Work,* 38(1): 56–63.

Ireland, K. (1993) 'Sexual exploitation of children and international travel and tourism', *Child Abuse Review,* 2(4): 263–70.

Iskander, R. (1989) 'In whose hands?', *Health Visitor,* 62: 264.

ITV (1997) 'Death of Childhood' – Episode One (Cleveland), Broadcast 28 May 1997.

Jackson, M. (1996) 'Infanticide: historical perspectives', *New Law Journal,* 146, 22 March: 416–17, 420.

Jackson, S., Sanders, R. and Thomas, N. (1994) *Protecting Children in Wales: The Role and Effectiveness of Area Child Protection Committees,* Swansea: University of Wales Swansea.

Jackson, S., Sanders, R. and Thomas, N. (1995), 'Setting Priorities in Child Protection: Perception of Risk and Agency Strategy', presented at ESRC Conference: 'Risk in Organisational Settings' on 16/17 May 1995.

James, G. (1994) *Study of Working Together 'Part 8' Reports*, Discussion Report for ACPC National Conference, London: Department of Health.

Johnson, B. (1997) 'The Limits of Personal Safety Education: Insights from an Australian Study', *Journal of Child Centred Practice*, 4(1): 83–92.

Johnson, O. (1981) 'The Socioeconomic Context of Child Abuse and Neglect in Native South America', Chapter 4 in Korbin, J. (ed.) *Child Abuse & Neglect: Cross-cultural perspectives*, Los Angeles: University of California Press.

Jones, A. and Bilton, K. (1994) *The Future Shape of Children's Services*, London: National Children's Bureau.

Jones, D. (1987) 'The Untreatable Family', *Child Abuse & Neglect*, 11: 409–20.

Jones, E. (1986) *Teenage Pregnancy in Industrialised Countries*, New Haven, CT: Yale University Press.

Jones, J. (1994) 'Towards an understanding of power relationships in institutional abuse', *Early Child Development and Care*, 100: 69–76.

Kahan, B. (ed.) (1989) *Child Care Research, Policy and Practice*, London: The Open University/Hodder & Stoughton.

Kane, R. A. (1980) 'Multidisciplinary teamwork in the U.S.: trends, issues and implications for the social worker', pp. 138–51 in Londsdale, S., Webb, A. and Briggs, T. (eds) *Teamwork in the personal social services and health care*, New York: Syracuse University Press.

Kauffman, C. and Neill, K. (1977) 'The hospitalised abused child: an inter-disciplinary approach', *Child Abuse & Neglect*, 1(1): 179–86.

Keller, R., Cicchinelli, L. and Gardner, D. (1989) 'Characteristics of Child Sexual Abuse Treatment Programs', *Child Abuse & Neglect*, 13: 361–8.

Kellmer Pringle, M. (1975) *The Needs of Children*, London: Hutchinson Educational.

Kempe, R.S. and Kempe, C.H. (1978) *Child Abuse*, London: Fontana/Open Books.

Kincheloe, J. and Steinberg, S. (1997) *Changing Multiculturalism*, Buckingham, UK: Open University.

Kirby, S. (1994) 'A Typical Child Molester?', *Police Review*, 6 May: 23–4.

Kohl, J. (1993) 'School-based child sexual abuse prevention programs', *Journal of Family Violence*, 8(2): 137–50.

Kolb, D.A. (1984) *Experiential Learning – Experiences as the Source of Learning and Development*, New Jersey: Prentice-Hall.

Konker, C. (1992) 'Rethinking child sexual abuse: An anthropological perspective', *American Journal of Orthopsychiatry*, 62(1): 147–53.

Korbin, J. (ed.) (1981) *Child Abuse & Neglect: Cross-cultural perspectives*, Los Angeles: University of California Press.

Korbin, J. (1991) 'Cross-Cultural Perspectives and Research Directions for the 21st Century', *Child Abuse & Neglect*, 15 (Supp. 1): 67–77.

Kotch, J., Chalmers, D., Fanslow, J., Marshall, S. (1993) 'Morbidity and death due to child abuse in New Zealand', *Child Abuse & Neglect*, 17(2): 233–47.

Kottak, C. (1997) *Anthropology: The Exploration of Human Diversity* (International edn), London: McGraw Hill.

Krishnan, V. and Morrison, K. (1995) 'An Ecological Model of Child Maltreatment in a Canadian Province', *Child Abuse & Neglect*, 19(1): 101–113.

Lambeth, Lewisham and Southwark Area Review Committee (1989) *The Doreen Aston Report*, London: Lewisham Social Services Department.

Langness, L.L. (1981) 'Child Abuse and Cultural Values: the case of New Guinea', Chapter 2 in Korbin, J. (ed.) *Child Abuse & Neglect: Cross-cultural perspectives*, Los Angeles: University of California Press.

Lardner, R. (1992) 'Factors affecting police/social work inter-agency co-operation in a child protection unit', *Police Journal*, 65: 213–28.

Lawrence-Karski, R. (1997) 'United States: California's Reporting System', Chapter 1 in Gilbert, N. (ed.) *Combating Child Abuse: International Perspectives and Trends*, Oxford, UK: Oxford University Press.

Lazoritz, S. and Shelman, E. (1996) 'Before Mary Ellen', *Child Abuse & Neglect*, 20(3): 235–7.

Lea-Cox, C. and Hall, A. (1991) 'Attendance of general practitioners at child protection case conferences', *British Medical Journal*, 302: 1378–9.

Lealman, G.T., Daigh, D., Phillips, J.M., Stoan, J. and Ord-Smith, C. (1983), 'Prediction and Prevention of Child Abuse – An Empty Hope?', *Lancet*, 8339, 25 June: 1423–4.

Leathard, A. (1994) *Going Inter-Professional: Working Together for Health and Welfare*, London: Routledge.

Lee, J., Campbell, C. and Feng, W. (1994) 'Infant and child mortality among the Qing nobility: implications for two types of positive check', *Population Studies*, 48 (3): 395–411.

Lee-Wright, P. (1990) *Child Slaves*, London: Earthscan.

Leonard, M. (1989) *The School Governors Handbook*, Oxford: Basil Blackwell.

Levine, M., Doueck, H., Freeman, J.B. and Compaan, C. (1996) 'African-American families and child protection', *Children and Youth Services Review*, 18(8): 693–711.

Levine, R. (1977) 'Child rearing as cultural adaptation', in Leiderman, P.H. and Tulin, S., and Rosenfeld, A. (eds) *Culture and infancy: variations in the human experience*, New York: Academic Press.

Levine, S. and Levine, R. (1981) 'Child Abuse and Neglect in Sub-Saharan Africa', Chapter 3 in Korbin, J. (ed.) *Child Abuse & Neglect: Cross-cultural perspectives*, Los Angeles: University of California Press.

Levy, A. and Kahan, B. (1991) *The Pindown Experience and the Protection of Children*, Stafford: Staffordshire County Council.

Lewington, F. and Olsen, A. (1994) 'International Police Cooperation on Crimes Committed Against Children: An Introduction to the Work of the Interpol Standing Working Party on Offences against Minors', *Child Abuse Review*, 3(2): 145–7.

Liddell, M. (1989) 'Policy development in child abuse and neglect in Victoria: the search for villains', *Journal of Social Welfare Law*, 4: 207–16.

Lie, G. and McMurtry, S. (1991) 'Foster Care for Sexually Abused Children: A Comparative Study', *Child Abuse & Neglect*, 15: 111–21.

Lindsey, D. and Hawkins, W. (1994) 'Should the Police have Greater Authority in Investigating Cases of Suspected Abuse? Yes', in Gambrill, E. and Stein, T. (eds) *Controversial Issues in Child Welfare*, London: Allyn and Bacon.

Lindsey, D. and Trocmé, N. (1994) 'Rejoinder to McDonald', in Gambrill, E. and Stein, T. (eds) *Controversial Issues in Child Welfare*, London: Allyn and Bacon.

Lloyd, S. and Burman, M. (1996) 'Specialist Police Units and the Joint Investigation of Child Abuse', *Child Abuse Review*, 5(1): 4–17.

Lock, J. (1993) 'The Baby Killer', *Police Review*, 28 May: 24–45.

London Borough of Bexley and Bexley Area Health Authority (1982) *Report and panel of Inquiry* (Lucie Gates), London Borough of Bexley and Bexley Area Health Authority.

London Borough of Brent and Brent Health Authority (1985), *A Child in trust: the report of the panel of inquiry into the circumstances surrounding the death of Jasmine Beckford*, London Borough of Brent.

London Borough of Greenwich (1987) *A Child in Mind: protection of children in a responsible society* (report of the public inquiry into the death of Kimberley Carlile), London Borough of Greenwich.

London·Borough of Hammersmith and Fulham (1984) *Report on the death of Shirley Woodcock*, London Borough of Hammersmith and Fulham.

London Borough of Hillingdon (1986) *Report of the review panel of the London Borough of Hillingdon Area Review Committee on Child Abuse into the death of Heidi Koseda*, London Borough of Hillingdon.

London Borough of Lambeth (1987) *Whose child? The report of the public inquiry into the death of Tyra Henry*, London Borough of Lambeth.

Lynch, M. (1996) 'The paediatric role: Providing assessment, treatment and continuity', Chapter 5 in Batty, D. and Cullen, D. (eds) *Child Protection: The therapeutic option*, London: British Agencies for Adoption and Fostering.

Lynch, M. and Roberts, J. (1982) *Consequences of Child Abuse*, London: Academic Press.

Lyon, C. and de Cruz, P. (1993) *Child Abuse* (2nd edn), Family Law: Bristol.

Macadem, E. (1945) *The Social Servant in the Making*, Boston: Allen & Unwin.

Macaskill, C. (1991) *Adopting or Fostering a Sexually Abused Child*, London: BAAF/Batsford.

Mackay, J. (1993) *The State of Health Atlas*, London: Simon and Schuster.

MacMillan, H.L., MacMillan, J.H., Offord, D.R., Griffith, L. and Macmillan, A. (1994a) 'Primary prevention of child physical abuse and neglect: a critical review', Part I, *Journal of Child Psychology and Psychiatry*, 35(5): 835–56.

MacMillan, H.L., MacMillan, J.H., Offord, D.R., Griffith, L. and Macmillan, A. (1994b) 'Primary prevention of child sexual abuse: a critical review', Part II, *Journal of Child Psychology and Psychiatry*, 35(5): 857–76.

Maden, M. (1993) 'Dissolution in All but Name', in Brynin, M. (ed.) *Pressure on Education*, Aldershot: Avebury.

Mahoney, T. (1988) *Governing Schools: Power Issues and Practice*, Basingstoke: Macmillan Education.

Maluccio, A.N., Fein, E. and Olmsmtead, K.A. (1986) *Permanency Planning for Children: Concepts and Methods*, London: Tavistock.

Marneffe, C. (1992) 'The Confidential Doctor Centre – a new approach to child protection work', *Adoption & Fostering*, 16(4): 23–8.

Marneffe, C. (1996) 'Does Mandatory Reporting Help to Protect Children? – Against', *Abstracts of ISPCAN Eleventh International Congress on Child Abuse and Neglect*, 42.

Marneffe, C. and Broos, P. (1997) 'Belgium: An Alternative Approach to Child Abuse Reporting and Treatment', Chapter 7 in Gilbert, N. (ed.) *Combating Child Abuse: International Perspectives and Trends*, Oxford: Oxford University Press.

Marvick, E.W. (1976) 'Nature Versus Nurture: Patterns and Trends in Seventeenth-Century French Child-Rearing', Chapter 6 in DeMause, L. (ed.) *The History of Childhood*, London: Souvenir Press.

Maslow, A. (1943) 'A dynamic theory of human motivation', *Psychological Review*, 50: 370–96.

Masson, J. (1997) 'Introducing non-punitive approaches into child protection: Legal issues', Chapter 6 in Parton, N. (ed.) *Child Protection and Family Support: Tensions, contradictions and possibilities*, London: Routledge.

Mather, M., Humphrey, J. and Robson, J. (1997) 'The statutory medical and health needs of looked after children', *Adoption & Fostering*, 36–40.

Mathias, P. and Thompson, T. (1997) 'Preparation for Interprofessional Work: Trends in Education, Training and the Structure of Qualifications in the United Kingdom' in Øvreteit, J., Mathias, P. and Thompson, T. (eds) *Interprofessional Working for Health and Social Care*, Basingstoke: Macmillan.

Maynard, A. (1986) 'Performance Incentives' in Teeling Smith, G. (ed.) *Health Education and General Practice*, London: Office of Health Economics.

McBeath, G. and Webb, S. (1991) 'Social work, modernity and postmodernity', *Sociological Review*, 39(4): 745–62.

McDonald, T. (1994) 'Should the Police have Greater Authority in Investigating

Cases of Suspected Abuse? No', in Gambrill, E. and Stein, T. (eds) *Controversial Issues in Child Welfare*, London: Allyn and Bacon.

McFarlane, T. (1993) 'Promoting inter-professional understanding and collaboration', Chapter 9 in Owen, H. and Pritchard, J. (eds) *Good Practice in Child Protection: A manual for professionals*, London: Jessica Kingsley.

McIntosh, J. and Dingwall, R. (1978) 'Teamwork in theory and practice', in Dingwall, R. and McIntosh, J. (eds), *Readings in the Sociology of Nursing*, Edinburgh: Churchill Livingstone.

McMurray, J. (1989) 'Case conferences', *British Medical Journal*, 299: 500–501.

McQuillan, I. (1994) 'Child's Play', *Police Review*, 8 April: 22–4.

Melton, G.B. (1991) 'Preserving the dignity of children around the world: the U.N. Convention on the Rights of the Child', *Child Abuse & Neglect*, 15(4): 343–50.

Metcalf, A. (1979) 'Family reunion: Networks and treatment in a Native American community', *Journal of Group Psychotherapy, Psychodrama and Sociometry*, 32: 179–89.

Metropolitan Police and London Borough of Bexley (1987) *Child Sexual Abuse: Joint Investigative Programme: Bexley Experiment*, London: HMSO.

Midwinter, E. (1994) *The Development of Social Welfare in Britain*, Buckingham: Open University.

Mills, C. and Vine, P. (1990) 'Critical Incident Reporting – an Approach to Reviewing the Investigation and Management of Child Abuse', *British Journal of Social Work*, 20: 215–20.

Milner, J.S. (1986) *The Child Abuse Potential Inventory: Manual* (2nd edn), Webster, NC: Psytec Corporation.

Milner, J.S. (1989) 'Physical Child Abuse Perpetrator Screening and Evaluation', *Criminal Justice and Behaviour*, 18(1): 47–63.

Minturn, L. and Lambert, W. (1964) *Mothers of Six Cultures*, New York: Wiley.

Moorehead, C. (1989) *Betrayal: Child Exploitation in Today's World*, London: Barrie & Jenkins.

Morris, R. (ed.) (1990) *Central and Local Control of Education After the Education Reform Act 1988*, Harlow: Longman.

Mrazek, P.B., Lynch, M. and Bentovim, A. (1981) 'Recognitions of Sexual Abuse in the United Kingdom', in Mrazek, P.B. and Kempe, C.H. (eds) *Sexually Abused Children and their Families*, Oxford: Pergamon Press.

Muldkjaer, F. (1997) 'National Council on Children's Rights', *Journal of Child Centred Practice*, 4(1): 101-105.

Munns, G. (1994) 'A Social Service?', *Police Review*, 27 May: 32–3.

Murray, K. and Hill, M. (1991) 'The recent history of Scottish child welfare', *Children & Society*, 5: 266–81.

Myers, J. (1994) 'Definitions and Origins of the Backlash Against Child

Protection', Chapter 2 in Myers, J.B. (ed.) *The Backlash: Child Protection under Fire*, London: Sage.

Myers, J. and Cooper, B. (1996) 'Creating and sustaining an inter-agency training pool', *Child Abuse Review*, 5(4): 289–93.

Narducci, T. (1992) 'Race, culture and child protection', Chapter 2 in Cloke, C. and Naish, J. (eds) *Key Issues in Child Protection for Health Visitors & Nurses*, Harlow: Longman.

Nash, C. (1997) 'Cause-for-concern criteria in child protection', *Health Visitor*, 70(7): 260–1.

Nelson, B. (1984) *Making an Issue of Child Abuse: Political Agenda Setting*, Chicago: University of Chicago.

Newberger, E.H. and Bourne, J.D. (1979) 'The medicalisation and legalisation of child abuse', in Bourne, J.D. and Newberger, E.H. (eds) *Critical perspectives on child abuse*, Lexington, MA: Heath & Co.

Newell, P. (1989) *Children are People Too: The case against physical punishment*, London: Bedford Square Press.

Newell, P. (1991) *The UN Convention and Children's Rights in the UK*, London: National Children's Bureau.

Newlands, M. and Emery, J. (1991) 'Child Abuse and Cot Deaths', *Child Abuse & Neglect*, 15: 275–8.

Ney, P., Fung, T. and Wickett, A. (1994) 'The Worst Combinations of Child Abuse and Neglect', *Child Abuse & Neglect*, 18(9): 705–14.

NHS Executive/SSI (National Health Service Executive/Social Services Inspectorate) (1995) *Community Care Monitoring Report 1994*, London: NHSE/SSI.

NHS Executive (1994) *Managing the New NHS: Functions and Responsibilities in the New NHS*, Leeds, NHSE.

NHS Executive (1996) *Child Health in the Community: A Guide to Good Practice*, London: Department of Health.

Nicol, A. (1989) 'Role of the Child Psychiatry Team', *British Medical Journal*, 299, 12 August: 451–2.

Nixon, S. and Hicks, C. (1987) 'Experiencing accusations of abuse', *Foster Care*, December: 10–11.

Nixon, S. and Verity, P. (1996) 'Allegations against foster families', *Foster Care*, 84: 11–14.

Nixon, S., Hicks, C. and Ells, S. (1986) 'Support for foster parents accused of child abuse', *Foster Care*, December: 8–10.

Noble, M. and Smith, T. (1994) '"Children in Need": Using Geographical Information Systems to inform strategic planning for social service provision', *Children & Society*, 8(4): 360–76.

Nottingham Area Review Committee (1985) *Report of inquiry into the case of Reuben Carthy (d.o.b. 7.4.82)*, Nottingham.

NSPCC (National Society for the Prevention of Cruelty to Children) (1996) *Messages from the NSPCC – a contribution to the 'Refocusing Debate'*, London: NSPCC.

OFSTED (Office for Standards in Education) (1995) *Framework for the Inspection of Nursery, Primary, Middle, Secondary and Special Schools*, London: HMSO.

O'Hagan, K. (1993) *Emotional and Psychological Abuse of Children*, Buckingham: Open University Press.

O'Kane, C. (1996, unpublished) 'The Phenomenon of Child Abuse in India and the UK'.

Okine, E. (1992) 'A Misassessment of black families in child abuse work', Chapter 7 in Moore, J. (ed.) *The ABC of Child Protection*, Aldershot: Ashgate.

Olson, E. (1981) 'Socioeconomic and Psychocultural Contexts of Child Abuse and Neglect in Turkey', Chapter 6 in Korbin, J. (ed.) *Child Abuse & Neglect: Cross-cultural perspectives*, Los Angeles: University of California Press.

Orr, J. (1992a) 'Assessing Individual and Family Health Needs', Chapter 4 in Luker, K. and Orr, J. (eds) *Health Visiting: Towards Community Health Nursing* (2nd edn), Oxford: Blackwell Scientific Publications.

Orr, J. (1992b) 'Health Visiting and the Community', Chapter 3 in Luker, K. and Orr, J. (eds) *Health Visiting: Towards Community Health Nursing* (2nd edn), Oxford: Blackwell Scientific Publications.

Packman, J., Randall, J. and Jacques, N. (1986) *Who Needs Care? Social Work Decisions about Children*, London: Blackwell.

Parton, N. (1985) *The Politics of Child Abuse*, London: Macmillan.

Parton, N. (1991) *Governing the Family: Child Care, Child Protection and the State*, London: Macmillan.

Parton, N. (1994) 'A Lost Opportunity', *Community Care*, 21–27 July: 18.

Parton, N. (1996) 'Child protection, family support and social work: a critical appraisal of the Department of Health research studies in child protection', *Child & Family Social Work*, 1(1): 3–13.

Parton, N. (1997) 'Child protection and family support: current debates and future prospects', Chapter 1 in Parton, N. (ed.) *Child Protection and Family Support: Tensions, contradictions and possibilities*, London: Routledge.

Parton, C. and Parton, N. (1989) 'The law and dangerousness' in Stevenson, O. (ed.) *Child Abuse: Public Policy and Professional Practice*, New York: Harvester Wheatsheaf.

Payne, G.H. (1928) *The Child in Human Progress*, New York: Sears.

Pelton, L.H. (1978) 'Child Abuse and Neglect: The Myth of Classlessness', *American Journal of Orthopsychiatry*, 48: 608–17.

Pettifer, E.W. (1939) *Punishments of Former Days*, Bradford: Clegg & Son.

Plotnikoff, J. and Woolfson, R. (1995) *Prosecuting Child Abuse: An Evaluation of the Government's Speedy Progress Policy*, London: Blackstone.

Poertner, J., Smith, P. and Fields, J. (1991) 'Quality control in child abuse prevention programs', *Children and Youth Services Review*, 13(1-2): 29–39.

Poffenberger, T. (1981) 'Child Rearing and Social Structure in Rural India: Toward a Cross-Cultural Definition of Child Abuse and Neglect', Chapter 5 in Korbin, J. (ed.) *Child Abuse & Neglect: Cross-cultural perspectives*, Los Angeles: University of California Press.

Pollock, L. (1993) *Forgotten Children: Parent–Child relations from 1500–1900*, Cambridge: Cambridge University Press.

Pollock, L. and West, E. (1984) 'On being a woman and a psychiatric nurse', *Senior Nurse*, 1(17): 333–48.

Pollock, L. (1986) 'The multi-disciplinary team', in C. Hume and I. Pullen (eds) *Rehabilitation in Psychiatry: An Introductory Handbook*, Edinburgh: Churchill Livingstone.

Prior, V., Lynch, M. and Glaser, D. (1994) *Messages from Children: Children's evaluations of the professional response to child sexual abuse*, London: NCH Action for Children.

Radbill, S. (1974) 'A history of child abuse and infanticide', in Helfer, R.E. and Kempe, C.H. (eds) *The battered child* (2nd edn), Chicago: University of Chicago Press.

Radbill, S. (1980) 'Children in a World of Violence: A History of Child Abuse', in Kempe, C.H. and Heifer, R.E. (eds) *The Battered Child* (3rd edn), Chicago: University of Chicago Press.

Rae, R. (1992) 'One step ahead', *Community Care*, 30: 21–3.

Reder, P., Duncan, S. and Gray, M. (1993), *Beyond Blame: Child Abuse Tragedies Revisited*, Routledge: London and New York.

Robbins, D. (1990) *Child Care Policy: Putting it in Writing*, London: SSI/HMSO.

Robertson, C. (1991) *Health Visiting in Practice* (2nd edn), London: Churchill Livingstone.

Robinson, J.A. (1979) 'Interdisciplinary in-service education and training', *Child Abuse & Neglect*, 3: 3–4, 749–55.

Robinson, R. (1994) 'Introduction' to Robinson, R. and LeGrand, J. (eds) *Evaluating the NHS Reforms*, Newbury, Berkshire: Kings Fund Institute/Policy Journals.

Rodwell, M.K. and Chambers, D.E. (1989) 'Promises, Promises: Child Abuse Prevention in the 1980's', *Policy Studies Review*, 8 (Summer): 749–73.

Roelofs, M. and Baartman, H. (1997) 'The Netherlands: Responding to Abuse – Compassion or Control?', Chapter 8 in Gilbert, N. (ed.) *Combating Child Abuse: International Perspectives and Trends*, Oxford: Oxford University Press.

Rose, L. (1986) *The massacre of the innocents: Infanticide in Britain 1800–1939*, London: Routledge and Kegan Paul.

Rose, S. (1985) *Recognition of Child Abuse and Neglect*, London: Gower Medical Publishing.

Rose, W. (1994) 'An Overview of the Developments of Services – The Relationship between Protection and Family Support and the Intentions of the Children Act 1989', Department of Health Paper for Sieff Conference, 5 September.

Rowbottom, R., Hey, A. and Billis, D. (1974) *Social Services Departments: Developing Patterns of Work and Organization*, London: Heinemann.

Royal College of Nursing (1994) *Nursing and Child Protection: An RCN Survey*, London: RCN.

Russell, D. (1983) 'The incidence and prevalence of intrafamilial and extra-familial sexual abuse of female children', *Child Abuse & Neglect*, 7: 133–46.

Rush, F. (1980) *The Best Kept Secret: Sexual Abuse of Children*, New York: McGraw-Hill.

Ruxton, S. (1996) *Children in Europe*, London: NCH Action for Children.

Ryan, G. and Lane, S. (eds) (1991) *Juvenile Sexual Offending – Causes, Consequences and Corrections*, Lexington, MA: Lexington Books.

Sadler, C. (1997) 'Caught on film', *Health Visitor*, 70(12): 447.

Salazar, M.C. (1991) 'Young workers in Latin America: protection or self-determination?', *Child Welfare*, 70: 269–83.

Sallis, J. (1988) *Schools, Parents and Governors: A New Approach to Accountability*, London: Routledge.

Salter, A., Richardson, C. and Martin, P., (1985) 'Treating Abusive Parents', *Child Welfare*, 64: 327–41.

Sanders, B. (1993) *The Children Act 1989: A Guide for Voluntary Organisations*, Caerphilly: Wales Council for Voluntary Action.

Sanders, B., Jackson, S. and Thomas, N. (1996a) 'A comparison of child protection local procedures handbooks', *Practice*, 8(3): 31–44.

Sanders, R., Jackson, S. and Thomas, N. (1996b) 'The Balance of Prevention, Investigation, and Treatment in the Management of Child Protection Services', *Child Abuse & Neglect*, 20(10): 899–906.

Sanders, R., Jackson, S. and Thomas, N. (1996c) 'The Police Role in the Management of Child Protection Services', *Policing and Society*, 6: 87–100.

Sanders, R., Jackson, S. and Thomas, N. (1997) 'Degrees of Involvement: The Interaction of Focus and Commitment in Area Child Protection Committees', *British Journal of Social Work*, 27: 871–92.

Sanders, R. and McAllen, A. (1995) 'Training Foster Carers of Children Who Have Been Sexually Abused – Issues and Dilemmas', *Child Abuse Review*, 4: 136–45.

Sanders, R. and Thomas., N. (1997) *Area Child Protection Committees*, Aldershot: Avebury.

Sawyer, R. (1988) *Children Enslaved*, London: Routledge.

Schultz, E. and Lavenda, R. (1990) *Cultural Anthropology: A Perspective on the Human Condition* (2nd edn), St. Paul, MN: West Publishing Co.

SCRCSSP (Steering Committee for the Review of Commonwealth/State Service Provision (1997) *Report on Government Service Provision*, Melbourne: SCRCSSP.

Secretaries of State for Health, Wales, Northern Ireland and Scotland (1989) *Working for Patients* (White Paper), London: HMSO.

Seebohm, Lord (chair) (1968) *Report of the Committee on Local Authority and Allied Personal Social Services*, Cmnd 3703, London: HMSO.

Selman, P. and Glendinning, C. (1996) 'Teenage Pregnancy: Do Social Policies Make a Difference?', Chapter 14 in Brannen, J. and O'Brien., M. (eds) *Children in Families: Research and Policy*, London: Falmer Press.

Seymour-Smith, C. (1986) *Macmillan Dictionary of Anthropology*, London: Macmillan.

Sharland, E., Jones, D., Aldgate, J., Seal, H. and Croucher, M. (1995) *Professional Intervention in Child Sexual Abuse*, London: HMSO.

Shaw, I. and Butler, I. (1998) 'Understanding Young People and Prostitution: A Foundation for Practice?', *British Journal of Social Work*, 28(2): 177–96.

Sharron, H. (1987) 'The influence of the Paterson factor', *Social Work Today*, 18, 30 March: 8–9.

Sherman, B. (1989) 'Confronting child abuse and neglect in New York State', *New York State Journal of Medicine*, 89(3): 163–5.

Simon, B. and Chitty, C. (1993) *SOS: Save Our Schools*, London: Lawrence & Wishart.

Simpson, C., Simpson, R., Power, K., Salter, A. and Williams, G-J. (1994) 'GPs' and Health Visitors' Participation in Child Protection Case Conferences', *Child Abuse Review*, 3: 211–30.

Sinclair, I. (1997) 'A Quality-control Perspective', Chapter VI.2 in Davies, M. (ed.) *The Blackwell Companion to Social Work*, Oxford: Blackwell.

Sloan, J. (1989) 'Child abuse in schools', *Educational and Child Psychology*, 6(1): 11–14.

Sluckin, A. and Dolan, R. (1989) 'Tackling child abuse in the EC', *Social Work Today*, 31/8/89: 14–15.

Smallwood, G. (1995) 'Child abuse and neglect from an indigenous Australian's perspective', *Child Abuse & Neglect*, 19(3): 281–9.

Smith., A. (1992) 'Police Reforms in Child Abuse Investigation: Their Success and Limitations in the Struggle to Uphold Children's Rights', *Children & Society*, 6(2): 104–10.

Smith, M., Bee, P., Heverin, A. and Nobes, G. (1995) *Parental Violence to Children within the Family: The Nature and Extent of Parental Violence to Children*, London: HMSO.

Smith., M. and Grocke, M. (1995) *Normal Family Sexuality and Sexual Knowledge in Children*, Royal College of Psychiatrists/Gorkill Press.

Smith, S. (1998) 'Child protection: are we going backwards?', *Community practitioner*, 71(3): 98–9.

Southall, D. (1997) 'Covert video recordings of life threatening child abuse: lessons for child protection', *Pediatrics*, 100(5): 735–60.

Spencer, J.R. and Flin, R. (1993) *The Evidence of Children: The Law and the Psychology* (2nd edn), London: Blackstone.

SSI (Social Services Inspectorate) (1986) *Inspection of the supervision of Social Workers in the assessment and monitoring of cases of child abuse*, London: DHSS.

SSI (Social Services Inspectorate) (1988) *Child Sexual Abuse: Survey Report*, London: DHSS.

SSI (Social Services Inspectorate) (1993) *Evaluating Performance in Child Protection: A framework for the inspection of local authority social services practice and systems*, London: HMSO.

SSI (Social Services Inspectorate) (1994a) *Report on the National Survey of Children's Services Plans – Progress Made During 1993*, Birmingham: SSI.

SSI (Social Services Inspectorate) (1994b) *Evaluating Child Protection Services: Findings and Issues – Inspections of Six Local Authority Child Protection Services 1993: Overview Report*, London: SSI.

SSI (Social Services Inspectorate) (1995a) *Evaluating Child Protection Services: Child Inspections 1993/94 – Overview Report*, London: SSI.

SSI (Social Services Inspectorate) (1995b) *Domestic Violence and Social Care: A report on two conferences held by the Social Services Inspectorate*, London: SSI.

SSI/DoH (Social Services Inspectorate/Department of Health) (1993) *Inspecting for Quality: Evaluating Peformance in Child Protection*.

SSI (Social Services Inspectorate) (North Western Region) (1990) *Inspection of Child Protection Services in Rochdale*, SSI(NW): Manchester.

SSI (Social Services Inspectorate) (Wales) (1992) *Alcohol Misuse and Child Mistreatment: Report of Second Training Initiative Developed from an Experimental Project published in April 1991*, SSI (Wales): Cardiff.

SSI (Social Services Inspectorate) (Wales) (1996) *Area Child Protection Committees and Local Government Reorganisation*, SSI (Wales): Cardiff.

Stainton Rogers, R. (1989) 'The Social Construction of Childhood', Chapter 1 in Stainton Rogers, W., Hevey, D. and Ash, E. (eds) *Child Abuse and Neglect: Facing the Challenge*, London: Open University/Batsford.

Stainton Rogers, W., Hevey, D. and Ash, E. (1989) (eds) *Child Abuse and Neglect: Facing the Challenge*, London: Open University/Batsford.

Stephens, M. (1994) 'Care and Control: The Future of British Policing', *Policing and Society*, 4: 237–51.

Stevenson, O. (1989) *Child Abuse: Public Policy and Professional Practice*, Hertfordshire: Harvester Wheatsheaf.

Stevenson, O. (1994) 'Child protection: Where now for inter-professional work?', Chapter 7 in Leathard, A. (ed.) *Going Inter-Professional: Working Together for Health and Welfare*, London: Routledge.

Strauss, M. Gelles, R. and Steinmetz, K. (1980) *Behind Closed Doors: Violence in the American Family*, New York: Anchor Press.

Summit, R.C. (1988) 'Hidden victims, hidden pain: societal avoidance of child sexual abuse' in Wyatt, G.E. and Powell, G.J. (eds), *Lasting Effects of Child Sexual Abuse*, Newbury Park: Sage.

Swan, H.L., Press, A.N. and Briggs, S.L. (1985) *Child Welfare*, 64: 395–405.

Swift, K. (1997) 'Canada: Trends and Issues in Child Welfare', Chapter 2 in Gilbert, N. (ed.) *Combating Child Abuse: International Perspectives and Trends*, Oxford: Oxford University Press.

Sylwander, L. (1997) 'The Children's Ombudsman in Sweden', *Journal of Child Centred Practice*, 4(1): 47–58

Tattersall, P. (1992) 'Communicating assertively to protect children in nursing practice', Chapter 6 in Cloke, C. and Naish, J. (eds) *Key Issues in Child Protection for Health Visitors & Nurses*, Harlow: Longman.

Taylor, S. and Tilley, N. (1990) 'Inter-agency conflict in child abuse work-reducing tensions between social workers and health visitors', *Adoption & Fostering*, 14(4): 13–17.

Thoburn, J., Lewis, A. and Shemmings, D. (1995) *Paternalism or Partnership? Family Involvement in the Child Protection Process*, London: HMSO.

Thomas, L. (1996) 'Working with Victims of Child Sexual Abuse' paper presented at BASPCAN (South Wales) Branch AGM, Cardiff, 9 January.

Thomas, M.P. (1972) 'Child abuse and neglect: Part 1, Historical overview., legal matrix, and social perspectives', *North Carolina Law Review*, 50: 293–349.

Thomas, N. (1995) 'Allegations of child abuse in local authority foster care', *Practice*, 7(3): 35–44.

Thomas, T. (1994) *The Police and Social Workers*, Aldershot: Arena.

Thompson, B. (1991) 'Child abuse in Sierra Leone: normative disparities', *International Journal of Law and the Family*, 5: 13–23.

Thompson-Cooper., I., Fugère, R. and Cormier, B. (1993) 'The Child Abuse Reporting Laws: An Ethical Dilemma for Professionals', *Canadian Journal of Psychiatry*, 38: 557–62.

Thorpe, D. (1994) *Evaluating Child Protection*, Buckingham: Open University.

Thorpe, D. (1997) 'Policing minority child-rearing practices in Australia: the consistency of "child abuse"', Chapter 4 in Parton, N. (ed.) *Child Protection and Family Support: Tensions, contradictions and possibilities*, London: Routledge.

Tite, R. (1994) 'Detecting the symptoms of child abuse: Classroom complications', *Canadian Journal of Education*, 19(1): 1–14.

Toth, P. (1996) 'Does Mandatory Reporting Help to Protect Children? – In Support', *Abstracts of ISPCAN Eleventh International Congress on Child Abuse and Neglect*, 41–2.

Tower, C.C. (1996) *Child Abuse and Neglect* (3rd edn), London: Allyn & Bacon.

Towle, C. (1973) *Common Human Needs*, London: George and Allen Unwin.

Trawick-Smith, J. (1997) *Early Child Development: A Multicultural Perspective*, New Jersey: Merrill/Prentice Hall.

Trute, B., Adkins, E. and MacDonald, G. (1992) 'Professional Attitudes Regarding the Sexual Abuse of Children: Comparing Police, Child Welfare and Community Mental Health', *Child Abuse & Neglect*, 16: 359–68.

Tyler, F., Tyler, S., Tommasello, A. and Connolly, M. (1992) 'Huckleberry Finn and Street Youth Everywhere: An Approach to Primary Prevention', Chapter 15 in Albee, G., Bond, L. and Cook Monsey, T. (eds) *Improving Children's Lives: Global Perspectives on Prevention*, London: Sage.

Urzi, M. (1977) *Cooperative approaches to child protection: a community guide*, St. Paul, MN: State Department of Public Welfare.

Uzodike, E. (1990) 'Child abuse and neglect in Nigeria – socio-legal aspects', *International Journal of Law and the Family*, 4: 83–96.

Van IJzendoorn, M. and Kroonenberg, P. (1988) 'Cross-cultural patterns of attachment: a meta-analysis of the Strange Situation', *Child Development*, 59: 147–56.

Verity, P. and Nixon, S. (1995) 'Allegations against foster families: survey results', *Foster Care*, (83): 13–16.

Waage, T. (1997) 'Monitoring the Convention on the Rights of the Child – The Role of the Ombudsman for Children in Norway', *Journal of Child Centred Practice*, 4(1): 107–22.

Wagatsuma, H. (1981) 'Child Abandonment and Infanticide: A Japanese Case', Chapter 7 in Korbin, J. (ed.) *Child Abuse & Neglect: Cross-cultural perspectives*, Los Angeles: University of California Press.

Wald, M. and Woolverton, M. (1990) 'Risk Assessment: The Emperor's New Clothes?', *Child Welfare*, 69(6): 483–511.

Walker, C.E., Bonner, B.L. and Kaufman, K.L. (1988) *The Physically and Sexually Abused Child: Evaluation and Treatment*, New York: Pergamon.

Walker, H. (1991) 'Family centres', in Carter, P., Jeffs, T. and Smith, M. (eds) *Social Work and Social Welfare*, Buckingham: Open University.

Walsh, K. (1991) 'Quality and Public Service', *Public Administration*, 69: 503–4.

Walvin, J. (1982) *A Child's World: A Social History of English Childhood 1800–1914*, Harmondsworth: Penguin.

Walzner, J. (1976) 'A Period of Ambivalence: Eighteenth-Century American Childhood', Chapter 8 in DeMause, L. (ed.) *The History of Childhood*, London: Souvenir Press.

Waterhouse, L. and Carnie, J. (1991) 'Social Work and Police Response to Child Sexual Abuse in Scotland', *British Journal of Social Work*, 21: 373–9.

Watkins, S. (1990) 'The Mary Ellen Myth: Correcting Child Welfare History',

Social Work, 35: 500-503.

Wattam, C. (1992) *Making a Case in Child Protection,* Harlow: Longman.

Webster, R. (1991) 'Issues in school-based child sexual abuse prevention', *Children and Society,* 5(2): 146–64.

Weisner, T. and Gallimore, R. (1977) 'My Brother's Keeper: Child and Sibling Caretaking', *Current Anthropology,* 18(2): 169–90.

Welsh Office (1995) *Protecting Children from Abuse: The Role of the Education Service,* Welsh Office Circular 52/95.

Whiting, B. and Whiting, J.W.M. (1975) *Children of Six Cultures,* Cambridge, MA: Harvard University Press.

Wigmore, J.H. (1970) *Evidence in trials at common law* (original published in 1904), Boston: Little, Brown.

Williams, J. (1992) 'Working Together II', *Journal of Child Law,* April: 68–71.

Williams of Mostyn, Lord (1996) *Childhood Matters: Report of the National Commission of Inquiry in the Prevention of Child Abuse,* London: The Stationery Office.

Wolfe, D. (1993) 'Child Abuse Prevention: Blending Research and Practice', *Child Abuse Review,* 2: 153–65.

Wonnacott, J. (1995) *Protecting Children in School: A handbook for developing child protection training,* London: National Children's Bureau.

Woodhead, M. (1998) '"Quality" in early childhood programmes – a contextually-appropriate approach', *International Journal of Early Years Education,* 6(1): 5–17.

Wooley, P.V. Jr. and Evans, W.A. Jr. (1955) 'Significance of skeletal lesions in infants resembling those of traumatic origin', *Journal of the American Medical Association,* 181: 17–24.

Yamamoto, J. and Iga, M. (1983) 'Emotional growth of Japanese-American children', in Powell, G. (ed.) *The psychosocial development of minority children,* New York: Brunner/Mazel.

Zigler, E. and Hall, N. (1989) 'Physical child abuse in America: past, present, and future', Chapter 2 in Cicchetti, D. and Carlson, V. (eds) *Child Maltreatment: Theory and research on the causes and consequences of child abuse and neglect,* Cambridge, MA: Cambridge University Press.

Index

abandonment 5, 7, 16, 60, 149
abortion 17
Abraham 2
abusers
    adult 13, 15, 42, 78, 121, 133, 134, 137,
        138, 165, 167, 175, 202, 205, 213,
        217, 241, 250
    juvenile 137, 165, 199, 241
adoption 36, 80, 88, 158, 215
Afghanistan 59
Africa 38, 59–61
African American 31, 69
African Network for the Prevention and
    Protection Against Child Abuse and
    Neglect (ANPPCAN) 61
Afro-Caribbean 68
age of consent 18
alcohol (misuse) 96, 142, 263
Allitt, Beverley: the case of 17
America 2, 4, 7, 13, 21, 22, 26, 32, 39, 46,
    47, 54, 62, 69
Amsterdam 65
Angola 59
anti-racist 70
appeals and complaints 22, 100, 124, 127,
    232
Area Child Protection Committee
    (ACPC) 73, 75, 83, 85, 91, 96, 98–101,
    113–115, 117–182, 196, 197, 202–204,
    209, 219, 225, 245–247, 250, 256, 259,
        260, 264, 269
    Annual Report 122, 139, 180–182
    budget 194–196
    chair 188, 189
    handbooks 122–124, 195, 225, 247
    Part 8 Reviews (see also fatality) 115,
        122, 126, 160–180, 187, 188, 224,
        225, 235, 236, 249
    subcommittees 126, 127, 154, 156, 189,
        191, 192, 209, 225, 247
Area Review Committee 157, 170, 197,
    198, 226, 245
Argentina 60
Aristotle 4
armed services 83, 119
Asia 52, 62–65
Association of Chief Police Officers 94
Aston, Doreen: the case of 157, 170, 226
attachment 29, 30
Attorney-General 205
Audit Commission 89, 95, 101–103, 141,
    221, 225, 227, 228, 246
Aukland, Susan: the case of 81
Australia 54–56, 59, 66, 67, 77, 209, 256
    Aboriginal people 65, 67
Austria 4, 49–51, 58, 59
autonomy 29–31, 48, 54, 85, 94, 120, 159,
    177, 217, 245, 246, 265

baby farming 8, 16, 17, 54
baby-sitting 31
Bangladesh 60
Barclay Report 1982 (UK) 147, 148
Barking 137
Barnsley 98
Battered-Child/Baby Syndrome 14, 75,
    130, 198, 228, 231
Beck, Frank: the case of 75, 193
Beckford, Jasmine: the case of 75, 81,
    142, 148, 166, 167, 201
Belgium 4, 40, 47, 48, 50–53, 58, 59
Bell, Stuart (MP) 80–82, 167
Bergh, Henry 9–11
Bexley Experiment 199, 202
Bible 1, 2
Birmingham, UK 64
Black Power movement (USA) 66
Boer War 220
Bolderkar affair, the (Netherlands) 53
Boston Society for the Prevention of
    Cruelty to Children 12, 13, 15, 21
Boston 32
Bowis, John, Parliamentary Under
    Secretary of State 108
Bradford, UK 64
Brewer, Wayne: the case of 81
British New Guinea 3
British Paediatric Association 228
Bronfenbrenner, Urie 144, 145
bullying 140, 252, 253
Burkina Faso 59

Caffey, Dr John, 14
California 41, 67, 69
Camberwell, London 17
Canada 26, 40, 41, 44, 58, 67, 198, 209,
    255, 258
capital punishment (of children) 37
Cardiff, Wales 64, 66
Care Proceedings/Care Orders 81, 106,
    125, 133, 186, 197, 206, 241, 258, 261
Carlile, Kimberley: the case of 84, 148,
    166, 167
Carthy, Reuben: the case of 245
Catholicism 5
centile charts 231
Central Council for Education and
    Training in Social Work (CCETSW)
    154

Chapman, Lester: the case of 81
Charity Organisation Society (COS) 22
chastise 8
Chicago Society for the Prevention of
    Cruelty to Children 12
child abduction 36, 37
child abuse inquiries 126, 148, 156, 160,
    162–170, 232
child Abuse Potential Inventory 79
Child Abuse Prevention and Treatment
    Act 1974 (USA) 14
child and adolescent mental health
    services 215, 240
child assessment order 83, 84, 125, 230,
    231, 241
child betrothal/marriage 38, 61, 63
child branding 63
Child Care Act 1980 (UK) 81, 86
Child Care and Protection Board
    (Netherlands) 53
child centred(ness) 44, 63, 235, 268
child health surveillance 102, 156, 221,
    225, 228, 244
child imprisonment 36, 37
child labour 6, 26, 36, 37, 54, 60–63
child pornography 14, 39, 71
child prostitution 6, 14, 18, 26, 34, 35, 39,
    60, 63–65
child protection conference 44, 45, 57, 73,
    85, 97, 107, 109, 110, 123, 126, 171,
    186–188, 190, 197, 198, 223, 224, 231,
    241, 245, 248, 254, 261, 264
child protection investigation 38, 41, 42,
    44, 45, 55, 56, 67, 83, 84, 97, 103, 109–
    114, 123, 124, 137–139, 141, 143, 157,
    158, 173, 178, 185, 186, 190, 192, 197–
    201, 214, 226, 243, 257–259, 261
child protection investigation (section
    47) 45, 84, 185, 193
child protection register 44, 45, 49, 50,
    57, 78, 83, 86, 97, 98, 102, 123, 126,
    161, 171, 173, 175, 187, 188, 204, 231,
    237, 264, 265
Child Protection Advisers (CPAs) 227
child protection coordinator 188–191
child protection trainer 154–156, 188,
    191, 192
child trafficking 36, 37
Child Welfare League of America 13
childhood 1, 2, 18, 67, 146, 250, 254

Children Act 1948 (UK) 139
Children Act 1975 (UK) 80, 81, 106
Children Act 1989 (UK) 81–84, 86, 88, 99,
    106, 113, 133, 139, 150–153, 184, 185,
    190, 197, 203, 210, 229, 230, 232, 266,
    267, 268
  child in need 22, 101–103, 150, 152,
    153, 184, 215, 251, 263, 267, 268
Children and Young Person's Act 1963
    (UK) 81
children in care (*see* looked after
    children)
Children's Bureau (USA) 12, 14, 40
Children's Protection Society (Australia)
    54
Children's Services Plans 89, 96
China 3, 30, 59
  foot-binding 28, 38, 63
  one-child policy 5, 63
cholera 16, 220
Civil Rights movement (USA) 66
class (socioeconomic) 12, 28, 34, 63, 144,
    222
Cleveland (UK) 21, 53, 75, 80–84, 106,
    108, 112, 113, 148, 149, 153, 157, 161,
    165, 167, 189, 190, 198, 199, 201, 202,
    230, 232, 234
Colwell, Maria: the case of 12, 75, 80, 84,
    160, 167, 192, 198, 200, 201
common sense 79, 130
community child health services 101,
    220, 228
community child health doctor 183, 219,
    228–239, 241
community development 146, 148, 149,
    151
Community Health Trusts 227
Community Practitioner's and Health
    Visitor's Association 227
community social work 148, 149
community workers 147–149
comprehensive assessments 97, 99, 113,
    123, 124, 136, 187, 230
concentration camps 27
Conference on the Care of Dependent
    Children (1909) 12
confidential doctor service 51–54
confidentiality 48, 161, 216, 217, 238,
    239, 244, 249, 259
Continuing Medical Education (CME)

tutor 156, 247
contraception 238
Coram, Thomas 5, 16
core groups 188
Cornwall, UK 260
corporal punishment 61, 144, 260
Court Committee Report 1976 (UK) 234
courts 9, 22, 95, 101, 103, 197, 207, 209,
    210, 229, 231, 234–236
covert video surveillance (CVS) 237, 238
Criminal Justice Act 1988 (UK) 208
Criminal Justice Act 1991 (UK) 203, 206–
    208, 210
Criminal Law Amendment Act 1885
    (UK) 18, 208
Crown Prosecution Service 186, 196, 197,
    204–214, 258
cultural relativism 27, 28, 71, 72, 269
Czech Republic 59

Darwin, Charles 10
Declaration of Geneva (1924) 35
Declaration of the Rights of the Child
    (1959) 35
definition of abuse 16, 33, 34, 54, 60, 61,
    65, 108, 109, 112, 269
Denmark 4, 35, 40, 49, 51, 58, 59
dental practitioners 119
Department for Education and
    Employment (UK) 88
Department of Education and Science
    (DES) (UK) 87
Department of Health (DoH) (UK) 73,
    82, 87, 88, 91, 95–97, 102, 104, 105,
    107, 108, 114, 125, 151, 161, 162, 170,
    173, 178, 181, 182, 187, 189, 191, 267
Department of Health and Social
    Security (DHSS) (UK) 105, 107, 117
designated teachers 94, 157, 254, 256–
    258, 260
Director of Public Prosecutions 205, 211
disability/handicap, child with 4, 33,
    36, 153, 158, 172, 175, 184, 214
discipline (of children) 6, 63, 221, 260
District Health Authorities 118, 218
domestic violence 67, 96, 173, 175, 202,
    204, 263
Dominican Republic 60
drugs 37, 142, 263
Dublin 5

Dutch Society for the Prevention of Cruelty to Children 52

ecological perspective/model 144–146
ecomaps 106
Economic and Social Research Council (ESRC) 105
Ecuador 60
Education (Schools) Act 1992 (UK) 93
Education Act 1993 (UK) 92
education, child's right to 37
education departments/agencies 83, 101, 119, 137, 155, 157, 164, 177, 178, 201, 215, 250–262
Education Reform Act 1988 (UK) 92, 251
education welfare/officers 240, 255
educational psychologists 240
Egypt 59
emergency protection order 83, 84, 125, 133, 185, 229, 231
Emotionally and Behaviourally Disturbed (EBD) 262
England 4, 7, 16–18, 25, 32, 40, 47, 48, 50, 54, 59, 86, 88, 114, 171, 235
England and Wales 3, 4, 7, 25, 39, 59, 64, 73, 89, 101, 137, 182, 183, 201
Epe incest case, the (Netherlands) 53
Essex 98
Estonia 59
ethnicity 26, 28, 29, 39, 65, 66, 68–71, 227, 231, 252, 264
ethnocentrism 27–29, 72, 269
Eurocentric 28, 70
Europe 4, 5, 7, 25, 26, 32, 40, 47–54, 59, 64–66, 251
evidence of children
  competency 207
  corroboration 207, 208
  method of giving evidence 207, 208
exclusion requirements 133, 134
expert witness 230, 231, 234, 235
exposure (of infants) 5, 7, 16
extrafamilial abuse 53, 60, 71, 186

failure to thrive 231
family centres 140, 149–153, 226
family group conferences 57, 66, 265
Family Health Services Authority (FHSA) 119, 156, 195, 219, 225
Family Law Act 1996 (UK) 133

Family Welfare Association 150
fatality/death, from child abuse 70, 75, 83, 99, 111, 148, 156, 160, 169, 170, 172, 177, 249
female circumcision 27, 38, 60, 61
feminism 13, 15
filtering in child protection 44, 45, 102
Finland 40, 49, 50, 51, 58, 59
Florida 136
force-feeding 38
foster care/fostering 17, 60, 68, 80, 112, 124, 132, 134, 135, 165, 175, 192–194, 232, 261
foundling hospitals 5, 16
Fox, John: the case of 11, 12
France 4, 33, 47, 50–52, 58, 59, 64, 67
Fraser, Richard: the case of 81
Freud, Sigmund 15

Gambia 59
Gates, Lucy: the case of 148
gender/role of women 5, 12, 15, 29, 33, 34, 63, 64, 78, 109, 120, 144, 159
General Medical Council (GMC) 216
general practitioner 23, 91, 119, 123, 137, 155, 156, 176, 183, 195, 219, 225, 227, 232, 238, 241, 243–249, 259
genograms 106, 169, 172, 177
geographical information systems 145
Germany 2–4, 40, 47, 48, 50, 51, 58, 60, 64
Gerry, Elbridge 12, 22
Gillick principle 238, 239, 248
government guidance 85–89, 100, 102, 177, 202
GP fundholding 90, 91, 219, 227, 228, 243, 244, 246
grant-maintained schools 92
Greece 3–6, 50, 51, 60
guardian ad litem 193, 235
Guatemala 32
Guinea 59
Guineau-Bisseau 59
Gwynedd (Wales) 57

Harris, Mary Jane: the case of 16
Health Advisory Service 241
health agencies 82, 83, 137, 158, 164, 178, 201, 214–250

health agency roles
  designated professionals 216–218, 225,
    233
  named professionals 217, 218, 225, 233
  senior officers 217, 218
health visiting 120, 140, 150, 155, 156,
    159, 183, 216, 218–227, 234, 244, 245
  family health needs model 220, 221
  prevention model 220, 221
Health Visitor's Association (*see*
  Community Practitioner's and
  Health Visitor's Association)
Henry, Tyra: the case of 70, 75, 148, 167
Her Majesty's Inspectors of
  Constabulary (HMIC) 89, 94, 95
Hereford and Worcester (England) 57, 98
Herod 1
Higgs, Dr Marietta 80
HM Customs and Excise 205
Home Office (UK) 73, 87, 88, 94, 95, 101,
    199, 204, 208
Homestart 140
homicide (child) 3, 4, 21
Hong Kong 58, 60, 62
Houghton Report (UK) 80, 84
Hounslow 99
housing 33, 142, 145, 175, 221
housing departments 119

illegitimacy 4, 5, 7, 16
incest 14, 15, 53
independent visitor scheme 193
India/Indians 5, 32, 33, 63, 66
infant welfare movement 220
infanticide 2–5, 7, 8, 60, 62, 63
Infanticide Act 1922 (UK) 5
Infanticide Act 1938 (UK) 5
Inland Revenue 205
Inservice Education and Training days
  (INSET) 155, 157, 258
Interdepartmental Group on Child
  Abuse 136
International Society for the Prevention
  and Treatment of Child Abuse and
  Neglect (ISPCAN) 14, 26, 60, 63, 71
interring (children) 3
Ireland (Eire) 50, 58, 60, 224
Isaac 2
Islington 99
Israel 30, 60

Italy 47, 50, 51, 60

Japan 3, 30, 31, 58–60, 62
Jericho 2, 3
Jesus Christ 2, 6
Joint Commissioning Council (JCC) 181
judges 48, 113, 167, 211, 241
judicial review 87
juvenile courts 13
juvenile justice 37, 48, 57

Kempe, Dr Henry 14, 78, 244
Kenya 32, 33, 60
key worker 173, 187, 188
kidnapping 36
Koseda, Heidi: the case of 75, 148

Law Commission 82
lawyers/solicitors 12, 109, 113, 119, 158,
    210, 230
Leicestershire 75, 99, 193
life expectancy 58, 59, 68
Liverpool 21, 66
Liverpool Society for the Prevention of
  Cruelty to Children 21
Local Authority Social Services Act 1970
  (UK) 86
Local Education Authorities (LEA) 92,
    93, 119, 214, 256, 257
Local Government Finance Act 1982
  (UK) 101
local management of schools 92, 93
Local Medical Committee (LMC) 119,
    219, 246
London 1, 3, 5, 16–18, 65, 70, 84, 87, 94,
    142, 148, 150, 166, 171, 199, 201, 243,
    244
London Society for the Protection of
  Young Females 18
looked after children/substitute care 22,
    64, 68, 80–82, 84, 86, 89, 102, 105–
    108, 124, 125, 132, 134, 135, 139, 156,
    192–194, 215, 231–233, 252

magistrates 82, 113, 208, 210
Malawi 59
Malaysia 60, 63
Mali 59
management information systems 129,
    144

Manchester 220
mandatory reporting 7, 39, 40–44, 46, 50, 51, 53, 55, 56, 71, 255
manslaughter 5
Maori 57, 65, 66
Massachussetts 7, 13, 15
media 11, 36, 73, 75–81, 93, 126, 160, 162, 167, 173, 178, 180, 206, 235
Medical Defence Union 232
medical examinations 83, 199, 228–230, 232–233, 236, 237
consent/refusal to submit 229–231, 233, 236, 248
Mellor, David (MP) 83
members of parliament (MPs) 73, 79
Memorandum of Good Practice (UK) 88, 191, 199, 204, 206, 209, 211, 213
videotaped evidence (UK) 199, 203, 206–208, 211–214, 230
Mexico 33
Michael Sieff Foundation/Conference 114, 261
midwives/midwifery 51, 140, 216, 218, 223
Mitchell, Alice: the case of (Australia) 54
Montreal 67
mortality
child 4
infant 4, 30, 36, 58, 59, 146, 220
under 5's 58, 59, 60
Moscow 5
Moses 2
Mozambique 58, 59
Mrs Jaggers, the case of 17
Mrs Waters, the case of 17
Munchausen Syndrome by Proxy 17

National Center for Child Abuse and Neglect 14
National Clearinghouse on Child Abuse and Neglect Information 40
National Health Service 89–91, 101, 148
National Health Service and Community Care Act 1990 (UK) 90, 101, 244
National Health Service Executive (NHSE) 89–91, 93, 220
National Society for the Prevention of Cruelty to Children (NSPCC) 21, 50, 73, 83, 118, 139, 144, 146, 158, 164, 185, 187, 212, 217
NSPCC National Commission of Inquiry into the Prevention of Child Abuse 73, 139, 144, 146
nationality, child's right to 36
Native American 3, 31, 67, 68
Native Canadians 66, 67
Native South Americans 62
NCH Action for Children 136
needs
children's 18, 22, 28, 29, 48, 70, 84, 102, 107, 110, 111, 129, 131, 138, 168, 212, 221, 222, 232, 241, 242
special education 101, 172, 175, 215
Netherlands/Holland 4, 30, 40, 47–53, 58, 60
networking 114, 115
New Guinea 62
New York 8–13, 21, 22, 75
New York Society for the Prevention of Cruelty to Children (NYSPCC) 12, 13, 22
New York Society for the Prevention of Cruelty to Animals (NYSPCA) 8, 9, 12
New Zealand 57, 60, 65, 66, 209, 255
Newham, London Borough of 87
Newpin 140
NHS Hospital Trusts 90
Nigeria 61
non-molestation order 133
normalisation 153
Norman, Agnes: the case of 17
North Tyneside 99
North Wales Abuse Inquiry 193
North Yorkshire 137
Northern Ireland 7, 25, 39, 64, 89, 244
Norway 4, 35, 60
nursing 119, 120, 146, 154–156, 159, 178, 216–219, 223–227, 239, 240, 255

O'Neil, Denis: the case of 192
occupational therapist 240
Office for Standards in Education (OFSTED) 89, 91–94
Office of Her Majesty's Chief Inspector of Schools in Wales (OHMCI) 91–94
Oldham 98
Oman 59

Ombudsman 35
Ontario, Canada 260
organised abuse 14, 162, 165, 199
Orkneys, the (Scotland) 75
Oude Pekela case, the (Netherlands) 53
over-representation of ethnic minorities
57, 66, 68–70
Owen, David (MP) 80
Oxford 137

Pacific Islands 66
Paediatrician/community paediatrician
14, 80, 82, 109, 156, 159, 178, 198,
210, 218, 219, 228–238, 244, 247, 249
Paedophile Information Exchange 18
Pakistan/Pakistani 60, 66
paramedics 154
Parents Anonymous 129
Paris 5, 65
Parliament 17, 18, 79–81, 83, 84, 86, 208
Paterson factor 234
permanency planning 80, 106, 200, 266
Philadelphia Society for the Prevention
of Cruelty to Children 12
Philippines, the/Filipino 35, 60, 64, 70
Pigot Report 1989 (UK) 206–209
Pindown (Staffordshire, UK) 75, 193
place of safety order 83, 106, 201, 229
play therapists 240
police 23, 52, 53, 73, 80–83, 89, 94, 95,
101, 103, 109, 113, 118, 119, 137, 155,
157, 158, 164, 166, 173, 175, 177, 178,
182, 183, 185, 186, 193, 195, 196–205,
206, 210, 212–215, 217, 226, 255, 257,
258, 259–261
Police Act 1964 (UK) 94
Police and Magistrates Courts Act 1994
(UK) 95, 101
police protection order/powers 125, 186,
203, 204
police – specialist child protection units
201, 202, 210
police surgeon 80, 82, 210, 234, 236
Post Office 205
poverty 18, 30, 33, 62, 63, 65, 67, 68, 71,
78, 103, 142, 144–146, 173, 175, 223
predictability in child abuse 78, 79, 141–
143, 145, 173, 174, 177, 250
prevention of child abuse 52, 62, 71, 122,
124, 126, 137–153, 177, 178, 181, 190,
195, 200–222, 225–227, 243, 253–256,
259, 258
Prevention of Cruelty to and Protection
of Children Act 1889 (UK) 21, 22
probation 83, 118, 119, 164, 215, 241, 250,
255
professional abuse of children 101, 165,
174, 192, 260, 262
Prohibition of Female Circumcision Act
1985 (UK) 38
Prosecution of Offences Act 1985 (UK)
205
protective factors 144, 296
psychiatric services
adult 119, 121, 122, 156, 170, 173, 174,
178, 183, 249, 250
child 119, 121, 122, 135, 138, 156, 183,
219, 229, 230, 240–243, 265
psychologist 230, 240
psychotherapists 240
Public Health Act 1872 (UK) 220
public opinion 51, 73, 75, 79
Puerto Rico 31, 136
purchaser/provider 89–91, 215, 217, 225

Quality (assurance/control) 33, 90, 93,
95, 97, 99, 126–129, 143, 172, 178,
188, 225, 227, 228

race 26, 57, 65–72, 124, 143
racism/racist 66, 68–71, 156
random audit 129, 179, 227
rate-capping 85
re-abuse 132
reflex anal dilatation 80, 234
refocusing 46, 114, 161, 168, 196, 248,
263, 267–269
refugee children 36
Regional Health Authority 181
reorganisation 147, 148, 173, 183, 217
Local Government Reorganisation
(LGR) 96, 114, 121, 191, 202, 268,
269
research 14, 21, 35, 63, 72, 75, 85, 88, 91,
94, 96, 103–112,128, 136, 143, 174,
179, 196, 224, 264
Richardson, Sue 80
ring-fenced funding 85, 112, 114, 153, 196
risk assessment/analysis/factors 60, 78,
103, 110, 140, 142–145, 160, 186, 241

ritual scarification 38
Rochdale (UK) 75, 96, 99
Romania 71
Rome 3–6
Roosevelt, Theodore 12
Rose, Wendy 114
Rowe, Jane 88, 107, 108
rule of optimism 169, 172
Russia 71

sacrifice (child) 2, 28, 64
Salford 220
Samoa 65, 66
school exclusion 140, 252, 253, 256, 262, 263
Scotland 7, 17, 25, 39, 40, 47, 48, 201, 205, 235
Seebohm Report 1968 (UK) 147, 149, 183
Seneca 4
Senior Clinical Medical Officer (SCMO) 218, 228
Sex Offenders Act 1997 (UK) 64
sex tourism 26, 35, 64, 71
Sexual Offences Act 1956 (UK) 238
Sheehy, Sir Patrick 95
Short Report 1984 (UK) 82, 141
siblings 174, 237, 265
    caretaking 31, 32
    placements 107
    relationships 107, 108, 151
Sierra Leone 59, 61
significant harm 46, 48, 84, 134, 186, 228, 241, 249, 264
Singapore 58, 60, 62
sleeper effects of abuse 130
social action 146
social interdependence 31
social security (child's right to) 37
social services 73, 79, 82, 89, 95, 96, 98, 100, 101, 103, 109, 114, 118, 124, 137, 140, 147, 148, 153–155, 157, 158, 164, 171, 177, 178, 182–201, 203, 210, 214–217, 226, 227, 239, 240, 242, 243, 245–247, 251, 252, 255–260, 263, 267
Social Services Inspectorate (SSI) 89, 91, 95–101, 120, 125, 128, 129, 159, 161, 162, 166, 170, 179, 180, 187
social work/social workers 9, 13, 15, 44, 47–49, 51, 69, 73, 80, 81, 83, 103–106, 108–110, 113, 128, 129, 132, 135, 146–

149, 154–156, 159, 166, 186, 187, 193, 194, 196, 198–201, 212, 222–224, 226, 240–242, 245, 267
South Africa 60
South America 62
South Korea 62
Spain 50, 51, 60
Special Assessment Teams (SATs) 199
Sri Lanka 35, 64
St Petersburg 5
Standard Spending Assessment 85
Strange Situation, the 29, 30
strategy discussion 185, 186, 213
street children 36, 60, 62
substance abuse 68
suicide 122, 142, 174, 178
Surrey 98
swaddling 64
Sweden 4, 30, 35, 40, 49–51, 58–60, 64, 238
Switzerland 58
system abuse 43, 206

Taiwan 58, 62
Tennessee 8
Thailand 64
Thompson, Emily: the case of 11
Toronto 67
torture 37
traditional/cultural practices 37, 38, 61–64
training 42, 48, 83, 85, 93, 97–99, 103, 105, 106, 112–114, 121–123, 126, 128, 135, 148, 151, 153–160, 164, 181, 190–192, 196, 201, 204, 218, 223–225, 233, 241, 247, 254, 255, 257
Training Support Programme (TSP) 83, 112–114, 153, 154
treatment for abused children/therapy 21, 38, 41, 47, 51, 53, 70, 71, 122, 124, 129–139, 143, 147, 178, 190, 195, 198, 200, 211, 212, 225, 229, 230, 232, 241–243, 259, 262, 264, 268
Tunisia 60
Turkey 31, 32, 59, 64
Ty Mawr Home (Wales) 193

United Arab Emirates 59

Valerio, Daniel: the case of (Australia) 55

Vancouver 67
Venezuela 33
voluntary organisations/agencies 48,
    49, 52, 65, 83, 88, 95, 112, 114, 119,
    120, 136, 141, 150–152, 193, 214, 219,
    226, 240
volunteers 154

Wakefield 99
Wales 57, 88, 89, 91–93, 96, 100, 112, 114,
    115, 119, 120, 121, 151, 161, 162, 174,
    181, 188, 193, 195, 202, 243
war 2, 37, 220
Welsh Office (UK) 87–89, 100, 101, 114, 125,

161, 162, 170, 174, 181, 182, 189, 260
West Bank, the 65
West Germany 30, 47
West Indians 66
West Sussex 99
Wheeler, Etta 9, 10, 11
white slavery 18
Wilson, Mary Ellen: the case of 7–12, 75,
    192
Wiltshire 98
Winsor, Charlotte: the case of 16, 17
witness care programmes 210, 212
Woodcock, Shirley: the case of 81, 148
Wright, John 12